APPLIED DEMAND ANALYSIS

SERIES ON ECONOMETRICS AND MANAGEMENT SCIENCES

This is one of a series of books on econometrics and the management sciences sponsored by the IC² Institute of the University of Texas at Austin, under the general editorship of W. W. Cooper and Henri Theil. In this series, econometrics and management sciences are to be interpreted broadly, providing an opportunity to introduce new topics that can influence future activities in these fields as well as allow for new contributions to establish lines of research in both disciplines. The books will be priced to make them available to a wide and diverse audience.

Volumes in the Series:

Volume 1: EXPLOITING CONTINUITY: Maximum Entropy Estimation of Continuous Distributions, *by Henri Theil and Denzil G. Fiebig*

Volume 2: CREATIVE AND INNOVATIVE MANAGEMENT: Essays in Honor of George Kozmetsky, *edited by A. Charnes and W. W. Cooper*

Volume 3: TRANSFORMATIONAL MANAGEMENT, *by George Kozmetsky*

Volume 4: FRONTIERS IN CREATIVE AND INNOVATIVE MANAGEMENT, *edited by Robert Lawrence Kuhn*

Volume 5: INNOVATION DIFFUSION MODELS OF NEW PRODUCT ACCEPTANCE, *edited by Vijay Mahajan and Yoram Wind*

Volume 6: ALLOCATION MODELS: Specification, Estimation, and Applications, *by Ronald Bewley*

Volume 7: APPLIED DEMAND ANALYSIS: Results from System-Wide Approaches, *by Henri Theil and Kenneth W. Clements*

APPLIED DEMAND ANALYSIS

Results from
System-Wide Approaches

Volume 7 of Series on
Econometrics and Management Sciences

HENRI THEIL
KENNETH W. CLEMENTS

1987

BALLINGER PUBLISHING COMPANY
Cambridge, Massachusetts
A Subsidiary of Harper & Row, Publishers, Inc.

International Standard Book Number: 0-88730-217-3

Library of Congress Catalog Card Number: 86-32230

Printed in the United States of America

Library of Congress Cataloging-in-Publication Data

Theil, Henri.
  Applied demand analysis.

  (Series on econometrics and management sciences ; v. 7)
  Includes bibliographies and index.
    1. Demand functions (Economic theory).   2. Consumption (Economics) — Econometric models.   3. Econometrics.
  I. Clements, Kenneth W., 1950-   . II. Title.
  III. Series.
  HB801.T489   1987   338.5′212   86-32230

  ISBN 0-88730-217-3

CONTENTS

LIST OF FIGURES

LIST OF TABLES

ACKNOWLEDGMENTS

The idea for this book originated when Kenneth Clements was visiting Henri Theil at the University of Florida as McKethan-Matherly Research Fellow, on study leave from the University of Western Australia. Theil wants to acknowledge the support from the McKethan-Matherly Eminent Scholar Chair as well as the contributions made by his former associates, particularly Renate Finke, Lennart Flood, and Mercedes Rosalsky. Clements would like to acknowledge the financial support of the University of Western Australia and of Theil's Chair in Florida. Both authors acknowledge the secretarial assistance of Bill Minter in Florida and of Mrs. Marie Green in Western Australia. Acknowledgments pertaining to individual chapters are given in those specific chapters.

July 1986   H.T.
                                                      K.W.C.

PROLOGUE

Henri Theil and Kenneth W. Clements

In a system-wide context, applied demand analysis is concerned with combining the theory of the utility-maximizing consumer with data to estimate systems of demand equations. The distinguishing characteristic of applied demand analysis is that it gives equal emphasis to theory and data. This area, which was initiated by Stone (1954) with the application of the linear expenditure sysem to British data, has expanded rapidly in the last fifteen years. For surveys, see Barten (1977), Brown and Deaton (1972), Deaton and Muellbauer (1980), Phlips (1974), Powell (1974), and Theil (1980).

This book presents a number of recent results that increase the usefulness of applied demand analysis. These results give rise to estimates of income and price elasticities that are reliable and plausible, thus obviating promises that such estimates will be available in the future. Accordingly, these estimates can be used with reasonable confidence by others. The quality of these estimates derives from the quality of the underlying data and the new econometric procedures that we employ.

For many applications, the analyst is interested in the income and price sensitivity of the demand for narrowly defined goods. An example is the effect of taxing beer on the consumption of wine. Here, the interest is in providing much more detail than is usually given by applied demand analysis in its focus on the broad aggregates. This book also shows how applied demand analysis can be adapted to deal with these issues. This material includes extensive applications with the demand for meats (beef, pork, chicken, and lamb) and alcoholic beverages (beer, wine, and spirits).

THE CONTENTS OF THIS BOOK

Chapter 1 sets the book's tone, beginning with a presentation of numerical values of income elasticities from Houthakker's (1957) famous study. It then gives a self-contained exposition of consumption theory, which is used in subsequent chapters. This material addresses utility theory (including the indirect utility function and the cost function), the differential approach to consumption theory, and the presentation of a number of demand systems.

Chapter 2 uses data on per capita consumption in thirty countries collected by Kravis, Heston, and Summers (1982) for the International Comparison Project. These researchers' painstaking care has ensured that the data, which exhibit great variability, are as comparable as possible across countries ranging from the United States to India. This variability and the overall quality of the data yield fairly precise estimates of a cross-country demand model for ten broad aggregates. The implications of this model are explored by presenting demand elasticities for the ten goods at the levels of the per capita incomes of each of the thirty countries, as well as for incomes below India's per capita level. Chapter 2 also includes an assessment of Frisch's (1959) conjecture about the income dependence of the income elasticity of the marginal utility of income, and indexes of the volume and quality of consumption across countries and time.

Chapter 3 examines the econometrics of demand systems. Until recently, the hypothesis of demand homogeneity (the absence of money illusion by the consumer) was almost universally rejected. This was particularly puzzling as homogeneity seems such a plausible restriction. The puzzle has now been satisfactorily resolved by Laitinen (1978), who showed that the rejections were just an artifact of the tests employed. The tests have only a large-sample justification and they perform particularly poorly with anything but small systems. Meisner (1979) obtained similar results for testing Slutsky symmetry (the symmetry of the substitution effects). These developments and others related to testing are surveyed in detail in this chapter.

Chapter 3 also provides an extensive analysis of the estimation of demand systems, including the estimation of nonlinear models by maximum likelihood and least squares, L_p-norm estimation, "bootstrapping" for standard errors, and instrumental variable estimation. Throughout the chapter, simulation experiments are used intensively to analyze how econometric procedures work under ideal circumstances where everything is known. This material clearly illustrates that simulation experiments provide an important new extension of econometrics. Originally, this field consisted of *two* components: econometric methodology and data analysis. *Simulation is now a third component of econometrics.* At the end of Chapter 3, we also consider Monte Carlo testing. This technique was proposed by G.A. Barnard in 1963, but it has not been widely used in econometrics. We believe that this technique is quite promising, particularly for systems of equations.

Chapters 1 through 3 address the demand for all n goods jointly. By contrast, Chapter 4 is concerned with a subset of goods. The chapter reviews various concepts of separability of the utility function that deal with the blocking of closely related goods into groups. It is shown that under appropriate conditions, the demand for members of a group can be analyzed in exactly the same way as before (as set out in Chapter 1), with real income reinterpreted as total (real) consumption of the group and the n prices replaced with those of the members of the group. This attractive result means that the prices of goods outside the group in question can be ignored. These results are illustrated with the demand for meats in the United States. The chapter also shows that the static demand equations are consistent with intertemporal utility maximization under appropriate separability conditions.

Chapter 5 continues the analysis of the demand for a group of goods by using data on the consumption of beer, wine, and spirits in Australia, the United Kingdom, and the United States. For each country, time series data are used to estimate a demand model. Using simulation experiments, the estimates are found to be of satisfactory quality. Demand elasticities for the three beverages are tabulated for each year of the sample and for each country. The results reveal a number of similarities in alcohol consumption patterns across countries: (1) drinkers in each country satisfy within-alcohol versions of homogeneity and symmetry; (2) beer is always a necessity and spirits a luxury; and (3) the price elasticities are not too different across countries. On the other hand, the data reject the hypothesis that tastes are identical across countries.

The Epilogue serves to avoid the impression that no further progress can be made. For instance, by applying a different grouping to the goods of the cross-country data of Kravis et al., we can study the demand for energy in a system-wide manner. In addition, we can look at the cross-country data of the successive phases of the International Comparison Project separately, but we can also consider successive phases simultaneously. We should expect the latter approach to yield more accurate estimates.

THE USES OF THIS BOOK

There are two distinct ways of using this book. The cover-to-cover reader will find the book to be well integrated and will not be frustrated by repetition, differing notation and terminology, or other inconsistencies. The reader with more specific interests will, in the main, be able to go straight to the relevant chapter (and, in some cases, the relevant section), without having to waste time covering nonessential material. Each chapter has been written so that it is more or less self-contained.

This book will be of interest to a varied audience. It provides economists with reliable numerical values for income and price elasticities of demand. These elasticities refer to (1) four broad aggregates in Japan; (2) ten broad aggregates in thirty countries ranging in affluence from the United States to India; (3) four types of meat in the United States; and (4) three alcoholic beverages in Australia, the United Kingdom, and the United States. The indexes of the volume and quality of consumption, which are comparable across countries and time, should also be of interest to the general economist.

Econometricians will be interested in Chapter 3 for the spectacular failure of asymptotic theory and for the new procedures introduced, particularly the simulation methodology. The extensive empirical applications will also appeal to econometricians with applied interests.

The book is also suitable for use in microeconomic courses at the graduate and advanced undergraduate levels. It can be used for both consumption theory and applications of demand analysis.

BIBLIOGRAPHY

Barnard, G.A. 1963. *Journal of the Royal Statistical Society,* Series B, 25, p. 294.

Barten, A.P. 1977. "The Systems of Consumer Demand Functions Approach: A Review." *Econometrica* 45: 23–51.

Brown, A., and A.S. Deaton. 1972. "Surveys in Applied Economics: Models of Consumer Behaviour." *Economic Journal* 82: 1145–1236.

Deaton, A.S., and J. Muellbauer. 1980. *Economics and Consumer Behaviour.* Cambridge: Cambridge University Press.

Frisch, R. 1959. "A Complete Scheme for Computing All Direct and Cross Demand Elasticities in a Model with Many Sectors." *Econometrica* 27: 177–96.

Houthakker, H.S. 1957. "An International Comparison of Household Expenditure Patterns, Commemorating the Centenary of Engel's Law." *Econometrica* 25: 532–51.

Kravis, I.B.; A.W. Heston; and R. Summers. 1982. *World Product and Income: International Comparisons of Real Gross Product.* Baltimore, Md.: The Johns Hopkins University Press.

Laitinen, K. 1978. "Why Is Demand Homogeneity So Often Rejected?" *Economics Letters* 1: 187–91.

Meisner, J.F. 1979. "The Sad Fate of the Asymptotic Slutsky Symmetry Test for Large Systems." *Economics Letters* 2: 231–33.

Phlips, L. 1974. *Applied Consumption Analysis*. Amsterdam: North-Holland Publishing Company. Second edition 1983.

Powell, A.A. 1974. *Empirical Analytics of Demand Systems*. Lexington, Mass.: D.C. Heath and Company.

Stone, R. 1954. "Linear Expenditure Systems and Demand Analysis: An Application to the Pattern of British Demand." *Economic Journal* 64: 511–27.

Theil, H. 1980. *The System-Wide Approach to Microeconomics*. Chicago: The University of Chicago Press.

1 ALTERNATIVE APPROACHES TO CONSUMPTION THEORY

Kenneth W. Clements

1.1 INTRODUCTION

One of the primary aims of applied demand analysis is to estimate systems of demand equations to discover empirical regularities in consumption patterns. With this objective in mind, Section 1.2 of this chapter presents income elasticities of four consumption categories for a large number of countries. All of the food elasticities are substantially less than unity, which gives strong support to Engel's law that the proportion of income devoted to food declines with increasing affluence.

Sections 1.3 through 1.13 deal mainly with the two utility-based ways of generating demand equations. The first, discussed in Sections 1.3 through 1.8, is based on the algebraic specification of some function as an *initial* step, be it the utility function, the indirect utility function, or the cost function. The second way of generating demand equations is the differential approach, discussed in Sections 1.9 through 1.13. This approach requires no initial algebraic specification of any function. As a result, the demand equations of this approach are completely general, having coefficients that are not necessarily constant. Of course, the estimation of these equations requires some parameterization, but this comes only as the *last* step. The flexibility

I am indebted to Antony Selvanathan and Henri Theil for helpful comments on an earlier draft of this chapter.

of the differential approach is illustrated in Sections 1.14 and 1.15, which contain two different parameterizations of differential demand equations.

The last three sections of this chapter present some further income elasticities and clarify some concepts introduced earlier.

1.2   DEMAND ANALYSIS WITHOUT UTILITY THEORY

The major approach to demand analysis emphasized in this book is utility based, or some variant thereof. This approach, to be explained in detail below, derives demand equations by postulating that the consumer behaves as if he chooses the consumption basket to maximize a utility function subject to a budget constraint. This approach gives rise to elegant and intuitive interpretations of the coefficients of the demand equations in terms of the utility function.

This, however, is not the only way of proceeding in demand analysis. There is an older tradition that uses demand equations directly, without any reference to the utility function; according to this approach, the demand equations are directly specified. In this pragmatic approach, the demand for the good is specified as a simple function of income and prices. This procedure, which goes back to Cassel (1932), has been used extensively by Stone (1954a) and others.

A popular example of directly specified demand equations is the *double-log system,*

$$\log q_i = \alpha_i + \eta_i \log M + \sum_{j=1}^{n} \eta_{ij} \log p_j \quad i = 1, \dots, n, \tag{2.1}$$

where q_i is the quantity demanded of good i $(i = 1, \dots, n)$; p_j is the price of good j;

$$M = \sum_{i=1}^{n} p_i q_i \tag{2.2}$$

is total expenditure, which we shall refer to as *income* for short; and α_i, η_i, and η_{ij} are constant coefficients. (All logarithms in this book are natural logarithms.)

The interpretation of (2.1) is straightforward. The coefficient of income is

$$\eta_i = \frac{\partial(\log q_i)}{\partial(\log M)}. \tag{2.3}$$

This is known as the *income elasticity* of demand for good i and answers the question, If income rises by 1 percent with prices constant, what is the percentage change in consumption of i? Commodities with income elasticities less than unity are called *necessities*, while those with income elasticities greater than unity are known as *luxuries*. If the income elasticity is negative, then the good is said to be *inferior* as its consumption falls with increasing income. Similarly, the coefficient η_{ij} is the percentage change in q_i resulting from a 1 percent change in p_j, income and the other prices remaining constant; η_{ij} is known as the elasticity of demand for i with respect to the price of j.

We define

$$w_i = \frac{p_i q_i}{M} \tag{2.4}$$

as the proportion of income devoted to good i, to be referred to as the *budget share* of this good. The budget shares are positive and, in view of (2.2), have a unit sum. Multiplication of the budget share by the corresponding income elasticity yields

$$w_i \eta_i = \frac{p_i q_i}{M} \frac{\partial(\log q_i)}{\partial(\log M)} = \frac{p_i q_i}{M} \frac{\partial q_i / q_i}{\partial M / M} = p_i \frac{\partial q_i}{\partial M} = \frac{\partial(p_i q_i)}{\partial M}, \tag{2.5}$$

where the last step follows from the fact the p_i is held constant. The term on the far right of (2.5) answers the question, If income rises by one dollar how much of this is spent on commodity i? We write this as

$$\theta_i = \frac{\partial(p_i q_i)}{\partial M}, \tag{2.6}$$

which shall be referred to as the ith *marginal share*. As the additional income is entirely spent, the marginal shares have a unit sum; this can be verified by differentiating both sides of (2.2) with respect to income. In contrast to the budget shares, the marginal shares are not always positive; θ_i is negative if i is inferior.

Combining (2.5) and (2.6) shows that the income elasticity can also be expressed as the ratio of the marginal share to the corresponding budget share,

$$\eta_i = \frac{\theta_i}{w_i}. \tag{2.7}$$

As the marginal shares have a unit sum, it follows from (2.7) that a budget-share weighted average of the income elasticities is equal to unity,

$$\sum_{i=1}^{n} w_i \eta_i = \sum_{i=1}^{n} \theta_i = 1. \tag{2.8}$$

In a household expenditure survey all participating families pay approximately the same price for each good, so that the ith equation of (2.1) reduces to

$$\log q_i = \alpha_i + \eta_i \log M, \tag{2.9}$$

where units are chosen such that the price of each good is unity, so that $\sum_j \eta_{ij} \log p_j = 0$. In a pioneering study, Houthakker (1957) used (2.9) to analyze a large number of household surveys, from a number of different countries. Table 1-1 summarizes a selection of Houthakker's data. The countries are ranked in terms of decreasing mean income per capita, given in column 4 of the table. Income in each country is expressed in terms of the common unit of United States dollars of 1950, making it comparable across countries. Accordingly, the middle class in the United Kingdom in 1938/39 was $1296/90 \approx 14$ times more affluent than the working class in 1927 Poland.

Houthakker distinguishes $n = 4$ goods: food (not including alcoholic beverages), clothing (including footwear), housing (including fuel and light but not furniture), and miscellaneous (everything else). Columns 5 through 8 of Table 1-1 give the budget shares of the four goods in each country, averaged over all families participating in the survey for each country. Thus we see that the middle-class British devoted 25 percent of their total spending to food consumption, while the Poles spent 64 percent. Although there are exceptions, there is a fairly systematic rise in the budget share of food as we go down column 5, which corresponds to decreasing affluence. This negative relationship between the food budget share and income is known as *Engel's law*, after Engel (1857).

Houthakker's estimates of the double-log model (2.9) are given in Table 1-2, where the countries are identical to those of Table 1-1. The income elasticity of food is always substantially less than unity, making food a necessity, which reflects Engel's law operating within each country. Given the diversity of the countries and time periods, it is truly remarkable that such an empirical regularity holds so strongly. Note also that there is some tendency for the food elasticity to rise with decreasing affluence. The same phenomena also occur within the three countries (the United Kingdom, Germany, and the Netherlands) where different social groups are distinguished. The income elasticities of clothing indicate that it is generally a modest luxury, housing is generally a necessity (but less of a necessity than food), and miscellaneous is always a luxury.

Table 1-1. Income Per Capita and Budget Shares in Twenty Household Expenditure Surveys.

Country (1)	Date (2)	Type of persons (3)	Mean income[a] per capita in $US of 1950 (4)	Mean budget shares (in percentage form)			
				Food (5)	Clothing (6)	Housing (7)	Miscellaneous (8)
United Kingdom	1938/39	Middle class	1296	25	12	19	44
Mexico	1931	City dwellers	579	40	—	—	—
Sweden	1955	Entire country	576	37	12	16	35
France	1951	City dwellers	544	49	10	9	32
Norway	1952	City dwellers	506	37	16	11	36
United Kingdom	1937/38	Working class	500	37	8	29	26
Germany	1928	Clerical workers	423	33	13	16	38
Germany	1928	Government officials	415	33	14	17	36
Germany	1907	City dwellers	395	45	10	20	25
Switzerland	1919	Entire country	391	46	10	17	27
Netherlands	1951	White-collar workers	362	29	14	13	44
Finland	1950/51	City dwellers	338	50	17	10	23
Ireland	1951/52	City dwellers	324	40	13	15	32
Austria	1954/55	City dwellers	313	53	10	11	26
Italy	1952/53	Entire country	275	46	15	—	—
Germany	1928	Manual workers	265	42	12	14	32
Latvia	1936/37	Urban and rural workers	231	34	15	15	36
Netherlands	1951	Manual workers	230	39	13	14	34
Japan	1955	Urban workers	150	45	10	11	34
Poland	1927	Working class	90	64	11	9	16

a. Income is total expenditure.
Source: Houthakker (1957; Tables I and IV).

Table 1-2.   Income Elasticities of Four Goods from Twenty Household Expenditure Surveys.

Country (1)	*Income elasticities η_i*			
	Food (2)	Clothing (3)	Housing (4)	Miscellaneous (5)
United Kingdom (middle class)	.34	1.34	.35	1.49
Mexico	.66	–	–	–
Sweden	.63	1.12	.80	1.45
France	.48	1.16	1.10	1.66
Norway	.52	1.27	.80	1.52
United Kingdom (working class)	.59	1.04	.55	1.79
Germany (1928 clerical workers)	.50	1.04	.88	1.47
Germany (1928 government officials)	.39	.92	.89	1.61
Germany (1907 city dwellers)	.54	1.50	.91	1.60
Switzerland	.46	1.45	.82	1.88
Netherlands (white-collar workers)	.49	1.06	.62	1.40
Finland	.62	1.62	.80	1.45
Ireland	.60	1.18	.71	1.48
Austria	.55	1.77	.74	1.62
Italy	.60	1.04	–	–
Germany (1928 manual workers)	.60	1.30	1.06	1.47
Latvia	.43	1.09	1.02	1.57
Netherlands (manual workers)	.71	1.63	.51	1.27
Japan	.56	1.59	.86	1.42
Poland	.73	1.78	.66	1.77

Source: Houthakker (1957: Table II).

Table 1-3 presents the marginal shares implied by the income elasticities and the budget shares. The marginal shares, like the budget shares, are pure numbers and thus comparable across commodities and countries. Looking at the first row of the table we see that for the middle-class British, 9 percent of an extra pound of income is spent on food, 16 percent on clothing, 7 percent on housing, and 66 percent on miscellaneous.

Although the double-log system is attractive in its simplicity, it does have a serious drawback. As prices are constant, it follows from (2.9) that the logarithmic change in expenditure on good i is a constant multiple η_i of the change in income,

$$d(\log p_i q_i) = \eta_i \, d(\log M).$$

Table 1-3. Marginal Shares of Four Goods from Twenty Household Expenditure Surveys.

Country (1)	Marginal shares $\theta_i \times 100$			
	Food (2)	Clothing (3)	Housing (4)	Miscellaneous (5)
United Kingdom (middle class)	9	16	7	66
Mexico	26	–	–	–
Sweden	23	13	13	51
France	24	12	10	53
Norway	19	20	9	55
United Kingdom (working class)	22	8	16	47
Germany (1928 clerical workers)	17	14	14	56
Germany (1928 government officials)	13	13	15	58
Germany (1907 city dwellers)	24	15	18	40
Switzerland	21	15	14	51
Netherlands (white-collar workers)	14	15	8	62
Finland	31	28	8	33
Ireland	24	15	11	47
Austria	29	18	8	42
Italy	28	16	–	–
Germany (1928 manual workers)	25	16	15	47
Latvia	15	16	15	57
Netherlands (manual workers)	28	21	7	43
Japan	25	16	9	48
Poland	47	20	6	28

Source: Computed from Tables 1-1 and 1-2.

Accordingly, if the income elasticity η_i exceeds unity, then expenditure on i increases at a faster rate than does income. If income rises sufficiently, expenditure on i will eventually exceed income, which violates the adding-up constraint (2.2). Therefore, the weakness of the model is that it does not satisfy the adding-up constraint for all values of income. This is why the marginal shares given in Table 1-3 do not sum to unity exactly.

Remark 1. Several kinds of price elasticities will be encountered in this book, and η_{ij} in (2.1) is one such elasticity. As this equation has money income M on the right side, the income effect of the change in the jth price is included in η_{ij}. This η_{ij} is called the *Cournot price elasticity*.

Remark 2. In Houthakker's application of (2.9), the dependent variable is $\log(p_i q_i)$ rather than $\log q_i$. As prices are the same across different households, this only affects the constant term on the right of (2.9). Houthakker also includes the logarithm of family size on the right of (2.9).

Remark 3. For a given country, expenditure on good i ($p_i q_i$) and income (M) are all expressed in terms of the local currency; the double-log system is then estimated for each country with these data. For the purpose of constructing income per capita given in column 4 of Table 1-1, the official exchange rate prevailing during the year of the survey is used to convert the local currency to U.S. dollars; this is then adjusted to U.S. prices of 1950 by using the U.S. cost-of-living index. In Section 2.3 it is shown that using the exchange rate in this manner tends to overstate the poverty of the poor. This bias should be taken into consideration when these income figures are compared.

1.3   SPECIFYING THE FORM OF THE UTILITY FUNCTION

Perhaps the most straightforward way of generating demand equations is to derive them by maximizing the utility function subject to the consumer's budget constraint. The utility function takes the form

$$u = u(q_1, \ldots, q_n), \tag{3.1}$$

where, as before, q_i is the quantity consumed of good i. We assume that this function is differentiable and that there is nonsatiation, so that each marginal utility is positive,

$$\frac{\partial u}{\partial q_i} > 0 \quad i = 1, \ldots, n. \tag{3.2}$$

We further assume that there is generalized diminishing marginal utility, so that the Hessian matrix of the utility function is negative definite. As Hessians are symmetric, we have

$$U = \left[\frac{\partial^2 u}{\partial q_i \, \partial q_j}\right] \text{ is a symmetric negative definite } n \times n \text{ matrix.} \tag{3.3}$$

Writing p_i for the price of good i, the budget constraint is that expenditure on the n goods $p_1 q_1 + \cdots + p_n q_n$ must equal a fixed total M,

$$\sum_{i=1}^{n} p_i q_i = M. \tag{3.4}$$

We shall continue to refer to M as income. Equation (3.4) is identical to (2.2), which we previously referred to as the adding-up constraint.

A popular choice for the form of the utility function (3.1) is

$$u = \sum_{i=1}^{n} a_i \log(q_i - b_i), \tag{3.5}$$

where the a_i's and b_i's are constants satisfying $\sum_i a_i = 1$ and $b_i < q_i$ for each i. Furthermore, (3.2) implies that each a_i is positive. The utility function (3.5) is known as the *Klein–Rubin*, after Klein and Rubin (1948). Under (3.5) utility is a weighted average of $\log(q_1 - b_1), ..., \log(q_n - b_n)$. This particular function will be further considered in Section 1.4.

Once the utility function is introduced, demand analysis becomes much richer in its implications and applications. The utility framework is the foundation for index number theory, which includes the measurement of real income, the measurement of the effects of distortions such as commodity taxation, and the division of goods into groups that are closely related. In addition, the utility function generates the three major predictions of demand analysis: (1) that the demand equations are homogeneous of degree zero in income and prices; (2) that the substitution effects will be symmetric; and (3) that the substitution matrix is negative semidefinite. A number of these topics are discussed at length in this book.

1.4   THE LINEAR EXPENDITURE SYSTEM

In this section we use the Klein–Rubin to illustrate how a specified form of the utility function can be used to derive the algebraic form of the demand equations. We commence by discussing in general terms a budget-constrained utility maximum and then apply the Klein–Rubin.

To maximize (3.1) subject to (3.4), we form the Lagrangian expression

$$u(q_1, ..., q_n) - \lambda \left(\sum_{i=1}^{n} p_i q_i - M \right), \tag{4.1}$$

where λ is a Lagrangian multiplier. The first-order conditions for a maximum of (4.1) are (3.4) and

$$\frac{\partial u}{\partial q_i} = \lambda p_i \quad i = 1, ..., n, \tag{4.2}$$

which states that each marginal utility is proportional to the corresponding price. As the prices are positive, it follows from (3.2) and (4.2) that $\lambda > 0$. By dividing both sides of (4.2) by p_i, we obtain $(\partial u/\partial q_i)/p_i = \lambda$, or $\partial u/\partial(p_i q_i) = \lambda$. This shows that a one-dollar increase in income causes utility to rise by λ when this increase is spent on any of the n goods. Accordingly, λ is known as the *marginal utility of income*. The second-order conditions for a maximum are satisfied by (3.3).

The first-order conditions (3.4) and (4.2) constitute $n+1$ equations, which can in principle be solved for the $n+1$ unknowns $q_1, ..., q_n$ and λ; we assume that the resulting quantities are unique and positive for relevant values of prices and income. The optimal quantities depend on income and the prices, so that we can write

$$q_i = q_i(M, p_1, ..., p_n) \quad i = 1, ..., n. \tag{4.3}$$

These are the *demand functions*.

Applying (4.2) to (3.5) and using the budget constraint to eliminate λ, we obtain

$$q_i = b_i + \frac{a_i}{p_i}\left(M - \sum_{j=1}^{n} p_j b_j\right) \quad i = 1, ..., n.$$

This is the algebraic form of the demand equations (4.3) associated with the Klein–Rubin utility function. We obtain a simpler result by multiplying both sides of the above by p_i,

$$p_i q_i = p_i b_i + a_i\left(M - \sum_{j=1}^{n} p_j b_j\right) \quad i = 1, ..., n. \tag{4.4}$$

As expenditure on good i is a linear function of the n prices and income, (4.4) is known as the *linear expenditure system*. If the b_i's are all positive, then (4.4) has the following interpretation. The consumer first purchases b_i units of good i at a cost of $p_i b_i$; this can be termed "subsistence consumption" of that commodity. The total cost of subsistence is $\sum_j p_j b_j$, which leaves $M - \sum_j p_j b_j$ as "supernumerary income." A fixed fraction a_i of supernumerary income is then spent on good i. The linear expenditure system was first applied to data by Stone (1954b); for other applications, see, for example, Deaton (1975) and Lluch and Powell (1975).

It follows from (4.4) that the marginal share θ_i [defined in (2.6)] implied by the linear expenditure system is equal to the constant coefficient a_i. Consequently, the income elasticity of i takes the form

$$\eta_i = \frac{a_i}{w_i}. \tag{4.5}$$

A rise in income with prices held constant causes the budget shares of necessities to fall and those of luxuries to rise. It then follows from (4.5) that increasing affluence causes the income elasticities of necessities to rise, while those of luxuries fall; the elasticities of both types of goods become closer to unity. Take the case of food, a necessity. The linear expenditure system implies that as the consumer becomes richer, the η_i for food increases, causing food to become less of a necessity or more of a luxury. This behavior of the elasticity is implausible as food should be less of a luxury for a richer consumer. See Section 2.5 for further discussion.

Recall that the coefficient a_i in the Klein–Rubin must be positive. As this coefficient is interpreted as the marginal share in (4.4), it follows that the linear expenditure system does not admit inferior goods.

1.5   PREFERENCE INDEPENDENCE

When the consumer's tastes can be described by a utility function that is the sum of n sub-utility functions, one for each good,

$$u = \sum_{i=1}^{n} u_i(q_i), \tag{5.1}$$

then the marginal utility of good i is independent of the consumption of j, $i \neq j$. Accordingly, (5.1) is known as *preference independence*. If the commodities are fairly broad groups, such as food, housing, clothing, and so on, then (5.1) could be a reasonable working hypothesis as it conveys the idea that total utility is obtained from the utility derived from food *and* utility from housing *and* utility from clothing *and* so on. These broad commodity groups can be interpreted as representing the "basic wants" of the consumer and could be expected to exhibit little interaction in the utility function. The Klein–Rubin utility function (3.5) is a special case of (5.1), with $u_i(q_i) = a_i \log(q_i - b_i)$. Weaker versions of preference independence will be analyzed in Chapter 4.

As will be described in detail in Section 1.12 below, the number of unknown coefficients in a general system of demand equations is of the order of n^2, where n is the number of commodities. This number of coefficients can be estimated precisely with data only when n is very small; even for moderate-sized systems (n in the vicinity of 6), it is impossible to estimate such a large number of coefficients from the data as they usually are observed. The hypothesis of preference independence comes to the rescue as it simplifies the form of the demand equations by greatly reducing the number of unknown coefficients to be estimated. Accordingly, there are two distinct justifications of preference independence: (1) the economic justification, in terms of preference independence being plausible when applied to broad aggregates; and (2) the statistical justification when n is not small. (A formal account of the implications for the demand equations of preference independence is given in Section 1.13 below.)

It can be easily shown that demand equations are invariant to monotonic transformations of the utility function. For example, we could replace the utility function (3.5) with

$$u^* = \Phi\left(\sum_{i=1}^{n} a_i \log(q_i - b_i)\right), \tag{5.2}$$

where $\Phi(\ )$ is any monotonically increasing function of its argument; the demand equations derived by the constrained-maximization of (5.2) are identical to (4.4), those associated with the original utility function (3.5). In other words, the utility function is only ordinal not cardinal. The consumer's tastes are said to be preference independent with respect to the n goods when these tastes can be represented by a utility function that is additive in these goods.

In the previous section we noted the incompatibility of the Klein–Rubin with inferior goods. This incompatibility applies to the general case of preference independence: All demand systems derived from a preference-independent utility function rule out inferior goods. See Section 1.13 for details.

1.6   SPECIFYING THE FORM OF THE INDIRECT UTILITY FUNCTION

Let $p = [p_i]$ and $q = [q_i]$ be vectors of the n prices and quantities and let $q = q(M, p)$ be the system of n demand equations (4.3). If we substitute the demand equations into the utility function (3.1), utility becomes a function of income and prices,

$$u = u(q(M, p)) = u_I(M, p). \tag{6.1}$$

The function $u_I(\ )$ is called the *indirect utility function;* it gives the maximum utility attainable corresponding to given values of income and prices. For example, it can be readily verified that the indirect utility function associated with the Klein–Rubin (direct) utility function (3.5) is

$$u_I(M, p) = k + \log\left(M - \sum_{i=1}^{n} p_i b_i\right) - \sum_{i=1}^{n} a_i \log p_i, \tag{6.2}$$

where $k = \sum_i a_i \log a_i$, which is a constant.

It can be shown (Theil 1980: App. B) that (6.1) has the following derivatives

$$\frac{\partial u_I}{\partial M} = \lambda, \qquad \frac{\partial u_I}{\partial p_i} = -\lambda q_i \quad i = 1, \dots, n, \tag{6.3}$$

where λ is the marginal utility of income. Taking the negative of the ratio of the price derivative to the income derivative, we obtain from (6.3)

$$q_i = -\frac{\partial u_I / \partial p_i}{\partial u_I / \partial M} \quad i = 1, \dots, n, \tag{6.4}$$

which is known as Roy's (1942) theorem.

Roy's theorem gives a second way of generating a system of demand equations, namely, specify an algebraic form of the indirect utility function and then apply (6.4). Christensen, Jorgenson, and Lau (1975) used this approach and introduced the translog indirect utility function,

$$u_I(M, p) = \sum_{i=1}^{n} \beta_i \log \frac{p_i}{M} + \frac{1}{2} \sum_{i=1}^{n} \sum_{j=1}^{n} \beta_{ij} \log \frac{p_i}{M} \log \frac{p_j}{M}, \tag{6.5}$$

where the β_i's and β_{ij}'s are constants. Application of (6.4) to (6.5) yields a result that can be expressed in terms of budget shares,

$$w_i = \frac{\beta_i + \sum\limits_{j=1}^{n} \beta_{ij} \log \dfrac{p_j}{M}}{\sum\limits_{k=1}^{n} \beta_k + \sum\limits_{k=1}^{n} \sum\limits_{j=1}^{n} \beta_{kj} \log \dfrac{p_j}{M}} \quad i = 1, \dots, n. \tag{6.6}$$

1.7 SPECIFYING THE FORM OF THE COST FUNCTION

The consumer's *cost function* is dual to the (direct) utility function in that it gives the minimum expenditure needed to reach a specified level of utility, given the prices. The cost function is also referred to as the *expenditure function*. We write the cost function as $C(u, p)$, which can be derived by substituting $C(\ )$ for M in the indirect utility function. Doing this for the indirect utility function (6.2), we obtain

$$C(u, p) = \sum_{i=1}^{n} p_i b_i + e^{u-k} \prod_{i=1}^{n} p_i^{a_i}. \tag{7.1}$$

This cost function consists of two parts, the first being the cost of subsistence $\sum_i p_i b_i$, which is independent of utility. The second part increases with utility and involves a weighted geometric mean of the prices, the weights being the marginal shares a_i.

Cost functions have the property that

$$\frac{\partial C}{\partial p_i} = q_i \quad i = 1, \ldots, n,$$
(7.2)

which is referred to as *Shephard's lemma*. Accordingly, a third approach to deriving demand equations is to specify the form of the cost function and then apply (7.2). As an example, Deaton and Muellbauer (1980a, b) suggested

$$C(u, p) = e^{a(p) + ub(p)},$$
(7.3)

where

$$a(p) = \sum_{i=1}^{n} \alpha_i \log p_i + \frac{1}{2} \sum_{i=1}^{n} \sum_{j=1}^{n} \gamma_{ij} \log p_i \log p_j,$$
(7.4)

$$b(p) = \beta_0 \prod_{i=1}^{n} p_i^{\beta_i},$$
(7.5)

with the α_i's, γ_{ij}'s, and β_i's all constants. Deaton and Muellbauer apply (7.2) to this cost function, which gives a demand system in terms of utility and prices. They then use the indirect utility function to express utility in terms of income and prices, which yields a demand system in terms of income and prices of the form

$$w_i = \alpha_i + \beta_i \log \frac{M}{P} + \sum_{j=1}^{n} \gamma_{ij} \log p_j \quad i = 1, \ldots, n,$$
(7.6)

where

$$\log P = \sum_{i=1}^{n} \alpha_i \log p_i + \frac{1}{2} \sum_{i=1}^{n} \sum_{j=1}^{n} \gamma_{ij} \log p_i \log p_j.$$
(7.7)

Deaton and Muellbauer refer to (7.6) as the almost ideal demand system, or AIDS for short.

1.8   WORKING'S MODEL

If prices are constant, as is approximately the case for a household expenditure survey, and if we choose units such that the price of each good is unity, then the AIDS model (7.6) simplifies to

$$w_i = \alpha_i + \beta_i \log M \quad i = 1, \ldots, n.$$
(8.1)

In words, the budget shares are linear functions of the logarithm of income, which was first proposed by Working (1943) to analyze household budget data. As the sum of the budget shares is unity, it follows from (8.1) that $\sum_i \alpha_i = 1$ and $\sum_i \beta_i = 0$. Choosing the income unit such that $M = 1$ for some household, α_i is then interpreted as the budget share of i for that household. The coefficient β_i gives us 100 times the change in the budget share of i ($\Delta w_i \times 100$) resulting from a 1 percent increase in income.

To derive the marginal shares implied by Working's model, we multiply (8.1) by M, which gives $p_i q_i = \alpha_i M + \beta_i M \log M$, and then differentiate with respect to M,

$$\frac{\partial(p_i q_i)}{\partial M} = \alpha_i + \beta_i(1 + \log M).$$

A comparison with (2.6) and (8.1) shows that this can be written as

$$\theta_i = w_i + \beta_i. \tag{8.2}$$

Thus under Working's model the ith marginal share exceeds the corresponding budget share by β_i; as the budget share is not constant with respect to income, neither is this marginal share.

Taking the ratio of the marginal share (8.2) to the corresponding budget share, we obtain for the income elasticity,

$$\eta_i = 1 + \frac{\beta_i}{w_i}. \tag{8.3}$$

This shows that a good with positive (negative) β_i is a luxury (necessity). As the budget share of a luxury increases with income, prices remaining constant, it follows from (8.3) that increasing income causes the η_i of such a good to fall toward 1. The income elasticity of a necessity also declines with increasing income under (8.3). Thus as the consumer becomes more affluent, all goods become less luxurious under Working's model, which is a plausible outcome. By contrast, under the linear expenditure system the income elasticities of necessities *increase*, which is implausible, as discussed previously.

If we rank goods according to their income elasticities, how does that ranking change with increasing income? Working's model implies that this ranking remains unchanged. To see this, let $\eta_i \gtrless \eta_j$. It follows from (8.3) that this implies $\beta_i/w_i \gtrless \beta_j/w_j$, or $w_j \beta_i \gtrless w_i \beta_j$. Using (8.1), we obtain

$$(\alpha_j + \beta_j \log M)\beta_i \gtrless (\alpha_i + \beta_i \log M)\beta_j,$$

or, after simplifications,

$$\alpha_j \beta_i \gtrless \alpha_i \beta_j.$$

As this last inequality does not involve income, the ranking of goods is invariant to income changes.

1.9   DIVISIA INDEXES

This and the next four sections are concerned with Theil's (1980) differential approach to consumption theory; the exposition in these five sections is based mainly on Theil (1975/76, 1980). We start by introducing the Divisia (1925) indexes that are used in this approach.

The differential of the budget constraint (3.4) is

$$\sum_{i=1}^{n} p_i \, dq_i + \sum_{i=1}^{n} q_i \, dp_i = dM.$$

Dividing both sides of this by M, using the identity $dx/x = d(\log x)$ and $w_i = p_i q_i / M$ we obtain

$$\sum_{i=1}^{n} w_i d(\log q_i) + \sum_{i=1}^{n} w_i d(\log p_i) = d(\log M).$$

We write this as

$$d(\log Q) + d(\log P) = d(\log M), \tag{9.1}$$

where

$$d(\log Q) = \sum_{i=1}^{n} w_i d(\log q_i) \tag{9.2}$$

is the *Divisia volume index,* and

$$d(\log P) = \sum_{i=1}^{n} w_i d(\log p_i) \tag{9.3}$$

is the *Divisia price index.*

Equation (9.1) decomposes the change in income into a volume and price index. The volume index defined in (9.2) is a weighted average of the n logarithmic quantity changes $d(\log q_1), \ldots, d(\log q_n)$, the weights being the budget shares. Similarly, the price index (9.3) is a weighted average of the price changes.

1.10   BARTEN'S FUNDAMENTAL MATRIX EQUATION

In this section and the next we apply the method of comparative statics to obtain information about the demand equations (4.3) in the form of partial derivatives. This involves the use of the first-order conditions (3.4) and (4.2) to ask, How do the values of the endogenous variables $q_1, \ldots, q_n, \lambda$ respond to changes in the exogenous variables $p_1, \ldots, p_n, M$? We proceed in three steps.

We *first* differentiate the budget constraint (3.4) with respect to p_j and M to yield

$$\sum_{i=1}^{n} p_i \frac{\partial q_i}{\partial p_j} = -q_j \quad j=1, \ldots, n, \quad \sum_{i=1}^{n} p_i \frac{\partial q_i}{\partial M} = 1.$$

These can be expressed in matrix form as

$$p' \frac{\partial q}{\partial p'} = -q', \qquad p' \frac{\partial q}{\partial M} = 1, \tag{10.1}$$

where $\partial q/\partial p' = [\partial q_i/\partial p_j]$ is the $n \times n$ matrix of price derivatives of the demand functions, and $\partial q/\partial M = [\partial q_i/\partial M]$ is the vector of n income slopes of the demand functions.

Second, we differentiate the proportionality conditions (4.2) with respect to p_j and M to give

$$\sum_{k=1}^{n} \frac{\partial^2 u}{\partial q_i \partial q_k} \frac{\partial q_k}{\partial p_j} = \lambda \delta_{ij} + p_i \frac{\partial \lambda}{\partial p_j} \quad i, j = 1, \ldots, n,$$

where δ_{ij} is the Kronecker delta ($=1$ if $i=j$, 0 otherwise), and

$$\sum_{k=1}^{n} \frac{\partial^2 u}{\partial q_i \partial q_k} \frac{\partial q_k}{\partial M} = p_i \frac{\partial \lambda}{\partial M} \quad i = 1, \ldots, n.$$

We write these in matrix form as

$$U \frac{\partial q}{\partial p'} = \lambda I + p \frac{\partial \lambda}{\partial p'}, \qquad U \frac{\partial q}{\partial M} = \frac{\partial \lambda}{\partial M} p, \tag{10.2}$$

where U is the Hessian matrix (3.3), I is the $n \times n$ identity matrix, and $\partial \lambda/\partial p' = [\partial \lambda/\partial p_i]$.

Third, we combine (10.1) and (10.2) to give

$$\begin{bmatrix} U & p \\ p' & 0 \end{bmatrix} \begin{bmatrix} \partial q/\partial M & \partial q/\partial p' \\ -\partial \lambda/\partial M & -\partial \lambda/\partial p' \end{bmatrix} = \begin{bmatrix} 0 & \lambda I \\ 1 & -q' \end{bmatrix}. \tag{10.3}$$

This is known as *Barten's fundamental matrix equation in consumption theory,* after Barten (1964). The matrix immediately to the left of the equal sign contains the derivatives of all the endogenous variables with respect to all exogenous variables. Our next objective is to solve (10.3) for this matrix.

1.11   SOLVING THE MATRIX EQUATION

The inverse of the matrix on the far left of (10.3) is

$$\begin{bmatrix} U & p \\ p' & 0 \end{bmatrix}^{-1} = \frac{1}{p'U^{-1}p} \begin{bmatrix} (p'U^{-1}p)U^{-1} - U^{-1}p(U^{-1}p)' & U^{-1}p \\ (U^{-1}p)' & -1 \end{bmatrix}.$$

Using this inverse the solution of (10.3) is

$$\begin{bmatrix} \partial q/\partial M & \partial q/\partial p' \\ -\partial\lambda/\partial M & -\partial\lambda/\partial p' \end{bmatrix}$$

$$= \frac{1}{p'U^{-1}p} \begin{bmatrix} (p'U^{-1}p)U^{-1} - U^{-1}p(U^{-1}p)' & U^{-1}p \\ (U^{-1}p)' & -1 \end{bmatrix} \begin{bmatrix} 0 & \lambda I \\ 1 & -q' \end{bmatrix}.$$

Carrying out the matrix multiplication block by block, we obtain

$$\frac{\partial q}{\partial M} = \frac{1}{p'U^{-1}p} U^{-1}p, \tag{11.1}$$

$$\frac{\partial q}{\partial p'} = \lambda U^{-1} - \frac{\lambda}{p'U^{-1}p} U^{-1}p(U^{-1}p)' - \frac{1}{p'U^{-1}p} U^{-1}pq', \tag{11.2}$$

$$\frac{\partial\lambda}{\partial M} = \frac{1}{p'U^{-1}p}, \tag{11.3}$$

$$\frac{\partial\lambda}{\partial p} = -\frac{\lambda}{p'U^{-1}p} U^{-1}p - \frac{1}{p'U^{-1}p} q. \tag{11.4}$$

To simplify these expressions we use (11.3) to substitute $\partial\lambda/\partial M$ for the reciprocal of $p'U^{-1}p$ in (11.1), (11.2), and (11.4). Equation (11.1) then becomes

$$\frac{\partial q}{\partial M} = \frac{\partial\lambda}{\partial M} U^{-1}p. \tag{11.5}$$

Next, we replace $U^{-1}p$ in (11.2) and (11.4) with $\partial q/\partial M$ divided by $\partial\lambda/\partial M$, which follows from (11.5). This yields

$$\frac{\partial q}{\partial p'} = \lambda U^{-1} - \frac{\lambda}{\partial\lambda/\partial M} \frac{\partial q}{\partial M} \frac{\partial q'}{\partial M} - \frac{\partial q}{\partial M} q', \tag{11.6}$$

$$\frac{\partial\lambda}{\partial p} = -\lambda \frac{\partial q}{\partial M} - \frac{\partial\lambda}{\partial M} q. \tag{11.7}$$

Equations (11.5) and (11.6) give the income and price derivatives of the demand functions. We write the latter equation in scalar form as

$$\frac{\partial q_i}{\partial p_j} = \lambda u^{ij} - \frac{\lambda}{\partial \lambda/\partial M} \frac{\partial q_i}{\partial M} \frac{\partial q_j}{\partial M} - \frac{\partial q_i}{\partial M} q_j \quad i,j = 1,...,n, \qquad (11.8)$$

where u^{ij} is the (i,j)th element of U^{-1}. This shows that the effect of a change in p_j on q_i, with income and the other prices constant, is made up of three terms. The third term on the right of (11.8), $-q_j(\partial q_i/\partial M)$, is the *income effect* of the price change. The remaining two terms thus represent the *total substitution effect,* the response of q_i to a change in p_j, with *real* income (and the other prices) held constant. This total substitution effect comprises the *specific substitution effect,* λu^{ij}, and the *general substitution effect,*

$$-\frac{\lambda}{\partial \lambda/\partial M} \frac{\partial q_i}{\partial M} \frac{\partial q_j}{\partial M},$$

with the terminology from Houthakker (1960). The latter effect is concerned with the competition of all goods for an extra dollar of the consumer's income, while the former deals with the interaction of goods i and j in the utility function.

For future reference, we write (11.5) in scalar terms as

$$\frac{\partial q_i}{\partial M} = \frac{\partial \lambda}{\partial M} \sum_{j=1}^{n} u^{ij} p_j \quad i = 1,...,n. \qquad (11.9)$$

1.12   A DIFFERENTIAL DEMAND SYSTEM

In this section we use the solution to the fundamental matrix equation to derive a general system of differential demand equations. Derivations of the results of this section are given in the next section.

The total differential of (4.3) is

$$dq_i = \frac{\partial q_i}{\partial M} dM + \sum_{j=1}^{n} \frac{\partial q_i}{\partial p_j} dp_j \quad i = 1,...,n.$$

We transform this to logarithmic-differential form by multiplying both sides by p_i/M and using $w_i = p_i q_i/M$,

$$w_i d(\log q_i) = \frac{\partial(p_i q_i)}{\partial M} d(\log M) + \sum_{j=1}^{n} \frac{p_i p_j}{M} \frac{\partial q_i}{\partial p_j} d(\log p_j). \qquad (12.1)$$

We use (11.8) to express the second term on the right of (12.1) as

$$\sum_{j=1}^{n} \frac{p_i p_j}{M} \frac{\partial q_i}{\partial p_j} d(\log p_j)$$

$$= \sum_{j=1}^{n} \frac{p_i p_j}{M} \left(\lambda u^{ij} - \frac{\lambda}{\partial \lambda/\partial M} \frac{\partial q_i}{\partial M} \frac{\partial q_j}{\partial M} - \frac{\partial q_i}{\partial M} q_j \right) d(\log p_j).$$

Substituting this in (12.1) and rearranging gives

$$w_i \, d(\log q_i) = \frac{\partial(p_i q_i)}{\partial M} \left[d(\log M) - \sum_{j=1}^{n} w_j \, d(\log p_j) \right]$$

$$+ \sum_{j=1}^{n} \left(\frac{\lambda p_i p_j u^{ij}}{M} - \frac{\lambda/M}{\partial \lambda/\partial M} \frac{\partial(p_i q_i)}{\partial M} \frac{\partial(p_j q_j)}{\partial M} \right) d(\log p_j). \tag{12.2}$$

In view of (9.1) and (9.3) the term in square brackets on the right of the above is the Divisia volume index $d(\log Q)$, which enables us to write

$$\frac{\partial(p_i q_i)}{\partial M} \left[d(\log M) - \sum_{j=1}^{n} w_j \, d(\log p_j) \right] = \theta_i \, d(\log Q) \tag{12.3}$$

where we have used (2.6).

To simplify the price substitution term of (12.2), we define

$$\phi = \frac{\lambda/M}{\partial \lambda/\partial M} = \left(\frac{\partial \log \lambda}{\partial \log M} \right)^{-1} < 0 \tag{12.4}$$

as the reciprocal of the income elasticity of the marginal utility of income. For brevity, we shall refer to ϕ as the *income flexibility*. We also define

$$\theta_{ij} = \frac{\lambda}{\phi M} p_i p_j u^{ij} \quad i, j = 1, \ldots, n, \tag{12.5}$$

which satisfies

$$\sum_{j=1}^{n} \theta_{ij} = \theta_i \quad i = 1, \ldots, n. \tag{12.6}$$

The substitution term of (12.2) can then be expressed as

$$\sum_{j=1}^{n} \left(\frac{\lambda p_i p_j u^{ij}}{M} - \frac{\lambda/M}{\partial \lambda/\partial M} \frac{\partial(p_i q_i)}{\partial M} \frac{\partial(p_j q_j)}{\partial M} \right) d(\log p_j)$$

$$= \phi \sum_{j=1}^{n} \theta_{ij} [d(\log p_j) - d(\log P')], \tag{12.7}$$

where

$$d(\log P') = \sum_{i=1}^{n} \theta_i \, d(\log p_i) \tag{12.8}$$

is the *Frisch (1932) price index*. This index is different from the Divisia price index (9.3), which uses budget shares as weights rather than marginal shares; we shall return to this difference in Section 1.18 below.

Using (12.3) and (12.7) in (12.2), the demand equation for good i becomes

$$w_i \, d(\log q_i) = \theta_i \, d(\log Q) + \phi \sum_{j=1}^{n} \theta_{ij} \, d\left(\log \frac{p_j}{P'} \right), \tag{12.9}$$

where $d[\log(p_j/P')]$ is interpreted as $d(\log p_j) - d(\log P')$. The variable on the left of (12.9) has two interpretations. First, it is the quantity component of the change in the ith budget share. This interpretation can be verified by taking the differential of $w_i = p_i q_i/M$,

$$dw_i = w_i d(\log p_i) + w_i d(\log q_i) - w_i d(\log M).$$

Only the quantity component of this change is endogenous from the consumer's viewpoint. The second interpretation of the left side variable of (12.9) is the contribution of good i to the Divisia volume index $d(\log Q)$ defined in (9.2).

The first term on the right of (12.9) gives the effect of real income on the demand for good i. This term is a multiple θ_i of the Divisia volume index $d(\log Q)$. As this volume index equals $d(\log M) - d(\log P)$, where $d(\log P)$ is the Divisia price index, it follows that the Divisia price index transforms the change in money income into the change in real income. Furthermore, as the Divisia price index is budget-share weighted, it follows that this index measures the income effect of the n price changes on the demand for the ith good.

The second term on the right of (12.9), $\phi \sum_j \theta_{ij} d[\log(p_j/P')]$, deals with the effects of relative prices. The Frisch price index acts as a deflator of each price change, so that we refer to $d[\log(p_j/P')]$ as the change in the *Frisch-deflated price of j*. It is shown in the next section that the substitution term can be written as the difference between $\phi \sum_j \theta_{ij} d(\log p_j)$, which is the specific substitution effect of the n prices on the demand for good i, and $\phi \theta_i d(\log P')$, which is the general substitution effect. Accordingly, the general substitution effect acts as the deflator of the specific effect by transforming absolute prices into Frisch-deflated prices.

In the substitution term of (12.9), $\phi \theta_{ij}$ is the coefficient of the jth relative price, which shall be called the (i, j)th price coefficient. We shall refer to the θ_{ij}'s as the *normalized price coefficients*; they are normalized since $\sum_i \sum_j \theta_{ij} = 1$, which follows from (12.6). If $\theta_{ij} < 0$, then, as ϕ is negative, an increase in the Frisch-deflated price of j causes consumption of i to increase. Consequently, we follow Houthakker (1960) and define goods i and j as *specific substitutes (complements)* if $\theta_{ij} < 0$ (> 0). We will have more to say about substitutes and complements in Section 1.17.

In contrast to the other approaches to generating demand equations discussed in this chapter, the differential approach requires no algebraic specification of the utility function, the indirect utility function, or the cost function. Consequently, the coefficients of the demand equations (12.9) need not be constant; they may be functions of income and prices. The decision how to parameterize differential demand equations comes as the final step, just before estimation. This principle is illustrated later in this chapter.

1.13 DERIVATIONS AND EXTENSIONS

Our first objective is to show that ϕ is negative, as stated in equation (12.4). We use (12.5) and (12.6) to write

$$\sum_{j=1}^{n} \frac{\lambda}{M} p_i p_j u^{ij} = \phi \theta_i \quad i = 1, ..., n.$$

In view of $\Sigma_i \theta_i = 1$, summing both sides of the above over $i = 1, ..., n$ yields

$$\phi = \frac{\lambda}{M} \sum_{i=1}^{n} \sum_{j=1}^{n} p_i p_j u^{ij}. \tag{13.1}$$

The right side is proportional to a quadratic form with matrix U^{-1} and vector p; in view of (3.3) this matrix is negative definite, so that the quadratic form is negative. As the factor of proportionality λ/M on the right of (13.1) is positive, we conclude that $\phi < 0$.

Constraint (12.6) can be verified by multiplying both sides of (11.9) by p_i, which yields

$$\theta_i = \frac{\partial \lambda}{\partial M} \sum_{j=1}^{n} p_i p_j u^{ij} \quad i = 1, ..., n,$$

and then using (12.4) to substitute $\lambda/\phi M$ for $\partial \lambda/\partial M$. After using (12.5), we obtain (12.6).

To verify (12.7) we use (2.6), (12.4), and (12.5) to express the substitution term of (12.2) as

$$\sum_{j=1}^{n} \left(\frac{\lambda p_i p_j u^{ij}}{M} - \frac{\lambda/M}{\partial \lambda/\partial M} \frac{\partial(p_i q_i)}{\partial M} \frac{\partial(p_j q_j)}{\partial M} \right) d(\log p_j)$$

$$= \phi \sum_{j=1}^{n} (\theta_{ij} - \theta_i \theta_j) d(\log p_j). \tag{13.2}$$

In view of (12.8), the right side of (13.2) can be written as

$$\phi \sum_{j=1}^{n} (\theta_{ij} - \theta_i \theta_j) d(\log p_j) = \phi \left[\sum_{j=1}^{n} \theta_{ij} d(\log p_j) - \theta_i d(\log P') \right]. \tag{13.3}$$

Substituting $\Sigma_j \theta_{ij}$ for θ_i [which follows from (12.6)] on the right side of (13.3) yields the right side of equation (12.7). Therefore (13.2) and (13.3) verify (12.7). Equation (13.3) also shows that the substitution term of (12.9) is the difference between $\phi \Sigma_j \theta_{ij} d(\log p_j)$ and $\phi \theta_i d(\log P')$.

To further interpret the θ_{ij}'s, we use (12.5) to define the $n \times n$ matrix

$$[\theta_{ij}] = \frac{\lambda}{\phi M} P^* U^{-1} P^*, \qquad (13.4)$$

where P^* is the diagonal matrix with $p_1, \ldots, p_n$ on the diagonal and U^{-1} is the inverse of the Hessian of the utility function. On the right in (13.4), $\lambda, M > 0$ and $\phi < 0$; P^* is a symmetric positive matrix and U^{-1} is symmetric negative definite. Therefore,

$$[\theta_{ij}] \text{ is a symmetric positive definite } n \times n \text{ matrix.} \qquad (13.5)$$

Inverting both sides of (13.4), we obtain

$$\theta^{ij} = \frac{\phi M}{\lambda} \frac{\partial^2 u}{\partial(p_i q_i) \partial(p_j q_j)} \quad i, j = 1, \ldots, n, \qquad (13.6)$$

where θ^{ij} is the (i, j)th element of $[\theta_{ij}]^{-1}$. Since $\partial u/\partial(p_i q_i)$ is the marginal utility of a dollar spent on i, $\partial^2 u/\partial(p_i q_i) \partial(p_j q_j)$ on the right in (13.6) is interpreted as the change in this marginal utility when spending on j increases by one dollar. Accordingly, (13.6) shows that $[\theta_{ij}]$ is inversely proportional to the Hessian matrix of the utility function in expenditure terms.

We now return to preference independence (5.1) and analyze the implications of this form of the utility function for the demand equation (12.9). Under (5.1), the Hessian matrix U and its inverse are both diagonal. As $u^{ij} = 0$ for $i \neq j$, it follows from (12.5) that $\theta_{ij} = 0$ for $i \neq j$. Equation (12.6) then implies $\theta_{ii} = \theta_i$, so that the demand equation (12.9) takes the simpler form

$$w_i d(\log q_i) = \theta_i d(\log Q) + \phi \theta_i d\left(\log \frac{p_i}{P'}\right). \qquad (13.7)$$

Therefore, preference independence implies that only the own-deflated price appears in each demand equation, rather than all n such prices. In other words, preference independence implies that no pair of goods (i, j) can be either a specific substitute or a specific complement. In addition, for $[\theta_{ij}]$ to be a positive definite matrix with diagonal elements $\theta_1, \ldots, \theta_n$ and off-diagonal elements zero, each marginal share θ_i must be positive. Consequently, the hypothesis of preference independence rules out inferior goods.

The substitution term of equation (12.9) is formulated in terms of deflated prices. We use (13.3) to express the substitution term in absolute (or undeflated) prices as

$$\phi \sum_{j=1}^{n} \theta_{ij} d\left(\log \frac{p_j}{P'}\right) = \sum_{j=1}^{n} \pi_{ij} d(\log p_j), \qquad (13.8)$$

where

$$\pi_{ij} = \phi(\theta_{ij} - \theta_i \theta_j) \quad i, j = 1, \ldots, n \tag{13.9}$$

is the (i, j)th *Slutsky* (1915) *coefficient*. This coefficient gives the total substitution effect on the demand for good i of a change in the jth price. It can be easily verified that

$[\pi_{ij}]$ is a symmetric negative semidefinite $n \times n$ matrix with rank $n-1$.

$$\tag{13.10}$$

Using (13.8) in (12.9) yields the demand equation for good i in terms of absolute prices,

$$w_i d(\log q_i) = \theta_i d(\log Q) + \sum_{j=1}^{n} \pi_{ij} d(\log p_j). \tag{13.11}$$

In the previous section we used the solution to the fundamental matrix equation (10.3) to analyze the change in consumption of each good. We now use the same approach to derive a simple result for the change in the marginal utility of income λ. As λ depends on income and prices we write $\lambda = \lambda(M, p)$, so that

$$d(\log \lambda) = \frac{\partial \lambda / \partial M}{\lambda / M} d(\log M) + \sum_{j=1}^{n} \frac{\partial \lambda}{\partial p_j} \frac{p_j}{\lambda} d(\log p_j)$$

$$= \frac{1}{\phi} d(\log M) + \sum_{j=1}^{n} \left(-\lambda \frac{\partial q_j}{\partial M} - \frac{\partial \lambda}{\partial M} q_j \right) \frac{p_j}{\lambda} d(\log p_j), \tag{13.12}$$

where the second step follows from (11.7) and (12.4). Using (2.4), (2.6), and (12.4), the second term on the right of (13.12) can be expressed as

$$\sum_{j=1}^{n} \left(-\lambda \frac{\partial q_j}{\partial M} - \frac{\partial \lambda}{\partial M} q_j \right) \frac{p_j}{\lambda} d(\log p_j)$$

$$= \sum_{j=1}^{n} \left(-\theta_j - \frac{1}{\phi} w_j \right) d(\log p_j) = -d(\log P') - \frac{1}{\phi} d(\log P),$$

where $d(\log P')$ is the Frisch price index (12.8) and $d(\log P)$ is the Divisia price index (9.3). Using the third member of the above in (13.12), and noting that $d(\log M) - d(\log P) = d(\log Q)$, the Divisia volume index, we obtain

$$d(\log \lambda) = \frac{1}{\phi} d(\log Q) - d(\log P'). \tag{13.13}$$

This shows how the change in λ depends on the change in real income and the price changes.

1.14 THE ROTTERDAM MODEL

Equation (12.9) is formulated in terms of infinitesimal changes; the Rotterdam model, due to Barten (1964) and Theil (1965), is a finite-change version of (12.9). We write $Dx_t = \log x_t - \log x_{t-1}$ for the finite log-change from period $t-1$ to t for any positive variable x. The variable $d(\log q_i)$ on the left in (12.9) becomes Dq_{it} and $d[\log(p_j/P')]$ becomes $Dp_{jt} - DP'_t$, where $DP'_t = \sum_i \theta_i Dp_{it}$ is a finite-change version of the Frisch price index. As the budget share w_i on the left in (12.9) does not involve a change, we could use $w_{i,t-1}$, w_{it}, or a combination thereof that treats t and $t-1$ symmetrically. The natural choice is to use the arithmetic average of $w_{i,t-1}$ and w_{it}, $\bar{w}_{it} = \frac{1}{2}(w_{i,t-1} + w_{it})$, which is midway between the two extremities. The finite-change version of (12.9) is then

$$\bar{w}_{it}Dq_{it} = \theta_i DQ_t + \sum_{j=1}^{n} \nu_{ij}(Dp_{jt} - DP'_t), \tag{14.1}$$

where $DQ_t = \sum_i \bar{w}_{it}Dq_{it}$ is a finite-change version of the Divisia volume index and

$$\nu_{ij} = \phi\theta_{ij} \tag{14.2}$$

is the coefficient of the jth relative price, to be referred to as the (i,j)th *price coefficient*.

When the coefficients of (14.1) θ_i and ν_{ij} are treated as constants, it is known as the ith demand equation of the *relative price version of the Rotterdam model*. In view of ϕ being negative and (13.5), the $n \times n$ matrix of price coefficients $[\nu_{ij}]$ is symmetric negative definite; these coefficients also satisfy

$$\sum_{j=1}^{n} \nu_{ij} = \phi\theta_i \quad i = 1, \ldots, n, \tag{14.3}$$

which follows from (12.6). Constraint (14.3) and the constancy of the coefficients ν_{ij} and θ_i imply that ϕ is also a constant in the model.

The second version of the Rotterdam model takes as its starting point the differential demand equation in absolute prices (13.11). The finite-change version of that equation is

$$\bar{w}_{it}Dq_{it} = \theta_i DQ_t + \sum_{j=1}^{n} \pi_{ij}Dp_{jt}, \tag{14.4}$$

where π_{ij} is the Slutsky coefficient defined in (13.9). We write this coefficient in the equivalent form

$$\pi_{ij} = \nu_{ij} - \phi\theta_i\theta_j \quad i, j = 1, \ldots, n. \tag{14.5}$$

When the coefficients θ_i and π_{ij} are specified as constants, (14.4) is known as the ith equation of the *absolute price version of the Rotterdam model*.

In view of (13.10), the Slutsky coefficients are symmetric in i and j,

$$\pi_{ij} = \pi_{ji} \quad i, j = 1, \ldots, n, \tag{14.6}$$

which is known as *Slutsky symmetry*. These coefficients also satisfy

$$\sum_{j=1}^{n} \pi_{ij} = 0 \quad i = 1, \ldots, n, \tag{14.7}$$

which follows from (14.3) and (14.5). Constraint (14.7) reflects the homogeneity postulate that a proportionate change in all prices has no effect on the demand for any good under the condition that real income is constant. Accordingly, (14.7) is known as *demand homogeneity*. As stated in (13.10), the Slutsky matrix $[\pi_{ij}]$ is symmetric negative semidefinite with rank $n-1$; the cause of the singularity is (14.7).

The two versions of the model both have their attractions. The absolute price version and the constraints (14.6) and (14.7) are linear in the parameters, which makes estimation and testing straightforward. However, when n becomes larger, the number of π_{ij}'s grows rapidly, making the absolute price version of the model suitable for small systems only. For larger models, it is necessary to use the relative price version of the model (which is nonlinear in the parameters) with suitable constraints on the ν_{ij}'s. These constraints take the form of postulating that certain goods do not interact in the utility function; a special case of this is preference independence when no good interacts with any other. Under preference independence the utility function takes the form (5.1), so that all second-order cross-derivatives vanish. Therefore, in view of (12.5), (14.2), and (14.3), $\nu_{ij} = 0$ for $i \neq j$ and $\nu_{ii} = \phi\theta_i$. The relative price version of the Rotterdam model (14.1) then takes the form

$$\bar{w}_{it}Dq_{it} = \theta_i DQ_t + \phi\theta_i(Dp_{it} - DP'_t). \tag{14.8}$$

The number of unconstrained coefficients in (14.8) for $i = 1, \ldots, n$ is n, which is made up of $n-1$ unconstrained θ_i's (one is constrained by $\sum_i \theta_i = 1$) and ϕ. Note that (14.8) is simply a finite-change version of (13.7).

Remark 1. Barnett (1979) analyzed the issue of aggregation over consumers in the context of differential demand equations. He started with each individual consumer possessing his own system of demand equations in the form of (13.11) with nonconstant coefficients; tastes are allowed to differ across consumers. Then, using the convergence approach to aggregation over consumers (Theil 1971: Sec. 11.4), Barnett obtains the Rotterdam model (14.4) with constant coefficients as a Taylor series approximation to the aggregate (per capita) demand equations. This result is obtained under extremely weak conditions; in particular, the result holds even when there is no individual consumer whose differential demand equations have constant coefficients.

Remark 2.   It follows from (14.5) that the constancy of the coefficients θ_i, ν_{ij}, and ϕ in the relative price version of the Rotterdam model implies that the Slutsky coefficients π_{ij} are also constant in the absolute price version.

1.15   WORKING'S MODEL FURTHER CONSIDERED

The Rotterdam model is a particular parameterization that uses the results of the differential approach. In this section we illustrate the usefulness of the differential approach as a general tool in demand analysis by giving a further parameterization using this approach. This parameterization involves endowing Working's model (8.1) with a substitution term under the assumption of preference independence.

We return to the general differential demand equation under preference independence (13.7) and recall that Working's model implies that the marginal share of good i equals the corresponding budget share plus a constant, $\theta_i = w_i + \beta_i$ [see equation (8.2)]. For a time-series application we write this marginal share as $\bar{w}_{it} + \beta_i$, where $\bar{w}_{it} = \frac{1}{2}(w_{i,t-1} + w_{it})$. To obtain the finite-change version of (13.7) we replace (1) w_i with $\bar{w}_{it}$, (2) $d(\log q_i)$ with Dq_{it}, (3) $d(\log Q)$ with $DQ_t = \sum_i \bar{w}_{it} Dq_{it}$, (4) θ_i with $\bar{w}_{it} + \beta_i$, and (5) $d(\log p_i)$ with Dp_{it}. After minor rearrangement, this yields

$$\bar{w}_{it}(Dq_{it} - DQ_t) = \beta_i DQ_t + \phi(\bar{w}_{it} + \beta_i)\left[Dp_{it} - \sum_{j=1}^{n}(\bar{w}_{jt} + \beta_j)Dp_{jt}\right]. \qquad (15.1)$$

Here the β_i's and ϕ are constant coefficients. Model (15.1) is the ith demand equation of Working's model with a substitution term added under preference independence with a constant income flexibility. For brevity, we shall refer to (15.1) as *Working's model under preference independence.*

Equation (15.1) can be compared to the AIDS model (7.6), which reduces to Working's model when prices are constant; see the discussion at the beginning of Section 1.8. There are two basic differences between (15.1) and AIDS. First, (15.1) is formulated in terms of changes over time, whereas AIDS is in levels; this is the reason for the absence of intercept terms in

(15.1). Second, the substitution term of AIDS is much more complicated as it involves double-subscripted parameters; (15.1) has only single-subscripted parameters. Thus, the number of γ_{ij}'s in the AIDS substitution term is of the order n^2, while in Working's model there are only $n-1$ β_i's (the constraint $\sum_i \beta_i = 0$ eliminates one β_i) and ϕ.

1.16   THE BEHAVIOR OF IMPLIED INCOME ELASTICITIES

In this chapter we have presented six systems of demand equations: the double-log model (2.1); the linear expenditure system (4.4); the translog model (6.6); AIDS (7.6); the two versions of the Rotterdam model (14.1) and (14.4); and Working's model under preference independence (15.1). As these all describe the demand for the n goods in one form or another, they are competitive specifications. The choice between them is generally made on the basis of statistical criteria such as goodness of fit or likelihood ratios. A different criterion, recommended by Flood, Finke, and Theil (1984), is the economic plausibility of the behavior of the income elasticities implied by the competing models.

To apply this procedure, Flood, Finke, and Theil (1984) and Finke, Flood, and Theil (1984) used annual Japanese data (1951–1972) to estimate by maximum likelihood the translog model (6.6), as well as Working's model under preference independence (15.1) for $n = 4$ goods: food (including beverages and tobacco); clothing (including footwear); housing (including furniture); and miscellaneous (everything else). For the estimation of the two models, normal error terms are added to the right sides of (6.6) and (15.1); see Sections 2.8 and 2.9 for details of the procedure of obtaining the ML estimates of Working's model.

The income elasticity of i is

$$1 + \frac{\sum\limits_{k=1}^{n} \sum\limits_{j=1}^{n} \beta_{kj} - (1/w_{it}) \sum\limits_{j=1}^{n} \beta_{ij}}{-1 + \sum\limits_{k=1}^{n} \sum\limits_{j=1}^{n} \beta_{kj} \log \dfrac{p_j}{M}} \tag{16.1}$$

under the translog and (8.3) under Working's model. These elasticities are given in Table 1–4. As can be seen, the two models imply substantially different elasticities. The translog elasticity of food *increases* from 0.42 in the early 1950s to 0.75 in the early 1970s. By contrast, the food elasticity under Working's model starts off at 0.72 and gradually *declines* to 0.54. The increase in

Table 1-4. The Behavior of Income Elasticities under Alternative Models: Japan, 1951–1972.

	Income elasticities implied by							
	Translog model				Working's model			
Year (1)	Food (2)	Clothing (3)	Housing (4)	Miscellaneous (5)	Food (6)	Clothing (7)	Housing (8)	Miscellaneous (9)
1951	.42	.42	3.74	2.01	—	—	—	—
1952	.46	.47	3.06	1.85	.72	1.02	1.80	1.39
1953	.48	.49	2.71	1.74	.71	1.02	1.72	1.37
1954	.50	.50	2.65	1.69	.71	1.02	1.68	1.35
1955	.51	.51	2.46	1.66	.70	1.02	1.65	1.33
1956	.52	.52	2.27	1.61	.70	1.02	1.61	1.32
1957	.54	.53	2.17	1.56	.69	1.02	1.58	1.32
1958	.55	.54	2.05	1.52	.68	1.02	1.55	1.31
1959	.56	.55	1.94	1.48	.67	1.03	1.50	1.31
1960	.59	.57	1.80	1.42	.65	1.03	1.45	1.30
1961	.61	.59	1.71	1.38	.64	1.02	1.43	1.29
1962	.62	.61	1.62	1.34	.62	1.02	1.42	1.28
1963	.64	.63	1.56	1.30	.61	1.03	1.42	1.26
1964	.66	.65	1.48	1.26	.60	1.02	1.39	1.26
1965	.67	.66	1.47	1.25	.59	1.03	1.38	1.25
1966	.68	.67	1.42	1.23	.59	1.03	1.37	1.25
1967	.70	.68	1.38	1.21	.58	1.03	1.36	1.24
1968	.71	.70	1.35	1.19	.58	1.03	1.35	1.24
1969	.72	.71	1.32	1.18	.57	1.03	1.34	1.24
1970	.73	.72	1.30	1.16	.55	1.03	1.33	1.24
1971	.74	.73	1.28	1.16	.55	1.03	1.32	1.23
1972	.75	.74	1.26	1.15	.54	1.03	1.32	1.23

this elasticity under the translog model means that the increased affluence of the Japanese over this period caused food to become *more* luxurious, which is implausible. It is much more plausible for food to become *less* of a luxury with increased affluence, as it does under Working's model. Note also that the translog elasticity values for housing in the early years seem too high. Moreover, these values decline by more than 50 percent over the period (from 3.7 to 1.3), while the corresponding values under Working's model are more stable. On the basis of the behavior of these elasticities, the conclusion is that Working's model is more acceptable than the translog.

1.17   MORE ON SUBSTITUTES AND COMPLEMENTS

We return to the general differential demand equation (12.9) and recall that the signs of the normalized price coefficients θ_{ij} indicate the pattern of substitutability/complementarity according to the Houthakker definition. As ϕ is negative, goods i and j are said to be specific substitutes (complements) if $\theta_{ij} < 0$ (> 0). This definition of substitutability is based on the sign of u^{ij}, the (i, j)th element of the inverse of the Hessian matrix of the utility function, and thus relates to the nature of the interaction of goods in the utility function.

By contrast, Hicks' (1946) definition is based on the sign of the total substitution effect, the sum of the specific and general effects. As the Slutsky coefficients defined in (13.9) combine the latter two effects, their signs reflect substitutability/complementarity in Hicks' sense. If $\pi_{ij} > 0$, then it follows from (13.11) that a rise in the absolute price of j causes consumption of i to increase, real income and other prices remaining constant. Accordingly, goods i and j are said to be *Hicksian substitutes (complements)* if $\pi_{ij} > 0$ (< 0).

To clarify this distinction, consider the following example, from Theil (1980). Let the matrix of normalized price coefficients for $n = 3$ goods be

$$[\theta_{ij}] = \begin{bmatrix} .5 & .1 & -.1 \\ .1 & .4 & -.2 \\ -.1 & -.2 & .5 \end{bmatrix} \begin{matrix} \text{good 1} \\ \text{good 2.} \\ \text{good 3} \end{matrix} \tag{17.1}$$

This matrix is symmetric in accordance with (13.5) and the sum of all the elements is unity. Its sign pattern indicates that goods 1 and 2 are specific complements; goods 1 and 3 are specific substitutes; and goods 2 and 3 are specific substitutes. Application of (12.6) yields the marginal shares as the row sums of (17.1):

$$[\theta_i] = \begin{bmatrix} .5 \\ .3 \\ .2 \end{bmatrix} \begin{matrix} \text{good 1} \\ \text{good 2.} \\ \text{good 3} \end{matrix} \qquad (17.2)$$

Let the three budget shares be

$$[w_i] = \begin{bmatrix} .2 \\ .3 \\ .5 \end{bmatrix} \begin{matrix} \text{good 1} \\ \text{good 2} \\ \text{good 3} \end{matrix} \qquad (17.3)$$

so that, in view of (2.7), the income elasticities are

$$[\eta_i] = [\theta_i/w_i] = \begin{bmatrix} 2.5 \\ 1.0 \\ .4 \end{bmatrix} \begin{matrix} \text{good 1} \\ \text{good 2.} \\ \text{good 3} \end{matrix}$$

Good 1 is a luxury and 3 a necessity, while 2 is a borderline case.

If we divide both sides of (12.9) by w_i, we obtain $\phi\theta_{ij}/w_i$ as the elasticity of consumption of good i with respect to the Frisch-deflated price of j. This is known as the *Frisch price elasticity*. Using $\phi = -0.5$, (17.1) and (17.3) yield the following Frisch price elasticity matrix:

$$[\phi\theta_{ij}/w_i] = \begin{bmatrix} -1.25 & -.25 & .25 \\ -.17 & -.67 & .33 \\ .10 & .20 & -.50 \end{bmatrix} \begin{matrix} \text{good 1} \\ \text{good 2.} \\ \text{good 3} \end{matrix}$$

Thus, a 1 percent increase in the Frisch-deflated price of good 1, other Frisch-deflated prices and income remaining constant, causes consumption of that good to fall by 1.25 percent; consumption of good 2 falls by 0.17 percent (as 1 and 2 are specific complements); and that of good 3 rises by 0.10 percent (1 and 3 are specific substitutes).

Using (17.1), (17.2), and $\phi = -0.5$ in (13.9) gives the following matrix of Slutsky coefficients:

$$[\pi_{ij}] = \phi[\theta_{ij} - \theta_i\theta_j] = \begin{bmatrix} -.13 & .03 & .10 \\ .03 & -.16 & .13 \\ .10 & .13 & -.23 \end{bmatrix} \begin{matrix} \text{good 1} \\ \text{good 2.} \\ \text{good 3} \end{matrix} \qquad (17.4)$$

As all the off-diagonal elements are positive, the three goods are pairwise substitutes in Hicks' sense. Dividing both sides of (13.11) by w_i, we find that π_{ij}/w_i is the elasticity of demand for i with respect to the jth absolute price, which is known as the *Slutsky price elasticity*. Using (17.3) and (17.4), the Slutsky elasticity matrix is

$$[\pi_{ij}/w_i] = \begin{bmatrix} -.65 & .15 & .50 \\ .10 & -.53 & .43 \\ .20 & .26 & -.46 \end{bmatrix} \begin{matrix} \text{good 1} \\ \text{good 2.} \\ \text{good 3} \end{matrix}$$

Accordingly, when real income and the other prices are held constant, a 1 percent increase in the absolute price of good 1 leads to a 0.65 percent fall in consumption of that good and increases in the consumption of the other two goods of 0.10 and 0.20 percent, respectively.

1.18   DIVISIA MOMENTS

The Divisia price index $d(\log P)$ is defined in (9.3) as a budget-share weighted average of the n logarithmic price changes $d(\log p_1), ..., d(\log p_n)$. This can be viewed as a weighted first-order moment of the price changes. The corresponding second-order moment is the *Divisia price variance*,

$$\Pi = \sum_{i=1}^{n} w_i[d(\log p_i) - d(\log P)]^2 = \sum_{i=1}^{n} w_i\left[d\left(\log \frac{p_i}{P}\right)\right]^2. \qquad (18.1)$$

This Π vanishes when all prices change proportionately and it increases when the prices change more disproportionately. In other words, Π is a measure of the changes in relative prices.

Similarly, the Divisia volume index $d(\log Q)$, defined in (9.2), is the Divisia (i.e., budget-share weighted) mean of the quantity changes. There is also the *Divisia quantity variance*,

$$K = \sum_{i=1}^{n} w_i[d(\log q_i) - d(\log Q)]^2 = \sum_{i=1}^{n} w_i\left[d\left(\log \frac{q_i}{Q}\right)\right]^2, \qquad (18.2)$$

and the *Divisia price-quantity covariance*,

$$\Gamma = \sum_{i=1}^{n} w_i d\left(\log \frac{p_i}{P}\right) d\left(\log \frac{q_i}{Q}\right), \qquad (18.3)$$

which measures the co-movement of prices and quantities. As those commodities having above-average price increases would tend to experience below-average increases in consumption and vice versa, Γ will usually be negative.

Using $w_i = p_i q_i/M$, we obtain

$$d(\log w_i) = d(\log p_i) + d(\log q_i) - d(\log M)$$

$$= [d(\log p_i) - d(\log P)] + [d(\log q_i) - d(\log Q)], \qquad (18.4)$$

where the second step follows from the decomposition

$$d(\log M) = d(\log Q) + d(\log P);$$

see equation (9.1). Using (18.1) through (18.4), we obtain

$$\sum_{i=1}^{n} w_i [d(\log w_i)]^2 = \Pi + K + 2\Gamma. \tag{18.5}$$

The term on the left of the above is the Divisia second moment of the logarithmic changes in the budget shares. In view of $\sum_i w_i = 1$, the corresponding Divisia mean is

$$\sum_{i=1}^{n} w_i d(\log w_i) = \sum_{i=1}^{n} w_i \frac{dw_i}{w_i} = 0.$$

Consequently, the left side of (18.5) is the *Divisia variance of the budget shares*. Equation (18.5) shows that this variance is equal to the sum of the price and quantity variances plus twice the price-quantity covariance.

The above Divisia moments provide convenient summary measures of the price-quantity changes. We now analyze two other applications of Divisia moments. First, consider the n income elasticities $\eta_1, \ldots, \eta_n$. It follows from (2.8) that their Divisia mean is unity, $\sum_i w_i \eta_i = 1$. The Divisia variance is

$$\sum_{i=1}^{n} w_i (\eta_i - 1)^2,$$

which is a measure of dispersion of these elasticities.

Next, consider the Divisia covariance of the income elasticities and the logarithmic price changes,

$$\Psi = \sum_{i=1}^{n} w_i (\eta_i - 1) [d(\log p_i) - d(\log P)]$$

$$= \sum_{i=1}^{n} (\theta_i - w_i) [d(\log p_i) - d(\log P)]$$

$$= \sum_{i=1}^{n} \theta_i d(\log p_i) - \sum_{i=1}^{n} w_i d(\log p_i), \tag{18.6}$$

where the first step follows from $\eta_i = \theta_i / w_i$ and the second from $\sum_i \theta_i = \sum_i w_i = 1$. In view of (9.3) and (12.8), we have

$$\Psi = d(\log P') - d(\log P).$$

In words, the Divisia income elasticity–price covariance is equal to the excess of the Frisch price index over the corresponding Divisia index. This excess is positive when the covariance Ψ is positive. From (18.6), $\Psi > 0$ when, on average, (1) the relative prices of luxuries ($\eta_i > 1$) increase and (2) the relative prices of necessities fall. The price of good i receives a weight θ_i in

$d(\log P')$ and w_i in $d(\log P)$. As $\theta_i > w_i$ for luxuries, these goods are more heavily weighted in the Frisch price index. Consequently, a rise in the relative prices of luxuries means that $d(\log P') > d(\log P)$, and similarly for a fall in the relative prices of necessities.

Remark 1. For further details of Divisia moments, see Theil (1975/76: Chap. 11).

Remark 2. Below equation (18.3) it is stated that the price-quantity covariance Γ is usually negative. However, as Γ includes a real-income component, in certain cases it may be positive. See Theil (1975/76: Chap. 11).

BIBLIOGRAPHY

The publications listed below are those referred to in Chapter 1, supplemented by some other publications that are directly related to the topics discussed.

Barnett, W.A. 1979. "Theoretical Foundations for the Rotterdam Model." *Review of Economic Studies* 46: 109–30.
Barten, A.P. 1964. "Consumer Demand Functions Under Conditions of Almost Additive Preferences." *Econometrica* 32: 1–38.
———. 1977. "The Systems of Consumer Demand Functions Approach: A Review." *Econometrica* 45: 23–51.
Brown, A., and A.S. Deaton. 1972. "Surveys in Applied Economics: Models of Consumer Behaviour." *Economic Journal* 82: 1145–1236.
Cassel, G. 1932. *The Theory of Social Economy*. Rev. ed. Translated from the 5th German ed. by S.L. Barrow. New York: Harcourt, Brace.
Christensen, L.R.; D.W. Jorgenson; and L.J. Lau. 1975. "Transcendental Logarithmic Utility Functions." *American Economic Review* 65: 367–83.
Deaton, A.S. 1975. *Models and Projections of Demand in Post-War Britain*. London: Chapman and Hall.
Deaton, A.S., and J. Muellbauer. 1980a. *Economics and Consumer Behavior*. Cambridge: Cambridge University Press.
———. 1980b. "An Almost Ideal Demand System." *American Economic Review* 70: 312–26.
Divisia, F. 1925. "L'indice monétaire et la théorie de la monnaie." *Revue d'Economie Politique* 39: 980–1008.
Engel, E. 1857. "Die Productions—und Consumtionsverhältnisse des Könichreichs Sachsen." *Zeitschrift des Statistischen Büreaus des Königlich Sächsischen Ministeriums des Innern* 8–9: 1–54. Reprinted in the *Bulletin de l'Institut International de Statistique* 9, 1895.
Finke, R.; L.R. Flood; and H. Theil. 1984. "Maximum Likelihood and Instrumental Variable Estimation of a Consumer Demand System for Japan and Sweden." *Economics Letters* 15: 13–19.

Flood, L.R.; R. Finke; and H. Theil. 1984. "An Evaluation of Alternative Demand Systems by Means of Implied Income Elasticities." *Economics Letters* 15: 21-27.

Frisch, R. 1932. *New Methods of Measuring Marginal Utility.* Tübingen: J.C.B. Mohr.

Hicks, J.R. 1946. *Value and Capital.* 2d ed. Oxford: Oxford University Press.

Houthakker, H.S. 1957. "An International Comparison of Household Expenditure Patterns, Commemorating the Centenary of Engel's Law." *Econometrica* 25: 532-51.

———. 1960. "Additive Preferences." *Econometrica* 28: 244-57.

Klein, L.R., and H. Rubin. 1948. "A Constant-Utility Index of the Cost of Living." *Review of Economic Studies* 15: 84-87.

Lluch, C., and A.A. Powell. 1975. "International Comparisons of Expenditure Patterns." *European Economic Review* 5: 275-303.

Lluch, C.; A.A. Powell; and R.A. Williams. 1977. *Patterns in Household Demand and Saving.* Oxford: Oxford University Press.

Phlips, L. 1974. *Applied Consumption Analysis.* Amsterdam: North-Holland Publishing Company.

Powell, A.A. 1974. *Empirical Analytics of Demand Systems.* Lexington, Mass.: D.C. Heath and Company.

Roy, R. 1942. *De l'utilité.* Paris: Hermann et Cie.

Slutsky, E. 1915. "Sulla Teoria del Bilancio del Consumatore." *Giornale degli Economisti* 51: 1-26. Translation, "On the Theory of the Budget of the Consumer." In *Readings in Price Theory,* edited by G.J. Stigler and K.E. Boulding, Chapter 2. Chicago: Richard D. Irwin, 1952.

Stone, R. 1954a. *The Measurement of Consumers' Expenditure and Behaviour in the United Kingdom, 1920-1938.* Vol. 1. Cambridge: Cambridge University Press.

———. 1954b. "Linear Expenditure Systems and Demand Analysis: An Application to the Pattern of British Demand." *Economic Journal* 64: 511-27.

Theil, H. 1965. "The Information Approach to Demand Analysis." *Econometrica* 33: 67-87.

———. 1967. *Economics and Information Theory.* New York: American Elsevier Publishing Company, and Amsterdam: North-Holland Publishing Company.

———. 1971. *Principles of Econometrics.* New York: John Wiley and Sons.

———. 1975/76. *Theory and Measurement of Consumer Demand.* 2 vols. Amsterdam: North-Holland Publishing Company.

———. 1980. *The System-Wide Approach to Microeconomics.* Chicago: The University of Chicago Press.

Theil, H., and F.E. Suhm. 1981. *International Consumption Comparisons: A System-Wide Approach.* Amsterdam: North-Holland Publishing Company.

Working, H. 1943. "Statistical Laws of Family Expenditure." *Journal of the American Statistical Association* 38: 43-56.

2 EVIDENCE FROM INTERNATIONAL CONSUMPTION COMPARISONS

Henri Theil

2.1   INTRODUCTION

This chapter presents evidence, in the form of income and price elasticities at various levels of real income, of the income and price sensitivity of the demand for broad groups of consumer goods. The underlying data are per capita data collected by Irving Kravis, Alan Heston, and Robert Summers of the University of Pennsylvania for a number of countries at quite different levels of affluence. These researchers published their results in three successive volumes. Kravis et al. (1975) considered ten countries: Colombia, France, Germany (West), Hungary, India, Italy, Japan, Kenya, the United Kingdom, and the United States. Kravis, Heston, and Summers (1978) extended the results to sixteen countries by adding the following six: Belgium, Iran, Korea, Malaysia, the Netherlands, and the Philippines. Finally, Kravis, Heston, and Summers (1982) considered thirty-four countries; most of what follows in this chapter is based on the 1982 publication.

The big problem in the comparison of consumption data for different countries is that these data are expressed in different currencies. A simple solution is by conversion based on exchange rates, but this procedure is highly imperfect. As will be explained in Section 2.2, Kravis et al. selected a microeconomic approach by computing purchasing power parities for narrowly

Comments by Kenneth Clements on an earlier draft of this chapter are gratefully acknowledged.

defined groups of goods such as "fresh vegetables." This is followed by aggregation over these groups, after which the results for total consumption and GDP and for ten broad groups of consumer goods will be presented in Sections 2.3 and 2.4.

The next problem is the formulation of a system of cross-country demand equations for these ten "goods." It is, of course, not at all self-evident that such a system is feasible (different countries may have different tastes). However, Theil and Suhm (1981) obtained some success when applying Working's model to the earlier cross-country data of Kravis et al. (1978); Section 2.5 shows that this model continues to be attractive. It should also be noted that if such a simple model is at least approximately correct, the use of per capita data of such countries as India and the United States has the great advantage of a large variation in the independent variables (real income and relative prices). The reader who is interested in earlier work in international consumption economics, including that of Colin Clark and of Houthakker, may want to consult the monograph of Lluch, Powell, and Williams (1977).

The implementation of the model is discussed in Sections 2.6 through 2.9. The remainder of the chapter deals mainly with implications of the model (such as income and price elasticities at different levels of real income) and with extensions and directions for further research.

2.2   THE COUNTRY-PRODUCT-DUMMY METHOD

Kravis and his colleagues divide each country's gross domestic product into more than 150 so-called detailed categories. One of these is fresh vegetables, which consists of the twenty individual items shown in Table 2-1. Let p_{ic} be the price of item i in country c, expressed in that country's currency. The country-product-dummy (CPD) method describes the natural logarithm of p_{ic} as the sum of an item effect A_i and a country effect B_c. If there are no missing data, and if this relation is estimated by least squares, the estimate of B_c is the mean over all items of log p_{ic}, and hence the antilog of this estimate equals the geometric mean of p_{ic} over $i = 1, ..., 20$. Similarly, the estimate of A_i is then equal to the mean of log p_{ic} over c, but the A_i's will play no further role in our analysis.

It is not the case, however, that there are no missing price data. Actually, there are numerous missing prices, indicated by $-$ in Table 2-1. The approach followed by Kravis et al. in such a case is a weighted form of least squares, the weight of each country being selected so as to correct for the

Table 2-1. Prices Per Kilogram of Fresh Vegetables in Ten Countries in 1970.

	Colombia (Peso)	France (Franc)	Germany (West) (D. Mark)	Hungary (Florint)	India (Rupee)	Italy (Lira)	Japan (Yen)	Kenya (Shilling)	United Kingdom (Pound)	United States (Dollar)	Coefficient A_i
1. Artichokes	–	2.75	3.26	–	–	646	–	–	–	2.22	.56
2. Beets	3.90	–	–	–	–	–	–	–	.07	.42	–.89
3. Brussels sprouts	–	2.35	1.69	–	–	485	–	–	–	1.89	–.23
4. Cabbage	1.41	.98	.55	2.9	.91	157	75.4	.47	.08	.32	–1.02
5. Cauliflower	5.33	1.90	1.13	–	1.27	195	156.6	2.58	.17	.63	–.18
6. Carrots	2.10	.93	.86	3.2	.75	172	115.1	2.58	.07	.39	–.67
7. Celery, pascal	4.49	–	–	–	–	–	–	–	–	.44	–.59
8. Cucumbers	–	–	–	4.7	.87	–	173.3	–	–	.61	–.39
9. Eggplant	–	–	–	–	.72	–	–	–	–	.59	–.63
10. Escarole	–	1.82	.98	–	–	212	–	–	–	–	–.41
11. Green peppers	17.40	2.62	2.32	8.7	–	186	195.4	–	–	1.16	.14
12. Kunde greens	–	–	–	–	.56	–	–	.79	–	.67	–.78
13. Lettuce	4.82	3.23	2.27	9.3	–	239	218.1	.62	–	.53	–.21
14. Mushrooms	–	7.90	5.60	–	–	790	–	–	.54	1.95	1.00
15. Onions, yellow	5.59	1.18	.86	4.8	.67	127[a]	98.6	.77	.13	.35	–.66
16. Radishes	–	–	–	–	.55	–	–	–	–	.88	–.68
17. Red cabbage	–	1.27	.56	–	–	–	–	–	–	.12	–1.20
18. Spinach	4.71	–	–	–	–	–	133.8	–	–	1.24	–.29
19. Tomatoes	5.79	2.55	1.85	6.7	1.21	226	160.9	1.19	.31	.92	–.10
20. Yellow squash	2.29	–	–	1.5	.34	–	–	.57	–	.66	–1.22
Coefficient B_c	1.96	.92	.57	2.02	.34	5.68	5.32	.57	–1.56	.00	
Antilog	7.11	2.52	1.77	7.53	1.41	291.9	204.5	1.76	.21	1.00	

a. This entry represents a correction of the corresponding figure in Kravis et al.
Source: Kravis et al. (1975: 59).

number of items with missing price data in that country. The B_c's of the ten countries and their antilogs are shown in the last two lines of Table 2-1. These antilogs are estimated purchasing power parities (PPPs) of fresh vegetables in 1970. Thus, reading the last line of the table from right to left, one dollar's worth of fresh vegetables in the United States equals 0.21 pound's worth of fresh vegetables in the United Kingdom equals 1.76 shillings' worth of fresh vegetables in Kenya, and so on. (The unit value in the U.S. column results from the fact that the expression $A_i + B_c$ has one additive degree of freedom; this freedom has been used in Table 2-1 by putting $B_c = 0$ for $c =$ U.S.) By dividing the per capita expenditure on fresh vegetables by such a PPP, we obtain the implied per capita volume.

Aggregation over detailed groups is necessary to obtain prices (PPPs) and volumes per capita for broader groups of goods. However, before proceeding to this matter we should emphasize that the CPD method illustrated in Table 2-1 was not the only one used. Sometimes goods can be narrowly defined, but not always. An example of a narrowly defined good is eggs: "fresh chicken eggs, large size (weighing at least 680.4 grams per dozen), white or brown shell. Not the best quality, but close to it. The white is less thick and high than the best quality; the yolk must be firm, high, and not easily broken" (Kravis, Heston, and Summers 1982: 38). But there are "comparison-resistant" services for which procedures other than the CPD method were used (Kravis, Heston, and Summers 1982: Chap. 5). The reader who is interested in these and similar matters should consult the original (1982) source: the work of national and U.N. price experts (p. 38); prices of construction and consumer durables (pp. 47–49); automobile and rent regressions (pp. 50–56); and a regional aspect in the application of the CPD method (Chap. 4).

2.3   TOTAL CONSUMPTION AND GDP PER CAPITA: THIRTY-FOUR COUNTRIES IN 1975

The objective of Kravis, Heston, and Summers (1982) is to provide multilateral base-invariant price and volume comparisons at various levels of aggregation for their thirty-four countries. The method used is that proposed by Geary (1958) and amended by Khamis (1967, 1970, 1972). This procedure yields volumes in the form of expenditures expressed in "international dollars." Such volumes are additive across expenditure categories, while prices can be obtained by dividing expenditures in national currency by those in international dollars. Columns 2 and 3 of Table 2-2 provide the results for the per capita volumes of total consumption and gross domestic product in

Table 2-2. Consumption and GDP Per Capita, Thirty-four Countries in 1975.

Country (1)	Consumption per capita[a] (2)	Gross domestic product per capita		
		International dollars[b] (3)	Same, U.S. = 100[c] (4)	Exchange rate converted[c] (5)
United States	4954.5	7176.0	100	100
Luxembourg	3934.6	5883.4	82.0	90.2
Denmark	3887.2	5910.9	82.4	104.5
France	3745.6	5876.9	81.9	89.6
Germany	3743.4	5952.7	83.0	94.7
Austria	3721.4	4994.8	69.6	69.8
Belgium	3715.1	5574.1	77.7	87.8
Netherlands	3398.1	5397.2	75.2	84.5
United Kingdom	3173.9	4587.9	63.9	57.6
Spain	3001.0	4010.2	55.9	41.0
Japan	2912.7	4906.7	68.4	62.3
Italy	2636.4	3861.1	53.8	47.9
Hungary	2313.2	3558.9	49.6	29.6
Ireland	2299.3	3048.8	42.5	37.2
Uruguay	2234.4	2844.3	39.6	18.2
Poland	2154.8	3597.9	50.1	36.0
Mexico	1839.4	2487.3	34.7	20.4
Yugoslavia	1712.6	2591.4	36.1	23.2
Romania	1435.6	2386.8	33.3	24.3
Iran	1345.3	2704.6	37.7	22.1
Jamaica	1333.0	1722.6	24.0	19.6
Syria	1295.4	1794.2	25.0	10.0
Colombia	1265.3	1608.7	22.4	7.9
Brazil	1219.0	1811.2	25.2	16.0
Korea	1019.4	1484.1	20.7	8.1
Malaysia	939.5	1540.6	21.5	10.9
Thailand	699.3	936.1	13.0	5.0
Philippines	693.6	946.3	13.2	5.2
Sri Lanka	510.1	667.7	9.3	2.6
Pakistan	441.8	590.3	8.2	2.6
Zambia	415.8	737.8	10.3	6.9
Kenya	364.6	470.5	6.6	3.4
India	338.0	470.5	6.6	2.0
Malawi	274.9	351.7	4.9	1.9

a. Sum of line numbers 1–107 (not including 108, net expenditure of residents abroad) of Kravis, Heston, and Summers (1982), summary multilateral Table 6–4.

b. Sum of line numbers 1–151 (same table).

c. Kravis, Heston, and Summers (1982; 12).

1975. The thirty-four countries are listed in the order of declining consumption volumes.

There are substantial differences between the exchange-rate converted figures and those which Kravis et al. obtain using their preferred method; not surprisingly, such differences tend to be larger when the two countries compared are more different in affluence. This matter is pursued in columns 4 and 5 of Table 2-2, which compare the PPP-based estimates of GDP per capita with those based on exchange rates, both as a percentage of the U.S. value. Using exchange rates tends to overstate the poverty of poor nations considerably. For example, when we use exchange rates, the ratio of the U.S. GDP per capita to its Indian counterpart is $100/2.0 = 50$, but it is only $100/6.6 \cong 15$ when we use the Kravis approach. A major reason for this sizeable difference is that services, which are cheaper relative to commodities in poorer countries, are only modestly represented in international trade and hence also in exchange rates.

Of course, an additional disadvantage of the use of exchange rates is their considerable variability during the late 1970s and 1980s. There is no reason why the consumption expenditures in national currencies should reflect this variability exactly. Converting these expenditures by such wildly fluctuating exchange rates would yield highly spurious results.

2.4   A TEN-GOOD CONSUMPTION CLASSIFICATION

Table 2-3 shows the volumes of consumption per capita of ten goods: food; beverages and tobacco; clothing and footwear; gross rent and fuel; house furnishings and operations; medical care; transport and communications; recreation; education; and other consumption expenditures. The last column of Table 2-3 is the sum of the ten earlier columns; it is identical to column 2 of Table 2-2. The ten goods are the same as those of Theil and Suhm (1981), based on the earlier data of Kravis et al. (1978), except that beverages and tobacco are now separated from food and, similarly, education from recreation.

By dividing the per capita expenditure in national currency by the corresponding volume in Table 2-3 we obtain the price p_{ic}: the price of good i in country c. Using the same numerator and dividing it by the sum of the per capita expenditures on all ten goods, we obtain the budget share w_{ic}. These shares are shown in percentage form in Table 2-4. The dominating position of food in poor countries should be noted; its budget share exceeds 50 percent in several cases.

Table 2-3. Volume of Consumption Per Capita of Ten Goods in Thirty-Four Countries in 1975.

Country (1)	Food (2)	Beverages, tobacco (3)	Clothing, footwear (4)	Gross rent, fuel (5)	House furnishings, operations (6)	Medical care (7)	Transport, communications (8)	Recreation (9)	Education (10)	Other (11)	Total (12)
United States	748.2	199.4	383.0	851.3	367.4	401.3	845.9	332.6	244.2	581.2	4954.5
Luxembourg	803.4	197.2	272.4	581.0	447.8	297.1	521.1	153.5	115.7	545.4	3934.6
Denmark	680.8	262.2	202.6	888.1	388.8	294.7	399.9	279.1	246.6	244.4	3887.2
France	799.0	202.9	227.1	519.0	447.9	386.6	429.3	215.5	132.7	385.6	3745.6
Germany	646.5	186.3	344.3	542.1	447.5	400.4	445.3	264.3	143.1	323.6	3743.4
Austria	677.6	296.4	391.5	518.6	324.5	323.9	339.1	184.1	138.3	527.4	3721.4
Belgium	838.2	186.1	255.5	475.0	482.0	319.6	423.3	182.6	164.2	388.6	3715.1
Netherlands	699.7	211.5	291.3	468.5	405.3	251.6	325.5	303.4	166.5	274.8	3398.1
United Kingdom	639.4	134.0	234.3	479.1	216.4	328.3	305.2	264.1	135.1	438.0	3173.9
Spain	942.6	149.1	248.2	405.8	165.7	240.3	223.5	131.4	138.0	356.4	3001.0
Japan	653.4	131.9	264.3	340.0	164.0	335.3	285.3	237.3	152.9	348.3	2912.7
Italy	764.1	159.1	221.2	336.8	159.0	244.0	277.1	115.7	128.3	231.1	2636.4
Hungary	600.1	179.9	171.6	167.5	161.8	286.4	123.7	191.5	138.9	291.8	2313.2
Ireland	656.7	87.8	156.5	211.7	157.1	239.7	148.3	144.8	127.5	369.2	2299.3
Uruguay	893.1	208.8	119.9	260.9	86.5	154.5	140.5	80.5	106.9	182.8	2234.4
Poland	580.8	124.1	189.7	278.1	166.3	245.1	100.6	131.7	171.8	166.6	2154.8
Mexico	663.6	55.5	168.1	225.4	212.7	83.1	164.7	35.7	101.5	129.1	1839.4

Table 2-3 continued.

Country (1)	Food (2)	Beverages, tobacco (3)	Clothing, footwear (4)	Gross rent, fuel (5)	House furnishings, operations (6)	Medical care (7)	Transport, communications (8)	Recreation (9)	Education (10)	Other (11)	Total (12)
Yugoslavia	461.3	107.6	139.3	188.8	127.6	179.4	120.0	102.5	120.6	165.5	1712.6
Romania	446.9	62.3	142.2	258.2	68.2	150.2	47.6	50.1	107.3	102.6	1435.6
Iran	414.2	23.1	194.6	239.7	91.9	56.7	97.6	25.0	99.1	103.4	1345.3
Jamaica	369.2	109.0	50.6	92.9	80.6	64.4	133.0	59.4	108.2	265.7	1333.0
Syria	612.7	48.0	134.6	163.4	63.5	51.7	42.5	21.9	85.3	71.8	1295.4
Colombia	403.4	76.2	134.8	105.5	73.3	45.9	121.6	34.0	129.7	140.9	1265.3
Brazil	488.5	31.9	90.0	105.0	77.2	71.2	99.4	41.5	101.7	112.6	1219.0
Korea	332.7	115.4	125.8	77.2	28.9	46.3	79.1	36.2	77.7	100.1	1019.4
Malaysia	308.1	42.7	69.5	102.6	59.5	49.7	85.7	49.5	82.9	89.3	939.5
Thailand	316.6	59.2	67.1	37.5	29.4	34.0	42.0	21.4	54.2	37.9	699.3
Philippines	290.5	47.5	52.8	73.2	31.7	39.7	15.3	7.6	86.0	49.3	693.6
Sri Lanka	229.3	26.1	33.0	41.5	24.0	27.0	28.3	18.0	56.8	26.1	510.1
Pakistan	229.7	12.1	53.3	28.6	19.6	19.7	16.8	19.6	28.6	13.8	441.8
Zambia	182.7	6.4	22.8	42.5	20.8	16.9	15.4	9.7	57.8	40.8	415.8
Kenya	132.8	22.6	18.2	26.2	48.5	8.7	18.4	6.5	65.4	17.3	364.6
India	165.9	7.2	16.6	27.4	7.4	16.7	27.0	5.2	44.5	20.1	338.0
Malawi	161.4	11.3	12.6	8.3	19.0	10.0	8.6	6.6	29.5	7.6	274.9

Table 2-4. Budget Shares (in Percentage Form) of Ten Goods in Thirty-Four Countries in 1975.

Country (1)	Food (2)	Beverages, tobacco (3)	Clothing, footwear (4)	Gross rent, fuel (5)	House furnishings, operations (6)	Medical care (7)	Transport, communications (8)	Recreation (9)	Education (10)	Other (11)
United States	12.76	3.10	6.52	17.52	6.65	12.67	13.42	6.26	8.93	12.18
Luxembourg	18.78	3.50	8.27	16.94	10.00	6.02	12.20	3.75	7.05	13.48
Denmark	15.78	7.71	5.35	19.55	7.66	5.15	11.91	7.12	12.19	7.57
France	18.89	3.97	7.46	14.32	9.97	10.57	11.41	6.10	5.63	11.68
Germany	15.21	4.75	8.67	14.64	9.64	12.65	12.18	6.75	6.14	9.37
Austria	16.67	6.56	10.18	11.29	8.20	9.38	12.36	5.69	4.91	14.76
Belgium	18.79	3.76	7.70	14.56	11.51	8.06	10.45	5.02	8.34	11.82
Netherlands	16.66	5.00	8.22	12.35	9.22	10.29	9.66	8.26	10.19	10.15
United Kingdom	16.40	6.15	7.62	17.25	6.55	5.91	11.83	7.51	7.23	13.55
Spain	29.80	2.91	9.48	12.38	7.90	8.43	9.76	4.99	3.95	10.41
Japan	22.28	3.85	7.45	14.44	5.84	8.93	8.77	7.28	7.30	13.85
Italy	29.02	5.07	8.37	12.49	5.89	8.02	10.20	5.21	6.45	9.27
Hungary	26.34	10.27	10.65	7.42	9.10	5.89	7.34	7.09	5.47	10.43
Ireland	23.07	6.40	7.26	10.10	6.83	8.98	8.62	5.53	7.51	15.70
Uruguay	31.85	10.07	7.14	11.02	7.92	6.31	9.70	5.29	3.15	7.55
Poland	28.68	10.57	12.77	7.81	8.81	5.82	6.33	5.81	6.22	7.19
Mexico	36.83	1.53	9.88	9.49	10.77	5.81	7.92	2.95	5.76	9.05

Table 2-4 continued.

Country (1)	Food (2)	Beverages, tobacco (3)	Clothing, footwear (4)	Gross rent, fuel (5)	House furnishings, operations (6)	Medical care (7)	Transport, communications (8)	Recreation (9)	Education (10)	Other (11)
Yugoslavia	28.37	6.65	9.28	8.14	9.46	7.23	9.18	5.44	6.34	9.92
Romania	35.17	6.33	14.58	6.82	7.23	5.06	6.58	4.15	5.43	8.67
Iran	32.33	1.69	10.42	16.84	7.73	6.71	6.85	2.95	7.51	6.98
Jamaica	31.49	8.80	3.88	10.25	5.55	4.18	11.16	3.49	4.97	16.22
Syria	47.50	3.93	11.58	12.09	6.25	3.43	3.80	2.02	4.14	5.27
Colombia	33.87	5.19	9.21	7.74	6.22	5.21	9.26	3.53	8.15	11.62
Brazil	33.94	2.87	9.35	10.66	8.30	5.38	10.71	5.15	3.67	9.96
Korea	44.43	9.36	9.38	7.70	3.11	3.89	6.82	2.84	4.91	7.56
Malaysia	34.16	6.07	5.91	10.33	6.00	4.27	13.29	4.91	7.41	7.66
Thailand	42.84	8.24	7.87	5.79	4.76	5.78	6.89	5.61	5.44	6.78
Philippines	54.13	6.76	6.75	8.98	4.57	3.33	2.09	1.52	5.50	6.36
Sri Lanka	59.99	8.15	6.27	4.94	2.84	2.56	6.12	2.64	2.90	3.60
Pakistan	56.80	2.57	10.77	11.53	4.15	4.72	1.93	3.18	1.92	2.42
Zambia	37.93	2.72	6.77	9.72	5.86	5.60	6.50	3.17	10.73	11.01
Kenya	36.87	7.08	6.86	11.30	8.42	4.79	7.30	2.10	9.63	5.64
India	60.33	3.78	7.52	6.10	2.77	3.22	6.49	1.66	3.61	4.51
Malawi	52.86	5.20	7.01	6.18	9.41	1.92	7.52	2.66	3.89	3.35

2.5 CROSS-COUNTRY DEMAND ANALYSIS: PRELIMINARY DISCUSSION

Kravis, Heston, and Summers (1982: Chap. 9) performed some cross-country demand analyses at various levels of aggregation. There are 103 detailed consumption categories, for each of which a log-linear demand equation was fitted. This yields an estimated income elasticity of bread and of rice equal to 1.26 and −0.80, respectively (with standard errors of 0.20 and 0.36). The former elasticity is far too high and the latter is algebraically much too low. These numerical results simply reflect the fact that "rich" countries favor bread and "poor" countries (mostly near the equator) favor rice. As was suggested in Section 2.1, it is not self-evident that cross-country demand analysis is feasible, because different countries may have different tastes. The assumption of approximately equal tastes is more acceptable when we apply it to broader groups of goods. For example, Kravis, Heston, and Summers (1982: Table 9-3) combine bread and rice with three other detailed categories into one summary category labeled "bread and cereals," and they obtain for this group an estimated income elasticity of 0.06 (standard error 0.07). This is a much more realistic result.

The numerical results discussed in the previous paragraph are based on a single-equation approach. Kravis et al. also applied a system-wide approach by fitting a linear expenditure system, but this is an unfortunate choice because of the assumption of constant marginal shares. The income elasticities, being equal to the ratio of the marginal to the budget shares, are then inversely proportional to the budget shares. Column 2 of Table 2-4 shows that the budget share of food is about five times higher for India than for the United States. The implication is that the income elasticity of the demand for food in the United States exceeds that in India by a factor of five, which is clearly unrealistic.

Theil and Suhm (1981) were more successful when they applied Working's model to the earlier data of Kravis, Heston, and Summers (1978), although they had to eliminate Kenya from their sixteen-country data set. As was discussed in Section 1.8, this model describes the budget share of each good as a linear function of the logarithm of total expenditure. Figure 2-1 fits budget shares of food (column 2 of Table 2-4) against the natural logarithm of total real per capita consumption (column 2 of Table 2-2). The fit is satisfactory except that all three African countries (Malawi and Zambia in addition to Kenya) appear to deviate from the general pattern. Kravis, Heston, and Summers indicate that there are numerous data problems for these countries,

Figure 2-1.   Working's Model for Food, 1975.

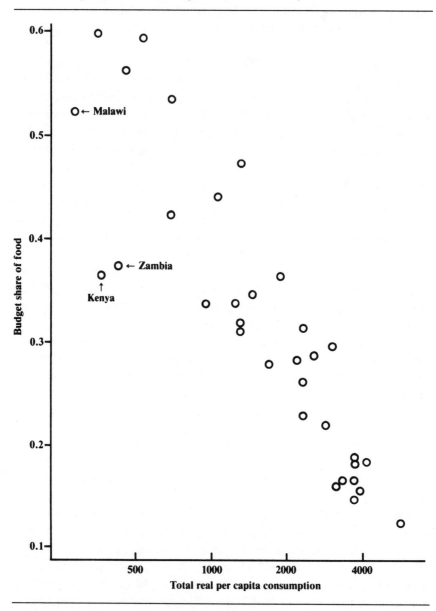

particularly regarding adequate representation of rural areas and the estimates for rent and medical care (1982: 42, 44–45, 54, and 57). We shall
therefore delete these three countries. We shall also delete Jamaica, thus
reducing the sample size from thirty-four to thirty, because of that country's

suspiciously large budget share of "other" consumption expenditure (column 11 of Table 2-4). It seems likely that the hotel and restaurant components of this category refer mainly to expenditures by foreign tourists rather than by domestic consumers.

2.6   WORKING'S MODEL AT GEOMETRIC MEAN PRICES

Although Working's model looks promising for our thirty countries, we must recognize that it does not involve prices. Following Theil and Suhm (1981), we postulate that the model holds at the geometric mean of the prices of each good across the thirty countries; the fact that each country's observations refer to that country's prices (rather than the geometric means) will enable us to endow the model with a substitution term.

We write $\bar{p}_i$ for the geometric mean of the prices of good i:

$$\log \bar{p}_i = \frac{1}{30} \sum_{c=1}^{30} \log p_{ic}. \tag{6.1}$$

Working's model for good i is now written as

$$\hat{w}_{ic} = \alpha_i + \beta_i \log Q_c + \epsilon_{ic}, \tag{6.2}$$

where Q_c is per capita real income of country c (specified as the total consumption figure in column 2 of Table 2-2), ϵ_{ic} is a random disturbance, and $\hat{w}_{ic}$ is the budget share of good i at the prices $\bar{p}_1, \bar{p}_2, \ldots$ and the observed Q_c. Therefore,

$$w_{ic} = \alpha_i + \beta_i \log Q_c + (w_{ic} - \hat{w}_{ic}) + \epsilon_{ic}, \tag{6.3}$$

where w_{ic} is the observed share of i in country c (Table 2-4).

The difference $w_{ic} - \hat{w}_{ic}$ in (6.3) results from the difference between the price vectors $[p_{ic}]$ and $[\bar{p}_i]$. It is shown in Section 2.7 that we can write $w_{ic} - \hat{w}_{ic}$ as the sum of two terms,

$$w_{ic} - \hat{w}_{ic} = w_{ic} \left(\log \frac{p_{ic}}{\bar{p}_i} - \sum_{j=1}^{10} w_{jc} \log \frac{p_{jc}}{\bar{p}_j} \right) + \sum_{j=1}^{10} \pi_{ij} \log \frac{p_{jc}}{\bar{p}_j}, \tag{6.4}$$

where π_{ij} is a Slutsky coefficient. The first term on the right in (6.4) shows how the budget share is affected by the change from $[\bar{p}_i]$ to $[p_{ic}]$ even when the consumer decides to buy the same quantities in spite of the price change. The second term recognizes that the consumer will not buy the same quantities because he will react to the price change by substitution.

We shall find it appropriate to reduce the number of parameters by postulating preference independence with a constant income flexibility ϕ. The (tentative) economic justification of this assumption is that for broad groups of goods the marginal utility of each is largely independent of the consumption of the others, but there is also a statistical justification (as discussed in Section 3.19). Under preference independence we can express the substitution component of (6.4) in terms of marginal shares. Also, recall that under Working's model the marginal share of good i equals the budget share plus the constant β_i. Similarly to the procedure used in Section 1.15, we thus write the marginal share of good i in country c as $w_{ic} + \beta_i$. The substitution term in (6.4) can then be written as

$$\phi(w_{ic} + \beta_i)\left[\log \frac{p_{ic}}{\bar{p}_i} - \sum_{j=1}^{10} (w_{jc} + \beta_j) \log \frac{p_{jc}}{\bar{p}_j}\right], \tag{6.5}$$

where the sum inside the brackets represents the Frisch price index of the change from $[\bar{p}_i]$ to $[p_{ic}]$.

By substituting (6.4) and (6.5) into (6.3) we obtain

$$y_{ic} = \alpha_i + \beta_i \log Q_c$$

$$+ \phi(w_{ic} + \beta_i)\left[\log \frac{p_{ic}}{\bar{p}_i} - \sum_{j=1}^{10} (w_{jc} + \beta_j) \log \frac{p_{jc}}{\bar{p}_j}\right] + \epsilon_{ic}, \tag{6.6}$$

where

$$y_{ic} = w_{ic} - w_{ic}\left(\log \frac{p_{ic}}{\bar{p}_i} - \sum_{j=1}^{10} w_{jc} \log \frac{p_{jc}}{\bar{p}_j}\right). \tag{6.7}$$

Note that the first right-hand term in (6.4), which contains no unknown parameters, has been combined with the budget share on the left. The estimation of the model (6.6) is considered in Section 2.8.

Remark 1. Suppose that country c changes its currency unit so that p_{ic} becomes $k_c p_{ic}$ for each i and for some $k_c > 0$ (as was the case for France when old francs were replaced by new francs, each being worth 100 old francs). Thus, from (6.1), $\log \bar{p}_i$ increases by $(1/30) \log k_c$ for each i so that $\log(p_{ic}/\bar{p}_i)$ increases by $(29/30) \log k_c$. Nevertheless, the expression in parentheses in (6.4) does not change, nor does the substitution term on the far right. This invariance reflects the fact that only relative price changes matter.

Remark 2. Our application of Working's model uses per capita data. An aggregation analysis shows that this requires an amendment of (6.6): β_i in the second term on the right should be multiplied by the sum of $\log Q_c$ and a measure of the income inequality in country c; see Muellbauer (1975) and Theil and Suhm (1981: 119–20) for details. Ignoring the inequality term will primarily affect the constant α_i, although probably not much.

2.7   DERIVATION OF THE MODEL

Our strategy will be to use the differential approach to find the change in the budget share of good i caused by the change from the price vector $[\bar{p}_i]$ to $[p_{ic}]$ when real income remains unchanged (at the level Q_c). For this purpose we go back to Sections 1.12 and 1.13. We use the total differential of w_i,

$$dw_i = w_i \, d(\log p_i) + w_i \, d(\log q_i) - w_i \, d(\log M), \tag{7.1}$$

and we note that the differential demand equations can now be written as

$$w_i \, d(\log q_i) = \sum_{j=1}^{n} \pi_{ij} \, d(\log p_j) \tag{7.2}$$

because the assumption of a constant real income implies that the income term in the differential demand equation vanishes. Also, this assumption implies that the Divisia decomposition of Section 1.9 can be written as

$$d(\log M) = \sum_{j=1}^{n} w_j \, d(\log p_j). \tag{7.3}$$

Substitution of (7.2) and (7.3) into (7.1) gives

$$dw_i = w_i \left[d(\log p_i) - \sum_{j=1}^{n} w_j \, d(\log p_j) \right] + \sum_{j=1}^{n} \pi_{ij} \, d(\log p_j). \tag{7.4}$$

Next we specify $n = 10$ and we interpret $d(\log p_i)$ as $\log p_{ic} - \log \bar{p}_i = \log(p_{ic}/\bar{p}_i)$. We apply the mean value theorem of differential calculus to (7.4),

$$w_{ic} - \hat{w}_{ic} = w_i \left(\log \frac{p_{ic}}{\bar{p}_i} - \sum_{j=1}^{10} w_j \log \frac{p_{jc}}{\bar{p}_j} \right) + \sum_{j=1}^{10} \pi_{ij} \log \frac{p_{jc}}{\bar{p}_j},$$

where the w_i's and π_{ij}'s on the right are the budget shares and Slutsky coefficients, respectively, evaluated at income Q_c and at relative prices between those of $[\bar{p}_i]$ and $[p_{ic}]$. The specifications (6.4) and (6.5), which involve w_{ic} instead of this w_i, should be viewed as first-order Taylor approximations of this result.

2.8   MAXIMUM LIKELIHOOD ESTIMATES

We proceed to use the data of the thirty countries to estimate the α_i's, β_i's, and ϕ of the model (6.6) by maximum likelihood under the assumption that the disturbance vectors $(\epsilon_{1c}, \epsilon_{2c}, \dots)$ for $c = 1, \dots, 30$ are independent and

Table 2-5.   Cross-Country ML Parameter Estimates of Working's Model.

Good	α_i	β_i
Food	.162 (.012)	−.154 (.010)
Beverages, tobacco	.056 (.006)	.001 (.005)
Clothing, footwear	.084 (.006)	−.005 (.005)
Gross rent, fuel	.145 (.008)	.032 (.006)
House furnishings, operations	.098 (.005)	.025 (.004)
Medical care	.089 (.004)	.024 (.003)
Transport, communications	.118 (.007)	.030 (.005)
Recreation	.069 (.004)	.019 (.003)
Education	.054 (.006)	−.004 (.005)
Other	.126 (.007)	.033 (.006)

multivariate normal with zero means and the same covariance matrix. Details on the estimation procedure follow in Section 2.9. The ML estimate of ϕ (with the asymptotic standard error in parentheses) is

$$\hat{\phi} = -0.526 \ (0.037). \tag{8.1}$$

The small standard error suggests that ϕ has been precisely estimated (we shall come back to this matter in Section 3.11). The ML estimates of the α_i's and β_i's are shown in Table 2-5. The β_i of food is negative as we expect it to be. There are two other negative point estimates of β_i's, but neither of these is significant. The implied income elasticities will be considered in Section 2.10. Note that the estimates of the α's add up to 1 and those of the β's to 0.

Recall that Working's model (including a substitution term with a constant ϕ) was fitted to Japanese time series data in Section 1.16. We considered there the behavior of the income elasticities that are implied by the ML parameter estimates of the model. Here it is of interest to compare these estimates with the cross-country estimates discussed in the previous paragraph. The Japanese ϕ estimate is

$$\hat{\phi} = -0.642 \ (0.096), \tag{8.2}$$

which is clearly not significantly different from the estimate shown in (8.1). The time series version of Working's model contains no α_i's, only β_i's. Also, the time series application has only four consumption categories. This requires that we add the β_i's of the relevant goods of Table 2-5: Food is com-

Table 2–6. Cross-Country and Japanese Time Series
Parameter Estimates.

Good	Cross-country	Japan, time series
Food, beverages, tobacco	−.153	−.153 (.013)
Clothing, footwear	−.005	.004 (.014)
Housing, furniture	.057	.069 (.014)
Miscellaneous	.101	.080 (.015)

bined with beverages and tobacco; gross rent and fuel are combined with house furnishings and operations; and the last five goods emerge collectively as "miscellaneous." The results shown in Table 2-6 indicate that there is satisfactory agreement, particularly when we take into consideration that the consumption categories of the two samples are not identical (even after aggregation).

2.9   THE MAXIMUM LIKELIHOOD PROCEDURE

We eliminate α_{10} and β_{10} using the constraints $\alpha_1 + \cdots + \alpha_{10} = 1$ and $\beta_1 + \cdots + \beta_{10} = 0$. We define

$$x_{ic} = \log \frac{p_{ic}}{\bar{p}_i} - \log \frac{p_{10,c}}{\bar{p}_{10}}. \tag{9.1}$$

It is then readily verified that (6.6) can be simplified to

$$y_{ic} = \alpha_i + \beta_i q_c + \phi z_{ic} + \epsilon_{ic}, \tag{9.2}$$

where $q_c = \log Q_c$ and

$$z_{ic} = (w_{ic} + \beta_i) \left[x_{ic} - \sum_{j=1}^{9} (w_{jc} + \beta_j) x_{jc} \right]. \tag{9.3}$$

Since $\epsilon_{1c} + \cdots + \epsilon_{10,c} = 0$ holds with probability 1, we confine ourselves to (9.2) for $i = 1, \ldots, 9$. We define α and β as the column vectors $[\alpha_1 \ldots \alpha_9]'$ and $[\beta_1 \ldots \beta_9]'$, respectively. Then we can write (9.2) in vector form as

$$y_c = X_c \theta + \epsilon_c, \tag{9.4}$$

where y_c and ϵ_c are nine-element column vectors, the ith element being y_{ic} and ϵ_{ic}, respectively, while θ is the nineteen-element parameter vector (consisting of α, β, ϕ) and X_c can be written in partitioned form as $[I_9, q_c I_9, z_c]$, where I_9 is the 9×9 unit matrix and z_c is a column vector with z_{ic} as ith element.

If $\epsilon_1, ..., \epsilon_{30}$ are independent normal vectors with zero mean and non-singular covariance matrix Σ, the log-likelihood function is

$$L = \text{constant} + 15 \log|\Sigma^{-1}| - \frac{1}{2} \sum_{c=1}^{30} (y_c - X_c\theta)'\Sigma^{-1}(y_c - X_c\theta),$$

which has the following derivatives with respect to Σ^{-1} and θ':

$$\frac{\partial L}{\partial \Sigma^{-1}} = 15\Sigma' - \frac{1}{2} \sum_{c=1}^{30} (y_c - X_c\theta)(y_c - X_c\theta)', \tag{9.5}$$

$$\frac{\partial L}{\partial \theta'} = \sum_{c=1}^{30} (y_c - X_c\theta)'\Sigma^{-1} \frac{\partial(X_c\theta)}{\partial \theta'}. \tag{9.6}$$

It follows from the definitions of X_c and θ that the derivative on the far right in (9.6) can be written in partioned form as

$$\frac{\partial(X_c\theta)}{\partial \theta'} = [I_9, q_c I_9 + \phi(\partial z_c/\partial \beta'), z_c], \tag{9.7}$$

where $\partial z_c/\partial \beta'$ is a 9×9 matrix with diagonal elements of the form,

$$\frac{\partial z_{ic}}{\partial \beta_i} = (1 - w_{ic} - \beta_i)x_{ic} - \sum_{j=1}^{9} (w_{jc} + \beta_j)x_{jc},$$

and off-diagonal elements $\partial z_{ic}/\partial \beta_j = -(w_{ic} + \beta_i)x_{jc}$.

We conclude from (9.6) and from the zero expectation of the vector $y_c - X_c\theta = \epsilon_c$ that the matrix $\partial^2 L/\partial\theta_r \, \partial\Sigma^{-1}$ has zero expectation for each element θ_r of the parameter vector θ. Therefore, the information matrix of the ML procedure is block-diagonal with respect to the elements of θ and those of Σ^{-1} so that the asymptotic covariance matrix of the ML estimator of θ is equal to minus the inverse of the expectation of the derivative $\partial^2 L/\partial\theta\partial\theta'$. This derivative is obtained by differentiating (9.6) with respect to θ, which yields

$$K = -\sum_{c=1}^{30} \frac{\partial(X_c\theta)'}{\partial\theta} \Sigma^{-1} \frac{\partial(X_c\theta)}{\partial\theta'} \tag{9.8}$$

plus a matrix that is linear in $(y_c - X_c\theta)'$ for $c = 1, ..., 30$. The latter matrix has zero expectation, where K is nonrandom. Hence, the asymptotic co-variance matrix of the ML estimator of θ is $-K^{-1}$.

The ML estimates of Table 2–5 were obtained by means of Newton's method based on successive estimates of K. The asymptotic standard errors were computed from the diagonal elements of $-K^{-1}$, with ML estimates substituted for the unknown parameters in K. Note that Q_c is measured with the U.S. value as unit (which is obtained by dividing the entries in column 2 of Table 2-2 by 4954.5). Hence, the α_i's have the interpretation of expected budget shares at the U.S. per capita income and geometric mean prices (apart from what is implied by Remark 2 at the end of Section 2.6). Also note the simplifying assumption that the presence of w_{ic} in (9.3) does not affect the exogeneity of z_{ic}.

The ML procedure for the time series model in Table 2-6 is analogous. For $n = 4$ goods we write the demand equations as

$$y_{it} = \beta_i DQ_t + \phi(\bar{w}_{it} + \beta_i)\left[x_{it} - \sum_{j=1}^{3}(\bar{w}_{jt} + \beta_j)x_{jt}\right] + \epsilon_{it},$$

where $y_{it} = \bar{w}_{it}(Dq_{it} - DQ_t)$ and $x_{it} = Dp_{it} - Dp_{4t}$. This equation is similar to (9.2) and (9.3), but note the absence of constant terms.

2.10   A CROSS-COUNTRY TABULATION OF INCOME ELASTICITIES

We proceed to present the income elasticities of the ten goods at the per capita income levels of the thirty countries. We shall do so at geometric mean prices, which means that the two price terms in (6.6) and (6.7) vanish. Next, by taking the expectation in (6.6) so that ϵ_{ic} becomes zero, we obtain

$$\bar{w}_{ic} = \alpha_i + \beta_i \log Q_c, \tag{10.1}$$

where $\bar{w}_{ic}$ stands for the expected budget share of good i at income Q_c and prices $\bar{p}_1, ..., \bar{p}_{10}$. As we know from Section 1.8, the income elasticity of the demand for this good at this point is

$$\frac{\bar{w}_{ic} + \beta_i}{\bar{w}_{ic}} = 1 + \frac{\beta_i}{\bar{w}_{ic}}. \tag{10.2}$$

These elasticities (with ML estimates substituted for the α_i's and β_i's) are shown in columns 4 through 13 of Table 2-7. Column 2 shows Q_c, normalized so that the U.S. value equals 1. Columns 3 and 14 will be discussed later in this section.

All income elasticities in Table 2-7 decline as we move to higher income levels. Also, the ranking of the ten goods according to increasing income elasticities is the same at all levels of income. Both features confirm what we know from Section 1.8. The most luxurious good is recreation (column 11);

Table 2-7.   A Cross-Country Tabulation of Income Elasticities

						Income
Country (1)	Income (2)	Food, beverages, tobacco (3)	Food (4)	Beverages, tobacco (5)	Clothing, footwear (6)	Gross rent, fuel (7)
India	.068	.76	.73	1.02	.95	1.52
Pakistan	.089	.74	.71	1.02	.95	1.46
Sri Lanka	.103	.73	.70	1.02	.95	1.43
Philippines	.140	.70	.67	1.02	.95	1.38
Thailand	.141	.70	.67	1.02	.95	1.38
Malaysia	.190	.68	.63	1.02	.95	1.34
Korea	.206	.67	.62	1.02	.95	1.33
Brazil	.246	.65	.59	1.02	.95	1.31
Colombia	.255	.64	.59	1.02	.95	1.31
Syria	.261	.64	.58	1.02	.95	1.31
Iran	.272	.63	.58	1.02	.95	1.30
Romania	.290	.62	.56	1.02	.95	1.30
Yugoslavia	.346	.60	.53	1.02	.95	1.28
Mexico	.371	.59	.51	1.02	.95	1.28
Poland	.435	.56	.47	1.02	.95	1.27
Uruguay	.451	.55	.46	1.02	.95	1.26
Ireland	.464	.54	.45	1.02	.95	1.26
Hungary	.467	.54	.45	1.02	.95	1.26
Italy	.532	.51	.41	1.02	.95	1.25
Japan	.588	.49	.37	1.02	.95	1.25
Spain	.606	.48	.36	1.02	.95	1.24
United Kingdom	.641	.46	.33	1.02	.95	1.24
Netherlands	.686	.44	.30	1.02	.95	1.24
Belgium	.750	.41	.25	1.02	.95	1.23
Austria	.751	.41	.25	1.02	.95	1.23
Germany	.756	.41	.25	1.02	.95	1.23
France	.756	.41	.25	1.02	.95	1.23
Denmark	.785	.40	.23	1.02	.95	1.23
Luxembourg	.794	.39	.22	1.02	.95	1.23
United States	1.000	.30	.05	1.02	.94	1.22

the most basic necessity is food (column 4). The behavior of the income elasticity of the demand for food is the most spectacular, declining from 0.7 at the per capita income levels of Southeast Asia to about one-quarter at the Western European levels to one-twentieth at the U.S. level. When income increases beyond the U.S. per capita level, the income elasticity of the demand for food moves toward zero and then becomes negative, thus implying that food is an inferior good. This is not necessarily unrealistic, since

of Demand.

elasticity of the demand for

House furnishings, operations (8)	Medical care (9)	Transport, communications (10)	Recreation (11)	Education (12)	Other (13)	Divisia variance (14)
1.84	1.94	1.76	2.12	.94	1.86	.1740
1.68	1.75	1.63	1.86	.94	1.70	.1527
1.62	1.68	1.58	1.77	.94	1.64	.1450
1.52	1.56	1.49	1.62	.93	1.53	.1341
1.52	1.56	1.49	1.62	.93	1.53	.1338
1.45	1.48	1.43	1.52	.93	1.46	.1286
1.43	1.46	1.41	1.50	.93	1.44	.1279
1.40	1.43	1.39	1.46	.93	1.41	.1272
1.40	1.42	1.38	1.45	.93	1.40	.1273
1.39	1.41	1.38	1.45	.93	1.40	.1273
1.39	1.41	1.37	1.44	.93	1.39	.1275
1.38	1.40	1.36	1.43	.93	1.38	.1278
1.35	1.37	1.34	1.40	.93	1.36	.1298
1.35	1.36	1.33	1.39	.93	1.35	.1310
1.33	1.34	1.32	1.36	.93	1.33	.1345
1.32	1.34	1.31	1.36	.93	1.33	.1355
1.32	1.33	1.31	1.36	.93	1.32	.1364
1.32	1.33	1.31	1.36	.93	1.32	.1365
1.31	1.32	1.30	1.34	.93	1.31	.1412
1.30	1.31	1.29	1.33	.93	1.30	.1455
1.30	1.31	1.29	1.33	.93	1.30	.1470
1.29	1.30	1.28	1.32	.93	1.29	.1499
1.29	1.30	1.28	1.31	.93	1.29	.1540
1.28	1.29	1.27	1.30	.93	1.28	.1601
1.28	1.29	1.27	1.30	.93	1.28	.1602
1.28	1.29	1.27	1.30	.93	1.28	.1606
1.28	1.29	1.27	1.30	.93	1.28	.1607
1.27	1.28	1.27	1.30	.93	1.28	.1636
1.27	1.28	1.27	1.30	.93	1.28	.1646
1.26	1.27	1.25	1.28	.92	1.26	.1885

food according to the definition of Kravis et al. is food consumed at home. Affluent Americans may increase their restaurant expenditures (which fall under "other" expenditures) when their income increases and reduce the expenditures on food consumed at home. However, the presence of an inferior good is incompatible with the assumption of preference independence (see Section 1.13). An obvious remedy is to let the two categories (at home and away from home) be specific substitutes, but we shall not pursue this matter here.

The budget-share weighted mean (or Divisia mean), with the $\bar{w}_{ic}$'s as weights, of the income elasticities (10.2) is obviously 1 (see Section 1.18). The corresponding Divisia variance is a measure of dispersion among the income elasticities. It takes the form

$$V_c = \sum_{i=1}^{10} \bar{w}_{ic} \left(\frac{\beta_i}{\bar{w}_{ic}} \right)^2 = \sum_{i=1}^{10} \frac{\beta_i^2}{\bar{w}_{ic}}, \tag{10.3}$$

and it is shown in the last column of Table 2-7. The results indicate that the dispersion among the income elasticities is not a monotonic function of income. When income increases from a low level, V_c declines until the per capita income of Brazil and then it increases again. This V_c plays an important role in the analysis of the consumer's demand for quality (see Section 2.15).

The income elasticity of the demand for food at the Japanese per capita income level is 0.37 (column 4 of Table 2-7), which is much smaller than the elasticity values shown for that country in column 6 of Table 1-4 in Section 1.16. However, this comparison is inappropriate because the latter elasticities refer to food combined with beverages and tobacco. Column 3 of Table 2-7, which deals with this combination in the cross-country context, provides a more appropriate comparison. The income elasticity of food, beverages, and tobacco at the Japanese per capita income level is 0.49. Since this income level refers to 1975, and since the corresponding figures in Table 1-4 are declining with a value of 0.54 in 1971/72 (the last year), the agreement is almost perfect. The elasticities in column 3 of Table 2-7 are obtained from (10.2) by interpreting β_i as $\beta_F + \beta_B$ and $\bar{w}_{ic}$ as $\bar{w}_{Fc} + \bar{w}_{Bc}$ (F = food, B = beverages and tobacco). Note that the difference between columns 3 and 4 is much larger for affluent than for poor countries.

2.11   A CROSS-COUNTRY TABULATION OF OWN-PRICE ELASTICITIES

Our next objective is to present the own-price elasticities of the demand for the ten goods; again, we shall do so at geometric mean prices. Three such elasticities will be considered. The simplest way to explain these elasticities is by means of the differential demand equations of Section 1.13. Under preference independence such an equation takes the form

$$w_i d(\log q_i) = \theta_i d(\log Q) + \phi \theta_i [d(\log p_i) - d(\log P')],$$

where θ_i is a marginal share and $d(\log P') = \sum_i \theta_i d(\log p_i)$ is the Frisch price index. We divide both sides by w_i so that we obtain the change in the logarithm of the quantity on the left:

$$d(\log q_i) = \frac{\theta_i}{w_i} d(\log Q) + \frac{\phi\theta_i}{w_i} [d(\log p_i) - d(\log P')]. \tag{11.1}$$

The two terms on the right show that θ_i/w_i is the income elasticity of good i and $\phi\theta_i/w_i$ its Frisch own-price elasticity: the elasticity with respect to the Frisch-deflated price of good i. This is equivalent to the own-price elasticity when the marginal utility of income remains constant. Since θ_i/w_i under Working's model is specified as shown in (10.2), we shall analogously specify the Frisch own-price elasticity as

$$F = \frac{\phi(\bar{w}_{ic} + \beta_i)}{\bar{w}_{ic}}. \tag{11.2}$$

The Slutsky own-price elasticity refers to the situation in which real income remains constant, $d(\log Q) = 0$, in spite of the price increase. To evaluate this elasticity we merge the Frisch deflator in (11.1) with $d(\log p_i)$. The substitution term then takes the form

$$\frac{\phi\theta_i}{w_i} \left[(1 - \theta_i)d(\log p_i) - \sum_{j \neq i} \theta_j d(\log p_j) \right], \tag{11.3}$$

which shows that the Slutsky own-price elasticity is $\phi\theta_i(1 - \theta_i)/w_i$. We implement this in the form

$$S = \frac{\phi(\bar{w}_{ic} + \beta_i)(1 - \bar{w}_{ic} - \beta_i)}{\bar{w}_{ic}}. \tag{11.4}$$

Finally, the Cournot own-price elasticity of the demand for good i refers to the situation in which money income remains constant, $d(\log M) = 0$. The Divisia decomposition of Section 1.9 can then be written as

$$d(\log Q) = - \sum_{j=1}^{n} w_j d(\log p_j),$$

so that the income term in (11.1) becomes $-\theta_i d(\log p_i)$ as far as the price of good i is concerned. Therefore, the Cournot own-price elasticity (C) is obtained from the Slutsky elasticity by subtracting the marginal share. We implement this in the form

$$C = \frac{\phi(\bar{w}_{ic} + \beta_i)(1 - \bar{w}_{ic} - \beta_i)}{\bar{w}_{ic}} - (\bar{w}_{ic} + \beta_i). \tag{11.5}$$

These three price elasticities are shown in Table 2–8 for the ten goods and the per capita income levels of the thirty countries. Unknown parameters are all replaced by ML estimates. The most striking feature is the large difference between the behavior of the own-price elasticities of food and those

Table 2-8.   A Cross-Country Tabulation of Own-Price Elasticities

Country (1)	Income (2)	Food			Beverages, tobacco		
		F (3)	S (4)	C (5)	F (6)	S (7)	C (8)
India	.068	−.39	−.22	−.64	−.53	−.51	−.56
Pakistan	.089	−.37	−.23	−.61	−.53	−.51	−.56
Sri Lanka	.103	−.37	−.24	−.59	−.53	−.51	−.56
Philippines	.140	−.35	−.24	−.55	−.53	−.50	−.56
Thailand	.141	−.35	−.24	−.55	−.53	−.50	−.56
Malaysia	.190	−.33	−.24	−.51	−.53	−.50	−.56
Korea	.206	−.33	−.24	−.50	−.53	−.50	−.56
Brazil	.246	−.31	−.24	−.47	−.53	−.50	−.56
Colombia	.255	−.31	−.24	−.46	−.53	−.50	−.56
Syria	.261	−.31	−.24	−.45	−.53	−.50	−.56
Iran	.272	−.30	−.24	−.45	−.53	−.50	−.56
Romania	.290	−.30	−.24	−.44	−.53	−.50	−.56
Yugoslavia	.346	−.28	−.23	−.40	−.53	−.50	−.56
Mexico	.371	−.27	−.23	−.39	−.53	−.50	−.56
Poland	.435	−.25	−.21	−.35	−.53	−.50	−.56
Uruguay	.451	−.24	−.21	−.34	−.53	−.50	−.56
Ireland	.464	−.24	−.21	−.33	−.53	−.50	−.56
Hungary	.467	−.24	−.21	−.33	−.53	−.50	−.56
Italy	.532	−.21	−.19	−.30	−.53	−.50	−.56
Japan	.588	−.19	−.18	−.27	−.53	−.50	−.56
Spain	.606	−.19	−.17	−.26	−.53	−.50	−.56
United Kingdom	.641	−.17	−.16	−.24	−.53	−.50	−.56
Netherlands	.686	−.16	−.15	−.21	−.53	−.50	−.56
Belgium	.750	−.13	−.13	−.18	−.53	−.50	−.56
Austria	.751	−.13	−.13	−.18	−.53	−.50	−.56
Germany	.756	−.13	−.12	−.17	−.53	−.50	−.56
France	.756	−.13	−.12	−.17	−.53	−.50	−.56
Denmark	.785	−.12	−.11	−.16	−.53	−.50	−.56
Luxembourg	.794	−.12	−.11	−.15	−.53	−.50	−.56
United States	1.000	−.03	−.02	−.03	−.53	−.50	−.56

of all other goods. For the latter, the Frisch and Cournot elasticities are typically close to each other, and the Slutsky elasticity is a bit smaller in absolute value. For food, the Frisch and Cournot elasticities decline toward zero when the country is more affluent, which confirms Timmer's (1981) proposition, but the Cournot elasticity is much larger than the Frisch elasticity of Demand.

Clothing, footwear			Gross rent, fuel			House furnishings, operations		
F (9)	S (10)	C (11)	F (12)	S (13)	C (14)	F (15)	S (16)	C (17)
−.50	−.45	−.55	−.80	−.73	−.82	−.97	−.91	−.97
−.50	−.45	−.55	−.77	−.69	−.80	−.89	−.83	−.89
−.50	−.46	−.54	−.75	−.67	−.78	−.85	−.80	−.86
−.50	−.46	−.54	−.73	−.64	−.76	−.80	−.74	−.82
−.50	−.46	−.54	−.73	−.64	−.76	−.80	−.74	−.81
−.50	−.46	−.54	−.71	−.62	−.74	−.76	−.70	−.78
−.50	−.46	−.54	−.70	−.61	−.74	−.75	−.70	−.78
−.50	−.46	−.54	−.69	−.60	−.73	−.74	−.67	−.76
−.50	−.46	−.54	−.69	−.60	−.73	−.73	−.67	−.76
−.50	−.46	−.54	−.69	−.60	−.73	−.73	−.67	−.76
−.50	−.46	−.54	−.69	−.59	−.73	−.73	−.66	−.75
−.50	−.46	−.54	−.68	−.59	−.73	−.72	−.66	−.75
−.50	−.46	−.54	−.67	−.58	−.72	−.71	−.64	−.74
−.50	−.46	−.54	−.67	−.57	−.72	−.71	−.64	−.74
−.50	−.46	−.54	−.67	−.57	−.72	−.70	−.63	−.73
−.50	−.46	−.54	−.66	−.56	−.72	−.70	−.62	−.73
−.50	−.46	−.54	−.66	−.56	−.71	−.69	−.62	−.73
−.50	−.46	−.54	−.66	−.56	−.71	−.69	−.62	−.73
−.50	−.46	−.54	−.66	−.56	−.71	−.69	−.61	−.72
−.50	−.46	−.54	−.66	−.55	−.71	−.68	−.61	−.72
−.50	−.46	−.54	−.65	−.55	−.71	−.68	−.61	−.72
−.50	−.46	−.54	−.65	−.55	−.71	−.68	−.60	−.72
−.50	−.46	−.54	−.65	−.54	−.71	−.68	−.60	−.71
−.50	−.46	−.54	−.65	−.54	−.71	−.67	−.59	−.71
−.50	−.46	−.54	−.65	−.54	−.71	−.67	−.59	−.71
−.50	−.46	−.54	−.65	−.54	−.71	−.67	−.59	−.71
−.50	−.46	−.54	−.65	−.54	−.71	−.67	−.59	−.71
−.50	−.46	−.54	−.65	−.54	−.71	−.67	−.59	−.71
−.50	−.46	−.54	−.65	−.54	−.71	−.67	−.59	−.71
−.50	−.46	−.54	−.64	−.53	−.70	−.66	−.58	−.70

except for the most affluent countries. On the other hand, the Slutsky own-price elasticity of the demand for food remains virtually constant as long as income remains below 40 percent of the U.S. per capita level.

To clarify the latter result we take the logarithmic income derivative of (11.4), using (10.1):

Table 2-8 continued.

Country	Income	Medical care F (18)	Medical care S (19)	Medical care C (20)	Transport, communication F (21)	Transport, communication S (22)	Transport, communication C (23)
India	.068	−1.02	−.97	−1.02	−.93	−.86	−.93
Pakistan	.089	−.92	−.87	−.92	−.86	−.79	−.87
Sri Lanka	.103	−.88	−.83	−.89	−.83	−.76	−.84
Philippines	.140	−.82	−.77	−.83	−.79	−.71	−.80
Thailand	.141	−.82	−.76	−.83	−.78	−.71	−.80
Malaysia	.190	−.78	−.72	−.79	−.75	−.68	−.78
Korea	.206	−.77	−.71	−.79	−.74	−.67	−.77
Brazil	.246	−.75	−.69	−.77	−.73	−.65	−.76
Colombia	.255	−.75	−.69	−.77	−.73	−.65	−.76
Syria	.261	−.74	−.68	−.76	−.72	−.65	−.75
Iran	.272	−.74	−.68	−.76	−.72	−.64	−.75
Romania	.290	−.74	−.67	−.76	−.72	−.64	−.75
Yugoslavia	.346	−.72	−.66	−.75	−.71	−.62	−.74
Mexico	.371	−.72	−.65	−.74	−.70	−.62	−.74
Poland	.435	−.71	−.64	−.73	−.69	−.61	−.73
Uruguay	.451	−.70	−.64	−.73	−.69	−.60	−.73
Ireland	.464	−.70	−.64	−.73	−.69	−.60	−.73
Hungary	.467	−.70	−.64	−.73	−.69	−.60	−.73
Italy	.532	−.69	−.63	−.72	−.68	−.59	−.72
Japan	.588	−.69	−.62	−.72	−.68	−.59	−.72
Spain	.606	−.69	−.62	−.72	−.68	−.59	−.72
United Kingdom	.641	−.68	−.62	−.72	−.67	−.58	−.72
Netherlands	.686	−.68	−.61	−.71	−.67	−.58	−.72
Belgium	.750	−.68	−.61	−.71	−.67	−.58	−.71
Austria	.751	−.68	−.61	−.71	−.67	−.57	−.71
Germany	.756	−.68	−.61	−.71	−.67	−.57	−.71
France	.756	−.68	−.61	−.71	−.67	−.57	−.71
Denmark	.785	−.68	−.60	−.71	−.67	−.57	−.71
Luxembourg	.794	−.68	−.60	−.71	−.67	−.57	−.71
United States	1.000	−.67	−.59	−.70	−.66	−.56	−.71

$$\frac{\partial \log(S/\phi)}{\partial \log Q_c} = \frac{-\beta_i[\bar{w}_{ic}^2 + \beta_i(1-\beta_i)]}{\bar{w}_{ic}(\bar{w}_{ic} + \beta_i)(1 - \bar{w}_{ic} - \beta_i)}.$$

If good i is a luxury ($\beta_i > 0$), the numerator on the right is negative so that the Slutsky elasticity declines in absolute value as the country becomes more affluent. But if i is a necessity ($\beta_i < 0$), $-\beta_i$ is positive and the expression in

Recreation			Education			Other		
F (24)	S (25)	C (26)	F (27)	S (28)	C (29)	F (30)	S (31)	C (32)
−1.12	−1.07	−1.11	−.49	−.46	−.52	−.98	−.91	−.98
−.98	−.93	−.98	−.49	−.46	−.52	−.89	−.82	−.90
−.93	−.89	−.93	−.49	−.46	−.52	−.86	−.79	−.87
−.85	−.81	−.86	−.49	−.46	−.52	−.81	−.73	−.82
−.85	−.81	−.86	−.49	−.46	−.52	−.80	−.73	−.82
−.80	−.76	−.81	−.49	−.46	−.52	−.77	−.69	−.79
−.79	−.74	−.80	−.49	−.46	−.52	−.76	−.68	−.78
−.77	−.72	−.78	−.49	−.46	−.52	−.74	−.66	−.77
−.76	−.72	−.78	−.49	−.46	−.52	−.74	−.65	−.77
−.76	−.71	−.78	−.49	−.46	−.52	−.74	−.65	−.77
−.76	−.71	−.77	−.49	−.46	−.52	−.73	−.65	−.76
−.75	−.70	−.77	−.49	−.46	−.52	−.73	−.64	−.76
−.74	−.69	−.75	−.49	−.46	−.52	−.71	−.63	−.75
−.73	−.68	−.75	−.49	−.46	−.52	−.71	−.62	−.75
−.72	−.67	−.74	−.49	−.46	−.52	−.70	−.61	−.74
−.72	−.66	−.74	−.49	−.46	−.52	−.70	−.61	−.74
−.71	−.66	−.73	−.49	−.46	−.52	−.70	−.60	−.74
−.71	−.66	−.73	−.49	−.46	−.52	−.70	−.60	−.74
−.70	−.65	−.73	−.49	−.46	−.51	−.69	−.59	−.73
−.70	−.64	−.72	−.49	−.46	−.51	−.68	−.59	−.73
−.70	−.64	−.72	−.49	−.46	−.51	−.68	−.59	−.73
−.69	−.64	−.72	−.49	−.46	−.51	−.68	−.58	−.73
−.69	−.63	−.72	−.49	−.46	−.51	−.68	−.58	−.72
−.69	−.63	−.71	−.49	−.46	−.51	−.67	−.57	−.72
−.69	−.63	−.71	−.49	−.46	−.51	−.67	−.57	−.72
−.69	−.63	−.71	−.49	−.46	−.51	−.67	−.57	−.72
−.69	−.63	−.71	−.49	−.46	−.51	−.67	−.57	−.72
−.68	−.63	−.71	−.49	−.46	−.51	−.67	−.57	−.72
−.68	−.63	−.71	−.49	−.46	−.51	−.67	−.57	−.72
−.67	−.61	−.70	−.49	−.46	−.51	−.66	−.56	−.72

brackets may also be positive so that the numerator is then positive too. In particular, this will happen for $i =$ food when $\bar{w}_{ic}$ is sufficiently large (as is the case for Q_c sufficiently small). The implication is that a rising Q_c will also raise the S of food in absolute value, but a further increase will ultimately yield a smaller absolute S.

2.12   INCOME AND PRICE ELASTICITIES AT LOW INCOME LEVELS

The income levels considered in Tables 2–7 and 2–8 are the per capita incomes of the thirty countries of the sample, but there is no reason why we should confine ourselves to these sample values. In particular, it is interesting to see how the model behaves when we apply it to incomes below India's per capita income (which is the lowest Q_c in the sample). Table 2–9 provides an answer in terms of the implied income and own-price elasticities at incomes that vary between 3 and 10 percent of the U.S. per capita level. When income declines below 3 percent of this level, the budget share of recreation computed from (10.1) becomes negative, thus invalidating Working's model. (This 3 percent is approximately equivalent to 40 percent of India's per capita income.) The very high values of the income elasticities near the top of the table should be noted. Such goods are truly luxuries at very low levels of affluence.

The remainder of Table 2–9 deals with the same three own-price elasticities as those considered in Table 2–8. None of the goods except food shows substantial differences among these three elasticities at given levels of income. For food the picture is different: When income increases from 3 to 10 percent of the U.S. per capita level, the Frisch and Slutsky own-price elasticities of food remain virtually constant around −0.4 and −0.2, respectively, whereas the Cournot own-price elasticity declines in absolute value from about −0.75 to −0.6. The large Cournot values for poor consumers reflect the importance of food in their budget.

The exceptional role of food makes it worthwhile to analyze the relation of food and nonfood. This is done in Table 2–10 for the income elasticities in columns 2 and 3 and for the own-price elasticities in columns 4 through 9. The income elasticity of the demand for nonfood declines gradually as income rises, and so do the Frisch and Slutsky own-price elasticities of nonfood. The picture of the nonfood Cournot elasticity is different; this results from the increasing budget share of nonfood with increasing income.

The last two columns of Table 2–10 deal with cross-price elasticities. The Frisch cross-price elasticities vanish because of the assumption of preference independence. It follows from the substitution term (11.3) that when there are only two goods (food and nonfood), the Slutsky elasticity of the demand for good i with respect to the price of j equals minus the Slutsky own-price elasticity of i. Thus, there is no need to present the Frisch and Slutsky cross-price elasticities of food and nonfood. The Cournot elasticity

Table 2-9. Income and Own-Price Elasticities at Low Income Levels.

Income[a] (1)	Food (2)	Beverages, tobacco (3)	Clothing, footwear (4)	Gross rent, fuel (5)	House furnishings, operations (6)	Medical care (7)	Transport, communication (8)	Recreation (9)	Education (10)	Other (11)
					Income elasticities					
0.03	.78	1.02	.95	1.92	3.67	5.05	3.05	15.19	.94	3.96
0.04	.77	1.02	.95	1.73	2.51	2.87	2.29	3.79	.94	2.60
0.05	.75	1.02	.95	1.63	2.13	2.32	2.00	2.72	.94	2.18
0.06	.74	1.02	.95	1.56	1.94	2.06	1.85	2.31	.94	1.97
0.07	.73	1.02	.95	1.52	1.82	1.91	1.75	2.09	.94	1.84
0.08	.72	1.02	.95	1.48	1.74	1.81	1.68	1.95	.94	1.76
0.09	.71	1.02	.95	1.46	1.68	1.74	1.63	1.86	.94	1.70
0.10	.70	1.02	.95	1.44	1.63	1.69	1.59	1.78	.94	1.65
					Frisch own-price elasticities					
0.03	−.41	−.53	−.50	−1.01	−1.93	−2.65	−1.60	−7.99	−.49	−2.08
0.04	−.40	−.53	−.50	−.91	−1.32	−1.51	−1.20	−1.99	−.49	−1.37
0.05	−.40	−.53	−.50	−.85	−1.12	−1.22	−1.05	−1.43	−.49	−1.15
0.06	−.39	−.53	−.50	−.82	−1.02	−1.09	−.97	−1.21	−.49	−1.04
0.07	−.38	−.53	−.50	−.80	−.96	−1.01	−.92	−1.10	−.49	−.97
0.08	−.38	−.53	−.50	−.78	−.91	−.95	−.88	−1.03	−.49	−.92
0.09	−.37	−.53	−.50	−.77	−.88	−.92	−.86	−.98	−.49	−.89
0.10	−.37	−.53	−.50	−.76	−.86	−.89	−.84	−.94	−.49	−.87

Table 2-9 continued.

Income[a] (1)	Food (2)	Beverages, tobacco (3)	Clothing, footwear (4)	Gross rent, fuel (5)	House furnishings, operations (6)	Medical care (7)	Transport, communication (8)	Recreation (9)	Education (10)	Other (11)
					Slutsky own-price elasticities					
0.03	-.19	-.51	-.45	-.94	-1.86	-2.58	-1.53	-7.82	-.46	-1.99
0.04	-.20	-.51	-.45	-.84	-1.26	-1.45	-1.14	-1.94	-.46	-1.29
0.05	-.21	-.51	-.45	-.78	-1.07	-1.17	-.99	-1.39	-.46	-1.08
0.06	-.22	-.51	-.45	-.75	-.97	-1.04	-.91	-1.17	-.46	-.97
0.07	-.22	-.51	-.45	-.72	-.90	-.96	-.86	-1.06	-.46	-.90
0.08	-.23	-.51	-.45	-.70	-.86	-.90	-.82	-.99	-.46	-.85
0.09	-.23	-.51	-.45	-.69	-.83	-.87	-.79	-.93	-.46	-.82
0.10	-.24	-.51	-.46	-.68	-.80	-.84	-.77	-.90	-.46	-.79
					Cournot own-price elasticities					
0.03	-.73	-.56	-.55	-1.01	-1.90	-2.61	-1.58	-7.84	-.53	-2.03
0.04	-.70	-.56	-.55	-.91	-1.31	-1.49	-1.19	-1.97	-.53	-1.35
0.05	-.68	-.56	-.55	-.87	-1.11	-1.21	-1.05	-1.42	-.52	-1.14
0.06	-.66	-.56	-.55	-.84	-1.02	-1.08	-.97	-1.21	-.52	-1.03
0.07	-.64	-.56	-.55	-.82	-.96	-1.01	-.93	-1.10	-.52	-.97
0.08	-.63	-.56	-.55	-.80	-.92	-.96	-.89	-1.03	-.52	-.93
0.09	-.61	-.56	-.55	-.79	-.89	-.92	-.87	-.98	-.52	-.90
0.10	-.60	-.56	-.55	-.78	-.87	-.89	-.85	-.94	-.52	-.88

a. Expressed as a fraction of the U.S. per capita income in 1975.

Table 2-10. Income and Price Elasticities of Food and Nonfood at Different Levels of Affluence.

Income[a] (1)	Income elasticities		Own-price elasticities						Cross-price elasticities	
			Frisch		Slutsky		Cournot		Cournot	
	food (2)	nonfood (3)	food (4)	nonfood (5)	food (6)	nonfood (7)	food (8)	nonfood (9)	food (10)	nonfood (11)
0.03	.78	1.52	-.41	-.80	-.19	-.44	-.73	-.89	-.05	-.63
0.04	.77	1.45	-.40	-.76	-.20	-.39	-.70	-.88	-.06	-.57
0.05	.75	1.41	-.40	-.74	-.21	-.35	-.68	-.88	-.07	-.53
0.06	.74	1.38	-.39	-.73	-.22	-.32	-.66	-.88	-.08	-.50
0.07	.73	1.36	-.38	-.72	-.22	-.30	-.64	-.88	-.09	-.48
0.08	.72	1.34	-.38	-.71	-.23	-.28	-.63	-.88	-.09	-.46
0.09	.71	1.33	-.37	-.70	-.23	-.27	-.61	-.89	-.10	-.44
0.10	.70	1.32	-.37	-.69	-.24	-.25	-.60	-.89	-.10	-.43
0.20	.62	1.26	-.33	-.66	-.24	-.17	-.50	-.91	-.12	-.35
0.40	.49	1.22	-.26	-.64	-.22	-.10	-.37	-.95	-.12	-.27
0.60	.36	1.20	-.19	-.63	-.17	-.05	-.26	-.97	-.10	-.23
0.80	.21	1.19	-.11	-.63	-.11	-.03	-.15	-.98	-.06	-.21
1.00	.05	1.18	-.03	-.62	-.02	-.00	-.03	-1.00	-.02	-.19

a. Expressed as a fraction of the U.S. per capita income in 1975.

of the demand for i with respect to the price of j is the sum of two terms, $-\phi\theta_i\theta_j/w_i$ and $-\theta_i w_j/w_i$, where θ_i is the marginal share of i, which is specified as $w_i + \beta_i$, with $w_i = \alpha_i + \beta_i \log Q$ ($Q =$ income measured as a fraction of the 1975 U.S. per capita level).

Column 10 of Table 2-10 shows the Cournot elasticity of the demand for food with respect to the price of nonfood. This elasticity takes small negative values. Column 11 contains the Cournot elasticity of the demand for nonfood with respect to the food price. This elasticity is much larger, particularly at low levels of income, which reflects the large budget share of food at a low level of affluence.

2.13   FRISCH'S CONJECTURE ON THE INCOME FLEXIBILITY

Until this point we have not questioned the assumption that the income flexibility ϕ can be viewed as a constant. Recall from Section 1.12 that the reciprocal of this flexibility, $1/\phi$, is the income elasticity of the marginal utility of income. Frisch (1959: 189) denies that this elasticity is a constant. In fact, he conjectures the following numerical values of the income elasticity of the marginal utility of income at different levels of affluence:

-10 for an extremely poor and apathetic part of the population,
-4 for the slightly better off but still poor part of the population with a fairly pronounced desire to become better off,
-2 for the middle income bracket, "the median part" of the population,
-0.7 for the better off part of the population,
-0.1 for the rich part of the population with ambitions toward "conspicuous consumption".

Frisch goes on to say that it would be a very promising research project to obtain the income elasticity of the marginal utility of income for different countries and different types of populations. He argues that a universal atlas of the values of this elasticity should be constructed and that it would serve an extremely useful purpose in demand analysis. It is not difficult to accept this proposition, at least under preference independence, because the Frisch own-price elasticities are then proportional to the income elasticities, with ϕ as proportionality coefficient. Thus, knowledge of ϕ is all we need to obtain these price elasticities once we know the income elasticities of the n goods.

However, accepting the numerical values of $1/\phi$ quoted above is quite another matter. To assess the implications of these values, recall from Table

2-10 that when income rises from 3 percent of the 1975 U.S. per capita value to a level ten times higher, the Frisch own-price elasticity of the demand for food declines slightly, from about -0.4 to -0.3. These elasticity values are based on the assumption of a constant ϕ. Therefore, let us now proceed under the condition that Frisch's conjecture is correct. More specifically, let the "extremely poor and apathetic part of the population" earn 3 percent of the above-mentioned U.S. level, so that its ϕ equals $1/(-10) = -0.1$. Let "the median part of the population" have an income equal to the per capita income in Northwestern Europe at the time when Frisch wrote his article; this amounts to about 35 percent of the 1975 U.S. level (see Table 2-13 in Section 2.14), so that the corresponding ϕ equals $1/(-2) = -0.5$. Thus, ϕ is about five times larger for the latter group. When we combine this with the income elasticities of food in column 2 of Table 2-10 (about 0.8 for $Q = 0.03$ and 0.5 for $Q = 0.35$), we conclude that the Frisch own-price elasticity of food must be about three times higher at $Q = 0.35$ than at $Q = 0.03$. This increased price sensitivity at higher income levels should be contrasted with the opposite picture in column 4 of Table 2-10.

Most analysts would agree that such a fast increase in the price sensitivity of the demand for food is not realistic. Nevertheless, Clements, Finke, and Theil (1984) decided to use the cross-country data in order to verify the proposition that ϕ takes larger negative values at a higher income level. They divided the thirty countries into two groups, one consisting of the fifteen countries with the lowest Q_c's and the other consisting of the fifteen with the highest Q_c's. The ML procedure was applied to each group separately, but it did not converge for one of the groups. Some further experimentation with other groupings suggests that the convergence problem results from insufficient variation of the per capita incomes within the group. Accordingly, Clements et al. decided to use one group consisting of the twenty countries with the lowest Q_c's and another consisting of the twenty with the highest Q_c's, but we should emphasize that this involves an overlap of ten middle-income countries. The results are shown in columns 3 and 4 of Table 2-11; column 2 provides the estimates based on all thirty countries and is reproduced from Table 2-5 (with a fourth digit added). The income flexibility estimates in the last row of Table 2-11 provides no support for Frisch's conjecture that ϕ increases in absolute value with income.

An alternative procedure, from Theil and Suhm (1981: 43), is to use the entire sample and to allow the income flexibility to vary systematically with Q_c. The relationship selected is

$$\phi(Q_c) = \phi_0 + \phi_1 \log Q_c. \tag{13.1}$$

Table 2–11. First Test of Frisch's Conjecture on the Income Flexibility.

| | *ML estimates and asymptotic standard errors* | | |
Parameter (1)	All 30 countries (2)	20 poorest countries (3)	20 richest countries (4)
α_i Food	.1620 (.0121)	.1808 (.0224)	.1522 (.0143)
Beverages, tobacco	.0558 (.0064)	.0743 (.0125)	.0502 (.0068)
Clothing, footwear	.0839 (.0058)	.0932 (.0107)	.0707 (.0062)
Gross rent, fuel	.1448 (.0078)	.1107 (.0109)	.1514 (.0112)
House furnishings, operations	.0982 (.0050)	.0948 (.0087)	.0982 (.0074)
Medical care	.0888 (.0041)	.0884 (.0055)	.0896 (.0055)
Transport, communications	.1179 (.0067)	.0990 (.0130)	.1342 (.0044)
Recreation	.0692 (.0042)	.0743 (.0066)	.0706 (.0054)
Education	.0535 (.0059)	.0495 (.0080)	.0535 (.0063)
Other	.1260 (.0068)	.1350 (.0109)	.1294 (.0100)
β_i Food	−.1543 (.0098)	−.1498 (.0149)	−.1474 (.0204)
Beverages, tobacco	.0008 (.0050)	.0112 (.0081)	−.0036 (.0091)
Clothing, footwear	−.0046 (.0048)	.0010 (.0072)	−.0317 (.0089)
Gross rent, fuel	.0315 (.0063)	.0119 (.0071)	.0436 (.0163)
House furnishings, operations	.0253 (.0040)	.0226 (.0058)	.0227 (.0103)
Medical care	.0237 (.0034)	.0244 (.0036)	.0217 (.0079)
Transport, communications	.0295 (.0055)	.0186 (.0088)	.0580 (.0061)
Recreation	.0193 (.0033)	.0230 (.0043)	.0212 (.0074)
Education	−.0040 (.0053)	−.0019 (.0056)	−.0213 (.0098)
Other	.0328 (.0056)	.0391 (.0073)	.0368 (.0145)
ϕ Income flexibility	−.5259 (.0369)	−.5504 (.0410)	−.4550 (.0360)

A negative value of ϕ_1 would be in qualitative agreement with Frisch's conjecture. The extension of the ML procedure that is needed to incorporate (13.1) is straightforward; see Theil and Suhm (1981: 45–47). The ML estimates and their asymptotic standard errors of ϕ_0 and ϕ_1 are

$$\hat{\phi}_0 = -0.498 \ (0.060), \qquad \hat{\phi}_1 = -0.003 \ (0.053). \tag{13.2}$$

Although the sign of the ϕ_1 estimate points to Frisch's conjecture, the standard error is such that the support given to this conjecture is actually minimal.

The computations discussed in the previous paragraph were made at a time when beverages and tobacco were not yet separated from food. Some additional results are shown in Table 2-12. In the first row we use the entire sample of thirty countries. Columns 2 and 3 show the estimates (13.2) and the others give the ML estimates of the β_i's; note that these are close to those shown in column 2 of Table 2-11 in spite of the use of nine rather than ten goods. In the next thirty lines of Table 2-12 we present the ML estimates for twenty-nine countries, one country being deleted each time. The results in column 3 show clearly how little the sample can tell us about the value of ϕ_1 in spite of the large income variation in this sample.

2.14   A CROSS-COUNTRY TIME SERIES PICTURE OF CONSUMPTION

Until this point, we have confined ourselves to cross-country comparisons based on ten goods in 1975. If we also have annual time series data for a number of years (including 1975) and for the same ten goods and the same countries (or for a subset of these countries), we can obtain a combined cross-country time series picture. For example, suppose that we have per capita quantities q_{it} and budget shares w_{it} for some country and for each $i = 1, ..., 10$. Then we can compute the Divisia volume index of consumption per capita,

$$DQ_t = \sum_{i=1}^{10} \bar{w}_{it} Dq_{it},$$ (14.1)

where $\bar{w}_{it} = (w_{i, t-1} + w_{it})/2$. In Table 2-13 we use for 1975 the consumption figures of column 2 of Table 2-2 (normalized so that the U.S. value equals 100) and we apply the Divisia index (14.1) for each country in the successive later years (1976, 1977, . . .) and in the successive earlier years (1974, 1973, . . .). The results enable us to compare the standard of living of any of the twelve countries in any year with that of any other country in any year. For example, the U.S. standard of living in 1964 was approximately equal to the Dutch level in 1977; the Dutch standard of living in 1960 was approximately equal to the Italian level in 1964; and both levels were about one-half of the German level in 1972. Note that these comparisons avoid the tricky issue of currency conversion.

    The time series data underlying Table 2-13 are from OECD (1983) except those for the Netherlands, which were directly obtained from the Dutch Central Bureau of Statistics; for details see Finke and Theil (1985) and Theil and Finke (1985b). Data on ten goods were available for eight of the twelve countries. For Ireland and Luxembourg the expenditures on recreation and

Table 2–12.   Second Test of Frisch's Conjecture.[a]

Country deleted (1)	ϕ_0 (2)	ϕ_1 (3)	Food, beverages, tobacco (4)	Clothing, footwear (5)
None	−4978 (597)	−33 (528)	−1530	−46
India	−5163 (642)	−515 (581)	−1565	−108
Pakistan	−4401 (584)	551 (576)	−1556	−24
Sri Lanka	−4508 (608)	562 (562)	−1495	−66
Philippines	−5535 (539)	−531 (485)	−1498	−58
Thailand	−4889 (605)	63 (543)	−1528	−49
Malaysia	−4960 (594)	126 (534)	−1579	−59
Korea	−5166 (604)	−264 (528)	−1511	−40
Brazil	−5118 (596)	14 (532)	−1548	−48
Colombia	−5143 (593)	−437 (524)	−1513	−44
Syria	−5082 (610)	−134 (533)	−1507	−40
Iran	−5091 (592)	−251 (516)	−1539	−37
Romania	−5092 (619)	42 (550)	−1536	−36
Yugoslavia	−4930 (607)	4 (534)	−1532	−46
Mexico	−4947 (596)	−112 (530)	−1524	−46
Poland	−5004 (630)	−39 (540)	−1531	−48
Uruguay	−5099 (628)	−302 (531)	−1542	−44
Ireland	−4874 (557)	118 (496)	−1528	−40
Hungary	−4931 (618)	−3 (527)	−1537	−47
Italy	−4663 (593)	193 (525)	−1540	−45
Japan	−5142 (603)	−92 (531)	−1526	−46
Spain	−4917 (612)	2 (534)	−1550	−47
United Kingdom	−5263 (577)	−158 (515)	−1514	−42
Netherlands	−4307 (615)	401 (521)	−1527	−46
Belgium	−4960 (604)	−6 (533)	−1535	−39
Austria	−5069 (601)	−69 (529)	−1531	−58
Germany	−5079 (597)	−101 (528)	−1515	−50
France	−4825 (590)	91 (523)	−1534	−38
Denmark	−5130 (617)	−133 (543)	−1521	−32
Luxembourg	−4659 (558)	223 (503)	−1531	−41
United States	−5638 (698)	−495 (593)	−1503	−36

a. All entries to be divided by 10^4.

education are combined; for Germany and Italy we have both this combination and that of food with beverages and tobacco. Accordingly, in the columns of Table 2–13 for these four countries we replace 10 in (14.1) by 9 or 8.

Gross rent, fuel (6)	House furnishings, operations (7)	Medical care (8)	Transport, communications (9)	Recreation (10)	Education (11)	Other (12)
322	255	237	299	197	−58	325
348	248	250	356	197	−64	337
364	268	252	292	211	−109	302
302	254	234	322	202	−72	319
339	248	232	261	179	−29	325
300	254	243	305	207	−56	324
322	257	234	327	203	−39	334
314	245	232	296	194	−57	327
315	256	234	303	197	−39	336
319	253	230	295	193	−59	325
328	252	231	287	191	−58	316
343	256	232	294	188	−57	319
326	252	239	289	194	−50	322
324	256	237	299	197	−58	324
327	253	234	300	196	−62	322
327	252	239	301	194	−65	330
329	252	238	300	197	−56	326
322	258	236	298	199	−60	315
333	254	241	306	191	−60	321
321	264	234	302	199	−62	327
320	261	232	305	191	−54	318
323	259	236	304	201	−52	326
299	260	249	290	192	−50	317
328	255	232	315	189	−79	335
322	240	239	301	205	−58	327
333	258	233	298	200	−42	309
320	248	221	294	194	−50	337
320	249	229	299	200	−53	328
288	259	253	294	192	−78	345
306	250	256	292	216	−63	314
306	267	230	268	198	−57	327

2.15 THE QUALITY OF CONSUMPTION

The quality of consumption can be measured in several ways. The most direct approach enumerates the attractive features of a good, such as the horse-

Table 2-13. Divisia Volume Index of Consumption Per Capita for Twelve OECD Countries.

	United States	Luxembourg	Denmark	France	Germany	Belgium	Netherlands	United Kingdom	Spain	Japan	Italy	Ireland
1952	—	—	—	—	—	—	25.2	—	—	—	—	—
1953	—	—	—	—	—	—	26.9	—	—	—	—	—
1954	—	—	—	—	—	—	28.9	—	—	—	—	—
1955	—	—	—	—	—	—	30.3	—	—	—	—	—
1956	—	—	—	—	—	—	32.7	—	—	—	—	—
1957	—	—	—	—	—	—	32.3	—	—	—	—	—
1958	—	—	—	—	—	—	31.6	—	—	—	—	—
1959	—	—	—	—	—	—	33.1	—	—	—	—	—
1960	—	—	—	—	—	—	35.2	—	—	—	—	—
1961	—	—	—	—	—	—	37.0	—	—	—	—	—
1962	—	—	—	—	—	—	39.0	—	—	—	—	—
1963	—	—	—	—	—	—	42.1	—	—	—	—	—

Year												
1964	75.4	—	—	49.2	51.6	49.5	43.7	51.9	36.4	—	35.7	—
1965	78.7	—	—	50.9	53.6	51.0	46.5	52.3	38.2	—	36.5	—
1966	81.9	—	67.0	52.9	55.4	52.2	47.1	53.2	40.4	—	38.9	—
1967	83.5	—	68.7	55.1	55.9	53.5	48.5	54.3	42.4	—	41.4	—
1968	87.3	—	69.1	56.6	58.3	56.3	50.8	56.0	44.4	—	43.1	—
1969	89.6	65.1	72.9	59.8	62.0	59.0	53.9	56.2	46.9	47.8	45.7	—
1970	90.5	68.1	74.8	62.1	66.1	61.4	57.7	57.6	48.3	50.0	48.7	44.4
1971	92.7	70.5	74.1	65.4	69.0	64.1	59.5	59.3	50.2	54.0	49.7	45.3
1972	97.0	73.4	75.1	68.9	71.6	67.7	61.8	62.7	53.7	58.2	51.0	46.5
1973	100.3	76.5	78.5	72.1	72.4	72.7	64.5	65.6	57.4	57.1	53.5	49.2
1974	98.9	79.4	76.8	73.8	72.8	74.9	66.1	64.5	59.8	58.8	54.4	49.4
1975	100.0	81.8	78.5	75.6	75.6	75.0	68.6	64.1	60.6	60.1	53.2	46.4
1976	104.6	83.8	84.3	79.6	78.9	78.6	71.8	64.5	62.8	61.7	54.7	47.0
1977	108.4	85.5	85.5	83.0	81.8	80.3	74.5	64.6	63.7	63.9	55.7	49.2
1978	111.9	88.7	85.7	86.3	84.9	82.3	—	68.0	—	67.0	57.1	51.2
1979	113.6	91.5	86.3	88.6	87.3	86.0	—	70.9	—	67.5	60.0	51.2
1980	112.7	—	83.2	89.3	88.3	86.9	—	70.2	—	67.5	62.5	50.6
1981	113.8	—	82.8	89.1	87.5	85.7	—	70.3	—	—	62.4	—

Sources: OECD (1983); Finke and Theil (1985); and Theil and Finke (1985b).

power and the size of an automobile, and also the unattractive features. This is the approach used in the theory of hedonic price indexes to explain price differentials of automobiles and other durables; see, for example, Griliches (1971). However, this approach is less practical when the analyst is interested in several goods simultaneously, particularly when he wants to summarize quality by means of one single number.

One such approach, suggested independently by Houthakker (1953) and Theil (1953), is based on the average price paid for a composite (nonhomogeneous) good. Let tea be such a good, consisting of various grades. Since high-quality tea commands a higher price than low-quality tea, the average price that a household pays for a pound of tea (the total expenditure on tea divided by the total quantity in pounds) is a measure of the quality of the tea bought by this household. Such an indicator is useful for a cross-section study when the prices of the individual grades are approximately constant during the short period covered by such a study. However, this method is applicable only to narrowly defined composite goods, since dimensional considerations prevent us from averaging the prices of tea and, say, legal services. It is clearly more attractive to measure quality in terms of dimensionless concepts.

The distinction between luxuries and necessities based on income elasticities provides a solution. By way of introduction, consider the excess of the Frisch price index over the Divisia price index:

$$\sum_{i=1}^{n} \theta_i d(\log p_i) - \sum_{i=1}^{n} w_i d(\log p_i) = \sum_{i=1}^{n} w_i \left(\frac{\theta_i}{w_i} - 1 \right) d(\log p_i).$$

The right side is the Divisia covariance (i.e., the budget-share weighted covariance) of the income elasticities and the logarithmic price changes. This covariance is positive when the prices of luxuries increase relative to those of necessities. Now consider the same equation for quantities rather than prices:

$$\sum_{i=1}^{n} \theta_i d(\log q_i) - \sum_{i=1}^{n} w_i d(\log q_i) = \sum_{i=1}^{n} w_i \left(\frac{\theta_i}{w_i} - 1 \right) d(\log q_i). \tag{15.1}$$

Here the right side is the Divisia covariance of the income elasticities and the logarithmic quantity changes; it is positive (negative) when the quantities consumed of luxuries increase (decrease) relative to those of necessities. The consumer reveals by his behavior that he considers luxuries more desirable than necessities; he does so by spending a larger fraction of his income on the former goods and a smaller fraction on the latter when he becomes more affluent. Accordingly, we refer to the covariance (15.1) as the *quality index* of the consumer's basket in differential form.

Under preference independence we can write the differential demand equations as

$$w_i d(\log q_i) = \theta_i d(\log Q) + \phi \theta_i [d(\log p_i) - d(\log P')] + \epsilon_i.$$

By substituting the right side into that of (15.1) we find, after minor rearrangements, that the quality index can be written as the sum of a real-income, a substitution, and a residual component:

Real income: $d(\log Q) \sum_{i=1}^{n} w_i \left(\dfrac{\theta_i}{w_i} - 1 \right)^2$

Substitution: $\phi \sum_{i=1}^{n} \theta_i [d(\log p_i) - d(\log P')] \dfrac{\theta_i}{w_i}$

Residual: $\sum_{i=1}^{n} \dfrac{\theta_i}{w_i} \epsilon_i$

The real-income component is thus equal to the Divisia volume index multiplied by the Divisia variance of the income elasticities, while the substitution component is a multiple ϕ of the Frisch covariance (i.e., the marginally weighted covariance) of the income elasticities and the logarithmic price changes. The former component reflects the increase in quality that results from an increase in real income, whereas the latter component shows (given $\phi < 0$) that an increase in the prices of luxuries relative to those of necessities reduces the demand for quality. Recall from (10.3) that we considered there the Divisia variance of the income elasticities under Working's model; the present developments indicate that this variance may be viewed as the income elasticity of the demand for quality.

We return to the quality index in differential form given in (15.1). The left side of that equation equals $\sum_i \beta_i d(\log q_i)$ under Working's model, which becomes $\sum_i \beta_i \log(q_{ic}/q_{id})$ when we use it to compare the consumption patterns of countries c and d. The implied quality index in level form (rather than differential form) is

$$\prod_{i=1}^{n} (q_{ic}/q_{id})^{\beta_i}. \tag{15.2}$$

Column 2 of Table 2–14 shows this index for the thirty countries (base U.S. = 1) based on our $n = 10$ goods, with the β_i's specified as the ML estimates. The next three columns contain the three component indexes; the quality index in column 2 is the *product* of the latter indexes. Not surprisingly, the dominant force behind the quality index is its real-income component (column 3). For the derivation of the component indexes see Finke (1983); she used the methodology of Theil and Suhm (1981: Chap. 5).

Table 2-14.   The Quality Index and Its Components in 1975.

| Country (1) | Quality index (2) | Component indexes | | |
		Real income (3)	Relative prices (4)	Residual (5)
United States	1.000	1.000	1.000	1.000
Luxembourg	.956	.957	1.009	.990
Denmark	.967	.962	1.008	.997
France	.950	.949	1.000	1.002
Germany	.978	.953	1.000	1.027
Austria	.959	.951	.996	1.011
Belgium	.936	.949	.999	.986
Netherlands	.940	.938	.998	1.005
United Kingdom	.956	.928	1.004	1.026
Spain	.860	.917	.993	.945
Japan	.926	.914	1.002	1.011
Italy	.876	.902	1.003	.968
Hungary	.886	.884	1.011	.991
Ireland	.883	.883	.996	1.004
Uruguay	.797	.880	.978	.927
Poland	.871	.877	1.020	.974
Mexico	.823	.861	.997	.959
Yugoslavia	.884	.849	1.007	1.034
Romania	.823	.826	1.015	.982
Iran	.831	.821	.994	1.018
Syria	.744	.825	.997	.905
Colombia	.827	.817	.995	1.018
Brazil	.802	.812	.979	1.009
Korea	.811	.798	1.025	.991
Malaysia	.846	.787	1.007	1.068
Thailand	.748	.758	.979	1.008
Philippines	.752	.759	1.023	.967
Sri Lanka	.758	.735	1.055	.978
Pakistan	.719	.718	1.019	.984
India	.736	.693	1.030	1.032

Table 2-15 shows the quality index for the same twelve countries as those of Table 2-13. The entries in the 1975 row of Table 2-15 are identical to the relevant entries in column 2 of Table 2-14 (except that the normalization is now U.S. = 100). The entries for years other than 1975 are obtained from the corresponding 1975 value by means of a time series interpretation of (15.2): $d = 1975$, $c =$ other year, and $\beta_i =$ cross-country ML estimate. The

Table 2–15. Quality Index for Twelve OECD Countries.

	United States	Luxembourg	Denmark	France	Germany	Belgium	Netherlands	United Kingdom	Spain	Japan	Italy	Ireland
1952	—	—	—	—	—	—	83.3	—	—	—	—	—
1953	—	—	—	—	—	—	83.2	—	—	—	—	—
1954	—	—	—	—	—	—	83.4	—	—	—	—	—
1955	—	—	—	—	—	—	84.3	—	—	—	—	—
1956	—	—	—	—	—	—	84.2	—	—	—	—	—
1957	—	—	—	—	—	—	84.3	—	—	—	—	—
1958	—	—	—	—	—	—	83.9	—	—	—	—	—
1959	—	—	—	—	—	—	84.5	—	—	—	—	—
1960	—	—	—	—	—	—	84.8	—	—	—	—	—
1961	—	—	—	—	—	—	84.8	—	—	—	—	—
1962	—	—	—	—	—	—	85.3	—	—	—	—	—
1963	—	—	—	—	—	—	85.7	—	—	—	—	—
1964	95.6	—	—	89.9	94.5	89.3	87.1	92.2	80.5	—	84.2	—
1965	95.7	—	—	90.2	94.9	89.8	87.7	92.2	81.2	—	84.3	—
1966	96.1	—	93.8	90.7	95.1	89.7	87.7	92.1	82.3	—	84.3	—

Table 2-15 continued.

	United States	Luxembourg	Denmark	France	Germany	Belgium	Netherlands	United Kingdom	Spain	Japan	Italy	Ireland
1967	96.2	—	93.9	91.0	94.9	89.6	88.3	92.5	82.7	—	84.8	—
1968	96.6	—	94.1	91.2	95.2	90.2	89.2	93.0	83.6	—	85.0	—
1969	97.0	—	95.1	91.8	96.1	90.8	90.6	93.1	84.2	—	85.5	—
1970	97.0	91.9	95.1	92.3	96.4	90.9	91.6	93.4	84.5	90.8	85.9	87.5
1971	97.6	92.5	95.0	93.0	96.7	91.2	91.5	94.1	85.2	91.3	86.3	87.8
1972	98.5	93.0	95.7	93.7	97.0	92.2	91.8	95.4	86.2	91.6	86.9	88.5
1973	100.1	93.8	96.6	94.4	97.4	93.3	92.2	96.0	86.0	92.5	87.4	88.4
1974	100.2	94.7	95.8	94.7	97.5	93.2	92.9	95.9	85.8	92.8	87.4	87.8
1975	100.0	95.6	96.7	95.0	97.8	93.6	94.0	95.6	86.0	92.6	87.6	88.3
1976	100.0	96.3	97.1	95.9	98.2	94.2	94.1	95.6	86.4	92.6	88.0	89.6
1977	100.2	96.7	97.4	96.3	98.9	95.0	95.0	95.7	86.7	93.1	88.3	89.8
1978	101.0	97.4	97.0	96.8	99.0	95.0	—	96.0	—	93.8	88.4	90.2
1979	101.1	97.9	96.9	97.0	99.0	95.3	—	96.6	—	94.5	88.9	90.6
1980	100.5	98.6	96.4	97.2	98.8	95.1	—	96.5	—	94.4	89.2	90.0
1981	100.5	—	96.4	97.6	98.9	95.2	—	96.8	—	94.7	89.4	—

lowest quality level among the twelve countries is that of Spain in 1964, which is a bit higher than that of Brazil in 1975 (see Table 2–14). For most countries the quality index was subject to an upward trend, but for several the behavior became stationary toward the end of the period (such as the U.S. after 1973). For more details see Theil and Finke (1985b).

2.16 EXTENSIONS AND POSSIBILITIES FOR FUTURE RESEARCH

This final section of Chapter 2 summarizes miscellaneous topics. The subsections that follow are short and are mainly intended to whet the reader's appetite.

Cross-Country Coefficient Estimates Applied to Time Series Data

Recall from Section 2.8 that the Japanese time series data yield estimates of ϕ and of the β_i's of Working's model for $n = 4$ goods that are in satisfactory agreement with the cross-country estimates. Theil and Finke (1984a) extended this comparison to annual Dutch data (1952–1977) for $n = 10$ goods. These are the same data that were also used in the Dutch columns of Tables 2–13 and 2–15.

The ML estimates and their asymptotic standard errors obtained from these data are shown in column 2 of Table 2–16. For comparison, the corresponding estimates and standard errors obtained from the cross-country data are shown in column 3. On the whole, the pairwise agreement of the point estimates is satisfactory, but the asymptotic standard errors in column 2 are almost all much larger than those in column 3. Therefore, in the subsections that follow we shall use the cross-country ML estimates (the point estimates in column 3) to further analyze the Dutch time series data. (The largest discrepancy between the two sets of estimates is that of the β_i of gross rent and fuel. To some extent it can be explained by the fact that the Dutch time series category of transport and communications includes liquid fuel, whereas in fact some of this fuel is heating oil.)

Changes in Budget Shares

The budget shares of the ten goods in the first and the last year of the sample are shown (in percentage form) in columns 2 and 3 of Table 2–17, and their

Table 2-16. Dutch Time Series Estimates of the Parameters of Working's Model.

Parameter (1)	Time series (2)	Cross-country (3)
β_i Food	−.130 (.016)	−.154 (.010)
Beverages, tobacco	−.013 (.007)	.001 (.005)
Clothing, footwear	.026 (.022)	−.005 (.005)
Gross rent, fuel	−.020 (.011)	.032 (.006)
House furnishings, operations	.048 (.016)	.025 (.004)
Medical care	.009 (.013)	.024 (.003)
Transport, communications	.041 (.012)	.030 (.005)
Recreation	.016 (.007)	.019 (.003)
Education	.010 (.005)	−.004 (.005)
Other	.013 (.011)	.033 (.006)
ϕ Income flexibility	−.597 (.066)	−.526 (.037)

difference in column 4. Some of these changes are quite substantial. Can we use the demand model to say more about these changes? The last four columns of the table provide an answer. Each budget share change has four components: a real-income component; two price components similar to the two price terms in the right side of (6.4); and a residual component. The largest entry in these four columns is the real-income component −16.7 of food; it shows that the decline of the budget share of food is wholly accounted for by the increase in affluence. The second largest is the direct price component 6.2 of medical care, which reflects the increase in the relative price of that consumption category. The third is the direct price component −5.6 of house furnishings and operations; it results mainly from the decrease in the relative price of appliances (refrigerators, dishwashers, etc.).

Table 2-18 provides considerably more detail. For each pair of successive years we can define the net flow from good i to good j; see Theil (1980a: Sec. 12.6) for this definition and its justification. The upper part of the table shows, for each pair of goods (i, j), the sum of the net flow over all pairs of successive years from 1952 through 1977. The net flows with destination food are shown in the first column; they are all negative and their sum is −15.5, which is the change in the budget share of food from 1952 to 1977 (see column 4 of Table 2-17). The order of the goods has been rearranged in Table 2-18 in such a way that the net flow from good i to good j during the twenty-five-year period 1952–1977 is positive when $i < j$.

Table 2-17. Budget Shares and Their Changes:
The Netherlands, 1952–1977.

	Budget share			Components of the change			
					Substi-	Direct	
Good	1952	1977	Change	Income	tution	price	Residual
(1)	(2)	(3)	(4)	(5)	(6)	(7)	(8)
Food	33.7	18.1	−15.5	−16.7	.7	−2.2	2.7
Beverages, tobacco	6.9	5.2	−1.7	.1	1.0	−1.6	−1.1
Clothing, footwear	16.9	11.0	−6.0	−.5	1.8	−2.8	−4.4
Gross rent, fuel	10.8	12.5	1.7	3.4	−1.6	2.8	−2.8
House furnishings, operations	10.0	12.2	2.2	2.7	3.9	−5.6	1.2
Medical care	3.3	11.2	7.9	2.6	−4.2	6.2	3.4
Transport, communications	5.0	9.3	4.3	3.2	1.1	−1.2	1.2
Recreation	3.1	4.1	1.0	2.1	−.9	1.3	−1.4
Education	2.2	4.2	2.1	−.4	−.7	1.6	1.6
Other	8.1	12.1	4.0	3.6	−.9	1.7	−.3

As in Table 2–17 for the change in each budget share, each net flow consists of four components. Since the matrix of net flows and those of its components are all skew symmetric, it is sufficient to present only the elements above the main diagonal. Note that the substitution components all have a sign opposite to that of the corresponding direct price component. For further details see Finke and Theil (1984).

The Cost of Living at Different Levels of Affluence

The application of the theory of the true cost-of-living index typically requires the algebraic specification of the consumer's utility function, of his indirect utility function, or of his cost function. However, Theil (1968, 1976) has shown how the true index can be closely approximated without such an algebraic specification. In particular, the Divisia price index $DP_t = \sum_i \bar{w}_{it} Dp_{it}$ can be shown to be the change in the cost of living evaluated at the utility level that corresponds to the geometric means of the incomes and the prices of $t-1$ and t. Thus, by chaining successive Divisia price indexes we obtain a cost of living index. The result for the Dutch data from 1952 to 1977

Table 2-18. Net Flows among Ten Goods and Their Components: The Netherlands, 1952–1977.[a]

Net flows

	Food	Clothing, footwear	Beverages, tobacco	Gross rent, fuel	Recreation	House furnishings, operations	Other expenditures	Transport, communication	Education	Medical care	
	0	1.27	.63	2.54	1.08	1.88	2.54	1.65	.88	3.06	Food
	-1.27	0	.17	.95	.41	1.23	1.24	1.10	.48	1.67	Clothing
	-.63	-.17	0	.28	.14	.36	.44	.41	.19	.65	Beverages
	-2.54	-.95	-.28	0	.05	.26	.32	.52	.16	.72	Rent
	-1.08	-.41	-.14	-.05	0	.07	.09	.19	.04	.25	Recreation
	-1.88	-1.23	-.36	-.26	-.07	0	.16	.37	.27	.82	Furnishings
	-2.54	-1.24	-.44	-.32	-.09	-.16	0	.25	.09	.48	Other
	-1.65	-1.10	-.41	-.52	-.19	-.37	-.25	0	.03	.15	Transport
	-.88	-.48	-.19	-.16	-.04	-.27	-.09	-.03	0	.10	Education
	-3.06	-1.67	-.65	-.72	-.25	-.82	-.48	-.15	-.10	0	Medical

Real-income components

	Food	Clothing, footwear	Beverages, tobacco	Gross rent, fuel	Recreation	House furnishings, operations	Other expenditures	Transport, communication	Education	Medical care	
		2.36	1.10	2.70	1.12	2.81	2.52	1.95	.40	1.76	Food
			.05	.56	.33	.47	.58	.51	-.05	.42	Clothing
				.21	.13	.16	.22	.20	-.03	.16	Beverages
					.11	-.13	.06	.12	-.15	.06	Rent
						-.17	-.08	-.03	-.08	-.05	Recreation
							.18	.22	-.14	.14	Furnishings
								.07	-.15	.01	Other
									-.13	-.04	Transport
										.11	Education

Substitution components

	Food	Clothing	Beverages	Rent	Recreation	Furnishings	Other	Transport	Education
Food	-.45								
Clothing	-.68	-.07							
Beverages	-.39	-.12	.05						
Rent	-.48	-.08	.01	-.19					
Recreation	-.15	-.07	-.04	-.32	.24				
Furnishings	-1.03	-.01	.28	-.21	.27	-.13			
Other	-.47	-.22	.15	.04	.10	-.21	-.35		
Transport	-.52	-.07	-.23	.07	.76	-.12	-.50	.02	
Education	-.05	-.10	.22	-.66	.35	-.06	-.25	.00	.21

Direct price components

	Food	Clothing	Beverages	Rent	Recreation	Furnishings	Other	Transport	Education
Food	1.67								
Clothing	.94	.44							
Beverages	.55	.27	-.15						
Rent	.53	.16	-.04	.67					
Recreation	.14	.11	.06	.45	-1.07				
Furnishings	1.23	.02	-.28	.30	-.45	.41			
Other	.51	.39	-.13	-.04	-.15	.26	1.08		
Transport	.52	.11	.27	-.07	-.94	.15	.75	-.20	
Education	.08	.15	-.22	.78	-.36	.06	.36	-.01	-.65

Residual components

	Food	Clothing	Beverages	Rent	Recreation	Furnishings	Other	Transport	Education
Food	.08								
Clothing	.98	.12							
Beverages	.33	.38	-.20						
Rent	.61	.14	.61	-.46					
Recreation	.31	.28	.19	.54	-.10				
Furnishings	.48	.12	.40	.13	.94	-.32			
Other	.44	.24	.19	.26	.25	.04	-.89		
Transport	.18	.19	.12	.16	.56	-.02	.13	-.28	
Education	-.04	.11	.18	-.15	.25	-.07	-.04	.13	-.65

a. All entries to be divided by 100.

Table 2-19.   Divisia and Frisch Price Indexes and Cost-of-Living

			Changes in price indexes[a]		
				Cost-of-living index at	
Year t (1)	Divisia (2)	Frisch (3)	Low income (4)	Medium income (5)	High income (6)
1953	−.63	−.30	−.87	−.43	.02
1954	3.43	3.68	3.25	3.60	3.95
1955	1.07	1.28	.91	1.22	1.52
1956	.87	.92	.86	.91	.96
1957	5.56	5.86	5.23	5.67	6.10
1958	1.37	2.00	.69	1.57	2.44
1959	.52	.27	.84	.50	.17
1960	1.25	2.01	.48	1.52	2.57
1961	1.38	1.34	1.43	1.39	1.34
1962	1.52	1.52	1.51	1.51	1.51
1963	2.07	1.85	2.33	2.02	1.71
1964	6.17	5.82	6.53	6.05	5.58
1965	3.32	3.21	3.45	3.30	3.14
1966	5.55	5.86	5.16	5.58	6.01
1967	3.18	3.51	2.78	3.23	3.68
1968	2.98	3.14	2.80	3.02	3.24
1969	6.46	6.56	6.28	6.42	6.55
1970	2.92	2.98	2.84	2.91	2.99
1971	7.23	7.95	6.09	7.10	8.11
1972	6.87	7.27	6.23	6.79	7.34
1973	7.75	7.88	7.53	7.71	7.89
1974	8.66	9.25	7.73	8.56	9.38
1975	8.71	8.77	8.58	8.66	8.75
1976	8.09	7.86	8.52	8.20	7.88
1977	5.47	5.12	6.08	5.60	5.12

a. All entries in columns 2 to 6 to be divided by 100.

is shown in columns 2 and 7 of Table 2-19, which is reproduced in part from Finke and Lu (1984).

This procedure has the advantage of requiring exclusively observable data; it does not use estimates of unknown parameters, nor does it require the validity of a particular demand (or other) model that may be false. However, we should be aware of the fact that the utility or real-income level at which the Divisia price index evaluates the cost of living is not constant over

Indexes: The Netherlands, 1952–1977.

		Levels, base 1952 = 100		
			Cost-of-living index at	
Divisia (7)	Frisch (8)	Low income (9)	Medium income (10)	High income (11)
99.4	99.7	99.1	99.6	100.0
102.8	103.4	102.4	103.2	104.0
103.9	104.8	103.3	104.4	105.6
104.9	105.7	104.2	105.4	106.6
110.8	112.1	109.6	111.3	113.1
112.4	114.4	110.4	113.1	115.8
113.0	114.7	111.3	113.6	116.0
114.4	117.0	111.8	115.4	119.0
116.0	118.6	113.4	117.0	120.6
117.8	120.4	115.2	118.7	122.4
120.2	122.7	117.8	121.1	124.5
127.9	130.0	125.5	128.5	131.5
132.2	134.3	129.9	132.7	135.6
139.7	142.4	136.6	140.1	143.7
144.2	147.5	140.4	144.6	149.0
148.6	152.2	144.3	149.0	153.8
158.5	162.5	153.4	158.6	163.9
163.2	167.4	157.7	163.2	168.8
175.5	181.2	167.3	174.8	182.5
187.9	194.9	177.7	186.6	195.9
203.1	210.9	191.1	201.0	211.4
221.4	231.3	205.9	218.2	231.2
241.6	252.6	223.6	237.2	251.4
262.0	273.2	242.6	256.6	271.2
276.7	287.5	257.4	271.0	285.1

time. Indeed, these changes can be substantial. As Table 2–13 in Section 2.14 shows, the volume of per capita consumption in the Netherlands rose almost threefold during the twenty-five-year period, from 25.2 to 74.5. Is it possible to evaluate the cost of living at a constant real-income level?

An approximation procedure was developed by Theil (1976: Sec. 13.6), the results of which may be summarized as follows. Let R_t be the logarithmic change in real income from the $(t-1, t)$ level to that at which the cost of living is to be evaluated. Then the log-change in the cost of living is approximately

$$DP_t + \frac{R_t}{1+\frac{1}{2}R_t}(DP_t'-DP_t),\qquad(16.1)$$

where DP_t' is the Frisch price index. In particular, if we wish to evaluate the cost of living at a constant real-income level equal to a multiple c of real income in year $t=1$, then $R_1 = \log c - \frac{1}{2}DQ_1$ and $R_t = R_{t-1} - \frac{1}{2}(DQ_{t-1}+DQ_t)$ for $t>1$.

However, as B.M. Balk pointed out (private communication), (16.1) is derived from the assumption of constant marginal shares and it simplifies to

$$DP_t + R_t(DP_t'-DP_t)\qquad(16.2)$$

under Working's model. The results of Finke and Lu are accordingly corrected in columns 4 through 6 and 9 through 11 of Table 2-19. These columns refer to three levels of real income: a low level equal to one-half of the per capita income in 1952 ($c=\frac{1}{2}$); a medium level equal to twice this per capita income ($c=2$); and a high level equal to eight times this per capita income ($c=8$). In terms of the index values of Table 2-13, these levels are 12.6, 50.4, and 201.6. The lowest of these levels is between the 1975 per capita levels of Sri Lanka and the Philippines (see columns 1 and 2 of Table 2-7 in Section 2.10). The medium level corresponds approximately to the Dutch per capita level in 1968 (see Table 2-13), while the high level exceeds the 1980 per capita level of the United States by about 80 percent.

The implementation of (16.2) requires the Frisch price index, which does involve unknown parameters. It is shown in column 3 of Table 2-19, and it is computed as $DP_t + \sum_i \beta_i Dp_{it}$, with the β_i's specified as the cross-country ML estimates. The next three columns show (16.2) at the three income levels and the last four columns of the table contain the chain indexes implied by DP_t' and by the three specifications of (16.2). Note that the cost of living went up faster for the more well-to-do. Also note that columns 8 and 11 are virtually identical, that is, the cost of living at the high income level is closely approximated by the Frisch index.

Why Did the Cost of Living Increase Faster for the Rich?

The faster increase in the cost of living at higher income levels reflects the fact that on average luxuries increased in price relative to necessities. This fact is responsible for the difference $DP_t'-DP_t$ in (16.2) to be positive for most values of t. These differences are shown in column 2 of Table 2–20, with their standard errors in parentheses. These standard errors are computed from the asymptotic covariance matrix of the cross-country ML estimates of the β_i's. Note that a substantial majority of the entries in column 2 are significantly different from zero.

Recall from the discussion preceding equation (15.1) that the difference between the Frisch and the Divisia price index can be viewed as the Divisia covariance of the income elasticities and the price log-changes. This interpretation has the advantage of enabling us to assess the effect of deleting one good. When good i is deleted, the Divisia covariance for the remaining $n-1$ goods becomes

$$\sum_{j \neq i} \frac{\bar{w}_{jt}}{1 - \bar{w}_{it}} \left(Dp_{jt} - \sum_{k \neq i} \frac{\bar{w}_{kt}}{1 - \bar{w}_{it}} Dp_{kt} \right) \left(1 + \frac{\beta_j}{\bar{w}_{jt}} \right).$$

When we work this out, we find that it can be simplified to

$$\frac{DP_t' - DP_t}{1 - \bar{w}_{it}} - \frac{\beta_i (Dp_{it} - DP_t)}{(1 - \bar{w}_{it})^2}. \tag{16.3}$$

Thus, when good i is deleted, the Divisia covariance of the income elasticities and the price log-changes consists of two terms, the first of which has the same sign as the Divisia covariance when no good is deleted, while the sign of the second term depends on whether the deleted good is a luxury or a necessity ($\beta_i > 0$ or < 0) and on whether the price of this good increased or decreased relative to the Divisia index ($Dp_{it} - DP_t > 0$ or < 0).

The Divisia covariances (16.3) are shown in the last ten columns of Table 2–20. For example, when we delete house furnishings and operations in the first year (1953), the effect on the covariance is an increase to 0.42×10^{-2} from 0.33×10^{-2}, while deleting medical care reduces the covariance to 0.13×10^{-2}. Both goods are luxuries ($\beta_i > 0$); the effect of deleting these goods on the Divisia covariance reflects the relative price decrease of house furnishings in 1953 and the relative price increase of medical care in that year.

The cases just discussed refer to one particular year. A more convenient summary is provided by the arithmetic means that are shown at the bottom of each column. In column 2, where no good is deleted, this mean is 0.15×10^{-2}. In column 8, where medical care is deleted, the mean equals 0.06×10^{-2}, which is the smallest entry in the bottom row of the table. Thus, the relative price increase of medical care is primarily responsible for the faster increase of the cost of living of the more well-to-do. The next smallest entry in the bottom row is that in the food column. Since food is a necessity ($\beta_i < 0$), this effect refers to the relative price decrease of food from 1952 to 1977.

Table 2-20. Divisia Covariances of Income Elasticities and Price Log-Changes. [a]

Year t (1)	None (2)	Which good is deleted?									
		Food (3)	Beverages, tobacco (4)	Clothing, footwear (5)	Gross rent, fuel (6)	House furnishings, operations (7)	Medical care (8)	Transport, communication (9)	Recreation (10)	Education (11)	Other expenditures (12)
1953	.33 (.03)	.38	.35	.39	.31	.42	.13	.31	.35	.34	.30
1954	.25 (.06)	.39	.27	.29	-.04	.31	.33	.36	.13	.25	.23
1955	.21 (.03)	.16	.23	.24	.14	.20	.28	.20	.21	.22	.16
1956	.05 (.04)	.58	.05	.02	-.04	.03	-.10	.04	.02	.05	.04
1957	.30 (.03)	.17	.32	.36	.24	.44	.19	.26	.35	.31	.31
1958	.63 (.05)	.14	.68	.74	.44	.73	.62	.69	.66	.66	.64
1959	-.25 (.02)	.02	-.27	-.30	-.25	-.25	-.29	-.22	-.26	-.25	-.25
1960	.76 (.05)	.26	.82	.90	.63	.90	.61	.87	.74	.78	.77
1961	-.03 (.02)	.08	-.04	-.04	-.06	-.03	-.12	.03	-.04	-.04	-.02
1962	-.00 (.02)	.07	-.00	-.01	-.02	.03	-.01	.04	-.06	.01	-.04

1963	−.22 (.02)	−.01	−.23	−.26	−.33	−.19	−.21	−.13	−.22	−.22	−.25
1964	−.35 (.05)	.00	−.38	−.42	−.30	−.30	−.53	−.24	−.39	−.35	−.38
1965	−.11 (.03)	.10	−.12	−.13	−.10	−.05	−.27	−.02	−.14	−.11	−.16
1966	.31 (.05)	.09	.33	.35	.41	.44	.18	.20	.31	.32	.35
1967	.32 (.05)	.12	.35	.38	.41	.52	.10	.33	.31	.35	.29
1968	.16 (.04)	.04	.17	.18	.17	.22	.02	.31	.12	.18	.13
1969	.10 (.05)	.05	.11	.12	.20	.16	.08	.21	−.07	.12	−.01
1970	.06 (.04)	.10	.06	.06	.10	.14	−.16	.08	.02	.08	.09
1971	.72 (.07)	−.03	.77	.85	.94	.82	.64	.67	.69	.77	.83
1972	.40 (.04)	.05	.43	.46	.42	.55	.27	.50	.38	.43	.38
1973	.13 (.04)	.11	.15	.16	.15	.27	.08	.01	.12	.15	.14
1974	.59 (.06)	.04	.63	.70	.74	.79	.58	.43	.58	.63	.63
1975	.06 (.05)	−.10	.07	.08	.03	.19	−.06	.25	.07	.09	−.05
1976	−.23 (.04)	.11	−.24	−.28	−.39	−.14	−.35	−.26	−.23	−.24	−.21
1977	−.35 (.05)	−.07	−.37	−.38	−.51	−.31	−.41	−.21	−.40	−.36	−.39
Mean	.15	.11	.17	.18	.13	.23	.06	.19	.13	.17	.14

a. All entries to be divided by 100.

Both goods (food and medical care) contributed to positive covariances of the income elasticities and the price log-changes. The effect of house furnishings and operations went in the other direction, but it was more than compensated.

The Decline of the Marginal Utility of the Guilder

Recall from Section 1.13 that the logarithmic differential of the marginal utility of income consists of two components:

$$d(\log \lambda) = (1/\phi)d(\log Q) - d(\log P').$$

The first component measures the impact on λ of the change in real income and the second gives the effect of price changes for a constant real income. We can implement this result in the form

$$D\lambda_t = (1/\phi)DQ_t - DP'_t, \tag{16.4}$$

where $D\lambda_t$ stands for the log-change in the marginal utility of income from year $t-1$ to year t.

Theil and Finke (1984b) applied (16.4) to the Dutch data, using the cross-country ML estimates of ϕ and of the β_i's of Working's model. The two terms on the right in (16.4) are shown in columns 4 and 5 of Table 2–21. The left side of (16.4) is defined as the sum of these two terms and is shown in column 2. Note that $D\lambda_t$ is negative in all years except only one. Column 3 provides the marginal utility in level form, as an index with base 100 in 1952. Twenty-five years later, in 1977, this index has dropped about 95 percent. Thus, the marginal utility of one guilder in 1952 is approximately equivalent to the marginal utility of twenty guilders in 1977.

Columns 4 and 5 of Table 2–21 show that, with very few exceptions, both the real-income and price components contributed to the decline of the marginal utility of the guilder. To assess which of these two factors was more important, we cumulate the log-changes in columns 2, 4, and 5. The results are shown in Table 2–22, the first line of which indicates that for the twenty-five-year period as a whole the increased affluence accounts for about two-thirds of the decline of the marginal utility of the guilder, and (hence) the increased prices for about one-third. The next five lines deal with successive five-year periods and show that this decomposition gradually changed over time. In the first ten years about 80 percent of the decline was accounted for by increased affluence; in the next ten years this percentage dropped to less than 70, and in the last five years to less than 50. Thus, the change in the

Table 2-21.   The Marginal Utility of the Guilder, 1952–1977.

Year t (1)	Marginal utility		Components of change	
	Change (2)	Level, 1952 = 100 (3)	Real income (4)	Price level (5)
1953	−.120	88.7	−.123	.003
1954	−.172	74.7	−.135	−.037
1955	−.108	67.1	−.095	−.013
1956	−.154	57.5	−.145	−.009
1957	−.035	55.5	.024	−.059
1958	.021	56.7	.041	−.020
1959	−.089	51.9	−.086	−.003
1960	−.134	45.4	−.114	−.020
1961	−.110	40.6	−.097	−.013
1962	−.115	36.2	−.100	−.015
1963	−.166	30.7	−.148	−.019
1964	−.129	27.0	−.071	−.058
1965	−.148	23.2	−.116	−.032
1966	−.083	21.4	−.024	−.059
1967	−.090	19.5	−.055	−.035
1968	−.120	17.3	−.089	−.031
1969	−.177	14.5	−.112	−.066
1970	−.160	12.4	−.130	−.030
1971	−.138	10.8	−.059	−.079
1972	−.145	9.3	−.072	−.073
1973	−.159	7.9	−.080	−.079
1974	−.141	6.9	−.049	−.092
1975	−.157	5.9	−.069	−.088
1976	−.165	5.0	−.087	−.079
1977	−.122	4.4	−.071	−.051

marginal utility of income provides a simple measure of the extent to which the "heat" in the economy comes from prices or from quantities.

The Consumer's Demand for Diversity

If a consumer is quite poor, he will spend most of his income on food and little on other goods and services. When income rises, however, the share of food declines, because of Engel's law, and other goods play a more important

Table 2–22.   Cumulated Log-Changes.

Period		Change in marginal utility	Income component	Price component
All twenty-five years:	1952–1977	−3.12	−2.06	−1.06
Subperiods:	1952–1957	−.59	−.47	−.11
	1957–1962	−.43	−.36	−.07
	1962–1967	−.62	−.41	−.20
	1967–1972	−.74	−.46	−.28
	1972–1977	−.74	−.36	−.39

role in the consumer's budget. Thus, we should expect an increasing diversity of spending as income increases. One way of measuring this effect is by means of the entropy of the budget shares,

$$H = - \sum_{i=1}^{n} w_i \log w_i, \qquad (16.5)$$

which varies from zero (when one budget share equals 1 and hence the $n-1$ others vanish) to a maximum of $\log n$ (when all shares are equal to $1/n$).

Theil and Finke (1983) applied (16.5) to the observed w_{ic}'s of the thirty countries for our $n = 10$ goods. The results are shown in column 3 of Table 2–23. The entries in this column clearly show an increasing trend, thus indicating a greater diversity at a higher level of real income. The maximum value is $\log 10 \cong 2.303$; the entropies of eight of the nine richest countries are all less than 0.1 below this maximum.

Column 4 shows the entropy (16.5) when w_i is interpreted as $\bar{w}_{ic}$ defined in (10.1). Since $\bar{w}_{ic}$ is determined by the per capita income Q_c, this entropy is written as $H(Q_c)$. Note that columns 3 and 4 are in broad agreement; the deviations result from differences in relative prices and the residuals in the demand equations. Next, by differentiating

$$H(Q) = - \sum_{i=1}^{n} (\alpha_i + \beta_i \log Q) \log(\alpha_i + \beta_i \log Q)$$

with respect to $\log Q$, we obtain

$$\frac{\partial H}{\partial \log Q} = - \sum_{i=1}^{n} \beta_i \log(\alpha_i + \beta_i \log Q). \qquad (16.6)$$

If we identify the antilog of H with diversity, we can view (16.6) as the income elasticity of the demand for diversity. When evaluated at $Q = Q_c$, this

Table 2-23.   Diversity Measured by the Entropy of the Budget Shares, 1975.

Country (1)	Q_c (2)	H_c (3)	$H(Q_c)$ (4)	Elasticity[a] (5)
India	.068	1.51	1.56	.441
Pakistan	.089	1.53	1.68	.398
Sri Lanka	.103	1.52	1.73	.376
Philippines	.140	1.65	1.84	.334
Thailand	.141	1.93	1.84	.332
Malaysia	.190	2.05	1.94	.294
Korea	.206	1.86	1.96	.283
Brazil	.246	2.04	2.01	.261
Colombia	.255	2.06	2.02	.256
Syria	.261	1.76	2.02	.253
Iran	.272	2.02	2.03	.248
Romania	.290	2.03	2.05	.240
Yugoslavia	.346	2.16	2.09	.217
Mexico	.371	1.98	2.10	.208
Poland	.435	2.14	2.14	.187
Uruguay	.451	2.09	2.14	.182
Ireland	.464	2.19	2.15	.178
Hungary	.467	2.18	2.15	.177
Italy	.532	2.13	2.17	.159
Japan	.588	2.18	2.19	.145
Spain	.606	2.09	2.19	.140
United Kingdom	.641	2.22	2.20	.132
Netherlands	.686	2.26	2.21	.122
Belgium	.750	2.21	2.22	.108
Austria	.751	2.24	2.22	.107
Germany	.756	2.24	2.22	.106
France	.756	2.21	2.22	.106
Denmark	.785	2.21	2.22	.100
Luxembourg	.794	2.17	2.22	.098
United States	1.000	2.21	2.24	.058

a. Income elasticity of the demand for diversity defined in (16.6).

elasticity equals $-\sum_i \beta_i \log \bar{w}_{ic}$, which is shown in column 5 for $n = 10$ and for each of the thirty countries. These elasticity values are about 0.4 for the poorest countries in Southeast Asia; they decrease with increasing real income until they are on the order of 0.1 for countries in Western Europe and about one-half of that level for the United States. See Theil and Finke (1983) for further details, including price and residual components of the entropy and also on the use of the Hirschman–Herfindahl index as an (inverse) measure of diversity.

The Demand for Leisure

Consumption theory can be extended to include the household's demand for leisure. We write q_0 for the quantity of leisure (measured in time units) and p_0 for its price, so that the household's "full income" is

$$M = p_0 q_0 + p_1 q_1 + \cdots + p_n q_n,$$

which includes the market value of the household's time. By postulating that the utility function has now $n+1$ arguments, $u(q_0, q_1, \ldots, q_n)$, we have the same formal structure as before.

Barnett (1979, 1981) extended the Rotterdam model to include the demand for leisure and applied it to annual U.S. data of the period 1890–1955, using a five-good classification: services, perishables, semidurables, durables, and leisure. He found that the price coefficient matrix of the model can be viewed as block-diagonal, the first two goods forming one block and the last three forming a second block. Here we are particularly interested in the latter block. The following matrix is the ML estimate of the normalized price coefficient matrix of the three-good group (normalized within the group):

$$\begin{bmatrix} 0.501 & 0.042 & -0.342 \\ 0.042 & 0.560 & -0.419 \\ -0.342 & -0.419 & 1.378 \end{bmatrix} \begin{matrix} \text{Semidurables} \\ \text{Durables} \\ \text{Leisure} \end{matrix} \qquad (16.7)$$

The negative elements in the last row and column imply that semidurables and durables are both specific substitutes of leisure. This is not entirely surprising, since many durables are time-saving goods. Examples are vacuum cleaners, washing machines, dishwashers, and word processors.

The Preference Independence Transformation

In this chapter, the matrix (16.7) provides the first specification that deviates from preference independence. We shall have more to say about the dominance of the independence assumption in Section 3.19. Here we call the reader's attention to the fact that if there is no such independence, we can always apply the preference-independence transformation so that the transformed goods are independent. This transformation, together with the analogous input- and output-independence transformations in the theory of the firm, is discussed in Chapters 10 and 11 of Theil (1980a). Here we confine ourselves to a brief discussion in conjunction with the normalized price coefficient matrix (16.7).

The transformation yields a different set of goods in such a way that none of these is a specific substitute or complement of any of the others. This is achieved subject to two invariance constraints: The total amount spent on the transformed goods is identical to that spent on the original (observed) goods, and the Divisia price and volume indexes of the two sets of goods are also identical. The transformation can be conveniently described by means of the so-called composition matrix. An example, from Flinn, Laitinen, and Theil (1978), is the following composition matrix based on the normalized price coefficient matrix (16.7):

	Semidurables	Durables	Leisure	Total
T_1	0.082	0.117	0.795	0.994
T_2	0.018	0.016	-0.028	0.006
T_3	0.004	-0.005	0.002	0.000
Total	0.104	0.127	0.769	1.000

The columns of the composition matrix refer to the observed goods (semidurables, durables, and leisure in this case). The entries in the bottom row add up to 1; they are the expenditure shares of the observed goods. The rows of the matrix refer to the transformed goods. The sum column on the far right shows that more than 99 percent of the expenditure on the three-good group is allocated to the transformed good labeled T_1, whereas virtually nothing (less than one-twentieth of 1 percent) is allocated to T_3. The first and second rows of the matrix indicate that all three observed goods contribute positively to T_1 but that T_2 is a contrast between the two durables categories and leisure. Hence, when the household buys T_2, it gives up leisure so that at least some of the household members supply more labor.

The mathematics of the preference independence transformation involves a simultaneous diagonalization of the normalized price coefficient matrix Θ and the (diagonal) expenditure-share matrix W: $X'\Theta X = \Lambda$ and $X'WX = I$, where Λ is diagonal and X is square. The composition matrix is determined by X, while the diagonal elements of Λ provide the income elasticities (all positive) of the transformed goods. In the example discussed in the previous paragraph, the income elasticity (the elasticity with respect to full income) of T_2 is about six times as large as that of T_1. See Rossi (1979), Theil (1980c), and Theil and Laitinen (1981) for other developments not included in Theil (1980a).

BIBLIOGRAPHY

The publications listed below are those referred to in Chapter 2, supplemented by some other publications that are directly related to the topics discussed.

Barnett, W.A. 1979. "The Joint Allocation of Leisure and Goods Expenditure." *Econometrica* 47: 539–63.

———. 1981. *Consumer Demand and Labor Supply: Goods, Monetary Assets, and Time.* Amsterdam: North-Holland Publishing Company.

Clements, K.W.; R. Finke; and H. Theil. 1984. "Frisch's Conjecture and the Own-Price Elasticity of the Demand for Food." *Economics Letters* 15: 1–4.

Finke, R. 1983. "A New Cross-Country Tabulation of the Quality Index of Consumption." *Economics Letters* 13: 11–14.

———. 1984. "Consumption Data for Ten Goods and Divisia Moments of Consumption for the Netherlands, 1952–1977." McKethan–Matherly Discussion Paper MM3, Graduate School of Business, University of Florida.

Finke, R., and W.-H. Lu. 1984. "The Behavior of the Cost of Living at Different Levels of Real Income." *Economics Letters* 15: 223–28.

Finke, R.; W.-H. Lu; and H. Theil. 1984. "A Cross-Country Tabulation of Own-Price Elasticities of Demand." *Economics Letters* 14: 137–42.

Finke, R.; M.C. Rosalsky; and H. Theil. 1983. "A New Cross-Country Tabulation of Income Elasticities of Demand." *Economics Letters* 12: 391–96.

Finke, R., and H. Theil. 1984. "Budget Share Transitions in the Netherlands, 1952–1977." *Economics Letters* 16: 7–13.

———. 1985. "A Cross-Country Time-Series Analysis of the Volume and Quality of Consumption." *Economics Letters* 17: 11–14.

Flinn, C.; K. Laitinen; and H. Theil. 1978. "New Results on the Preference Independence Transformation." *Economics Letters* 1: 179–81.

Frisch, R. 1959. "A Complete Scheme for Computing All Direct and Cross Demand Elasticities in a Model with Many Sectors." *Econometrica* 27: 177–96.

Geary, R.C. 1958. "A Note on the Comparison of Exchange Rates and Purchasing Power Between Countries." *Journal of the Royal Statistical Society,* Series A, 121, Part 1, pp. 97–99.

Griliches, Z., ed. 1971. *Price Indexes and Quality Change.* Cambridge, Mass.: Harvard University Press.

Houthakker, H.S. 1953. "Compensated Changes in Quantities and Qualities Consumed." *Review of Economic Studies* 19: 155–64.

Isenman, P. 1980. "Inter-Country Comparisons of 'Real' (PPP) Incomes: Revised Estimates and Unresolved Questions." *World Development* 8 (January 1980): 61–72.

Khamis, S.H. 1967. "Some Problems Relating to the International Comparability and Fluctuations of Production Volume Indicators." *Bulletin of the International Statistical Institute* 42, Part 1, pp. 213–30.

———. 1970. "Properties and Conditions for the Existence of a New Type of Index Numbers." Sankhyā, Series B, 32, pp. 81–98.

————. 1972. "A New System of Index Numbers for National and International Purposes." *Journal of the Royal Statistical Society,* Series A, 135, Part 1, pp. 96–121.

Kravis, I.B.; A.W. Heston; and R. Summers. 1978. *International Comparisons of Real Product and Purchasing Power.* Baltimore, Md.: The Johns Hopkins University Press.

————. 1982. *World Product and Income: International Comparisons of Real Gross Product.* Baltimore, Md.: The Johns Hopkins University Press.

Kravis, I.B.; Z. Kenessey; A.W. Heston; and R. Summers. 1975. *A System of International Comparisons of Gross Product and Purchasing Power.* Baltimore, Md.: The Johns Hopkins University Press.

Lluch, C.; A.A. Powell; and R.A. Williams. 1977. *Patterns in Household Demand and Saving.* New York: Oxford University Press.

Lu, W.-H. and R. Finke. 1984. "Predicting the Change in the Cost of Living." *Economics Letters* 16: 315–19.

Muellbauer, J. 1975. "Aggregation, Income Distribution and Consumer Demand." *Review of Economic Studies* 42: 525–43.

OECD, 1983. *National Accounts of OECD Countries, 1964–1981.* Vol. 2, Detailed Tables. Paris: OECD.

Rossi, P.E. 1979. "The Independence Transformation of Specific Substitutes and Specific Complements." *Economics Letters* 2: 299–301.

Theil, H. 1953. "Qualities, Prices and Budget Enquiries." *Review of Economic Studies* 19: 129–47.

————. 1968. "On the Geometry and the Numerical Approximation of the Cost of Living and Real Income Indices." *De Economist* 116: 677–89.

————. 1976. *Theory and Measurement of Consumer Demand.* Vol. 2. Amsterdam: North-Holland Publishing Company.

————. 1980a. *The System-Wide Approach to Microeconomics.* University of Chicago Press.

————. 1980b. *System-Wide Explorations in International Economics, Input–Output Analysis, and Marketing Research.* Amsterdam: North-Holland Publishing Company.

————. 1980c. "The Independence Transformation Under Almost Additivity." *Economics Letters* 5: 281–84.

————. 1983. "World Product and Income: A Review Article." *Journal of Political Economy* 91: 505–17.

Theil, H., and R. Finke. 1983. "The Consumer's Demand for Diversity." *European Economic Review* 23: 395–400.

————. 1984a. "A Time Series Analysis of a Demand System Based on Cross-Country Coefficient Estimates." *Economics Letters* 15: 245–50.

————. 1984b. "The Decline of the Marginal Utility of the Guilder, 1952–1977." *De Economist* 132: 497–502.

————. 1985a. "Income and Price Elasticities of Demand at Low Levels of Real Income." *Economics Letters* 18: 1–5.

————. 1985b. "An Extended Cross-Country Time-Series Analysis of the Volume and Quality of Consumption." *Economics Letters* 18: 117–20.

Theil, H., and K. Laitinen. 1981. "The Independence Transformation: A Review and Some Further Explorations." In *Essays in the Theory and Measurement of Consumer Behaviour,* edited by A.S. Deaton, 73–112. New York: Cambridge University Press.

Theil, H., and F.E. Suhm. 1981. *International Consumption Comparisons: A System-Wide Approach.* Amsterdam: North-Holland Publishing Company.

Timmer, C.P. 1981. "Is There 'Curvature' in the Slutsky Matrix?" *Review of Economics and Statistics* 63: 395–402.

3 THE ECONOMETRICS OF DEMAND SYSTEMS

Henri Theil

3.1 INTRODUCTION

In recent years considerable new insight has been obtained in the problems of statistical inference in systems of demand equations. Originally there was the impression that this topic was well understood because it is in the domain of "seemingly unrelated regressions"; also, that if there are nonlinearities in the parameters, the maximum likelihood method can be relied upon to produce superior results, at least for large samples. But how large is large?

The first breakthrough came in the late 1970s at the University of Chicago, when Laitinen and Meisner convincingly showed, using simulation experiments, that the numerous rejections of demand homogeneity and Slutsky symmetry published in the literature are at least in part due to the inadequacy of the large-sample tests of these hypotheses. I continued to stimulate this work when I left Chicago and moved to the University of Florida in 1981. A major objective of this chapter is to summarize the results of that work. Indeed, I believe that simulation experiments provide an important extension of econometrics. Originally this field consisted of two components: econometric methodology (mainly mathematical statistics) and data

Comments by Kenneth Clements and Antony Selvanathan on an earlier draft of this chapter are gratefully acknowledged.

analysis. Simulation is now a third component; it shows how econometric methods work under ideal circumstances. This is particularly relevant when theoretical results are confined to large-sample approximations.

Section 3.2 provides the starting point for testing when the demand system is linear in the parameters and when the error distribution is multivariate normal. Sections 3.3 and 3.4 deal with Laitinen's and Meisner's work on homogeneity and symmetry testing. The main cause of the failure of such tests is the fact that the error covariance matrix Σ is unknown. In Section 3.5 we extend the scene by experimenting with error distributions that are fat-tailed rather than normal. Next, in Sections 3.6 to 3.8, we introduce a priori specifications of Σ and we experiment with tests based on such specifications, both under the null hypothesis and under the alternative hypothesis. The remainder of the chapter deals with estimation rather than testing, including L_p-norm estimation and "bootstrapping" for standard errors, but we do consider Barnard's Monte Carlo tests briefly at the end of Section 3.20.

3.2   TESTING FOR HOMOGENEITY OF DEMAND

Recall from Section 1.14 that the absolute price version of the Rotterdam model takes the form

$$\bar{w}_{it} Dq_{it} = \theta_i DQ_t + \sum_{j=1}^{n} \pi_{ij} Dp_{jt} + \epsilon_{it}. \tag{2.1}$$

We want to test the hypothesis of demand homogeneity. For (2.1) this hypothesis takes the form $\pi_{i1} + \cdots + \pi_{in} = 0$ or $v'\beta_i = 0$, where

$$v' = [0 \ 1 \ \ldots \ 1], \qquad \beta_i = [\theta_i \ \pi_{i1} \ \ldots \ \pi_{in}]'. \tag{2.2}$$

Since $\epsilon_{1t} + \cdots + \epsilon_{nt} = 0$ holds with probability 1, we shall consider (2.2) for $i = 1, \ldots, n-1$ only and we do so in vector form,

$$y = (I_{n-1} \otimes X)\beta + \epsilon, \tag{2.3}$$

where β, y, and ϵ are all vectors consisting of $n-1$ subvectors, namely, β_i, $y_i = [\bar{w}_{it} Dq_{it}]$ and $\epsilon_i = [\epsilon_{it}]$ for $t = 1, \ldots, T$ (the sample size), while I_{n-1} is the unit matrix of order $n-1$ and X is a $T \times (n+1)$ matrix whose tth row equals $(DQ_t, Dp_{1t}, \ldots, Dp_{nt})$. Homogeneity of the entire system can then be written as

$$R\beta = 0, \quad \text{where} \quad R = I_{n-1} \otimes v'. \tag{2.4}$$

To test the validity of (2.4) we assume that the ϵ_{it}'s are normally distributed with zero means and a constant contemporaneous covariance matrix; also, that they are independent over time. The vector ϵ in (2.3) is then normal with zero mean and covariance matrix $\Sigma \otimes I_T$, where Σ is the covariance matrix of $(\epsilon_{1t}, ..., \epsilon_{n-1,t})$ for each $t = 1, ..., T$. We assume that Σ is non-singular and write σ^{ij} for elements of Σ^{-1}.

The F test for (2.4) is a multiple of the ratio of two quadratic forms. The form in the numerator is

$$b'R'\{R[\Sigma \otimes (X'X)^{-1}]R'\}^{-1}Rb = \frac{b'R'\Sigma^{-1}Rb}{v'(X'X)^{-1}v}, \qquad (2.5)$$

where b is the LS estimator of β; it consists of $n-1$ subvectors of the form $b_i = (X'X)^{-1}X'y_i$. The quadratic form in the denominator is

$$\sum_{i=1}^{n-1} \sum_{j=1}^{n-1} \sigma^{ij} e_i' e_j = (T - n - 1) \operatorname{tr} \Sigma^{-1} S, \qquad (2.6)$$

where $e_i = y_i - Xb_i$ is the LS residual vector of the ith equation and S is a square matrix (of order $n-1$) whose elements are $s_{ij} = e_i' e_j / (T - n - 1)$. This S is an unbiased estimator of Σ.

The quadratic form (2.6) is distributed as χ^2 with $(n-1)(T-n-1)$ degrees of freedom, while (2.5) is distributed as χ^2 with $n-1$ degrees of freedom if the null hypothesis (2.4) is true. The ratio of (2.5) to (2.6), each divided by its degrees of freedom, is

$$\frac{b'R'\Sigma^{-1}Rb/v'(X'X)^{-1}v}{\operatorname{tr} \Sigma^{-1} S}, \qquad (2.7)$$

which is distributed as F with $n-1$ and $(n-1)(T-n-1)$ degrees of freedom under (2.4). A problem in the application of this F ratio is that we usually do not know Σ. The standard solution is to approximate Σ by S, which changes the denominator of the ratio (2.7) into a constant: $\operatorname{tr} S^{-1} S = n - 1$. Therefore, the test is reduced to the numerator with Σ replaced by S,

$$b'R'S^{-1}Rb/v'(X'X)^{-1}v, \qquad (2.8)$$

which is asymptotically $(T \to \infty)$ distributed as $\chi^2(n-1)$.

When we apply this result to annual Dutch data published by Theil (1975: 264–65) for $n = 14$ and $T = 31$, we obtain a value of 267.85 for (2.8). This is quite unacceptable for $\chi^2(13)$. We must therefore reject the homogeneity assumption if we believe in the validity of the test.

3.3   A SIMULATION EXPERIMENT FOR HOMOGENEITY TESTING

This negative result for the seemingly innocent assumption of demand homogeneity does not stand in isolation. Several other researchers have indicated that their data reject homogeneity, including Barten (1969), Byron (1970), Christensen, Jorgenson, and Lau (1975), Deaton (1974), and Lluch (1971). The problem appears to be particularly serious when n is large or moderately large. For small n the rejections are much less numerous. Laitinen (1978: 188) computed the statistic (2.8) for several sets of data published by Theil (1975, 1976) with $n = 4$ and obtained values ranging from 2.3 to 7.2. These values are all quite acceptable for $\chi^2(3)$.

Laitinen decided to pursue this matter by means of a simulation experiment. The design of such an experiment includes numerically specified coefficients and T values of each of the independent variables (the price logchanges and the Divisia volume index) as well as a distribution from which the T disturbance vectors are pseudo-randomly drawn. The distribution selected is normal with zero mean and a numerically specified covariance matrix Σ. The coefficients are selected so that homogeneity is satisfied.

Having drawn independently T times from the disturbance distribution ($T = 31$ in this case), we can combine these numerical results with the specified coefficients and values of the independent variables to compute a new vector y from (2.3) and then a new test statistic (2.8) for this artificial sample. When this is done 100 times, the statistic should be about 5 times in the 5 percent rejection region because the null hypothesis is true by construction. However, the actual results obtained by Laitinen, reproduced in the left half of Table 3–1, show that this hypothesis is far too often rejected. The experiment includes demand systems of different sizes, for $n = 5$, 8, 11, and 14

Table 3–1. Rejections of Homogeneity and Symmetry.

	Rejections of homogeneity		Rejections of symmetry	
	5 percent	1 percent	5 percent	1 percent
$n = 5$	14	6	9	3
$n = 8$	30	16	26	8
$n = 11$	53	35	50	37
$n = 14$	87	81	96	91

Table 3-2.   Rejections of Homogeneity by Three Tests.

	Exact F tests based on Σ		Asymptotic χ^2 tests based on S		Exact χ^2 tests based on Σ	
	5 percent	1 percent	5 percent	1 percent	5 percent	1 percent
$n = 5$	7	1	14	6	8	1
$n = 8$	8	2	30	16	5	2
$n = 11$	5	2	53	35	5	1
$n = 14$	4	2	87	81	6	1

goods. There are too many rejections for each n, both at the 5 percent and at the 1 percent level, and the rejection percentage increases with increasing n. The right half of the table pertains to the test for Slutsky symmetry and will be discussed in Section 3.4.

A simulation experiment has the advantage that everything is known, including the matrix Σ. We can thus use the same 100 trials to compute the F ratio (2.7). The numbers of rejections are shown in the left part of Table 3-2 with those based on (2.8) in the middle; the latter are reproduced from Table 3-1 to facilitate the comparison. Evidently, the rejection percentages are now quite close to the corresponding significance levels, thus indicating that the F test would work quite well if we could apply it (i.e., if we knew Σ). To verify this matter further we also show (in the last two columns of Table 3-2) the rejections for the same 100 trials that result from the χ^2 distribution with $n-1$ degrees of freedom of the quadratic form (2.5); recall that (2.5) is identical to the test statistic (2.8) except that (2.5) uses the true Σ. Evidently, knowing Σ leads to an almost perfect result.

Laitinen succeeded in deriving the exact distribution of the statistic (2.8) under the null hypothesis (2.4). This distribution is a multiple

$$\frac{(n-1)(T-n-1)}{T-2n+1}$$

of F with $n-1$ and $T-2n+1$ degrees of freedom. For $T = 31$ and $n = 14$ this is $52F(13, 4)$; since the 5 percent critical value of $F(13, 4)$ is 5.89, the exact 5 percent critical value for the statistic (2.8) is thus $52 \times 5.89 \approx 306.3$. Recall from the last paragraph of Section 3.2 that the value of (2.8) for the Dutch data is 267.85; hence, this value is not evidence against homogeneity at all. Table 3-3 contains for $T = 31$ the critical values of the asymptotic χ^2 distribution of the statistic (2.8) and also the exact critical values. The discrepancies

Table 3-3.   Additional Results on Homogeneity Testing.

| | Asymptotic critical values | | Exact distribution of (2.8) | | | |
| | | | Critical values | | Rejections | |
	5 percent	1 percent	5 percent	1 percent	5 percent	1 percent
$n=5$	9.5	13.3	12.8	19.6	6	2
$n=8$	14.1	18.5	25.6	38.8	7	1
$n=11$	18.3	23.2	56.6	92.1	5	1
$n=14$	22.4	27.7	306.3	744.1	3	1

are sizeable, particularly when n is not very small. The last two columns of the table show the numbers of rejections by the exact test for our 100 trials. These numbers are close to 5 and to 1, as they should be.

3.4   TESTING FOR SLUTSKY SYMMETRY

Here we impose homogeneity by writing π_{in} as $-\pi_{i1}-\cdots-\pi_{i,n-1}$, so that (2.1) becomes

$$\bar{w}_{it}Dq_{it} = \theta_i DQ_t + \sum_{j=1}^{n-1} \pi_{ij}(Dp_{jt}-Dp_{nt})+\epsilon_{it}. \qquad (4.1)$$

As before, we write (4.1) for $i=1,...,n-1$ in the form (2.3), but this re-quires some modifications: X is now the $T \times n$ matrix whose tth row equals $(DQ_t, Dp_{1t}-Dp_{nt}, \ldots, Dp_{n-1,t}-Dp_{nt})$; and the subvectors β_i of β con-sist now of n elements each, π_{in} being deleted, so that β has $n(n-1)$ ele-ments. Also, the typical element of the unbiased estimator S of Σ is now $e_i'e_j/(T-n)$, while the quadratic form in the left side of (2.6) becomes

$$\sum_{i=1}^{n-1} \sum_{j=1}^{n-1} \sigma^{ij}e_i'e_j = (T-n)\,\text{tr}\,\Sigma^{-1}S, \qquad (4.2)$$

which is distributed as χ^2 with $(n-1)(T-n)$ degrees of freedom.

Our objective is to test the hypothesis of Slutsky symmetry, $\pi_{ij}=\pi_{ji}$, given homogeneity. The total number of symmetry relations in (4.1) for $i=1,...,n-1$ is $q=\frac{1}{2}(n-1)(n-2)$. As in (2.4) we shall write this null hypoth-esis as $R\beta=0$, but R is now a $q \times n(n-1)$ matrix, each row of R consisting of zeros except for a 1 and a -1 corresponding to π_{ij} and π_{ji} for some $i \neq j$. For example, R takes the following 3×15 form for $n=4$:

$$
\begin{array}{cccccccccccc}
\theta_1 & \pi_{11} & \pi_{12} & \pi_{13} & \theta_2 & \pi_{21} & \pi_{22} & \pi_{23} & \theta_3 & \pi_{31} & \pi_{32} & \pi_{33}
\end{array}
$$

$$
\begin{bmatrix}
0 & 0 & 1 & 0 & 0 & -1 & 0 & 0 & 0 & 0 & 0 & 0 \\
0 & 0 & 0 & 1 & 0 & 0 & 0 & 0 & 0 & -1 & 0 & 0 \\
0 & 0 & 0 & 0 & 0 & 0 & 0 & 1 & 0 & 0 & -1 & 0
\end{bmatrix}.
$$

With R thus interpreted, the quadratic form

$$
b'R'\{R[\Sigma \otimes (X'X)^{-1}]R'\}^{-1}Rb \tag{4.3}
$$

is distributed as $\chi^2(q)$ if the null hypothesis is true. The ratio of (4.3) to (4.2), each divided by its degrees of freedom, is

$$
\frac{b'R'\{R[\Sigma \otimes (X'X)^{-1}]R'\}^{-1}Rb}{[q/(n-1)]\,\mathrm{tr}\,\Sigma^{-1}S}, \tag{4.4}
$$

which is distributed as F with q and $(n-1)(T-n)$ degrees of freedom under the null hypothesis.

Again we must face the problem of an unknown Σ. If we replace it by S, the denominator of the ratio (4.4) becomes a constant so that the test is reduced to the numerator with Σ replaced by S,

$$
b'R'\{R[S \otimes (X'X)^{-1}]R'\}^{-1}Rb, \tag{4.5}
$$

which is asymptotically $(T \to \infty)$ distributed as $\chi^2(q)$ under the null hypothesis. How well does this asymptotic procedure work?

Meisner (1979) answered this question by means of a simulation experiment of the same design as that of Laitinen for homogeneity. The right half of Table 3–1 shows the rejections (out of 100 trials) that result from the asymptotic $\chi^2(q)$ distribution of the test statistic (4.5). As in the case of homogeneity testing, the rejections are too numerous, but note that their excess over the significance levels is smaller than that for homogeneity testing as long as n takes small values ($n = 5$ or 8). At $n = 11$ the numbers of rejections of homogeneity and symmetry are about equal, but at $n = 14$ they are clearly larger for symmetry, thus reflecting the fast increase of q when n increases. Table 3–4, which is similar to Table 3–2, compares the rejections based on (4.5) with those based on (4.4) and (4.3).

3.5   TESTING WITH FAT-TAILED ERROR DISTRIBUTIONS

Until this point we have assumed that the ϵ_{it}'s are normally distributed. Many analysts believe it is more realistic to assume that the error distribution has fatter tails than those of the normal distribution. How do the homogeneity and symmetry tests perform when the ϵ_{it}'s have fat tails?

Table 3-4.   Rejections of Symmetry by Three Tests.

	Exact F tests based on Σ		Asymptotic χ² tests based on S		Exact χ² tests based on Σ	
	5 percent	1 percent	5 percent	1 percent	5 percent	1 percent
$n = 5$	6	0	9	3	5	1
$n = 8$	5	2	26	8	5	1
$n = 11$	6	2	50	37	4	3
$n = 14$	4	2	96	91	6	0

Theil and Rosalsky (1985b) pursued this matter by generating a mixture of two normal distributions. A proportion $1 - p$ is picked from a normal distribution with zero mean and covariance matrix Σ, and a proportion p from a normal distribution with zero mean and covariance matrix $k\Sigma$, where k is a scalar ≥ 1. The mixture is then a random vector with zero mean and the following covariance matrix:

$$\Omega(k) = (1-p)\Sigma + p(k\Sigma). \tag{5.1}$$

For $k = 1$ this mixture is obviously normal, but for $k > 1$ it has a positive kurtosis coefficient (the fourth cumulant divided by the square of the variance) of the form

$$\frac{3p(1-p)(k-1)^2}{(1-p+pk)^2}, \tag{5.2}$$

which indicates fat tails.

To verify (5.2) it is sufficient to consider a standard normal distribution and a normal distribution with zero mean and variance k. A proportion $1 - p$ is picked from the former distribution and a proportion p from the latter. The mixture has zero mean, a variance equal to $1 - p + pk$, and a fourth moment equal to $3(1-p) + p(3k^2)$, so that the fourth cumulant (equal to the fourth moment minus three times the squared variance) is a multiple 3 of

$$1 - p + pk^2 - (1-p+pk)^2 = p(1-p)(k-1)^2,$$

from which the result (5.2) follows directly.

The experimental design is Laitinen's (see Section 3.3) with $T = 31$ observations. The value selected for p is 2/31, that is, two of the thirty-one error vectors are picked from a normal distribution with zero mean and covariance matrix $k\Sigma$. The kurtosis coefficient (5.2) is then zero for $k = 1$, 1.14 for

Table 3-5. Rejection Percentages for Homogeneity (Fat-tailed error distributions).

| | k = 1 | | k = 4 | | k = 9 | | k = 16 | |
| | 5 percent | 1 percent | 5 percent | 1 percent | 5 percent | 1 percent | 5 percent | 1 percent |
n								
			Using the true $\Omega(k)$					
5	6.8	1.2	6.0	2.0	7.4	3.2	8.4	4.0
8	5.4	1.0	7.4	3.2	10.0	6.4	12.8	7.8
11	4.8	0.6	5.4	1.6	7.2	2.8	9.6	4.2
14	5.6	1.4	6.0	1.2	10.2	4.2	12.2	7.8
			Using the LS estimate of $\Omega(k)$					
5	13.6	4.0	13.8	5.0	15.2	5.2	15.2	6.2
8	25.8	16.0	28.0	17.8	28.2	18.2	29.0	18.4
11	51.4	37.0	51.6	37.0	52.2	38.4	51.0	39.4
14	88.0	82.8	89.0	82.8	88.6	81.6	89.2	82.4

$k = 4$, 5.04 for $k = 9$, and 10.52 for $k = 16$. For $k = 1$ and each trial we generate thirty-one pseudo-normal error vectors with zero mean and covariance matrix Σ. For $k > 1$ we use the same vectors but we pick two of the thirty-one vectors at random and multiply them by the square root of k. (An alternative procedure is to pick, not two vectors with covariance matrix $k\Sigma$, but a random number whose expectation is 2. However, this makes no difference for the distribution of the sample moments and, therefore, for the kurtosis.)

The results are shown in Tables 3–5 and 3–6 in the form of rejection percentages out of 500 trials. The statistics used are (2.5) and (4.3) in the upper half of these tables, with Σ replaced by $\Omega(k)$, and (2.8) and (4.5) in the lower half. In all cases we applied the χ^2 distribution with the relevant degrees of freedom. This is exact, of course, only in the upper-left corner of the two tables ($k = 1$ using the true Ω), and it is asymptotically valid in the lower-left corners. The large rejection percentages in the latter corners corroborate the results of Table 3–1.

When k increases above 1, the χ^2 distribution is no longer applicable even when the true $\Omega(k)$ is used, the reason being that the error distribution is then no longer normal. The rejections at the 1 percent level tend to increase with k, particularly when n is not small. When the LS estimate rather than the true $\Omega(k)$ is used, the proportionate increase in the rejection percentage is much smaller. Yet, the results for $k = 16$ based on the true $\Omega(k)$ are not as bad as those for $k = 1$ based on the estimated $\Omega(k)$.

Table 3–6.   Rejection Percentages for Slutsky Symmetry
(Fat-tailed error distributions).

	$k = 1$		$k = 4$		$k = 9$		$k = 16$	
n	5 percent	1 percent	5 percent	1 percent	5 percent	1 percent	5 percent	1 percent
			Using the true $\Omega(k)$					
5	5.6	1.2	4.6	1.4	5.8	2.4	6.4	3.4
8	4.0	1.6	5.0	0.8	6.4	3.2	7.6	4.0
11	6.4	1.2	8.6	2.0	10.6	5.0	13.8	7.6
14	3.8	1.0	5.4	1.6	12.0	4.8	14.6	9.0
			Using the LS estimate of $\Omega(k)$					
5	8.0	2.8	7.2	3.0	8.2	2.4	8.4	2.6
8	24.2	12.0	25.6	12.4	25.8	12.0	26.2	11.6
11	54.0	37.2	55.0	38.4	56.6	40.2	58.0	41.4
14	94.2	87.6	93.4	88.0	93.0	88.4	94.0	88.8

3.6   ALTERNATIVE SPECIFICATIONS OF Σ

We return to the assumption of a normal error distribution and recall that
Laitinen succeeded in finding the exact distribution of the test statistic (2.8)
under the null hypothesis of homogeneity. The analogous problem of the
exact distribution of the statistic (4.5) for Slutsky symmetry is much more
complicated because symmetry is a cross-equation constraint. Another difference is that (2.8) requires the inverse of S whereas (4.5) does not. This
could be a major cause of the better behavior of the symmetry test relative
to the homogeneity test for small n (see Table 3–1). On the other hand, the
symmetry test based on S produces very bad results for larger n.

The tests based on S fall under what is frequently referred to as Wald
tests. Bera, Byron, and Jarque (1981) considered the asymptotically equivalent Lagrange multiplier and likelihood ratio tests, while Bewley (1983) ex-
perimented with iterative versions of S. Another possibility is to replace Σ
by a nonstochastic matrix in both the numerator and the denominator of a
ratio such as (4.4). The simplest specification would be the identity matrix
I_{n-1}, but that would violate the condition that the $n \times n$ augmented covariance matrix is singular (because $\epsilon_{1t} + \cdots + \epsilon_{nt} = 0$ holds with probability 1).
We can correct this by using Σ^*, defined as the square matrix of order $n-1$

whose diagonal elements are all $1 - 1/n$ and whose off-diagonal elements are all $-1/n$. It is easily verified that the $n \times n$ augmented version of Σ^* has rows and columns whose elements add up to zero (in agreement with $\epsilon_{1t} + \cdots + \epsilon_{nt} = 0$). In the next two sections we shall consider symmetry tests using matrices such as Σ^*. A justification of the use of such matrices is given in Section 3.20 in the discussion of rational random behavior.

3.7   A CROSS-COUNTRY SIMULATION DESIGN

To verify the merits of a specification such as Σ^* we follow Theil and Rosalsky (1984b) by adopting Meisner's (1981) cross-country simulation design. The underlying model is Working's as described in Section 2.6, but there are eight goods (not 10) and the substitution term is formulated in terms of Slutsky coefficients (π_{ij}'s) rather than w_{ic}'s and β_i's. Thus, the equation for good i in country c is

$$y_{ic} = \alpha_i + \beta_i \log Q_c + \sum_{j=1}^{8} \pi_{ij} \log \frac{p_{jc}}{\bar{p}_j} + \epsilon_{ic}. \tag{7.1}$$

The eight goods are the ten listed in Table 2–5 of Section 2.8 except that beverages and tobacco are merged with food and that recreation and education are similarly combined. The country index c takes fifteen values: the sixteen countries of Kravis, Heston, and Summers (1978) with Kenya deleted as an outlier. The sixteen countries are listed in the first paragraph of Section 2.1.

We shall be interested in testing for symmetry given homogeneity. Thus we replace (7.1) by

$$y_{ic} = \alpha_i + \beta_i \log Q_c + \sum_{j=1}^{7} \pi_{ij} \left(\log \frac{p_{jc}}{\bar{p}_j} - \log \frac{p_{8c}}{\bar{p}_8} \right) + \epsilon_{ic}, \tag{7.2}$$

which is of the same form as (4.1) except that (7.2) has a constant term. With appropriate adjustments, the F ratio has the form (4.4); its distribution is $F(21, 42)$, 21 being the number of symmetry relations $\pi_{ij} = \pi_{ji}$ in (7.2) for $i = 1, \ldots, 7$, and 42 being the number of degrees of freedom in the denominator of the F ratio. This 42 is the product of 7, which is the number of linearly independent equations, and $15 - 9$, which is the number of countries minus the number of coefficients adjusted in each equation.

In the simulation experiment we use the observed values of the independent variables of the fifteen countries and we specify the coefficients and

Table 3-7.   Rejections of Symmetry by Four Tests.

	Significance levels					
	10 percent	5 percent	2.5 percent	1 percent	0.5 percent	0.1 percent
	Rejection percentages, 500 trials					
Using Σ	8.8	4.2	2.0	.4	.2	0
Using S	91.4	89.4	86.6	82.4	80.0	76.6
Using Σ^*	9.2	5.4	2.4	1.2	.4	.2
Using Σ^{**}	11.4	7.2	3.4	1.0	.6	.2
	Rejection percentages, 1000 trials					
Using Σ	10.4	5.9	2.7	.9	.4	.3
Using Σ^*	8.6	6.3	4.0	2.4	1.1	.3
Using Σ^{**}	11.3	7.1	3.4	1.5	.7	.2

the covariance matrix Σ as was done by Meisner (1981: App. E). We generate fifteen independent pseudo-normal vectors with covariance matrix Σ and we compute the implied values of the dependent variables. Next, using the true Σ we compute the F ratio (4.4) as well as three other statistics (see the next paragraph). We repeat this 500 independent times and count the number of rejections at various significance levels. The result, shown in the first line of Table 3-7, indicates satisfactory agreement of the rejection percentage with the theoretical significance level.

Next we replace Σ in (4.4) by the unbiased LS estimator S, which implies that the F test is approximated by an asymptotic χ^2 test with 21 degrees of freedom. The result, shown in the second line of Table 3-7, is about as disastrous as that in the last line of Table 3-1. On the other hand, the third and fourth lines of Table 3-7 are much more promising because their rejection percentages are close to the significance level on top. The matrix underlying the rejections in the third line is Σ^* defined at the end of Section 3.6, and the distribution used is $F(21, 42)$. [Note that Σ^* may be multiplied by a scalar without affecting the ratio (4.4).] The matrix Σ^{**} of the fourth line has diagonal elements of the form $\bar{w}_i(1 - \bar{w}_i)$ and off-diagonal elements of the form $-\bar{w}_i\bar{w}_j$, where $\bar{w}_i$ is the arithmetic average of the w_{ic}'s over the fifteen countries. In this row $F(21, 42)$ is also used.

In the lower part of Table 3-7 the experiment is repeated for the specifications Σ, Σ^*, and Σ^{**} by means of a second (independent) set of 1000 trials.

The agreement with the corresponding lines in the upper part of the table appears to be satisfactory. See Theil and Rosalsky (1984b) for other specifications in addition to Σ, S, Σ^*, and Σ^{**}.

3.8   THE POWER OF ALTERNATIVE SYMMETRY TESTS

We proceed to evaluate the specifications Σ, Σ^*, and Σ^{**} under the alternative hypothesis of an asymmetric Slutsky matrix. We introduce asymmetry by changing the elements of the first row and the first column of this matrix, corresponding to food ($i = 1$), all elements outside this row and this column remaining unchanged. Since food includes beverages and tobacco in the present experimental design, we can in principle visualize the type of asymmetry selected here as the result of an aggregation error. (In other words, there would be symmetry if nine rather than eight goods had been used, beverages and tobacco being separated from food.)

More specifically, the π_{11} of Meisner's (1981: 180) symmetric specification equals -0.106, and the π_{1j}'s for $j \neq 1$ vary between 0.012 and 0.020. We introduce asymmetry by raising each π_{1j} in (7.2) by k and subtracting k from each π_{j1} ($j = 1, \ldots, 7$). In Table 3-8 we specify the asymmetry coefficient k as ± 25, ± 50, and ± 75 (all $\times 10^{-4}$), and we use the same 1000 trials as those in the lower part of Table 3-7. However, we multiplied the error covariance matrix Σ of Meisner's design by 1/9 in order to obtain a smaller ratio of errors to the independent variables (real income and relative prices). For comparison, we reproduce in Table 3-8 the results in the last three rows of Table 3-7 for $k = 0$. [The multiplication by 1/9 has no effect on the test statistic (4.4) under the null hypothesis.]

The results summarized in Table 3-8 indicate that, for a given significance level, the rejection percentage tends to go up when the asymmetry deviates more from zero. Table 3-9 makes this comparison a bit easier by expressing the rejection percentages under asymmetry as deviations from the corresponding percentage under symmetry. Except when the significance level selected is very low, the increase in the rejection percentage with increasing asymmetry tends to be highest when the true Σ is used. Thus, as could be expected, using Σ^* or Σ^{**} entails a loss of power.

Before blaming these two specifications for this defect, we should recognize that their performance for the present data set is actually very good. To understand this we go back to (7.1) rather than (7.2), and we consider the use of the fifteen-country data set for the test of homogeneity. Since there

Table 3-8.   Rejection Percentages (out of 1000 trials) Under Asymmetry.

| Asymmetry | Significance levels | | | | | |
	10 percent	5 percent	2.5 percent	1 percent	0.5 percent	0.1 percent
			Using Σ			
−0.0075	47.6	34.7	23.8	14.7	8.6	2.0
−0.0050	25.0	16.8	8.8	3.6	1.7	.3
−0.0025	14.0	6.8	2.8	1.0	.4	.1
0	10.4	5.9	2.7	.9	.4	.3
0.0025	13.2	6.7	3.8	1.2	.5	.3
0.0050	26.6	15.7	9.0	3.9	1.8	.5
0.0075	51.7	36.1	25.3	14.4	8.8	2.3
			Using Σ^*			
−0.0075	33.0	23.6	17.3	10.3	6.7	3.1
−0.0050	17.5	10.9	7.1	3.5	2.5	.6
−0.0025	9.7	5.2	3.3	1.5	.9	.3
0	8.6	6.3	4.0	2.4	1.1	.3
0.0025	10.6	6.1	3.8	2.0	1.0	.4
0.0050	20.1	12.0	7.5	4.4	2.6	1.0
0.0075	37.5	26.2	18.3	11.6	8.0	3.1
			Using Σ^{**}			
−0.0075	34.3	22.8	15.6	9.5	6.7	3.4
−0.0050	20.0	13.3	8.4	5.4	3.5	1.0
−0.0025	14.2	8.3	4.8	2.7	1.6	.6
0	11.3	7.1	3.4	1.5	.7	.2
0.0025	13.5	7.0	4.2	2.0	1.4	.5
0.0050	20.4	12.8	7.0	3.6	2.1	.9
0.0075	34.7	23.5	15.0	8.7	5.7	1.5

are ten unknown parameters in (7.1) for each i, the unbiased LS estimator S of the associated matrix Σ satisfies

$$(15-10)S = Y'[I_{15} - X(X'X)^{-1}X']Y, \tag{8.1}$$

where $Y = [y_1 \ldots y_7]$ and X consists of ten columns. Thus, the matrix in brackets on the right in (8.1) has rank $15 - 10 = 5$, which is less than the order (7×7) of S. Therefore, S is singular so that the statistic (2.8) does not exist. In other words, Laitinen's exact homogeneity test cannot be performed,

Table 3-9. Differences of Rejection Percentages.

	Significance levels					
Asymmetry	10 percent	5 percent	2.5 percent	1 percent	0.5 percent	0.1 percent
			Using Σ			
−0.0075	37.2	28.8	21.1	13.8	8.2	1.7
−0.0050	14.6	10.9	6.1	2.7	1.3	.0
−0.0025	3.6	.9	.1	.1	.0	−.2
0	0	0	0	0	0	0
0.0025	2.8	.8	1.1	.3	.1	.0
0.0050	16.2	9.8	6.3	3.0	1.4	.2
0.0075	41.3	30.2	22.6	13.5	8.4	2.0
			Using Σ^*			
−0.0075	24.4	17.3	13.3	7.9	5.6	2.8
−0.0050	8.9	4.6	3.1	1.1	1.4	.3
−0.0025	1.1	−1.1	−.7	−.9	−.2	.0
0	0	0	0	0	0	0
0.0025	2.0	−.2	−.2	−.4	−.1	.1
0.0050	11.5	5.7	3.5	2.0	1.5	.7
0.0075	28.9	19.9	14.3	9.2	6.9	2.8
			Using Σ^{**}			
−0.0075	23.0	15.7	12.2	8.0	6.0	3.2
−0.0050	8.7	6.2	5.0	3.9	2.8	.8
−0.0025	2.9	1.2	1.4	1.2	.9	.4
0	0	0	0	0	0	0
0.0025	2.2	−.1	.8	.5	.7	.3
0.0050	9.1	5.7	3.6	2.1	1.4	.7
0.0075	23.4	16.4	11.6	7.2	5.0	1.3

whereas the symmetry tests based on Σ^* or Σ^{**} do work and have approximately the correct size (Table 3-7) and seem to have tolerable power.

3.9 THE TWO PERILS OF SYMMETRY-CONSTRAINED ESTIMATION

Here we move from symmetry testing to the related topic of symmetry-constrained estimation. The account that follows is based on Fiebig and Theil (1983) and Theil and Rosalsky (1984a).

We write (7.2) for all countries ($c = 1, \ldots, 15$) as $y_i = X\delta_i + \epsilon_i$, where $\delta_i = [\alpha_i, \beta_i, \pi_{i1}, \ldots, \pi_{i7}]'$. We write Slutsky symmetry as $R\delta = 0$, where δ is a vector that contains δ_i as a subvector ($i = 1, \ldots, 7$) and R is a 21×63 matrix whose elements are all 0 or ± 1, each row of R corresponding to $\pi_{ij} = \pi_{ji}$ for some $i \neq j$. The LS estimator of δ_i is $d_i = (X'X)^{-1}X'y_i$; we write d for the vector with d_i as subvector ($i = 1, \ldots, 7$). This d does not satisfy Slutsky symmetry. The best linear unbiased estimator of δ constrained by symmetry is

$$\hat{\delta}(\Sigma) = d - C(\Sigma)R'[RC(\Sigma)R']^{-1}Rd, \tag{9.1}$$

and the covariance matrix of this estimator is

$$C(\Sigma) - C(\Sigma)R'[RC(\Sigma)R']^{-1}RC(\Sigma), \tag{9.2}$$

where $C(\Sigma) = \Sigma \otimes (X'X)^{-1}$. Note that the quadratic form (4.3) in the present notation is $d'R'[RC(\Sigma)R']^{-1}Rd$.

If Σ is known, as is the case in Meisner's (1981) simulation design, we can apply (9.1) and (9.2) directly. The results are shown in columns 4 through 6 of Table 3–10 for 500 trials, all obtained from independent quasi-normal error vectors with covariance matrix Σ. The estimated bias (the mean of the 500 estimates minus the true value) is close to zero, as it should be. The root-mean-squared error (the RMSE, computed from the true value) is close to the root-mean-squared standard error (RMSSE), thus indicating that the standard errors are on average of correct size. The RMSSE is obtained by summing each diagonal element of the covariance matrix (9.2) over the 500 trials, dividing the sum by 500, and then taking the square root.

In columns 7 through 9 we recognize that Σ is typically unknown and must be replaced by a known matrix. In these columns we use the unbiased LS estimator S, which is thus substituted for Σ in (9.1) to yield the vector $\hat{\delta}(S)$. Also, by substituting S for Σ in the matrix (9.2) and then taking square roots of the diagonal elements, we obtain approximate standard errors (ASEs) of $\hat{\delta}(S)$. Column 7 shows that bias is not much of a problem for $\hat{\delta}(S)$, but a comparison of columns 5 and 8 indicates that this estimator has a serious efficiency problem, its RMSEs being substantially larger than those of $\hat{\delta}(\Sigma)$. In addition, the root-mean squares of the approximate standard errors (the RMSASEs) shown in column 9 are all *below* the corresponding RMSSEs of column 6, and they are very much below the RMSEs in column 8.

These results illustrate the two perils of symmetry-constrained estimation when Σ is replaced by S: The coefficient estimates have an impaired efficiency and their approximate standard errors give an overly optimistic picture of their precision.

Table 3-10.   Symmetry-Constrained Estimation, 500 trials.[a]

		True	Using Σ			Using S		
i	j	value	Bias	RMSE	RMSSE	Bias	RMSE	RMSASE
(1)	(2)	(3)	(4)	(5)	(6)	(7)	(8)	(9)
			Coefficients β_i					
1	n.a.[b]	−1526	6	216	218	−7	309	172
2	n.a.	42	2	81	86	3	117	70
3	n.a.	261	5	121	124	6	135	117
4	n.a.	266	0	153	150	15	240	105
5	n.a.	258	−3	59	58	−6	74	49
6	n.a.	210	0	144	147	−8	173	131
7	n.a.	243	−5	116	112	3	174	84
			Diagonal Slutsky coefficients π_{ii}					
1	n.a.	−1061	−26	801	823	−75	1109	636
2	n.a.	−502	−3	175	174	2	223	134
3	n.a.	−785	−11	303	304	−8	331	277
4	n.a.	−546	−19	495	480	−56	818	309
5	n.a.	−492	−3	74	77	−3	94	63
6	n.a.	−580	9	447	459	4	510	404
7	n.a.	−713	5	220	211	−15	339	148
			Off-diagonal Slutsky coefficients π_{ij}					
1	2	121	9	271	270	3	385	199
1	3	203	9	314	324	16	379	272
1	4	133	22	499	495	66	805	338
1	5	119	9	183	182	1	238	140
1	6	142	−10	470	450	−28	546	362
1	7	181	−20	306	309	−4	486	209
2	3	82	8	142	145	7	176	125
2	4	54	−13	198	196	−20	313	133
2	5	48	8	83	83	16	115	63
2	6	58	4	196	201	20	243	163
2	7	73	−7	141	138	−13	212	96
3	4	90	−5	200	195	−5	256	169
3	5	80	−2	97	98	−5	120	85
3	6	96	3	257	260	0	287	225
3	7	123	−5	158	157	−5	201	138
4	5	53	0	124	127	4	184	91
4	6	63	9	283	293	24	411	222
4	7	80	12	244	244	−11	408	148
5	6	56	−15	134	141	−17	172	113
5	7	72	3	92	93	11	128	71
6	7	86	8	206	209	28	280	162

a. All entries are to be divided by 10^4.
b. n.a. = not applicable.

3.10   IS IT POSSIBLE TO AVOID THE TWO PERILS?

A natural question is whether the results are improved when we replace S by the matrices Σ^* or Σ^{**}, which we considered in Sections 3.7 and 3.8 in the context of symmetry testing. Accordingly, Table 3-11 summarizes the results of $\hat{\delta}(\Sigma^*)$ and $\hat{\delta}(\Sigma^{**})$ for the same 500 trials as those underlying Table 3-10. Since Σ^* is nonstochastic, the covariance matrix of $\hat{\delta}(\Sigma^*)$ is $AC(\Sigma)A'$, where

$$A = I - C(\Sigma^*)R'[RC(\Sigma^*)R']^{-1}R.$$

We can estimate $AC(\Sigma)A'$ unbiasedly by $AC(S)A'$, from which standard errors are obtained by taking the square roots of the diagonal elements. The argument is not quite the same for Σ^{**}, because this matrix involves the average $\bar{w}_i$ of the w_{ic}'s that occur in the dependent variable y_{ic} of (7.2). Nevertheless, we shall compute approximate standard errors from the diagonal elements of $BC(S)B'$, where

$$B = I - C(\Sigma^{**})R'[RC(\Sigma^{**})R']^{-1}R.$$

A convenient summary is provided in Table 3-12. For each of the thirty-five coefficients (β_i's, π_{ii}'s and π_{ij}'s) we compute the ratio of the RMSE based on Σ to the RMSE based on any of the other specifications. The left half of Table 3-12 contains the quartiles of these thirty-five ratios for each method of estimation. Clearly, Σ^* and particularly Σ^{**} represent a considerable improvement in efficiency over S. In addition, the right half of the table shows the quartiles of the ratios of the RMSSEs (or RMSASEs) to the corresponding RMSEs. These quartiles are satisfactorily close to 1 for Σ and Σ^* and even for Σ^{**}, but they are quite low for S. The last line of the table pertains to the matrix $\hat{\Sigma}$, which we have not yet met (see the next paragraph). It is clearly the winner in the efficiency comparison but not in the standard error comparison.

The motivation of $\hat{\Sigma}$ may be summarized as follows. First, the matrix Σ is related to the canonical correlations of the dependent and the independent variables of the system (7.2): If ρ is such a canonical correlation, then $1 - \rho^2$ is a latent root of Σ in the metric of the covariance matrix of the dependent variables. Second, the inferior performance of the LS estimator S of Σ reflects the fact that sample canonical correlations are biased in zero direction. Such a bias is similar to that of the ordinary multiple correlation coefficient; in both cases a correction for bias is appropriate. Third, by working with sample moment matrices (consisting of mean squares and

Table 3-11. More on Symmetry-Constrained Estimation.[a]

i (1)	j (2)	Using Σ^*			Using Σ^{**}			Using $\hat{\Sigma}$		
		Bias (3)	RMSE (4)	RMSSE (5)	Bias (6)	RMSE (7)	RMSASE (8)	Bias (9)	RMSE (10)	RMSASE (11)
		Coefficients β_i								
1	n.a.[b]	7	259	261	7	245	249	19	235	328
2	n.a.	3	99	105	4	93	99	−1	90	85
3	n.a.	9	130	133	8	129	134	2	123	133
4	n.a.	−1	186	187	0	167	172	1	155	143
5	n.a.	−3	73	72	−4	68	67	−5	65	81
6	n.a.	4	168	168	−1	175	178	4	154	147
7	n.a.	−9	140	143	−8	133	137	−26	123	115
		Diagonal Slutsky coefficients π_{ii}								
1	n.a.	−28	868	895	−17	854	882	1	854	1294
2	n.a.	−7	192	193	−9	190	191	12	174	154
3	n.a.	−9	306	304	−8	309	305	−27	312	296
4	n.a.	−17	616	604	−20	547	540	0	497	411
5	n.a.	−4	88	90	−4	84	87	8	80	108
6	n.a.	10	491	513	18	493	514	−30	463	395
7	n.a.	12	266	265	10	263	264	52	240	208

Table 3-11 continued.

i (1)	j (2)	Using Σ^*			Using Σ^{**}			Using $\hat{\Sigma}$		
		Bias (3)	RMSE (4)	RMSSE (5)	Bias (6)	RMSE (7)	RMSASE (8)	Bias (9)	RMSE (10)	RMSASE (11)
		\multicolumn{10}{c}{Off-diagonal Slusky coefficients π_{ij}}								
1	2	0	350	356	8	298	301	2	310	290
1	3	11	323	327	6	324	334	-1	366	464
1	4	35	627	627	34	541	545	11	517	505
1	5	13	253	246	7	217	213	8	281	281
1	6	-8	501	479	-32	530	519	-10	536	535
1	7	-23	414	425	-20	354	373	-54	320	339
2	3	19	169	181	16	156	167	10	144	130
2	4	-16	233	232	-19	228	224	-21	200	168
2	5	10	97	101	10	92	95	-2	88	86
2	6	18	270	271	19	270	270	15	197	170
2	7	-10	165	166	-11	166	165	7	148	129
3	4	-12	229	226	-10	210	207	10	197	181
3	5	-7	149	146	-5	126	124	-4	111	123
3	6	8	266	270	13	274	278	6	255	229
3	7	-14	200	197	-13	194	193	-8	164	149
4	5	-3	149	156	-1	141	149	0	131	127
4	6	-7	359	370	2	334	348	24	295	254
4	7	19	305	313	16	281	296	15	242	216
5	6	-18	200	213	-16	190	203	-4	156	151
5	7	3	114	114	5	109	109	5	100	98
6	7	2	271	288	6	283	304	-7	207	193

a. All entries to be divided by 10^4.   b. n.a. = not applicable.

Table 3-12. Efficiency and Standard Error Comparisons.

	Efficiency comparison			*Standard error comparison*		
	Lower quartile	*Median*	*Upper quartile*	*Lower quartile*	*Median*	*Upper quartile*
Using Σ	a	a	a	.99	1.01	1.02
Using S	.67	.74	.81	.48	.59	.69
Using Σ^*	.79	.83	.87	1.00	1.01	1.03
Using Σ^{**}	.84	.88	.92	.99	1.01	1.04
Using $\hat{\Sigma}$	.92	.95	.99	.89	.94	1.06

a. Equal to 1 by construction.

products of sample values) we do not exploit the knowledge that our variables have a continuous distribution, but the maximum entropy approach enables us to do so. The matrix $\hat{\Sigma}$ combines these lines of thought; see Theil and Fiebig (1984: Chap. 6) for details. Approximate standard errors are obtained from the matrix (9.2), with $\hat{\Sigma}$ substituted for Σ. As noted at the end of the last paragraph, this procedure seems to be less than satisfactory; we shall return to this matter in Section 3.15.

3.11 MAXIMUM LIKELIHOOD ESTIMATION OF NONLINEAR SYSTEMS

The poor performance of S as an estimator of Σ should cause concern for the maximum likelihood estimation of demand systems, because this S is not only the LS estimator but also (apart from a scalar multiplier) the ML estimator of Σ. Recall from Section 2.9, particularly equations (9.6) and (9.8), that Σ^{-1} plays a role in the first-order derivatives of the log-likelihood function and in the expectations of the second-order derivatives. Since Σ is unknown, Σ^{-1} in these two equations becomes the ML estimator S^{-1} (apart from a scalar). The poor quality of S^{-1} as an estimator of Σ^{-1} may have undesirable consequences for the ML coefficient estimates of the model.

Theil and Rosalsky (1985a) pursued this matter using a cross-country simulation design based on Working's model for the ten goods of Section 2.8. The data-based ML point estimates are selected as the true parameter values of the design; see column 2 of Table 3-13. Similarly, the data-based ML estimate of Σ is used as the true Σ of the experiment. We draw thirty independent

Table 3-13. Maximum Likelihood and Least-Squares Estimation of a Nonlinear System.

Parameter (1)	True value (2)	ML, known Σ			ML, unknown Σ			Unweighted LS		Weighted LS	
		Mean (3)	RMSE (4)	RMSASE (5)	Mean (6)	RMSE (7)	RMSASE (8)	Mean (9)	RMSE (10)	Mean (11)	RMSE (12)
α_i Food	.1620	.1626	.0124	.0121	.1626	.0125	.0115	.1626	.0126	.1626	.0125
Beverages, tobacco	.0558	.0560	.0061	.0064	.0560	.0062	.0061	.0559	.0064	.0559	.0063
Clothing, footwear	.0839	.0838	.0058	.0058	.0838	.0059	.0055	.0837	.0058	.0838	.0058
Gross rent, fuel	.1448	.1450	.0078	.0078	.1450	.0080	.0075	.1451	.0078	.1451	.0079
House furnishings, operations	.0982	.0978	.0051	.0050	.0977	.0052	.0048	.0978	.0052	.0978	.0052
Medical care	.0888	.0886	.0040	.0041	.0886	.0040	.0039	.0886	.0041	.0886	.0041
Transport, communication	.1179	.1177	.0064	.0067	.1177	.0065	.0063	.1176	.0065	.1177	.0065
Recreation	.0692	.0691	.0042	.0042	.0691	.0042	.0040	.0690	.0042	.0690	.0042
Education	.0535	.0536	.0060	.0059	.0536	.0063	.0053	.0538	.0071	.0537	.0063
Other	.1260	.1258	.0070	.0068	.1258	.0071	.0065	.1258	.0070	.1258	.0070

β_i											
Food	-.1543	-.1540	.0099	.0098	-.1540	.0101	.0092	-.1540	.0102	-.1540	.0100
Beverages, tobacco	.0008	.0009	.0049	.0050	.0009	.0050	.0047	.0009	.0051	.0009	.0051
Clothing, footwear	-.0046	-.0046	.0047	.0048	-.0046	.0048	.0045	-.0046	.0047	-.0046	.0047
Gross rent, fuel	.0315	.0318	.0063	.0063	.0318	.0065	.0060	.0319	.0064	.0319	.0064
House furnishings, operations	.0253	.0250	.0040	.0040	.0250	.0042	.0038	.0250	.0041	.0251	.0041
Medical care	.0237	.0234	.0031	.0034	.0234	.0032	.0032	.0234	.0033	.0234	.0032
Transport, communication	.0295	.0296	.0055	.0055	.0296	.0055	.0051	.0295	.0056	.0296	.0056
Recreation	.0193	.0191	.0033	.0033	.0191	.0034	.0032	.0190	.0034	.0190	.0034
Education	-.0040	-.0039	.0054	.0054	-.0039	.0058	.0048	-.0037	.0065	-.0039	.0057
Other	.0328	.0326	.0057	.0056	.0326	.0057	.0054	.0327	.0058	.0327	.0057
ϕ Income flexibility	-.5259	-.5288	.0393	.0369	-.5291	.0476	.0291	-.5291	.0649	-.5294	.0497

quasi-normal vectors with zero mean and covariance matrix Σ. When these are combined with the observed values of the independent variables of the thirty countries and with the above-mentioned parameter values, we obtain the implied values of the dependent variables. Using the latter values, we can reestimate the model by ML or by other methods. For example, if Σ is known, we can simplify the log-likelihood function of Section 2.9 to

$$L = \text{constant} - \frac{1}{2} \sum_{c=1}^{30} (y_c - X_c\theta)'\Sigma^{-1}(y_c - X_c\theta) \qquad (11.1)$$

because the term involving the determinant of Σ^{-1} is now a known constant. Note also that the expression after the summation sign in (11.1) is now a quadratic form with a known matrix Σ^{-1} so that this matrix no longer changes in successive iterations.

Table 3–13 provides the results for 500 trials and for four methods of estimation: ML with and without knowledge of Σ and two versions of LS (the discussion of which follows in Section 3.12). The means over the 500 trials, which are shown in columns 3 and 6, are so close to the true values in column 2 that we may conclude that bias is no problem. The RMSEs in column 7 exceed those in column 4, particularly for ϕ. The RMSASEs in column 8 are all *below* those in column 5 and also below the corresponding RMSEs in column 7. Thus, as in Section 3.9, there are two perils in not knowing Σ: The ML coefficient estimates have an impaired efficiency (larger RMSEs) and their asymptotic standard errors overstate their precision.

This result has immediate applicability to the interpretation of the asymptotic standard error of our data-based ϕ estimate. Recall from the first paragraph of Section 2.8 that this standard error is 0.037 and that we tentatively concluded that ϕ has been precisely estimated. But the ratio of the RMSASE to the RMSE for ϕ in Table 3–13 (ML, unknown Σ) is only $291/476 \approx 0.61$. If we correct the above-mentioned standard error of 0.037 by dividing by 0.61, we obtain about 0.06. This is still not bad relative to the ML point estimate $\hat{\phi} = -0.526$, but it is not nearly as good as the original value of 0.037.

Rosalsky, Finke, and Theil (1984) performed a simulation experiment using Laitinen's design based on the Rotterdam model. Although this design was formulated in terms of Slutsky coefficients for the purpose of homogeneity testing, it is actually in preference-independent form: $\pi_{ii} = \phi\theta_i(1-\theta_i)$ and $\pi_{ij} = -\phi\theta_i\theta_j$ $(i \neq j)$ with $\phi = -0.6$ [cf. (2.1)]. The parameters and their true values are shown in columns 1 and 2 of Table 3–14. Recall from the last paragraph of Section 2.9 that ML estimation of Working's time series model is a straightforward extension of its cross-country counterpart; the same is true for the Rotterdam model and it is also true when the contemporaneous

Table 3-14. ML Estimation of the Rotterdam Model, 100 trials.[a]

Parameter (1)	True value (2)	Σ known			Σ unknown		
		Mean (3)	RMSE (4)	RMSASE (5)	Mean (6)	RMSE (7)	RMSASE (8)
θ_i $i = 1$	55	56	24	23	55	30	19
$i = 2$	266	265	47	49	266	56	42
$i = 3$	369	382	72	67	372	84	54
$i = 4$	296	291	45	46	290	60	36
$i = 5$	661	650	73	71	648	90	55
$i = 6$	45	41	18	16	42	24	12
$i = 7$	352	352	51	55	353	63	46
$i = 8$	234	237	45	54	241	55	46
$i = 9$	272	276	59	53	278	63	44
$i = 10$	2371	2345	138	146	2338	169	121
$i = 11$	237	234	41	42	228	53	34
$i = 12$	2125	2139	145	160	2154	195	130
$i = 13$	478	479	71	74	478	90	61
$i = 14$	2240	2252	200	187	2260	237	155
ϕ	−6000	−5993	402	377	−5973	510	276

a. All entries to be divided by 10^4.

covariance matrix Σ is known. The results are shown in columns 3 through 8 for 100 trials. Again, bias is no problem, the means in columns 3 and 6 being close to the true values in column 2, but the RMSEs in column 7 are larger than those in column 4, and the RMSASEs in column 8 greatly understate the RMSEs in column 7. See Rosalsky, Finke, and Theil (1984) for similar (but not as drastic) results with systems consisting of 11, 8, and 5 equations.

3.12   LEAST SQUARES AND MAXIMUM LIKELIHOOD COMPARED

We return to the simulation experiment whose results are summarized in Table 3-13. The experimental design favors the ML method because of its use of normal error vectors. Nevertheless, the results of ML are not good at all when Σ is unknown. This raises the question of whether there are viable estimation methods (other than ML) that avoid estimating Σ. For example, we can simply minimize the sum of the squared residuals over all n equations and all countries. That is, if e_{ic} is such a residual (corresponding to the error or disturbance ϵ_{ic}), we minimize the sum over $c = 1, \ldots, 30$ of

$$\sum_{i=1}^{n} e_{ic}^2 = e_c' \Sigma^{*-1} e_c, \tag{12.1}$$

where $e_c = [e_{1c} \ldots e_{n-1,c}]'$ and Σ^* is the square matrix of order $n-1$ whose diagonal and off-diagonal elements are $1 - 1/n$ and $-1/n$, respectively (see the end of Section 3.6). To verify the equal sign in (12.1) we introduce ι as a column vector consisting of $n-1$ unit elements. Then $\Sigma^* = I_{n-1} - (1/n)\iota\iota'$ and $\Sigma^{*-1} = I_{n-1} + \iota\iota'$. The verification is completed when we note that $e_{nc} = -\iota'e_c$.

Alternatively, we may want to minimize a weighted sum of squared residuals of the form $e_{ic}^2/\bar{w}_i$, where $\bar{w}_i$ is the average (over the 30 countries) of the budget shares of good i. Thus, we minimize the sum over $c = 1, \ldots, 30$ of

$$\sum_{i=1}^{n} (e_{ic}^2/\bar{w}_i) = e_c' \Sigma^{**-1} e_c, \tag{12.2}$$

where Σ^{**} is a square matrix of order $n-1$ whose diagonal elements are of the form $\bar{w}_i(1 - \bar{w}_i)$ and whose off-diagonal elements are of the form $-\bar{w}_i\bar{w}_j$. The verification of the equal sign in (12.2) is left to the reader.

The two estimation methods discussed above are equivalent to the minimization of the quadratic form in (11.1) when Σ is appropriately interpreted (as Σ^* or as Σ^{**}). We can implement this minimization by means of Newton's method, using equations (9.6) and (9.8) of Section 2.9, given this interpretation of Σ. The numerical results are summarized in columns 9 and 10 of Table 3–13 for unweighted LS (based on Σ^*) and in columns 11 and 12 for weighted LS (based on Σ^{**}). The latter results tend to be better. A comparison of columns 7 and 12 shows convincingly that little if anything is gained by estimating the matrix Σ from the sample. Table 3–15 displays the 500 sampling errors of the four alternative ϕ estimators. The picture of ML with known Σ is the best, that of unweighted LS worst, and those of weighted LS and of ML with unknown Σ are about the same.

3.13 L_p-NORM ESTIMATION OF NONLINEAR SYSTEMS

Aasness and Nyquist (1983) were the first to consider L_p-norm estimators of systems of demand equations. Here we shall be particularly interested in the

Table 3-15.   Sampling Errors of Four Estimators of the Income Flexibility.

Interval	ML (Σ known)	ML (Σ unknown)	LS (unweighted)	LS (weighted)
−.20, −.18	0	0	1	0
−.18, −.16	0	0	6	0
−.16, −.14	0	0	5	0
−.14, −.12	0	0	10	5
−.12, −.10	1	9	15	9
−.10, −.08	15	14	26	18
−.08, −.06	23	38	29	40
−.06, −.04	42	51	48	35
−.04, −.02	85	70	56	69
−.02, 0	96	84	56	83
0, .02	106	86	57	75
.02, .04	64	61	68	77
.04, .06	36	34	41	45
.06, .08	19	31	34	21
.08, .10	13	14	20	13
.10, .12	0	4	17	6
.12, .14	0	4	6	4
.14, .16	0	0	3	0
.16, .18	0	0	2	0
.18, .20	0	0	0	0

performance of such estimators when the error distributions are fat-tailed mixtures of normal distributions. The account that follows is based on Theil, Rosalsky, and McManus (1985).

Recall the minimization of the sum over c of (12.2). The L_p-norm extension of this problem is the minimization of

$$\sum_{i=1}^{n} \sum_{c=1}^{30} |e_{ic}/\sqrt{\bar{w}_i}|^p. \tag{13.1}$$

For $p = 2$ this amounts to the weighted LS approach considered in the last two columns of Table 3-13. Here we shall extend this to $1 < p \le 2$. A simple way to achieve this numerically is by means of the following iterative LS procedure. We write (13.1) as

$$\sum_{i=1}^{n} \bar{w}_i^{-p/2} \sum_{c=1}^{30} |e_{ic}|^{p-2} e_{ic}^2. \tag{13.2}$$

Table 3-16. L_p-Norm Estimation of a Nonlinear System with

| Parameter (1) | True value (2) | RMSEs for k = 1 | | | |
		p = 2 (3)	p = 1.75 (4)	p = 1.5 (5)	p = 1.25 (6)
α_i Food	1620	125	125	127	131
Beverages	558	63	63	65	69
Clothing	839	58	58	60	63
Rent	1448	79	79	82	88
Furnishings	982	52	52	54	56
Medical	888	41	41	43	46
Transport	1179	65	65	66	70
Recreation	692	42	42	44	46
Education	535	63	63	65	68
Other	1260	70	70	72	75
β_i Food	− 1543	100	100	102	106
Beverages	8	51	51	53	56
Clothing	− 46	47	47	48	51
Rent	315	64	64	66	71
Furnishings	253	41	41	42	44
Medical	237	32	33	34	36
Transport	295	56	56	57	61
Recreation	193	34	34	34	36
Education	− 40	57	57	58	61
Other	328	57	58	59	62
ϕ Income flexibility	− 5259	497	496	504	525
Median RMSE ratio[b]	n.a.[c]	100	100.3	102.4	107.9

a. All entries (except those in the bottom row) to be divided by 10,000.
b. See text.
c. n.a. = not applicable.

Given fixed $|e_{ic}|^{p-2}$, the minimization of (13.2) is performed with Newton's method. Once the coefficient values have been obtained, we compute the associated $|e_{ic}|^{p-2}$ for each pair (i, c) and substitute this into (13.2). This procedure is continued until convergence.

Also recall the normal mixtures introduced in Section 3.5, with covariance matrix (5.1) and kurtosis coefficient (5.2). Our present sample size is thirty (rather than thirty-one). Again we select two observations at random which we multiply by the square root of k; the kurtosis is then zero for $k = 1$, 1.17 for $k = 4$ and 5.08 for $k = 9$. The results for 500 trials (the same as those

Fat-Tailed Error Distributions.[a]

RMSEs for $k = 4$				RMSEs for $k = 9$			
$p = 2$ (7)	$p = 1.75$ (8)	$p = 1.5$ (9)	$p = 1.25$ (10)	$p = 2$ (11)	$p = 1.75$ (12)	$p = 1.5$ (13)	$p = 1.25$ (14)
137	134	134	138	154	145	141	142
70	69	69	72	80	74	72	74
65	63	63	66	74	69	67	68
87	86	87	92	99	93	91	94
57	56	57	58	65	61	59	60
45	44	45	48	51	48	47	49
73	71	71	74	84	77	74	76
47	46	46	48	53	50	48	49
71	69	69	72	81	75	72	74
77	76	76	79	88	82	80	81
110	108	108	111	124	117	114	115
56	56	56	59	64	61	59	60
52	51	51	53	59	55	54	55
71	70	70	74	82	76	74	76
45	45	45	46	52	48	47	47
36	35	36	38	40	38	38	39
62	61	61	64	71	66	64	66
37	37	37	38	43	40	39	39
63	62	62	65	72	67	65	66
63	62	63	66	71	67	66	68
541	528	529	546	610	568	551	560
100	98.1	98.5	102.4	100	93.5	90.6	92.5

used in Table 3-13) are shown in Table 3-16 for these three values of k and for $p = 2$, 1.75, 1.5 and 1.25. Note that column 3 (for $k = 1$, $p = 2$) agrees, as it should, with the last column of Table 3-13. Since none of the methods considered in Table 3-16 exhibits significant biases, we do not report the means over the 500 trials but only the RMSEs around the true value.

RMSEs for $k = 1$ are shown in columns 3 through 6. Here the errors are normal. Simple weighted least squares (column 3) and L_p-norm estimators with $p = 1.75$ perform the best and have virtually identical RMSEs. The RMSEs of the L_p-norm estimators with $p = 1.5$ and $p = 1.25$ are almost all larger. The bottom row of the table provides a convenient summary: For each of the twenty-one coefficients (and for each k) we express the RMSE at $p = 1.75$, 1.5 and 1.25 as a percentage of the RMSE at $p = 2$, and the figures shown in that row are the medians of these twenty-one percentages.

Columns 7 through 10 give the RMSEs for $k = 4$. The tails of the error distribution are now fatter than for $k = 1$, and the L_p-norm estimators with $p = 1.75$ and $p = 1.5$ basically tie for the best estimator based on their RMSEs. The fattest tails are those underlying columns 11 through 14 where $k = 9$. All three L_p-norm estimators with $p < 2$ perform better than weighted least squares, and $p = 1.5$ is the clear winner overall. Apparently, the RMSEs are U-shaped between $p = 2$ and $p = 1$, and the value $p = 1.5$ seems to be near the minimum.

3.14   BOOTSTRAPPING FOR STANDARD ERRORS OF THE L_p NORM

Although the merits of L_p-norm estimators have been adequately demonstrated, we should emphasize that we have obtained only point estimators and no measure of variability such as a standard error. Fortunately, there is an interesting technique, called bootstrapping and proposed by Efron (1979), that enables us to obtain an approximate standard error numerically.

Consider again the L_p-norm estimator with $p = 1.5$ for a normal mixture with $k = 9$. The RMSEs of such estimators were shown in column 13 of Table 3–16, but here we consider only one such coefficient vector (consisting of $\hat{\alpha}_i$'s, $\hat{\beta}_i$'s, and $\hat{\phi}$) for one particular sample. Associated with these coefficients are thirty residual vectors ($e_{1c}, e_{2c}, \ldots$), one for each country. The bootstrapping method is a simulation experiment whose design is conventional with respect to the true coefficients (these are the $\hat{\alpha}_i$'s, ... of the sample drawn) and the values of the independent variables, but not with respect to the error distribution. The method assigns probability 1/30 to each of the thirty residual vectors ($e_{1c}, e_{2c}, \ldots$); it draws from this distribution thirty times independently with replacement and it combines the thirty vectors thus obtained with the coefficients and the values of the independent variables to obtain new values of the dependent variables. These new values constitute a bootstrap replication. For each such replication we can obtain the L_p-norm estimate with $p = 1.5$. If we do this a large number of times, we can compare the means over all replications with the true coefficient values of the experiment to assess whether bias is present. Similarly, the bootstrap standard error is computed as the RMSE of the coefficient estimates of the successive bootstrap replications from the same true value.

How well does this procedure work? This question is difficult to answer when we do not know the sampling distribution of the estimator (as is the case for L_p-norm estimators of a nonlinear system whose error distribution is a mixture of two normal distributions). However, the procedure described in the next paragraph, based on Freedman and Peters (1984) but in a different context, enables us to overcome this problem.

We choose the experimental design underlying column 13 of Table 3-16: $k = 9$ and $p = 1.5$. Columns 3 and 4 of Table 3-17 show the mean over 200 trials and their RMSE (around the true value given in column 2). These 200 trials are now viewed as constituting the outer loop of a new experiment. For each pass in this outer loop we use the bootstrap in order to approximate the RMSEs in column 4. Let $(e_{1c}, e_{2c}, \dots)$ be one of the thirty residual vectors of one such pass. We assign probability 1/30 to each of these vectors

Table 3-17. Bootstrapping for Standard Errors of L_p-Norm Estimates.

			Outer loop		Inner loop	
Parameter (1)		True value (2)	Mean (3)	RMSE (4)	Mean (5)	RMSE (6)
α_i	Food	0.1620	0.1619	0.0136	0.1620	0.0137
	Beverages, tobacco	0.0558	0.0557	0.0076	0.0558	0.0072
	Clothing, footwear	0.0839	0.0832	0.0071	0.0832	0.0066
	Gross rent, fuel	0.1448	0.1458	0.0092	0.1457	0.0088
	House furnishings, operations	0.0982	0.0986	0.0057	0.0986	0.0057
	Medical care	0.0888	0.0885	0.0046	0.0884	0.0047
	Transport, communication	0.1179	0.1183	0.0079	0.1182	0.0075
	Recreation	0.0692	0.0686	0.0045	0.0687	0.0048
	Education	0.0535	0.0540	0.0073	0.0541	0.0069
	Other	0.1260	0.1255	0.0077	0.1255	0.0078
β_i	Food	−0.1543	−0.1550	0.0112	−0.1551	0.0111
	Beverages, tobacco	0.0008	0.0009	0.0058	0.0010	0.0057
	Clothing, footwear	−0.0046	−0.0052	0.0059	−0.0052	0.0054
	Gross rent, fuel	0.0315	0.0316	0.0075	0.0316	0.0071
	House furnishings, operations	0.0253	0.0255	0.0047	0.0255	0.0046
	Medical care	0.0237	0.0236	0.0036	0.0235	0.0038
	Transport, communication	0.0295	0.0300	0.0064	0.0300	0.0061
	Recreation	0.0193	0.0193	0.0037	0.0193	0.0038
	Education	−0.0040	−0.0037	0.0068	−0.0036	0.0063
	Other	0.0328	0.0331	0.0065	0.0330	0.0065
ϕ	Income flexibility	−0.5259	−0.5274	0.0502	−0.5271	0.0508

and draw from this distribution thirty times with replacement. Using this new set of error vectors together with the coefficient estimates of this pass in the outer loop (and the original values of the independent variables), we obtain new values of the dependent variables from which new coefficient estimates can be computed. This is repeated fifty times for each of the 200 passes through the outer loop. We compute the mean of the fifty estimates and their RMSE (around the value of the corresponding pass through the outer loop). Column 5 of Table 3–17 contains the mean of the 200 means, and column 6 gives the RMS of the 200 RMSEs. The correspondence of columns 4 and 6 is encouraging, thus suggesting that the bootstrap provides a viable method for obtaining standard errors of L_p-norm coefficient estimates in nonlinear systems.

3.15   MORE ON BOOTSTRAPPING FOR STANDARD ERRORS

Although we introduced bootstrapping in Section 3.14 in the specific context of L_p-norm estimators, it should be obvious that the method has much wider applicability. For example, we concluded at the end of Section 3.10 that the approximate standard errors obtained from (9.2) by substituting $\hat{\Sigma}$ for Σ are unsatisfactory. But we do not have to compute standard errors in this way; we can use the residual vectors associated with $\hat{\delta}(\hat{\Sigma})$ to obtain bootstrap replications of this coefficient vector. Also, recall the second peril of symmetry-constrained estimation (Section 3.9) and the analogous problem of the asymptotic standard errors of ML estimates (Section 3.11). As we shall illustrate in this section, such problems can be avoided by bootstrapping, at least to a large degree.

In contrast to the earlier simulations discussed in this chapter, bootstrapping avoids distributional assumptions such as normality. The error distribution used by bootstrapping is discrete and it is based on the observed residuals; hence, the technique may be described as distribution free. But sometimes we do know that the error distribution has a particular form. Does this knowledge enable us to obtain more accurate standard errors than those obtained from ordinary bootstrapping?

We return to the ML estimation of the Rotterdam model according to Laitinen's experimental design; see Table 3–14 in Section 3.11. Theil, Rosalsky, and Finke (1984) used this design to answer the question raised in the previous paragraph. They followed Laitinen's approach by using systems of $n = 5, 8, 11$, and 14 equations; in Table 3–18 we present their results for $n = 5$ and 11, with the parameters and their true values shown in columns 1 and 2.

Table 3-18. A Comparison of Discrete and Normal Bootstraps.[a]

Parameter (1)	True value (2)	Outer loop		Inner loop (discrete)			Inner loop (normal)			Ratios			
		Mean (3)	RMSE (4)	Mean (5)	RMSE (6)	RMSASE (7)	Mean (8)	RMSE (9)	RMSASE (10)	6/4 (11)	9/4 (12)	7/4 (13)	10/4 (14)
					Five-equation system									
θ_i $i=1$	334	326	93	327	86	78	325	88	77	93	94	84	83
$i=2$	1615	1619	201	1619	197	174	1616	196	173	98	98	87	86
$i=3$	2240	2213	268	2218	248	214	2210	247	214	93	92	80	80
$i=4$	1797	1823	194	1822	170	149	1823	173	149	88	89	77	77
$i=5$	4013	4019	350	4015	334	286	4025	331	286	95	94	82	82
ϕ	−6000	−5972	313	−5991	308	277	−5991	315	277	99	101	89	89
					Eleven-equation system									
θ_i $i=1$	107	98	50	98	42	29	98	42	29	84	84	58	59
$i=2$	516	528	108	526	98	70	529	99	70	91	91	64	65
$i=3$	715	697	171	696	131	86	698	131	87	77	77	50	51
$i=4$	574	584	89	585	77	51	585	78	51	87	88	57	58
$i=5$	1282	1262	158	1263	135	87	1262	135	87	85	86	55	55
$i=6$	87	85	33	85	26	17	85	26	17	80	80	51	52
$i=7$	682	706	117	704	96	67	706	97	67	82	83	58	58
$i=8$	454	464	141	461	107	68	466	103	69	75	73	48	49
$i=9$	527	531	126	531	103	68	532	100	69	82	80	54	54
$i=10$	4597	4587	360	4592	281	178	4584	274	179	78	76	49	50
$i=11$	459	456	86	459	80	48	455	74	49	93	86	56	57
ϕ	−6000	−5977	463	−5996	375	233	−5992	370	235	81	80	50	51

a. All entries to be divided by 10^4 except those in the last four columns (which are ratios in percentage form).

As in Section 3.14, the bootstrap design consists of an outer loop and an inner loop. The outer loop, consisting of 100 trials, is obtained from quasi-normal error vectors with zero mean and the covariance matrix Σ of Laitinen's design. The means over the 100 trials and their RMSEs around the true value are shown in columns 3 and 4 of Table 3–18. Again, our objective is to verify how accurately these RMSEs are approximated by bootstrap methods.

Since the sample size of Laitinen's design is thirty-one, we assign mass 1/31 to each residual vector in each pass through the outer loop. There are 100 bootstrap replications for each such pass. We use these replications to compute means and RMSEs (around the value of the corresponding pass through the outer loop) and also RMSASEs (using the ML information matrix). There are 100 such means, RMSEs and RMSASEs because there are 100 passes through the outer loop. Columns 5 through 7 show the mean of the 100 means and the RMS of the 100 RMSEs and of the 100 RMSASEs.

Next we consider an inner loop that exploits the knowledge that the outer loop has normal error vectors. Each pass through the outer loop yields thirty-one ML residual vectors; in columns 8 through 10 we use these vectors exclusively in the form of their moment matrix. The inner loop trials are now obtained from pseudo-normal error vectors with zero mean and this particular moment matrix (which takes different values for different passes through the outer loop). A line-by-line comparison shows that the results are hardly different from those in columns 5 through 7 for the discrete bootstrap. Thus, in spite of the fact that the true error distribution is normal, it is not the case that the normal bootstrap yields any gain over the conventional discrete bootstrap.

The ratios in the last four columns of the table provide an easy comparison. In columns 11 and 12 we divide the RMSEs of the discrete and the normal bootstrap, respectively, by the corresponding RMSE of the outer loop. In columns 13 and 14 we use the same denominator, but the numerators are the RMSASEs in the inner loop. The results are pairwise virtually identical, thus confirming that exploiting normality yields no gain. The RMSASEs in columns 13 and 14 are clearly worse than the RMSEs in columns 11 and 12, but the latter are not perfect either; they, too, understate the RMSEs of the outer loop. See Theil, Rosalsky, and Finke (1984) for attempts to correct for this bias.

3.16   THE DISTANCE FROM THE EQUATOR AS AN INSTRUMENTAL VARIABLE

Until this point we have assumed that the independent variables of our demand systems (real income and relative prices) are measured without error.

This is obviously a simplifying assumption. An alternative procedure is to use an instrumental variable that is not subject to error. For example, we may question the accuracy of the per capita real incomes in our cross-country demand model. Theil and Finke (1983) introduced the distance of the country's capital from the equator as an instrumental variable for the logarithm of the country's per capita real income. In qualitative terms this means that poverty is considered as being approximately a tropical problem. Here we pursue this approach and we illustrate how the bootstrapping method can be used to yield standard errors for instrumental variable (IV) estimates.

We return to equation (9.2) of Section 2.9. Since we shall operate conditionally on ϕ, we subtract the substitution term from both sides:

$$y_{ic} - \phi z_{ic} = \alpha_i + \beta_i q_c + \epsilon_{ic}. \tag{16.1}$$

Let $y_i(\phi, \beta)$ be the vector whose cth element ($c = 1, \ldots, 30$) equals the left side of (16.1). We write this equation in matrix form as $y_i(\phi, \beta) = X\theta_i + \epsilon_i$, where $\theta_i = (\alpha_i, \beta_i)'$ and X is the 30×2 matrix whose cth row is $(1, q_c)$. Let Z be the 30×2 matrix of the instrumental variables, with cth row $(1, d_c)$, where d_c is the distance of the capital of country c from the equator. Then the IV estimator of θ_i given ϕ is $(Z'X)^{-1}Z'y_i(\phi, \beta)$, which depends on the β vector. The estimates presented in Table 3–19, for three values of ϕ, are obtained by iterating on β. The results are encouraging since most of the IV estimates are close to the ML estimates (shown in column 2). The major exception is the β_i of transport and communications; its IV estimates are about 50 percent below the ML estimate.

How accurate are the IV estimates? Finke and Theil (1984a) performed a bootstrap experiment to answer this question. They used the IV coefficient estimates (columns 3 through 5) as the true parameter values; they also used the associated residual vectors and the thirty values of per capita real income and of each of the ten prices. By assigning mass 1/30 to each of the residual vectors and then drawing from this distribution with replacement thirty times, we obtain a new vector $y_i(\phi, \beta)$ for the left variable of the ith IV equation. The IV technique is then applied again and this procedure is repeated 500 times. The means of the 500 bootstrap replications are so close to the corresponding true values (columns 3 through 5) that we do not reproduce them. The RMSEs are shown in columns 6 through 8, along with the asymptotic standard error of the data-based ML estimate in column 9. Not surprisingly, the bootstrap RMSEs of the IV estimates exceed this asymptotic standard error, particularly for $\phi = -0.7$, which is farthest from the ML estimate of ϕ. See Finke and Theil (1984a) for further details, and Theil (1979) for other aspects of observational errors in demand systems.

Table 3-19. Instrumental Variable Estimates.

| Parameter (1) | ML estimate (2) | IV estimates conditional on ϕ | | | Bootstrap RMSEs | | | Asymptotic standard error ML estimate (9) |
		$\phi = -0.5$ (3)	$\phi = -0.6$ (4)	$\phi = -0.7$ (5)	$\phi = -0.5$ (6)	$\phi = -0.6$ (7)	$\phi = -0.7$ (8)	
α_i Food	.162	.164	.162	.160	.016	.016	.017	.012
Beverages, tobacco	.056	.058	.058	.058	.009	.009	.010	.006
Clothing, footwear	.084	.090	.091	.092	.009	.009	.009	.006
Gross rent, fuel	.145	.151	.150	.149	.010	.010	.012	.008
House furnishings, operations	.098	.099	.097	.096	.006	.007	.006	.005
Medical care	.089	.094	.093	.092	.006	.005	.006	.004
Transport, communications	.118	.106	.105	.104	.010	.009	.009	.007
Recreation	.069	.073	.071	.069	.005	.005	.005	.004
Education	.054	.045	.051	.060	.008	.009	.012	.006
Other	.126	.121	.121	.120	.009	.009	.009	.007
β_i Food	−.154	−.152	−.155	−.158	.015	.015	.015	.010
Beverages, tobacco	.001	.003	.003	.003	.008	.008	.009	.005
Clothing, footwear	−.005	.002	.003	.004	.008	.008	.008	.005
Gross rent, fuel	.032	.038	.037	.037	.009	.009	.011	.006
House furnishings, operations	.025	.026	.025	.024	.006	.006	.006	.004
Medical care	.024	.029	.028	.027	.005	.005	.006	.003
Transport, communications	.030	.017	.017	.016	.009	.008	.008	.006
Recreation	.019	.023	.021	.020	.005	.004	.004	.003
Education	−.004	−.013	−.007	.001	.008	.009	.011	.005
Other	.033	.027	.028	.027	.008	.008	.009	.006

3.17   THE GOODNESS OF FIT OF A DEMAND SYSTEM

The standard measure of fit in econometrics is the multiple correlation coefficient. Although this coefficient refers to one equation, it can and has been used to measure the fit of individual demand equations that constitute a demand system. On the other hand, since the equations are fitted as a system, it is clearly attractive to measure the fit of a system as a whole. The multiple correlation coefficient can be generalized for an equation system. Actually, this can be done in several ways; see McElroy (1977) for a comparison of three different generalizations.

Here we discuss a measure from information theory that is specifically applicable to allocation models. Demand models fall under this category; the allocation proportions are budget shares that are nonnegative and add up to 1. Let w_{ic} be the observed budget share of good i in country c. As a measure of poorness of fit of the model with respect to these observed shares we use the information inaccuracy,

$$I_c = \sum_{i=1}^{n} w_{ic} \log \frac{w_{ic}}{\hat{w}_{ic}}, \tag{17.1}$$

where n is the number of goods ($n = 10$ in our case) and $\hat{w}_{ic}$ is the predicted budget share of good i in country c that is implied by the model. Always, $I_c \geq 0$; we have $I_c = 0$ if and only if the predictions are perfect ($\hat{w}_{ic} = w_{ic}$ for each i).

Column 2 of Table 3–20, from Finke (1983), shows I_c for each of the thirty countries of the sample. To obtain $\hat{w}_{ic}$ we substitute ML estimates for α_i, β_i, and ϕ in equation (6.6) of Section 2.6 and we replace ϵ_{ic} by zero. Next we add the price term in equation (6.7) of that section to both sides of (6.6), and we interpret all variables on the right (Q_c, p_{ic}, $\bar{p}_i$, and w_{ic}) as the observed values. The mean of the thirty values I_c, shown in line 31, is 249×10^{-4}. Three countries have an inaccuracy exceeding twice this mean: Iran, Syria, and Pakistan (lines 20, 21, and 29).

The entry in line 32, 311×10^{-4}, is the mean of the I_c's that are obtained when we ignore the price terms. (The model is then simplified to

$$\hat{w}_{ic} = \alpha_i + \beta_i \log Q_c,$$

with α_i, β_i specified as the ML estimates in Table 2–5.) The increase in the average inaccuracy, from 249×10^{-4} in line 31 to 311×10^{-4} in line 32, is about 25 percent, thus indicating that it is important to take into consideration that the ten goods have different relative prices in different countries.

Table 3-20. Information Inaccuracies Measuring the Fit of a Cross-Country Demand System.[a]

Country (1)	I_c (2)	Food (3)	Beverages, tobacco (4)	Clothing, footwear (5)	Gross rent, fuel (6)	House furnishings, operations (7)	Medical care (8)	Transport, communications (9)	Recreation (10)	Education (11)	Other (12)
						I_{ic}					
					The thirty countries of the sample						
United States	183	1	50	8	24	55	5	52	1	3	2
Luxembourg	195	3	23	2	17	14	33	20	66	18	17
Denmark	457	14	29	66	184	4	61	3	8	38	109
France	76	1	11	17	0	16	17	3	1	15	1
Germany	138	35	5	3	1	11	45	10	3	8	34
Austria	135	20	25	26	15	3	1	1	6	19	34
Belgium	97	8	19	7	0	54	1	0	16	0	1
Netherlands	89	6	0	0	3	10	2	4	50	3	20
United Kingdom	154	30	1	5	32	29	13	4	30	1	29
Spain	199	137	46	1	1	13	0	7	11	22	0
Japan	147	8	20	0	0	48	21	4	32	1	26
Italy	70	25	0	0	0	36	3	3	3	1	10
Hungary	295	4	99	1	117	4	0	38	53	0	8
Ireland	221	1	3	16	33	8	23	14	1	1	146
Uruguay	430	207	127	41	8	19	8	6	5	45	40
Poland	232	0	42	32	46	10	0	62	9	19	33
Mexico	388	57	173	5	9	105	14	1	57	1	5
Yugoslavia	137	58	12	0	32	23	19	0	9	6	4
Romania	133	1	0	81	27	0	0	33	1	4	0

Iran	523	49	185	81	195	8	0	5	34	15	10
Syria	534	232	27	28	16	2	56	139	80	9	64
Colombia	240	50	0	8	35	0	10	24	10	75	65
Brazil	142	0	86	3	2	11	2	27	1	8	12
Korea	405	22	265	35	15	71	12	2	9	0	9
Malaysia	344	147	0	40	8	4	4	156	28	31	8
Thailand	162	10	70	2	58	1	9	3	25	0	0
Philippines	316	6	31	18	14	0	5	175	44	38	4
Sri Lanka	178	30	27	37	23	13	9	28	5	16	17
Pakistan	552	13	84	40	40	6	33	136	34	126	74
India	289	1	52	53	5	0	19	158	0	1	16
Arithmetic means											
Including prices	249	39	50	22	32	19	14	37	21	17	27
Excluding prices	311	55	60	25	41	18	23	35	19	50	26
Outliers											
Malawi	539	25	1	94	2	358	6	55	38	6	0
Kenya	1536	708	17	75	58	621	17	65	1	362	19
Zambia	942	319	124	71	51	44	36	10	12	213	263
Jamaica	916	118	88	191	9	4	23	72	5	1	527
Soviet Union	1116	48	493	351	199	26	56	64	0	1	0

a. All entries to be divided by 10^4.
Source: Finke (1983).

Four of the last five lines of the table deal with the countries that were deleted from the original group of thirty-four: the three African countries and Jamaica. Their I_c's tend to be much higher than the mean in line 31, thus confirming their position as outliers. The last line of the table deals with the Soviet Union. Finke (1983) used data from Joint Economic Committee (1981) to obtain a Q_c of the Soviet Union equal to 34.4 percent of the 1975 U.S. value (comparable to the 1960 Dutch level and the 1964 Spanish and Italian levels in Table 2–13), but she could not use price data. Therefore, the entry 1116×10^{-4} in the last line should be compared with 311×10^{-4} in line 32, not with 249×10^{-4} in line 31; see Finke (1983) for further details.

The information inaccuracy defined in (17.1) refers to all $n = 10$ goods jointly. It is also possible to consider the predictive performance of the model with respect to good i only. This can be done by combining all goods other than i, yielding

$$I_{ic} = w_{ic} \log \frac{w_{ic}}{\hat{w}_{ic}} + (1 - w_{ic}) \log \frac{1 - w_{ic}}{1 - \hat{w}_{ic}}, \tag{17.2}$$

which is shown in columns 3 through 12 for each good i and each country c. The entries in this part of the table indicate that the major source of misfit is house furnishings and operations for Malawi (line 33), food for Kenya and Zambia, "other" expenditures for Jamaica, and beverages and tobacco for the Soviet Union.

Remark 1. For the computation of the information inaccuracy (17.1) it is important that the observed and predicted shares add up to 1 exactly: $\Sigma_i w_{ic} = \Sigma_i \hat{w}_{ic} = 1$. If this is only approximately true (e.g., because of rounding errors), the value obtained for (17.1) may be dominated by the extent to which the sum constraint is violated; it may even be negative. See Theil (1975: 220–21).

Remark 2. If the errors $\hat{w}_{ic} - w_{ic}$ are small, we can expand the logarithm in (17.1) by means of a Taylor series. The leading term in the expansion is quadratic,

$$I_c \cong \tfrac{1}{2} \sum_{i=1}^{n} \frac{(\hat{w}_{ic} - w_{ic})^2}{w_{ic}}, \tag{17.3}$$

which shows that the information inaccuracy is approximately proportional to a chi-square as long as the prediction errors are small.

Remark 3. It is intuitively obvious that the fit is improved when we select a model for which a large number of parameters is fitted. Thus, the average inaccuracy (249×10^{-4} in line 31 of Table 3-20) is probably reduced when we adjust more parameters. See Theil (1975: Sec. 6.5) for a correction, based on the quadratic approximation (17.3), of the average information inaccuracy for the parameters adjusted.

3.18   MORE ON GOODNESS OF FIT

Table 3-20 clearly illustrates the advantages of the information inaccuracy. Not only does this measure take into account that the model is an allocation model, but it also describes the fit for each of the thirty individual observations. For example, we may be interested in the question of whether the fit is worse for the centrally planned economies: Hungary, Poland, Yugoslavia, and Romania. As the entries in column 2 and lines 13, 16, 18, and 19 indicate, their fit is not worse on the average compared with the mean shown in line 31. See Podkaminer, Finke, and Theil (1984) for more details on demand systems and centrally planned economies.

As an alternative to I_{ic} defined in (17.2), Strobel (1982) proposes

$$I_{Sic} = \hat{w}_{ic} - w_{ic} + w_{ic} \log \frac{w_{ic}}{\hat{w}_{ic}}. \tag{18.1}$$

Both I_{ic} and I_{Sic} have the property of vanishing when the prediction is perfect and of being positive otherwise, but I_{Sic} has the additional property of summing to the n-good inaccuracy (17.1): $I_c = \sum_i I_{Sic}$. Thus the Strobel measure provides a simple decomposition of the information inaccuracy over its constituent equations.

Table 3-21, from Fiebig, Finke, and Theil (1984), provides the results for the Strobel measures. This table is identical to Table 3-20 except that (18.1) is substituted for (17.2) in columns 3 through 12. A comparison of corresponding entries in these two tables shows that $I_{Sic} \leq I_{ic}$ or, equivalently,

$$\hat{w}_{ic} - w_{ic} \leq (1 - w_{ic}) \log \frac{1 - w_{ic}}{1 - \hat{w}_{ic}}. \tag{18.2}$$

always holds. This is indeed generally true, which follows from $\log \zeta \leq \zeta - 1$ for $\zeta = (1 - \hat{w}_{ic})/(1 - w_{ic})$. When w_{ic} and $\hat{w}_{ic}$ are both small (as is the case for most goods other than food), this ζ will be close to 1 so that the two sides of (18.2) are not far apart. This explains why corresponding entries in columns 4 through 12 in Tables 3-20 and 3-21 tend to be close to each other.

By dividing I_{Sic} by I_c we obtain the proportion of the inaccuracy of the model that is accounted for by the misfit of the demand equation for good i. These ratios are shown in percentage form in columns 3 through 12 of Table 3-22. For example, the first line of the table (for the U.S.) indicates that the

Table 3-21. Information Inaccuracies and Strobel Measures.[a]

Country (1)	I_c (2)	Food (3)	Beverages, tobacco (4)	Clothing, footwear (5)	Gross rent, fuel (6)	House furnishings, operations (7)	Medical care (8)	Transport, communications (9)	Recreation (10)	Education (11)	Other (12)
						Strobel measures					
				The thirty countries of the sample							
United States	183	1	48	8	20	50	4	46	1	3	1
Luxembourg	195	2	22	2	14	12	30	18	63	16	15
Denmark	457	12	27	61	157	3	57	3	7	34	97
France	76	1	11	16	0	14	15	3	1	14	1
Germany	138	29	4	2	1	10	40	9	3	8	31
Austria	135	16	24	24	14	3	1	1	6	18	30
Belgium	97	7	18	7	0	49	1	0	15	0	1
Netherlands	89	5	0	0	3	9	16	3	46	3	18
United Kingdom	154	24	1	5	27	26	13	3	28	1	25
Spain	199	103	44	1	1	12	0	7	10	21	0
Japan	147	6	19	0	0	45	19	4	30	1	23
Italy	70	18	0	0	0	33	3	3	3	0	9
Hungary	295	3	91	1	105	3	0	34	50	0	7
Ireland	221	1	3	15	29	8	22	12	1	1	129
Uruguay	430	153	118	37	7	17	7	6	5	43	36
Poland	232	0	38	29	42	9	0	57	9	18	30
Mexico	388	38	166	5	8	97	13	1	55	1	5
Yugoslavia	137	40	11	0	28	21	18	0	9	5	4
Romania	133	0	0	72	25	0	0	30	1	4	0

Iran	523	32	177	75	171	8	0	5	32	14	9
Syria	534	139	26	25	14	2	53	130	77	8	60
Colombia	240	31	0	7	32	0	9	22	10	70	59
Brazil	142	0	82	2	2	10	2	24	1	8	11
Korea	405	12	250	32	13	68	11	2	9	0	8
Malaysia	344	88	0	37	7	3	4	140	27	29	7
Thailand	162	6	66	2	53	1	8	3	24	0	0
Philippines	316	3	30	16	13	0	5	167	43	36	4
Sri Lanka	178	13	25	34	21	13	8	27	5	16	16
Pakistan	552	6	81	37	36	6	31	131	33	121	71
India	289	0	50	48	5	0	18	151	0	1	16
Arithmetic means											
Including prices	249	26	48	20	28	18	13	35	20	16	24
Excluding prices	311	36	57	22	36	17	21	32	18	47	24
Outliers											
Malawi	539	11	1	85	1	340	6	52	37	5	0
Kenya	1536	359	16	68	52	599	17	62	1	343	18
Zambia	942	171	118	65	47	42	35	10	12	198	245
Jamaica	916	75	82	178	8	4	22	65	5	1	477
Soviet Union	1116	33	454	311	181	24	53	59	0	1	0

a. All entries to be divided by 10^4.
Source: Fiebig, Finke, and Theil (1984).

Table 3–22. Relative Strobel Measures and Their Entropy.

Country (1)	Entropy (2)	Food (3)	Beverages, tobacco (4)	Clothing, footwear (5)	Gross rent, fuel (6)	House furnishings, operations (7)	Medical care (8)	Transport, communications (9)	Recreation (10)	Education (11)	Other (12)
						Relative Strobel measures (percentages)					
					The thirty countries of the sample						
United States	1.68	0	26	4	11	27	2	25	1	2	1
Luxembourg	1.99	1	11	1	7	6	15	9	32	8	8
Denmark	1.81	3	6	13	34	1	12	1	2	7	21
France	1.84	1	14	21	0	19	20	3	1	19	2
Germany	1.85	21	3	2	1	7	29	7	2	6	22
Austria	1.97	12	18	17	10	2	1	0	4	13	22
Belgium	1.40	7	18	7	0	50	1	0	15	0	1
Netherlands	1.47	6	0	0	3	10	2	4	52	3	20
United Kingdom	1.97	16	1	3	17	17	8	2	18	1	16
Spain	1.41	52	22	1	1	6	0	3	5	10	0
Japan	1.79	4	13	0	0	30	13	3	20	1	16
Italy	1.42	26	0	0	0	47	4	4	5	1	13
Hungary	1.49	1	31	0	36	1	0	12	17	0	2
Ireland	1.41	0	1	7	13	4	10	6	0	1	58
Uruguay	1.75	36	27	9	2	4	2	1	1	10	8
Poland	1.94	0	16	12	18	4	0	24	4	8	13
Mexico	1.54	10	43	1	2	25	3	0	14	0	1
Yugoslavia	1.86	29	8	0	21	16	13	0	7	4	3
Romania	1.16	0	0	54	19	0	0	23	1	3	0

Iran	1.63	6	34	14	33	1	0	1	6	3	2
Syria	1.92	26	5	5	3	0	10	24	14	2	11
Colombia	1.83	13	0	3	13	0	4	9	4	29	25
Brazil	1.38	0	58	2	1	7	1	17	1	5	8
Korea	1.30	3	62	8	3	17	3	0	2	0	2
Malaysia	1.62	26	0	11	2	1	1	41	8	8	2
Thailand	1.44	4	41	1	33	1	5	2	14	0	0
Philippines	1.52	1	9	5	4	0	1	53	13	11	1
Sri Lanka	2.18	7	14	19	12	7	5	15	3	9	9
Pakistan	2.00	1	15	7	7	1	6	24	6	22	13
India	1.37	0	17	17	2	0	6	52	0	0	5
Arithmetic means											
Including prices	1.66	11	19	8	11	7	5	14	8	7	10
Excluding prices	1.65	12	18	7	12	5	7	10	6	15	8
Outliers											
Malawi	1.19	2	0	16	0	63	1	10	7	1	0
Kenya	1.58	23	1	4	3	39	1	4	0	22	1
Zambia	1.94	18	13	7	5	4	4	1	1	21	26
Jamaica	1.45	8	9	19	1	0	2	7	1	0	52
Soviet Union	1.51	3	41	28	16	2	5	5	0	0	0

demand equations for beverages and tobacco, for house furnishings and operations, and for transport and communications contribute about equally to the misfit of the model and that their total contribution is almost 80 percent.

Column 2 of Table 3–22 contains the entropy of these ratios,

$$-\sum_{i=1}^{n} \frac{I_{Sic}}{I_c} \log \frac{I_{Sic}}{I_c}, \tag{18.3}$$

which varies between 0 and $\log n = \log 10 \cong 2.30$. This entropy takes values close to the maximum when the 10 equations contribute about equally to the inaccuracy I_c, and smaller values when I_c is dominated by few equations. The largest entropy is that of Sri Lanka (line 28); none of the ten equations contributed more than 20 percent of that country's I_c, and only two contributed less than 7 percent. The smallest entropy is that of Romania (line 19); the worst equation contributed more than 50 percent to Romania's I_c, while as many as seven equations contributed only 3 percent or less.

We can use the average information inaccuracy also as a criterion for estimation. Suppose that we have time series data, w_{it} being the budget share of good i in year t ($i = 1, \ldots, n$; $t = 1, \ldots, T$). Let $\hat{w}_{it}(\theta)$ be the predicted budget share of a model, given that θ is the parameter selected for this model. The estimation procedure minimizes the average information accuracy,

$$\bar{I}(\theta) = \frac{1}{T} \sum_{t=1}^{T} \sum_{i=1}^{n} w_{it} \log \frac{w_{it}}{\hat{w}_{it}(\theta)}, \tag{18.4}$$

with respect to θ. For example, we may have an addilog model of the form

$$\hat{w}_{it}(\theta) = \beta_i (p_{it}/M_t)^{\alpha_i} \bigg/ \sum_{k=1}^{n} \beta_k (p_{kt}/M_t)^{\alpha_k}, \tag{18.5}$$

with the β_i's satisfying $\beta_1 + \cdots + \beta_n = 1$. In that case θ may be viewed as consisting of $\beta_1, \ldots, \beta_{n-1}, \alpha_1, \ldots, \alpha_n$. Let θ_0 be the true value of θ and let us generate observed budget shares by

$$w_{it} = \hat{w}_{it}(\theta_0) + \epsilon_{it}, \tag{18.6}$$

where ϵ_{it} is quasi-random and satisfies $\epsilon_{1t} + \cdots + \epsilon_{nt} = 0$.

Theil, Finke, and Flood (1984) referred to the estimation of θ based on minimizing the information inaccuracy (18.4) as *minimum information* (MI) estimation. They applied the design outlined in the previous paragraph to the $T = 22$ years of Japanese data on the $n = 4$ goods that were discussed earlier in Section 2.8. The true values of the β_i's and α_i's are shown in column 2 of Table 3–23. The next four columns are the result of 500 trials, the

Table 3-23.   ML and MI Estimation of an Addilog Model.

Parameter (1)	True value (2)	Maximum likelihood		Minimum information	
		Mean (3)	RMSE (4)	Mean (5)	RMSE (6)
β_i Food	.4270	.4269	.001460	.4270	.001430
Clothing	.1270	.1271	.001029	.1271	.001029
Housing	.1580	.1580	.001574	.1580	.001525
Other	.2880	.2879	.001063	.2879	.001072
α_i Food	.900	.903	.0524	.903	.0504
Clothing	.870	.871	.0422	.871	.0410
Housing	.378	.382	.0743	.381	.0708
Other	.517	.519	.0539	.518	.0519

vectors $(\epsilon_{1t}, ..., \epsilon_{4t})$ for $t = 1, ..., 22$ and for each trial being independently generated as quasi-normal vectors with zero means and the same covariance matrix. The ML method used in columns 3 and 4 treats this matrix as unknown. The RMSEs of the MI estimates in column 6 tend to be smaller than those of the ML estimates in column 4, thus indicating that MI is a viable method of estimation.

Note that the MI procedure is distribution free, since minimizing (18.4) involves no distributional assumptions such as normality. For extensions of MI estimation to models with fat-tailed error distributions see Flood, Finke, and Theil (1984). For bootstrapping as a method for estimating standard errors of MI estimates see Finke and Theil (1984b).

3.19   HOW GOOD (OR BAD) IS THE PREFERENCE INDEPENDENCE ASSUMPTION?

When discussing the preference independence transformation at the end of Section 2.16, we noted that most of the demand specifications discussed in Chapter 2 avoided relationships of specific substitutibility or complementarity. It will be impossible to avoid such relationships when the demand system deals with more narrowly defined goods, such as beer, wine, and spirits; more will be said about that topic in Chapter 4. It seems plausible that the use of broader groups makes the independence assumption more realistic, but it is not at all clear that this assumption is fully realistic even then. Can we truly guarantee that food and "other expenditures" are unrelated when the latter category includes food consumed away from home?

Of course, it is impossible to provide such a guarantee. The problem is, however, that as soon as we abandon the preference independence assumption, the specification that emerges has double-subscript parameters. The model is then easily overparameterized. An example of such double-subscript parameters is the π_{ij}'s of Table 3–10 in Section 3.9. The true coefficient values in column 3 of that table are the data-based ML estimates, and so is the true covariance matrix Σ. For the off-diagonal π_{ij}'s, the RMSEs in column 5 all exceed the true values, thus illustrating the extent of the overparameterization. The situation is even worse for the RMSEs that are obtained when a matrix different from Σ is used.

The Deaton–Muellbauer model (AIDS) provides another example. The income component of AIDS is Working's model. Our evidence on this component has been satisfactory; see Tables 2–6 and 2–16 (Sections 2.8 and 2.16) on the proximity of the Japanese and Dutch time series estimates to the cross-country estimates. However, the price component of AIDS involves double-subscript parameters, thus carrying the danger of overparameterization when the number of equations is not small.

The assumption of preference independence should be viewed as a convenient simplification when broad groups of goods are considered. Allowing such goods to be specific substitutes or complements will in many cases yield estimates that are even less precise. (Remember that asymptotic standard errors provide a picture of this precision that is too optimistic.) A convenient way of analyzing the stability of such estimates is by reestimation, deleting one observation at a time. The reader may want to go back to Table 2–12 in Section 2.13, where we applied this procedure to a different problem (that of Frisch's conjecture on the income flexibility).

3.20   EXTENSIONS AND POSSIBILITIES FOR FUTURE RESEARCH

This final section of Chapter 3 summarizes miscellaneous topics. As in the corresponding section of Chapter 2, the subsections that follow are designed mainly to whet the reader's appetite.

Aggregation Over Goods

Dividing the consumer's expenditures into n categories requires a number of decisions, including the specification of n. For example, let us return to equation (6.6) of Section 2.6 for n goods:

$$y_{ic} = \alpha_i + \beta_i \log Q_c$$

$$+ \phi(w_{ic} + \beta_i) \left[\log \frac{p_{ic}}{\bar{p}_i} - \sum_{j=1}^{n} (w_{jc} + \beta_j) \log \frac{p_{jc}}{\bar{p}_j} \right] + \epsilon_{ic}. \quad (20.1)$$

In Section 2.8 we applied maximum likelihood to $n = 10$ goods: 1, food; 2, beverages and tobacco; 3, clothing and footwear; 4, gross rent and fuel; 5, house furnishings and operations; 6, medical care; 7, transport and communications; 8, recreation; 9, education; and 10, other consumption expenditures. But what happens when we combine some of these goods to groups and then apply maximum likelihood?

Flood, Rosalsky, and Theil (1984) considered this question by first combining the last three goods (numbered 8 through 10) into one aggregate, which yields a system of $n = 8$ equations. Next they combined the last five (6 through 10), yielding $n = 6$; then they combined the last seven, yielding $n = 4$; finally, the last nine, yielding $n = 2$. Of course, $n = 2$ amounts to a system for food and nonfood; since (20.1) is an allocation model consisting of $n - 1$ linearly independent equations, $n = 2$ basically means that the demand system is reduced to only one demand equation (for food or for nonfood).

The upper part of Table 3–24 shows the results for ϕ of the simulations for 500 independent trials, the parameter specification of the experiment being the data-based ML estimates discussed in Section 2.8. Note that disaggregation yields higher precision (column 3). This should be ascribed (at

Table 3–24. Income Flexibility Estimates at Different Levels of Aggregation.

Size of the system (n) (1)	Mean (2)	RMSE (3)	RMSASE (4)	Ratio 4/3 (5)
Cross-country: true $\phi = -0.526$				
10	−.529	.049	.029	.60
8	−.532	.056	.038	.68
6	−.532	.084	.065	.77
4	−.530	.123	.104	.84
2	−.528	.236	.208	.88
Time series: true $\phi = -0.6$				
14	−.603	.052	.028	.54
9	−.603	.055	.036	.66
6	−.602	.055	.041	.75
4	−.598	.063	.052	.84
2	−.599	.129	.124	.96

least in part) to the fact that preference independence for a larger n imposes more restrictions on the consumer's preferences. The RMSASEs in column 4 are obtained from the information matrix of the ML procedure. The ratios in column 5 show that the overstatement of the precision of the ML estimate of ϕ by its asymptotic standard error increases with increasing n.

The lower part of the table shows similar results. It deals with an analogous experiment based on Laitinen's (1978) time series design for $n = 14$ goods. For details, also on parameters other than ϕ, see Flood, Rosalsky, and Theil (1984).

Rational Random Behavior

Given the difficulties we faced with the unknown error covariance matrix Σ, it is natural to ask whether it is possible to model this matrix by means of a small number of parameters. One answer is provided by the theory of rational random behavior. Details on this theory are given in Chapters 7 and 8 of Theil (1980); see also Bowman, Laitinen, and Theil (1979). A brief account and some illustrations follow here and in the next subsection.

The theory of rational random behavior is formulated in terms of *decision distributions*. Decisions are then random rather than fixed, which is in agreement with the random error terms that are introduced in the decision-maker's behavioral equations. When the consumer's behavior is random, he does not attain the budget-constrained utility maximum. Accordingly, the expected loss is one consideration for the selection of a decision distribution; in the consumer's case this expected loss is the expectation of the excess of the utility maximum over the utility level attained. The reason why the consumer does not actually attain the utility maximum is that he considers it too costly to seek information on the prices of all goods. Therefore, he minimizes the sum of the expected loss and the cost of information.

The approach of rational random behavior defines information in the way in which this is done in statistical information theory, similar to (17.1). The result is that the optimal decision distribution (which minimizes the sum of the expected loss and the cost of information) depends on the marginal cost of information. If this marginal cost is zero, the decisionmaker acquires as much information as is necessary to reduce the expected loss to zero. The decision made is then nonstochastic and equal to the *theoretically optimal decision*; that is, to the decision that would be optimal if information were costless. If the marginal cost of information is positive but small, we can apply an asymptotic expansion to obtain a multivariate normal decision distribution with a mean vector equal to the theoretically optimal decision and a covariance matrix that is known up to a scalar multiplier.

We proceed to illustrate this result for the addilog model. Recall from (18.5) that this model implies a budget share of good i equal to the ratio of $\beta_i(p_i/M)^{\alpha_i}$ to $\sum_k \beta_k(p_k/M)^{\alpha_k}$. We shall write this ratio as $\bar{w}_i$ to indicate that this is the theoretically optimal decision for the budget share of good i. For the actual values of these shares according to rational random behavior we have

$$\log \frac{w_i}{w_j} = \log \frac{\beta_i}{\beta_j} + \alpha_i \log \frac{p_i}{M} - \alpha_j \log \frac{p_j}{M} + u_i - u_j, \qquad (20.2)$$

where u_i and u_j are random variables. The asymptotic decision distribution is in this case equivalent to the independence and normality of $u_1, \ldots, u_n$ with zero means and variances proportional to $(1-\alpha_i)/\bar{w}_i$. The positive sign of these variances follows from $\alpha_i < 1$, which is a necessary and sufficient condition for the negative semidefiniteness with rank $n-1$ of the Slutsky matrix; see Theil (1975: 97–98).

Two Applications of Rational Random Behavior

Next we consider the Rotterdam model with a disturbance ϵ_{it} added:

$$\bar{w}_{it} Dq_{it} = \theta_i DQ_t + \sum_{j=1}^{n} \pi_{ij} Dp_{jt} + \epsilon_{it}. \qquad (20.3)$$

The consumer's decision variable is here the quantity component of the change in the ith budget share. This first-difference formulation implies that the theory of rational random behavior must be interpreted conditionally; that is, this theory describes the distribution of today's decision variables, given yesterday's values of the quantities bought.

The right side of (20.3) excluding ϵ_{it} is the theoretically optimal value of the ith decision variable. The asymptotic decision distribution of rational random behavior implies that $(\epsilon_{1t}, \ldots, \epsilon_{nt})$ is multivariate normal with zero means and a covariance matrix equal to a scalar multiple of the Slutsky matrix $[\pi_{ij}]$. Since the latter matrix is negative semidefinite and since ϕ is negative, we can write the covariance of ϵ_{it} and ϵ_{jt} as $\sigma^2 \pi_{ij}/\phi$, where σ^2 is a positive coefficient proportional to the marginal cost of information. Figure 3–1 provides some evidence based on variances $(i = j)$ for annual Dutch data on $n = 14$ goods. Along the horizontal axis we measure the estimates of π_{ii}/ϕ and along the vertical axis the mean squares of the associated residuals,

Figure 3-1. Rational Random Behavior for Fourteen Goods.

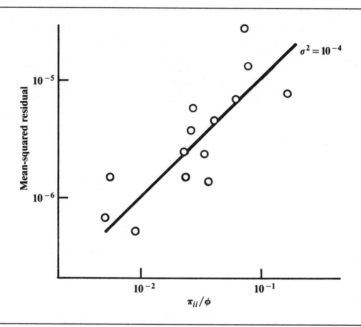

both on a logarithmic scale. The covariance matrix described above predicts a proportionality of var ϵ_{it} and π_{ii}/ϕ, with σ^2 as proportionality constant. On a double-log scale this proportionality becomes a linear relation with unit slope. The figure shows that the fourteen points are indeed scattered around such a line, which is encouraging; see Theil (1980: 87–89, 161–64) for more details.

Figure 3–2 provides another illustration of the covariance matrix under rational random behavior. The figure is based on annual U.S. data on beef (B), pork (P), chicken (C), and lamb (L). The underlying model is a conditional demand model within the meat group; further details on such models will follow in Chapter 4. In contrast to Figure 3–1, the figure for the four meats does not use a logarithmic scale. The four points labeled B, P, C, and L refer to the variances, while the other points carry two letters such as BP, which means that the point refers to the residual covariance of the equations for beef and pork. We have 10 points as a whole because four equations have 10 distinct variances and covariances. These 10 points are not far from the upward-sloping line through the origin. This line corresponds to the ML estimates obtained when the covariance structure of rational random behavior is imposed. The two sets of Slutsky estimates are shown in the last four columns of Table 3–25, which is from Theil and Laitinen (1979).

Figure 3-2.   Rational Random Behavior for Four Meats.

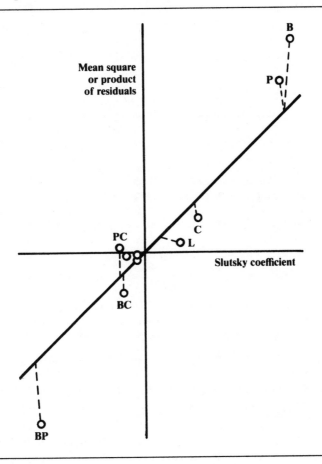

Under preference independence π_{ij} equals $\phi\theta_i(1-\theta_i)$ for $i = j$ and $-\phi\theta_i\theta_j$ for $i \neq j$. Thus, the covariance matrix $[\sigma^2\pi_{ij}/\phi]$ of rational random behavior has then diagonal elements of the form $\sigma^2\theta_i(1-\theta_i)$ and off-diagonal elements of the form $-\sigma^2\theta_i\theta_j$. Note that this particular covariance structure is similar to Σ^* and Σ^{**} discussed in Sections 3.6 and 3.7.

Predetermined Quantities

Until this point we have taken for granted that prices are predetermined variables in a demand system, but it is not difficult to formulate conditions under which prices are endogenous in a supply-and-demand system, while

Table 3-25.   Estimates of a Conditional Demand Model for Meats.

Meat	Marginal share	Slutsky coefficients			
		Beef	Pork	Chicken	Lamb
Symmetry-constrained estimates					
Beef	.692 (.049)	−.227 (.019)	.164 (.014)	.033 (.009)	.029 (.010)
Pork	.199 (.044)		−.214 (.014)	.038 (.007)	.012 (.004)
Chicken	.059 (.021)			−.084 (.009)	.013 (.005)
Lamb	.050 (.012)				−.055 (.014)
ML estimates under rational random behavior					
Beef	.703 (.040)	−.216 (.015)	.173 (.012)	.034 (.009)	.008 (.007)
Pork	.201 (.040)		−.216 (.013)	.035 (.008)	.007 (.004)
Chicken	.058 (.024)			−.079 (.010)	.009 (.005)
Lamb	.039 (.014)				−.024 (.008)

Source: Theil and Laitinen (1979).

quantities become predetermined. In fact, such a model originated with the Danish economist E.P. Mackeprang in his doctoral dissertation as early as 1906; see Theil (1976: 95–96) and Wold (1969).

One way of handling the assumption of predetermined quantity changes under the Rotterdam model is by means of the instrumental variable technique: Multiply both sides of (20.3) by $\bar{w}_{jt} Dq_{jt}$, sum over t, replace the disturbance term by zero, and interpret the parameters (the θ_i's and π_{ij}'s) as IV estimates. When we do this for all relevant values of j, we obtain IV estimates under the assumption of predetermined quantity changes. The π_{ij} estimates thus obtained do not form a symmetric matrix, but a procedure similar to (9.1) and (9.2) can be used to obtain symmetry-constrained IV estimates and their asymptotic standard errors.

When we apply this to the four meats, we obtain the results shown in the lower half of Table 3-26; the upper half contains the symmetry-constrained estimates of Table 3-25, which are reproduced here to facilitate the comparison. The estimates of the Slutsky coefficients in the lower half of Table 3-26 have the same sign as those in the upper half, but they are larger in absolute value. Thus, the assumption of predetermined quantity changes yields a picture of greater price sensitivity than does the assumption of predetermined price changes (which is not entirely surprising). Also, the asymptotic standard errors in the lower half of Table 3-26 are all larger than those

Table 3-26. Second Set of Estimates of a Conditional Demand Model for Meats.

Meat	Marginal share	Slutsky coefficients			
		Beef	Pork	Chicken	Lamb
Symmetry-constrained estimates of Table 3-25					
Beef	.692 (.049)	−.227 (.019)	.164 (.014)	.033 (.009)	.029 (.010)
Pork	.199 (.044)		−.214 (.014)	.038 (.007)	.012 (.004)
Chicken	.059 (.021)			−.084 (.009)	.013 (.005)
Lamb	.050 (.012)				−.055 (.014)
Symmetry-constrained IV estimates					
Beef	.669 (.057)	−.306 (.031)	.171 (.018)	.047 (.013)	.089 (.027)
Pork	.183 (.047)		−.239 (.015)	.040 (.008)	.028 (.009)
Chicken	.067 (.024)			−.105 (.011)	.018 (.009)
Lamb	.081 (.022)				−.135 (.035)

in the upper half. (It would be an interesting project to verify the validity of the asymptotic standard errors of the unconstrained and the symmetry-constrained IV estimates by means of a simulation experiment.) Note further that in both Table 3-25 and Table 3-26, the last column (for lamb) shows the largest changes; this may relate to the fact that lamb has the smallest expenditure shares among the four meats. See Theil (1976: Chap. 9) for more details on the IV technique under predetermined quantity changes.

Monte Carlo Testing in Demand Systems

Laitinen's exact test for demand homogeneity uses the test statistic (2.8), which involves the inverse of the LS estimator S of the contemporaneous covariance matrix Σ. Recall from the discussion at the end of Section 3.8 that S may be singular so that the test cannot be performed. When S is not singular, it may be ill conditioned, in which case we should expect the test to have little power. Earlier in this chapter we tried to avoid this problem by using nonstochastic specifications such as Σ^* and Σ^{**} rather than S. The procedure described below uses an entirely different way of avoiding this problem.

Let our objective be to test for homogeneity of the Rotterdam model (20.3), and let us write $\hat{\pi}_{ij}$ for the LS estimate of π_{ij}. We select

$$\hat{\tau}_i = \sum_{j=1}^{n} \hat{\pi}_{ij} \qquad (20.4)$$

as our test statistic for the homogeneity of the ith equation, and

$$\hat{\tau} = \sum_{i=1}^{n} |\hat{\tau}_i| \qquad (20.5)$$

as the test statistic for the homogeneity of all n equations jointly. Column 2 of Table 3-27, from Taylor, Shonkwiler, and Theil (1986), shows the values of these $n+1$ statistics for the Dutch time series data on $n = 14$ goods used in Laitinen's and Meisner's experiments.

To assess the significance of these outcomes we apply Barnard's (1963) Monte Carlo test procedure. In general terms this procedure can be explained as follows. Let T_1 denote the data-based value of a test statistic. Next we simulate data sets under the null hypothesis $N-1$ times, yielding N test statistics as a whole: the data-based statistic T_1 and $N-1$ statistics $T_2, ..., T_N$

Table 3-27. Monte Carlo and Bootstrap Tests of Homogeneity.

| | | | Rank of data-based statistic | |
Good (1)	$\hat{\tau}_i, \hat{\tau}$ (2)	Standard error (3)	Normal errors (4)	Bootstrap (5)
1. Bread	−.006	.005	13	19
2. Groceries	−.002	.010	44	44
3. Dairy products	.017	.011	90	89
4. Vegetables, fruit	−.004	.012	38	52
5. Meat	.024	.021	90	89
6. Fish	.002	.006	64	65
7. Beverages	.019	.008	97	96
8. Tobacco	.007	.007	90	90
9. Pastry, ice cream	−.013	.005	1	2
10. Textiles	−.100	.024	1	3
11. Footwear	.005	.004	93	91
12. Other durables	.045	.012	100	100
13. Water, light, heat	.010	.013	82	69
14. Other nondurables	−.002	.029	44	35
All fourteen goods	.256	a	98	96

a. Not calculated.
Source: Taylor, Shonkwiler, and Theil (1986).

corresponding to the simulated data sets. If we decide on the 5 percent significance level (say), we reject the null hypothesis for the observed sample if T_1 is among the N' largest values of the T_i's such that $N'/N = 0.05$. (More will be said about N and N' in the next subsection.)

To implement this procedure for the homogeneity test, Taylor et al. used the homogeneity-constrained form (4.1) in order to simulate data sets under the null hypothesis. They generated quasi-normal error terms with zero mean and a covariance matrix equal to the data-based unbiased LS estimate of the contemporaneous covariance matrix of the ϵ_{it}'s in (4.1). This was repeated $N-1 = 99$ times, and in each case the test statistics (20.4) and (20.5) were computed. Column 4 of Table 3-27 contains the rank of the data-based value among the 100 outcomes. Thus, the bottom row of the table shows that the data-based value 0.256 ranks ninety-eighth from the bottom, or third from the top, so that homogeneity is rejected at the 5 percent level but not at the 1 percent level.

The Monte Carlo test procedure can also be applied to $\hat{\tau}_i$ for each equation separately, thus indicating which equations are the troublemakers if homogeneity is in trouble. The first fourteen entries of column 4 in Table 3-27 show the ranking of the data-based $\hat{\tau}_i$ for each i. This ranking can be used for a two-tailed test of homogeneity of the ith equation: If we use the 6 percent significance level, we reject homogeneity when the rank is 1, 2, 3, 98, 99, or 100. The results clearly indicate that equations 9 (pastry and ice cream), 10 (textiles), and 12 (other durables) are the troublemakers. This is confirmed by the standard errors of the $\hat{\tau}_i$'s in column 3; they show that the $\hat{\tau}_i$'s for $i = 9$, 10, and 12 are the most significant ones.

More on Monte Carlo Testing

The simulation studies discussed in earlier sections of this chapter operate entirely within their simulated world. By contrast, the Monte Carlo test procedure uses both the data-based test statistic and the simulated values. Gentle (1985) provides a clear and concise introduction to Monte Carlo methods including the Monte Carlo test. As noted by Hope (1968) and Besag and Diggle (1977), the Monte Carlo test yields a "blurred" critical region in which values of the test statistic have a certain probability of being judged significant. This blurring effect, which leads to a loss of power, can be considerably reduced by choosing N or N' to be sufficiently large; Besag and Diggle (1977: 327) suggest that $N' = 5$ is adequate for most cases. See also Marriott (1979) and Ripley (1977).

The reader should note the flexibility of the Monte Carlo test with respect to the selection of the test statistic. In conventional testing such statistics typically have a form that is dictated by normal distribution theory. In the case of homogeneity testing this leads to the test statistic (2.8), which involves the troublesome inverse of the matrix S. The Monte Carlo test of the previous subsection uses the statistic (20.5), which avoids this inverse completely. Similarly, Theil, Shonkwiler, and Taylor (1985), when applying the Monte Carlo test for Slutsky symmetry, use a statistic of the form

$$\sum_{i=1}^{n} \sum_{j=1}^{n} |\hat{\pi}_{ij} - \hat{\pi}_{ji}|,$$

which also avoids the inverse of S. It appears that symmetry (given homogeneity) is an acceptable hypothesis for the Dutch data on $n = 14$ goods.

For both homogeneity and symmetry, the error terms in the simulations for the Monte Carlo tests have been generated as quasi-normal variates. If the assumption of error normality for the data is in question, the analyst may prefer not to use normal errors in these simulations. One way of doing this is by bootstrapping, given the data-based residual distribution. Returning to the Monte Carlo test of homogeneity summarized in Table 3–27, we write $\hat{\epsilon}_{it}$ for a data-based LS residual obtained from the homogeneity-constrained equation (4.1) and $\hat{\epsilon}_t$ for the vector whose ith element equals $\hat{\epsilon}_{it}$ multiplied by $T/(T-n)$, where $T = 31$ and $n = 14$. We assign probability $1/T$ to each of the vectors $\hat{\epsilon}_1, \ldots, \hat{\epsilon}_T$ and we draw from this distribution T times with replacement. Thus we avoid the normality assumption when we use these errors rather than the quasi-normal errors discussed in the previous subsection. The results, summarized in column 5 of Table 3–27, do not differ much from those of column 4, but the null hypothesis of homogeneity seems to fare a bit better because the rank of the data-based statistic $\hat{r}$ is reduced to the ninety-sixth.

At the beginning of the previous subsection we suggested that Laitinen's test may have little power. Shonkwiler and Theil (1986) pursued this problem empirically by comparing this test with the Monte Carlo and bootstrap tests of columns 4 and 5 of Table 3–27. Using Laitinen's experimental design (which satisfies homogeneity) 100 times, they counted the number of rejections at the 5 percent level. For all three methods, the number of rejections is satisfactorily close to 5 (see the first row of Table 3–28). Next they changed the design by subtracting 0.0005 from each π_{ij}, and then by subtracting another 0.0005. For Laitinen's test this raises the number of rejections from 3 to 28 to 90 (see column 2 of Table 3–28), but for the two other methods the increase is much faster (see columns 3 and 4), thus suggesting that the

Table 3-28.   Rejections of Homogeneity by Another Group of Three Tests.

(1)	Laitinen's test (2)	Monte Carlo test (3)	Bootstrap test (4)
Homogeneity is true	3	4	3
Homogeneity is false[a]	28	83	79
Homogeneity is quite false[a]	90	100	100

a. See text.

power of the latter two tests is greater than that of Laitinen's test. This result is not entirely surprising given that Laitinen's test involves an F with only four degrees of freedom in the denominator (see the end of Section 3.3).

BIBLIOGRAPHY

The publications listed below are those referred to in Chapter 3, supplemented by some other publications that are directly related to the topics discussed.

Aasness, J., and H. Nyquist. 1983. "Engel Functions, Residual Distributions and L_p-Norm Estimators." Memorandum from the Institute of Economics, University of Oslo.

Barnard, G.A. 1963. *Journal of the Royal Statistical Society,* Series B, 25, p. 294.

Barten, A.P. 1969. "Maximum Likelihood Estimation of a Complete System of Demand Equations." *European Economic Review* 1: 7-73.

Bera, A.K.; R.P. Byron; and C.M. Jarque. 1981. "Further Evidence on Asymptotic Tests for Homogeneity and Symmetry in Large Demand Systems." *Economics Letters* 8: 101-105.

Besag, J., and P.J. Diggle. 1977. "Simple Monte Carlo Tests for Spatial Pattern." *Applied Statistics* 26: 327-33.

Bewley, R.A. 1983. "Tests of Restrictions in Large Demand Systems." *European Economic Review* 20: 257-69.

Bowman, J.P.; K. Laitinen; and H. Theil. 1979. "New Results on Rational Random Behavior." *Economics Letters* 2: 201-204.

Byron, R.P. 1970. "The Restricted Aitken Estimation of Sets of Demand Equations." *Econometrica* 38: 816-30.

Christensen, L.R.; D.W. Jorgenson; and L.J. Lau. 1975. "Transcendental Logarithmic Utility Functions." *American Economic Review* 65: 367-83.

Deaton, A.S. 1974. "The Analysis of Consumer Demand in the United Kingdom, 1900–1970." *Econometrica* 42: 341–67.

Efron, B. 1979. "Bootstrap Methods: Another Look at the Jackknife." *Annals of Statistics* 7: 1–26.

Fiebig, D.G.; R. Finke; and H. Theil. 1984. "More on Goodness of Fit of Allocation Models." *Economics Letters* 15: 5–11.

Fiebig, D.G., and H. Theil. 1983. "The Two Perils of Symmetry-Constrained Estimation of Demand Systems." *Economics Letters* 13: 105–11.

Finke, R. 1983. "Goodness of Fit and Outliers in Cross-Country Demand Systems." *Economics Letters* 13: 303–307.

Finke, R.; L.R. Flood; and H. Theil. 1984. "Minimum Information Estimation of Allocation Models of Different Sizes." *Statistics and Probability Letters* 2: 279–83.

Finke, R., and H. Theil. 1984a. "Bootstrapping for Standard Errors of Instrumental Variable Estimates." *Economics Letters* 14: 297–301.

———. 1984b. "An Extended Version of Minimum Information Estimation of Allocation Models." *Economics Letters* 15: 229–33.

Flood, L.R.; R. Finke; and H. Theil. 1984. "Maximum Likelihood and Minimum Information Estimation of Allocation Models with Fat-Tailed Error Distributions." *Economics Letters* 16: 213–18.

Flood, L.R.; M.C. Rosalsky; and H. Theil. 1984. "Aggregation and the Estimation of Equation Systems." *Statistics and Probability Letters* 2: 187–91.

Freedman, D.A., and S.C. Peters. 1984. "Bootstrapping a Regression Equation: Some Empirical Results." *Journal of the American Statistical Association* 79: 97–106.

Gentle, J.E. 1985. "Monte Carlo Methods." In *Encyclopedia of Statistical Sciences,* Vol. 5, edited by S. Kotz, N.L. Johnson, and C.B. Read, 612–17. New York: John Wiley and Sons, Inc.

Hope, A.C.A. 1968. "A Simplified Monte Carlo Significance Test Procedure." *Journal of the Royal Statistical Society,* Series B, 30, pp. 582–98.

Joint Economic Committee, Congress of the United States (1981). *Consumption in the U.S.S.R.: An International Comparison.* Washington, D.C.: U.S. Government Printing Office.

Kravis, I.B.; A.W. Heston; and R. Summers. 1978. *International Comparisons of Real Product and Purchasing Power.* Baltimore, Md.: The Johns Hopkins University Press.

Laitinen, K. 1978. "Why Is Demand Homogeneity So Often Rejected?" *Economics Letters* 1: 187–91.

Lluch, C. 1971. "Consumer Demand Functions, Spain, 1958–1964." *European Economic Review* 2: 277–302.

Marriott, F.H.C. 1979. "Barnard's Monte Carlo Tests: How Many Simulations?" *Applied Statistics* 28: 75–77.

McElroy, M.B. 1977. "Goodness of Fit for Seemingly Unrelated Regressions." *Journal of Econometrics* 6: 381–87.

Meisner, J.F. 1979. "The Sad Fate of the Asymptotic Slutsky Symmetry Test for Large Systems." *Economics Letters* 2: 231–33.

Meisner, J.F. 1981. Appendix to *International Consumption Comparisons: A System-Wide Approach,* by H. Theil and F.E. Suhm. Amsterdam: North-Holland Publishing Company, 1981.

Podkaimer, L.; R. Finke; and H. Theil. 1984. "Cross-Country Demand Systems and Centrally Planned Economies." *Economics Letters* 16: 269–71.

Ripley, B.D. 1977. "Modelling Spatial Patterns." *Journal of the Royal Statistical Society,* Series B, 39, pp. 172–212.

Rosalsky, M.C.; R. Finke; and H. Theil. 1984. "The Downward Bias of Asymptotic Standard Errors of Maximum Likelihood Estimates of Non-Linear Systems." *Economics Letters* 14: 207–211.

Rossi, P.E. 1979. "The Cost of Search and Rational Random Behavior." *Economics Letters* 3: 5–8.

Shonkwiler, J.S., and H. Theil. 1986. "Some Evidence on the Power of Monte Carlo Tests in Systems of Equations." *Economics Letters* 20: 53–54.

Strobel, D. 1982. "Determining Outliers in Multivariate Surveys by Decomposition of a Measure of Information." *Proceedings of the American Statistical Association, Business and Economic Statistics Section,* pp. 31–35.

Taylor, T.G.; J.S. Shonkwiler; and H. Theil. 1986. "Monte Carlo and Bootstrap Testing of Demand Homogeneity." *Economics Letters* 20: 55–57.

Theil, H. 1975. *Theory and Measurement of Consumer Demand.* Vol. 1. Amsterdam: North-Holland Publishing Company.

———. 1976. *Theory and Measurement of Consumer Demand.* Vol. 2. Amsterdam: North-Holland Publishing Company.

———. 1979. "The Effect of Measurement Errors on the Estimation of Demand Systems." *Economics Letters* 3: 373–76.

———. 1980. *The System-Wide Approach to Microeconomics.* University of Chicago Press.

Theil, H., and D.G. Fiebig. 1984. *Exploiting Continuity: Maximum Entropy Estimation of Continuous Distributions.* Cambridge, Mass.: Ballinger Publishing Company.

Theil, H., and R. Finke. 1983. "The Distance from the Equator as an Instrumental Variable." *Economics Letters* 13: 357–60.

Theil, H.; R. Finke; and L.R. Flood. 1984. "Minimum Information Estimation of Allocation Models." *Economics Letters* 15: 251–56.

Theil, H., and K. Laitinen. 1979. "Maximum Likelihood Estimation of the Rotterdam Model Under Two Different Conditions." *Economics Letters* 2: 239–44.

Theil, H., and M.C. Rosalsky. 1984a. "More on Symmetry-Constrained Estimation." *Economics Letters* 15: 257–63.

———. 1984b. "Another Look at Symmetry Testing." *Economics Letters* 16: 225–30.

———. 1985a. "Least Squares and Maximum Likelihood Estimation of Non-linear Systems." *Economics Letters* 17: 119–22.

———. 1985b. "Homogeneity and Symmetry Testing When the Error Distribution Has Fat Tails." *Economics Letters* 18: 7–8.

Theil, H.; M.C. Rosalsky; and R. Finke. 1984. "A Comparison of Normal and Discrete Bootstraps for Standard Errors in Equation Systems." *Statistics and Probability Letters* 2: 175–80; erratum, 2: 255.

Theil, H.; M.C. Rosalsky; and W.S. McManus. 1985. "L_p-Norm Estimation of Nonlinear Systems." *Economics Letters* 17: 123–25.

Theil, H.; J.S. Shonkwiler; and T.G. Taylor. 1985. "A Monte Carlo Test of Slutsky Symmetry." *Economics Letters* 19: 331–32.

Theil, H., and F.E. Suhm. 1981. *International Consumption Comparisons: A System-Wide Approach.* Amsterdam: North-Holland Publishing Company.

Wold, H.O. 1969. "E.P. Mackeprang's Question Concerning the Choice of Regression: A Key Problem in the Evolution of Econometrics." In *Economic Models, Estimation and Risk Programming,* edited by K.A. Fox, J.K. Sengupta, and G.V.L. Narasimham, 325–41. New York: Springer Verlag.

4 THE DEMAND FOR GROUPS OF GOODS AND CONDITIONAL DEMAND

Kenneth W. Clements

4.1 INTRODUCTION

The previous three chapters deal largely with the demand for all n goods. It is frequently the case, however, that the analyst is concerned with the determinants of the demand for only a group of goods, rather than all the goods. Examples occur in marketing research where the focus is on the market shares of brands of a product, and in the analysis of the effects of differential taxation of the consumption of different members of the same group of goods, such as beer, wine, and spirits.

When the n goods are divided into groups that are appropriately separable in the consumer's utility function, it turns out that the demand for members of a given group can be analyzed in exactly the same way as before. The only difference between the previous differential demand equations for all n goods and those for the members of a given group is that (1) real income is replaced by total consumption of the group and (2) the n prices are replaced with the prices of the members of the group. Consequently, these demand equations for members of the group allow the analyst to confine his attention to variables pertaining to the group and ignore the role of prices of goods outside the group.

I am indebted to Antony Selvanathan and Henri Theil for helpful comments on an earlier draft of this chapter.

These developments, which were pioneered by Sono (1961) and Leontief (1947a, b), have been applied to the differential approach to consumption theory by Barten and Turnovsky (1966) and Theil (1975/76, 1980). The objective of this chapter is to provide a link between the first three chapters of the book and the subsequent chapter, which deals with applications of the differential approach to the demand for groups of goods. This chapter draws freely on Theil (1975/76, 1980).

4.2   A BRIEF REVIEW OF EARLIER RESULTS

This section, based on the material presented in Sections 1.9 through 1.13 of Chapter 1, summarizes those results of the differential approach to consumption theory that will be used subsequently in this chapter.

We start with the solution for the price derivatives of the demand functions, from the fundamental matrix equation,

$$\frac{\partial q_i}{\partial p_j} = \lambda u^{ij} - \frac{\lambda}{\partial \lambda / \partial M} \frac{\partial q_i}{\partial M} \frac{\partial q_j}{\partial M} - \frac{\partial q_i}{\partial M} q_j \quad i,j = 1, \ldots, n, \qquad (2.1)$$

where q_i is the quantity consumed of good i $(i = 1, \ldots, n)$; p_i is the corresponding price; λ is the marginal utility of income; u^{ij} is the (i, j)th element of the inverse of the Hessian matrix of the utility function $[\partial^2 u / \partial q_i \partial q_j]^{-1}$; and M is income. Equation (2.1) shows that the effect of a change in the price of good j on the consumption of i is made up of three components. First, λu^{ij} is the specific substitution effect, which deals with the utility interaction of goods i and j. Second,

$$-\frac{\lambda}{\partial \lambda / \partial M} \frac{\partial q_i}{\partial M} \frac{\partial q_j}{\partial M}$$

is the general substitution effect, which is concerned with the competition of all goods for an extra dollar of the consumer's income. These two components represent the total substitution effect, the response of q_i to a change in p_j with real income and other prices held constant. The third term on the right of (2.1), $-q_j(\partial q_i / M)$, is the income effect of the price change.

The differential approach uses the result (2.1) to express the demand equation for good i as

$$w_i \, d(\log q_i) = \theta_i \, d(\log Q) + \phi \sum_{j=1}^{n} \theta_{ij} \, d\left(\log \frac{p_j}{P'}\right), \qquad (2.2)$$

where $w_i = p_i q_i / M$ is the ith budget share, which satisfies $\sum_{i=1}^{n} w_i = 1$; $\theta_i =$

$\partial(p_i q_i)/\partial M$ is the marginal share of good i, with $\sum_{i=1}^{n} \theta_i = 1$; $d(\log Q) = \sum_{i=1}^{n} w_i \, d(\log q_i)$ is the Divisia volume index; $\phi < 0$ is the income flexibility; $d[\log(p_j/P')] = d(\log p_j) - d(\log P')$ is the change in the jth relative price, $d(\log P')$ being the Frisch price index defined as $\sum_{i=1}^{n} \theta_i \, d(\log p_i)$; and θ_{ij} is the (i,j)th normalized price coefficient defined as

$$\theta_{ij} = \frac{\lambda}{\phi M} p_i p_j u^{ij} \quad i,j = 1, \ldots, n. \tag{2.3}$$

These price coefficients satisfy

$$\sum_{j=1}^{n} \theta_{ij} = \theta_i \quad i = 1, \ldots, n \tag{2.4}$$

and

$$[\theta_{ij}] \text{ is a symmetric positive definite } n \times n \text{ matrix.} \tag{2.5}$$

The coefficients are normalized since $\sum_{i=1}^{n} \sum_{j=1}^{n} \theta_{ij} = 1$, which follows from (2.4) and $\sum_{i=1}^{n} \theta_i = 1$.

The variable on the left in (2.2) has the dual interpretation as the quantity component of the change in the ith budget share and the contribution of good i to the Divisia volume index $d(\log Q)$. The demand equation (2.2) explains this variable in terms of real income (as measured by the Divisia volume index) and relative prices. The real income term is a multiple θ_i of the Divisia volume index $d(\log Q)$. The marginal share θ_i in this term answers the question, If income rises by one dollar how much of this is spent on commodity i?

The term $\phi \sum_j \theta_{ij} d[\log(p_j/P')]$ on the right in (2.2) deals with the effects of relative prices and gives the total substitution effect of the n price changes on the demand for good i. The income flexibility ϕ has the interpretation as the reciprocal of the income elasticity of the marginal utility of income. The Frisch price index acts as deflator for each price change, so that $d[\log(p_j/P')]$ is known as the Frisch-deflated price of j. It can be shown (see Section 1.12) that the general substitution effect acts as the deflator of the specific effect by transforming absolute prices into Frisch-deflated prices.

In (2.2) $\phi\theta_{ij}$ is the coefficient of the jth relative price. If $\theta_{ij} < 0$, then, as $\phi < 0$, an increase in the Frisch-deflated price of j causes the consumption of i to rise, and goods i and j are said to be specific substitutes; if $\theta_{ij} > 0$ the two goods are specific complements. Finally, the matrix of normalized price coefficients $[\theta_{ij}]$ is interpreted as being inversely proportional to the Hessian matrix of the utility function in expenditure terms, $[\partial^2 u/\partial(p_i q_i)\partial(p_j q_j)]$.

4.3   PREFERENCE INDEPENDENCE AND BLOCK INDEPENDENCE

In Chapter 1 we analyzed the case when preferences can be represented by a utility function that is additive in the n goods,

$$u = \sum_{i=1}^{n} u_i(q_i). \tag{3.1}$$

This form of the utility function is known as preference independence as the marginal utility of good i is independent of the consumption of good j for $i \neq j$. Under (3.1) the Hessian matrix of the utility function and its inverse are both diagonal. It then follows from (2.3) and (2.4) that $\theta_{ij} = 0$ for $i \neq j$ and $\theta_{ii} = \theta_i$, so that the demand equation (2.2) simplifies to

$$w_i \, d(\log q_i) = \theta_i \, d(\log Q) + \phi \theta_i \, d\left(\log \frac{p_i}{P'}\right). \tag{3.2}$$

Accordingly, under preference independence only the own Frisch-deflated price appears in each demand equation, so that no pair of goods is either a specific substitute or complement. Note also that (2.5) implies that each θ_i is positive under preference independence, which rules out inferior goods.

As can be seen, the implications of the preference independence assumption are rather drastic. A weaker version of preference independence is *block independence,* whereby the additive specification (3.1) is applied to *groups* of goods rather than to individual goods. Let the n goods be divided into $G < n$ groups, written $S_1, \ldots, S_G$, such that each good belongs to only one group. Further, let the consumer's preferences be such that the utility function is the sum of G group utility functions, each involving the quantities of only one group,

$$u = \sum_{g=1}^{G} u_g(q_g^*), \tag{3.3}$$

where q_g^* is the vector of the q_i's that fall under S_g. Under (3.3), the marginal utility of a good depends only on the consumption of goods belonging to the same group. When the goods are numbered appropriately, the Hessian of the utility function and its inverse become block-diagonal. Accordingly, specification (3.3) is known as *block-independent preferences.*

In view of (2.3), block independence implies that $[\theta_{ij}]$ is block-diagonal. Therefore, if i belongs to S_g, equations (2.2) and (2.4) can now be written as

$$w_i\, d(\log q_i) = \theta_i\, d(\log Q) + \phi \sum_{j \in S_g} \theta_{ij}\, d\!\left(\log \frac{p_j}{P'}\right), \tag{3.4}$$

$$\sum_{j \in S_g} \theta_{ij} = \theta_i \quad i \in S_g. \tag{3.5}$$

Thus block independence implies that the only deflated prices that appear in the ith demand equation are those of goods belonging to the same group as the commodity in question. As $\theta_{ij} = 0$ for i and j in different groups, under block independence no good is a specific substitute or complement of any good that belongs to a different group.

4.4   THE DEMAND FOR GROUPS OF GOODS UNDER BLOCK INDEPENDENCE

We write

$$W_g = \sum_{i \in S_g} w_i, \qquad \Theta_g = \sum_{i \in S_g} \theta_i \tag{4.1}$$

for the budget and marginal shares of group g. The marginal share Θ_g tells us the increase in expenditure on S_g as a result of a one-dollar increase in income. Summing both sides of (3.5) over $i \in S_g$ shows that

$$\sum_{i \in S_g} \sum_{j \in S_g} \theta_{ij} = \Theta_g > 0, \tag{4.2}$$

where the inequality sign is based on the positive definiteness of the matrix $[\theta_{ij}]$. Accordingly, block independence means that no group as a whole can be inferior; members of the group can be inferior, however.

We define the group Divisia volume and Frisch price indexes as

$$d(\log Q_g) = \sum_{i \in S_g} \frac{w_i}{W_g}\, d(\log q_i), \tag{4.3}$$

$$d(\log P'_g) = \sum_{i \in S_g} \frac{\theta_i}{\Theta_g}\, d(\log p_i). \tag{4.4}$$

These two indexes aggregate consistently since a budget-share-weighted average of $d(\log Q_1), \ldots, d(\log Q_G)$ equals the Divisia volume index of all the n goods $d(\log Q)$; and a marginal-share-weighted average of $d(\log P'_1), \ldots, d(\log P'_G)$ equals the overall Frisch price index $d(\log P')$:

$$\sum_{g=1}^{G} W_g\, d(\log Q_g) = d(\log Q), \qquad \sum_{g=1}^{G} \Theta_g\, d(\log P'_g) = d(\log P').$$

We obtain the demand equation for the group S_g as a whole under block independence by simply adding over $i \in S_g$ both sides of the demand equation for good i under block independence, equation (3.4). In view of (4.1) and (4.3) this yields

$$W_g \, d(\log Q_g) = \Theta_g \, d(\log Q) + \phi \sum_{i \in S_g} \sum_{j \in S_g} \theta_{ij} \, d\left(\log \frac{p_j}{P'}\right). \qquad (4.5)$$

Our objective is to simplify the price substitution term of this equation. As θ_{ij} is symmetric in i and j [see equation (2.5)], (3.5) can be expressed as

$$\sum_{i \in S_g} \theta_{ij} = \theta_j \quad j \in S_g,$$

so that

$$\phi \sum_{i \in S_g} \sum_{j \in S_g} \theta_{ij} \, d\left(\log \frac{p_j}{P'}\right) = \phi \sum_{j \in S_g} \theta_j \, d\left(\log \frac{p_j}{P'}\right)$$

$$= \phi \Theta_g \, d\left(\log \frac{P'_g}{P'}\right),$$

where the second step is based on (4.1) and (4.4). Accordingly, (4.5) can be expressed as

$$W_g \, d(\log Q_g) = \Theta_g \, d(\log Q) + \phi \Theta_g \, d\left(\log \frac{P'_g}{P'}\right). \qquad (4.6)$$

This is the *composite demand equation* for S_g as a group.

Equation (4.6) shows that under block independence, the demand for a group of goods as a whole depends on real income and the relative price of the group $d[\log(P'_g/P')]$. This relative price is the Frisch-deflated Frisch price index of the group. It is to be noted that the relative prices of goods outside the group in question play no role in equation (4.6). By dividing both sides of this equation by W_g, we find that Θ_g/W_g is the income elasticity of demand for the group and that $\phi\Theta_g/W_g$ is the own-price elasticity; this latter elasticity is the elasticity of the Divisia volume index of the group with respect to the Frisch-deflated Frisch price index of the group.

It is instructive to compare equation (4.6) with (3.2), the demand equation for an individual good under preference independence. This comparison reveals that both equations have the same general form: $w_i \, d(\log q_i)$ on the left side of (3.2) becomes $W_g \, d(\log Q_g)$ in (4.6), and $\theta_i \, d(\log Q)$ and $\phi\theta_i \, d[\log(p_i/P')]$ on the right in (3.2) are replaced with $\Theta_g \, d(\log Q)$ and $\phi\Theta_g \, d[\log(P'_g/P')]$ in (4.6). Therefore in going from (3.2) to (4.6), each variable is replaced by the corresponding group concept, making the latter equation an "uppercase" version of the former. The reason for this is that the demand equation for the group (4.6) is based on block independence, while (3.2) holds under preference independence, and the utility function under block independence (3.3) exhibits preference independence with respect to *groups* of goods, rather than the individual commodities. Another way of expressing this is to note that if S_g consists of only one good, let it be the ith, then (4.6) for this group coincides with (3.2).

4.5   CONDITIONAL DEMAND EQUATIONS

As there are G groups of goods, there are G composite demand equations, each of the form (4.6). These equations give the allocation of income to each of the G groups. This allocation depends only on income and the G relative prices of the groups. Given the demand for a group, the next question is how is expenditure on the group allocated to the commodities within the group? This question is answered by the conditional demand equations. In this section we analyze the form of the conditional demand equations under the assumption of block independence.

To obtain the conditional demand equations, we first rearrange (4.6):

$$d(\log Q) = \frac{W_g}{\Theta_g} d(\log Q_g) - \phi d\left(\log \frac{P'_g}{P'}\right). \tag{5.1}$$

We then substitute the right side of this equation for $d(\log Q)$ in (3.4). In the next section it is shown that this yields for $i \in S_g$

$$w_i d(\log q_i) = \theta'_i W_g d(\log Q_g) + \phi \sum_{j \in S_g} \theta_{ij} d\left(\log \frac{p_j}{P'_g}\right), \tag{5.2}$$

where

$$\theta'_i = \frac{\theta_i}{\Theta_g} \quad i \in S_g \tag{5.3}$$

is the *conditional marginal share* of good i within the group S_g, with

$$\sum_{i \in S_g} \theta'_i = 1.$$

This share answers the question, If income increases by one dollar, resulting in a certain additional amount spent on the group S_g, what is the proportion of this additional amount that is allocated to commodity i?

Equation (5.2) is the demand equation for $i \in S_g$, given the demand for the group as a whole $W_g d(\log Q_g)$. It is known as the *conditional demand equation* for $i \in S_g$. This equation shows that the allocation of expenditure to goods within the gth group depends on the total consumption of the group, as measured by $W_g d(\log Q_g)$, and the relative prices of goods within the group. The deflator for these relative prices is the Frisch price index of the group $d(\log P'_g)$, defined in (4.4). Consumption of other groups and the prices of goods outside S_g do not appear in (5.2). Consequently, the within-group allocation of expenditure depends only on variables pertaining to the group in question. It follows from (2.5) that the normalized price coefficients are symmetric in i and j for commodities belonging to the same group,

$$\theta_{ij} = \theta_{ji} \quad i, j \in S_g. \tag{5.4}$$

The θ_{ij}'s within S_g are also constrained by (3.5) which we repeat here:

$$\sum_{j \in S_g} \theta_{ij} = \theta_i \quad i \in S_g. \tag{5.5}$$

The conditional demand equation (5.2) is to be contrasted with (3.4), which can be described as the corresponding *unconditional* demand equation. The left variables of these two equations are the same, but the real income term in (3.4), $\theta_i d(\log Q)$, is replaced by $\theta'_i W_g d(\log Q_g)$ in (5.2). Also, the price substitution terms are identical, except that the Frisch price index of all goods acts as the deflator in (3.4), while the corresponding group concept $d(\log P'_g)$ plays this role in (5.2).

Block-independent preferences imply that the consumer's problem can be solved in two steps. The first decision involves the allocation of income to the G groups, as described by the G group demand equations (4.6). Each of these demand equations contains real income and the relative price of the group in question but not the prices of the individual goods. Then in the second decision, for each of the groups, expenditure is allocated to the goods within the group. The conditional demand equations (5.2) describe this allocation and they contain total consumption of the group, as determined by the previous decision, and relative prices within the group. Accordingly, there is a decision hierarchy under block independence.

The conditional demand equations (5.2) were obtained under block independence. These results also hold, however, under the weaker condition of blockwise dependence. See Section 4.12 below.

4.6   DERIVATION OF THE CONDITIONAL DEMAND EQUATIONS

To derive the conditional demand equation (5.2) we first substitute the right side of (5.1) for $d(\log Q)$ in the unconditional equation (3.4). This yields

$$w_i \, d(\log q_i) = \frac{\theta_i}{\theta_g} W_g \, d(\log Q_g) - \phi \theta_i \, d(\log P_g') + \phi \theta_i \, d(\log P')$$

$$+ \phi \sum_{j \in S_g} \theta_{ij} \, d(\log p_j) - \phi \sum_{j \in S_g} \theta_{ij} \, d(\log P'). \qquad (6.1)$$

In view of (5.5), the second term on the right in (6.1) can be expressed as

$$-\phi \theta_i \, d(\log P_g') = -\phi \sum_{j \in S_g} \theta_{ij} \, d(\log P_g'),$$

and the third term becomes

$$\phi \theta_i \, d(\log P') = \phi \sum_{j \in S_g} \theta_{ij} \, d(\log P'),$$

so that it cancels with the last term. Consequently, (6.1) can be written as

$$w_i \, d(\log q_i) = \frac{\theta_i}{\theta_g} W_g \, d(\log Q_g) + \phi \sum_{j \in S_g} \theta_{ij} \, d(\log p_j) - \phi \sum_{j \in S_g} \theta_{ij} \, d(\log P_g')$$

$$= \theta_i' W_g \, d(\log Q_g) + \phi \sum_{j \in S_g} \theta_{ij} \, d\!\left(\log \frac{p_j}{P_g'}\right),$$

which is the conditional demand equation (5.2).

4.7   THE ROTTERDAM MODEL REVISITED

In the two sections following this one, we discuss Rotterdam-type parameterizations of the conditional demand equations. To set the scene, in this section we present in summary form the *un*conditional Rotterdam model; this model was previously analyzed in detail in Section 1.14 of Chapter 1.

The relative price version of the Rotterdam model is a finite-change version of the general differential demand equation (2.2). The ith equation of the model is

$$\bar{w}_{it} Dq_{it} = \theta_i DQ_t + \sum_{j=1}^{n} \nu_{ij}(Dp_{jt} - DP_t'), \qquad (7.1)$$

where $\bar{w}_{it} = \frac{1}{2}(w_{i,t-1} + w_{it})$ is the arithmetic average of the budget shares in periods $t-1$ and t; $Dq_{it} = \log q_{it} - \log q_{i,t-1}$ is the ith quantity log-change; $DQ_t = \sum_{i=1}^{n} \bar{w}_{it} Dq_{it}$ is a finite-change version of the Divisia volume index;

$$\nu_{ij} = \phi \theta_{ij} \qquad (7.2)$$

is the (i, j)th price coefficient; Dp_{jt} is the price log-change of j; and $DP_t' = \sum_{i=1}^{n} \theta_i Dp_{it}$ is a finite-change version of the Frisch price index. The marginal share and price coefficients in (7.1) are treated as constants in the model. The price coefficients satisfy

$$\sum_{j=1}^{n} v_{ij} = \phi\theta_i \quad i = 1, ..., n \tag{7.3}$$

and

$$[v_{ij}] \text{ is a symmetric negative definite } n \times n \text{ matrix.} \tag{7.4}$$

By combining Dp_j and DP' on the right in (7.1) we obtain the ith equation of the absolute price version of the Rotterdam model:

$$\bar{w}_{it} Dq_{it} = \theta_i DQ_t + \sum_{j=1}^{n} \pi_{ij} Dp_{jt}, \tag{7.5}$$

where

$$\pi_{ij} = v_{ij} - \phi\theta_i\theta_j \quad i, j = 1, ..., n \tag{7.6}$$

is the (i, j)th Slutsky coefficient. These Slutsky coefficients satisfy

$$\sum_{j=1}^{n} \pi_{ij} = 0 \quad i = 1, ..., n \tag{7.7}$$

and are symmetric in i and j,

$$\pi_{ij} = \pi_{ji} \quad i, j = 1, ..., n. \tag{7.8}$$

Constraint (7.7) is known as demand homogeneity as it reflects the homogeneity postulate that a proportionate change in all prices has no effect on the demand for any good when real income is held constant. Constraint (7.8) is referred to as Slutsky symmetry. The $n \times n$ Slutsky matrix $[\pi_{ij}]$ is symmetric negative semidefinite with rank $n-1$.

4.8   THE FIRST CONDITIONAL VERSION OF THE ROTTERDAM MODEL

Consider equation (5.2) in terms of finite changes:

$$\bar{w}_{it} dq_{it} = \theta_i' \bar{W}_{gt} DQ_{gt} + \sum_{j \in S_g} v_{ij}(Dp_{jt} - DP'_{gt}), \tag{8.1}$$

where $\bar{W}_{gt} DQ_{gt} = \Sigma_{i \in S_g} \bar{w}_{it} Dq_{it}$; $DP'_{gt} = \Sigma_{i \in S_g} \theta_i' Dp_{it}$ is the Frisch price index of the group in terms of finite changes; and the other notation is as before. When the conditional marginal share and price coefficients in (8.1) are treated as constants, it is known as the ith equation of the *first conditional version of the Rotterdam model;* it is the conditional demand equation for commodity i belonging to the group S_g.

Equation (8.1) is analogous to the unconditional Rotterdam model given in (7.1). The price coefficients ν_{ij} in these two equations are identical, and the constraint on the ν_{ij}'s within S_g, similar to (7.3), is

$$\sum_{j \in S_g} \nu_{ij} = \phi \Theta_g \theta_i' \quad i \in S_g, \tag{8.2}$$

which follows from (5.3), (5.5), and (7.2). Constraint (8.2) also follows from (5.3) and (7.3) as $\nu_{ij} = 0$ for i and j belonging to different groups. Furthermore, in view of (7.4), the price coefficients within the group are symmetric,

$$\nu_{ij} = \nu_{ji} \quad i, j \in S_g. \tag{8.3}$$

The absolute price version of (8.1) is

$$\bar{w}_{it} Dq_{it} = \theta_i' \bar{W}_{gt} DQ_{gt} + \sum_{j \in S_g} \pi_{ij}^g Dp_{jt}, \tag{8.4}$$

where

$$\pi_{ij}^g = \nu_{ij} - \phi \Theta_g \theta_i' \theta_j' \quad i, j \in S_g \tag{8.5}$$

is the (i, j)th *conditional Slutsky coefficient*. This coefficient measures the effect of a change in the price of good j on the consumption of i $(i, j \in S_g)$ under the condition that other prices and total consumption of the group remain constant. The conditional Slutsky coefficients satisfy demand homogeneity,

$$\sum_{j \in S_g} \pi_{ij}^g = 0 \quad i \in S_g, \tag{8.6}$$

which follows from (8.2), (8.5) and $\sum_{j \in S_g} \theta_j' = 1$; and are symmetric,

$$\pi_{ij}^g = \pi_{ji}^g \quad i, j \in S_g, \tag{8.7}$$

which follows from (8.3) and (8.5). Equation (8.4) is a conditional version of (7.5); and similarly (8.5), (8.6), and (8.7) are the conditional counterparts of (7.6), (7.7), and (7.8). It is to be noted that, in contrast to the price coefficients ν_{ij}, which are the same in the unconditional and conditional models, the Slutsky coefficients in (8.4) differ from those in (7.5).

4.9 THE SECOND CONDITIONAL VERSION OF THE ROTTERDAM MODEL

Consider the modification of the conditional demand equation (5.2) obtained by dividing both sides by W_g and multiplying and dividing the substitution term by Θ_g:

$$\frac{w_i}{W_g} d(\log q_i) = \theta_i' d(\log Q_g) + \frac{\phi \Theta_g}{W_g} \sum_{j \in S_g} \frac{\theta_{ij}}{\Theta_g} d\left(\log \frac{p_j}{P_g'}\right). \tag{9.1}$$

The first term on the left in this equation is

$$\frac{w_i}{W_g} = \frac{p_i q_i / M}{\sum_{j \in S_g} p_j q_j / M} = \frac{p_i q_i}{M_g}, \tag{9.2}$$

where $M_g = \sum_{j \in S_g} p_j q_j$ is total expenditure on the group S_g. Consequently, w_i / W_g is interpreted as the proportion of expenditure on S_g devoted to good i belonging to the group; this proportion is known as the *conditional budget share* of i within S_g, with $\sum_{i \in S_g} (w_i / W_g) = 1$. It follows from (9.2) that

$$d\left(\frac{w_i}{W_g}\right) = \frac{w_i}{W_g} d(\log p_i) + \frac{w_i}{W_g} d(\log q_i) - \frac{w_i}{W_g} d(\log M_g).$$

This shows that the left variable in (9.1) is the quantity component of the change in the conditional budget share of i. This variable is also the contribution of i to the Divisia volume index of S_g [see equation (4.3)]. These interpretations are, of course, the within-group versions of those pertaining to the unconditional demand equation (2.2).

The term $\phi \Theta_g / W_g$ before the summation sign in (9.1) is interpreted as the own-price elasticity of demand for the group S_g as a whole; see the discussion in the second last paragraph of Section 4.4. This own-price elasticity replaces ϕ when we use (9.1) rather than (5.2). It should also be noted that θ_{ij} / Θ_g in the substitution term of (9.1) amounts to normalizing the price coefficients within the group since $\sum_{i \in S_g} \sum_{j \in S_g} (\theta_{ij} / \Theta_g) = 1$, which follows from (4.1) and (5.5).

The *second conditional Rotterdam model* is the following finite-change version of (9.1):

$$\frac{\bar{w}_{it}}{\bar{W}_{gt}} Dq_{it} = \theta_i' DQ_{gt} + \sum_{j \in S_g} v_{ij}' (Dp_{jt} - DP_{gt}'), \tag{9.3}$$

where

$$v_{ij}' = \frac{v_{ij}}{W_g} \quad i, j \in S_g \tag{9.4}$$

is a new price coefficient, to be referred to as the (i, j)th *modified price coefficient*. These modified coefficients satisfy

$$\sum_{j \in S_g} v_{ij}' = \frac{\phi \Theta_g}{W_g} \theta_i' \quad i \in S_g \tag{9.5}$$

and

$$v_{ij}' = v_{ji}', \quad i, j \in S_g \tag{9.6}$$

which follow from (8.2) and (8.3).

In (9.3) the coefficients θ_i' and v_{ij}' are taken to be constants. Constraint (9.5) then implies that $\phi\Theta_g/W_g$ is also a constant. Summing both sides of (9.5) over $i \in S_g$ yields

$$\sum_{i \in S_g} \sum_{j \in S_g} v_{ij}' = \frac{\phi\Theta_g}{W_g}. \tag{9.7}$$

This shows that the sum of all the modified price coefficients within S_g equals the constant own-price elasticity of demand for the group.

The difference between (8.1) and (9.3) is twofold. First, the dependent variable of (8.1), $\bar{w}_{it}Dq_{it}$, becomes $(\bar{w}_{it}/\bar{W}_{gt})Dq_{it}$ in (9.3). Second, the two versions differ in their parameterization. In (8.1) the price coefficients v_{ij} are specified as constants, while it is the modified coefficients v_{ij}' that are constant in (9.3). As (9.3) can be obtained by dividing both sides of (8.1) by $\bar{W}_{gt}$, it follows that the parameterization adopted in the second version of the model implies that the original price coefficients v_{ij} are variable and proportional to $\bar{W}_{gt}$. As it is difficult to judge a priori which assumption is likely to be better, the choice between the two models can be made on the basis of a goodness-of-fit criterion. We illustrate the application of such a procedure in the next section.

The absolute price version of (9.3) is

$$\frac{\bar{w}_{it}}{\bar{W}_{gt}}Dq_{it} = \theta_i'DQ_{gt} + \sum_{j \in S_g} \pi_{ij}'Dp_{jt}, \tag{9.8}$$

where

$$\pi_{ij}' = v_{ij}' - \frac{\phi\Theta_g}{W_g}\theta_i'\theta_j' \quad i, j \in S_g \tag{9.9}$$

is the *modified conditional Slutsky coefficient* of the ith and jth commodities, with

$$\sum_{j \in S_g} \pi_{ij}' = 0 \quad i \in S_g, \tag{9.10}$$

$$\pi_{ij}' = \pi_{ji}' \quad i, j \in S_g. \tag{9.11}$$

In view of (9.9), the assumption that the coefficients v_{ij}', $\phi\Theta_g/W_g$ and θ_i' are constants implies that the coefficients π_{ij}' in (9.8) are also constants. A comparison of (9.8) with (8.4) shows that the second parameterization treats the original Slutsky coefficients π_{ij}^g as varying proportionally to $\bar{W}_{gt}$.

4.10   APPLICATION TO THE DEMAND FOR MEATS IN THE UNITED STATES

In this section we use the consumption of meats in the United States to illustrate the estimation of conditional demand equations. To do this we take meats to be block independent of all other commodities. The results of this section are from Theil (1975/76: Secs. 7.2 and 7.3).

The Data

The meat group, which we indicate by S_g, is made up of four meats, beef, pork, chicken, and lamb. The meats data, given in Theil (1975/76: Tables 7.2 and 7.3), are annual and cover the period 1950–1972. At sample means, the budget shares w_i for $i = 1, ..., 4$ are ($\times 100$)

Beef	2.76	
Pork	1.94	
Chicken	0.68	(10.1)
Lamb	0.15	
Total meat	5.53.	

Thus, beef accounts for 2.8 percent of total expenditure in the United States; pork, 1.9 percent; chicken, 0.7 percent; and lamb, 0.2 percent. Meats as a whole, then, absorb $2.8 + 1.9 + 0.7 + 0.2 \approx 5.5$ percent of the consumer's budget. The total meat budget share declines substantially over this period, from almost 7 percent in 1950 to less than 5 percent in 1972. As can be seen from (10.1), beef accounts for about half of total meat expenditure; pork, 35 percent; chicken, 12 percent; and lamb, 3 percent.

Estimates of the First Version of the Conditional Rotterdam Model

We now present estimates of the first version of the conditional Rotterdam model in absolute prices, equation (8.4) for $i = 1$ (beef), 2 (pork), 3 (chicken), and 4 (lamb). Estimation of the model involves adding to (8.4) zero-mean disturbances, which are serially uncorrelated and have a constant contemporaneous covariance matrix; the variables $\bar{W}_{gt} DQ_{gt}$ and the DP_{jt}'s are taken to be predetermined. The generalized least-squares estimates, constrained by (8.6) and (8.7), are given in Table 4–1.

The estimated conditional marginal shares given in Table 4–1 indicate that a one-dollar increase in expenditure on meat causes spending on beef to rise by 75 cents, pork by 15 cents, chicken by 5 cents, with the remaining 6 cents going to lamb. All the diagonal elements of the conditional Slutsky matrix $[\pi_{ij}^g]$ are negative, as they should be. It should be noted that most of the standard errors of the conditional Slutsky coefficients are small in compari-

Table 4-1.   First Set of Estimates of Conditional Demand
Equations for Meats – United States, 1950–1972:

$$\bar{w}_{it} Dq_{it} = \theta_i' \bar{W}_{gt} DQ_{gt} + \sum_{j=1}^{4} \pi_{ij}^g Dp_{jt}.^{a}$$

Meat	Conditional marginal share θ_i'	Conditional Slutsky coefficients $\times 10$			
		π_{i1}^g	π_{i2}^g	π_{i3}^g	π_{i4}^g
Beef	.746 (.053)	−.137 (.011)	.100 (.009)	.021 (.005)	.016 (.006)
Pork	.146 (.048)		−.127 (.009)	.020 (.004)	.007 (.002)
Chicken	.051 (.020)			−.048 (.005)	.007 (.003)
Lamb	.057 (.011)				−.030 (.007)

a. Standard errors in parentheses.

son with the corresponding point estimates. This high degree of precision is
due largely to the substantial variability of the prices of the four meats.

Estimates of the Second Version of the Model

The estimates of equation (9.8), the second version of the model, are given
in Table 4-2. The estimation procedure is constrained GLS, as before. It
should be noted that, while the marginal shares have the same interpretation
in the two models, the Slutsky coefficients do not.

Table 4-2.   Second Set of Estimates of Conditional Demand
Equations for Meats – United States, 1950–1972:

$$\frac{\bar{w}_{it}}{\bar{W}_{gt}} Dq_{it} = \theta_i' DQ_{gt} + \sum_{j=1}^{4} \pi_{ij}' Dp_{jt}.^{a}$$

Meat	Conditional marginal share θ_i'	Modified conditional Slutsky coefficients			
		π_{i1}'	π_{i2}'	π_{i3}'	π_{i4}'
Beef	.692 (.049)	−.227 (.019)	.164 (.014)	.033 (.009)	.029 (.010)
Pork	.199 (.044)		−.214 (.014)	.038 (.007)	.012 (.004)
Chicken	.059 (.021)			−.084 (.009)	.013 (.005)
Lamb	.050 (.012)				−.055 (.014)

a. Standard errors in parentheses.

Table 4-3. Average Information Inaccuracies for Meats: United States, 1950-1972.[a]

Meat (1)	Predictions based on (8.4) (2)	(9.8) (3)	No-change extrapolation (4)
All four meats	236.7	196.3	337.2
Beef	141.7	109.1	221.2
Pork	127.4	94.7	165.1
Chicken	47.0	42.1	71.0
Lamb	43.8	45.1	58.6

a. All entries are to be divided by 10^6.

Choosing between the Two Versions

We shall choose between (8.4) and (9.8) on the basis of which parameterization provides a better description of the meats data. For this purpose, we use the information inaccuracy that was introduced in Section 3.17.

Table 4-3 gives the averages over $t=1, \ldots, 22$ of

$$I_t = \sum_{i=1}^{4} \frac{w_{it}}{W_{gt}} \log \frac{w_{it}/W_{gt}}{\hat{w}_{it}/\hat{W}_{gt}},$$

$$I_{it} = \frac{w_{it}}{W_{gt}} \log \frac{w_{it}/W_{gt}}{\hat{w}_{it}/\hat{W}_{gt}} + \left(1 - \frac{w_{it}}{W_{gt}}\right) \log \frac{1 - w_{it}/W_{gt}}{1 - \hat{w}_{it}/\hat{W}_{gt}},$$

where $\hat{w}_{it}/\bar{W}_{gt}$ is the predicted conditional budget share of meat i. In columns 2 and 3 of the table the predictions are from the first and second versions of the model, (8.4) and (9.8) respectively. It can be shown that $\hat{w}_{it}/\hat{W}_{gt}$ from (9.8) is equal to the corresponding observed conditional budget share minus the residual from the demand equation for i; for (8.4) the residual needs to be divided by $\bar{W}_{gt}$ before being subtracted from w_{it}/W_{gt}. In column 4 of the table $\hat{w}_{it}/\hat{W}_{gt}$ is specified as $w_{i,t-1}/W_{g,t-1}$, which is no-change extrapolation.

As can be seen, (9.8) yields a lower inaccuracy than does (8.4) for three of the four meats as well as for all meats combined. On this basis (9.8) is the preferred version of the model. In addition, both versions dominate no-change extrapolation.

Table 4–4. Conditional Demand Elasticities of Meats: United States, 1950–1972.

Meat (1)	Conditional income elasticity $\theta_i' \bar{W}_g / \bar{w}_i$ (2)	Conditional price elasticities			
		$\pi_{i1}' \bar{W}_g / \bar{w}_i$ (3)	$\pi_{i2}' \bar{W}_g / \bar{w}_i$ (4)	$\pi_{i3}' \bar{W}_g / \bar{w}_i$ (5)	$\pi_{i4}' \bar{W}_g / \bar{w}_i$ (6)
Beef	1.39	−.45	.33	.07	.06
Pork	.57	.47	−.61	.11	.03
Chicken	.49	.27	.31	−.69	.11
Lamb	1.80	1.06	.44	.47	−2.00

The Demand Elasticities

By dividing both sides of (9.8) by $\bar{w}_{it}/\bar{W}_{gt}$, we obtain as the coefficient attached to the Divisia volume index

$$\frac{\theta_i'}{\bar{w}_{it}/\bar{W}_{gt}} = \frac{\theta_i/\bar{w}_{it}}{\Theta_g/\bar{W}_{gt}},$$

which is the ratio of the income elasticity of demand of i to that of the group as a whole. This shall be referred to as the *conditional income elasticity* of demand for i. We also obtain $\pi_{ij}'/(\bar{w}_{it}/\bar{W}_{gt})$ as $\partial(\log q_{it})/\partial(\log p_{jt})$, which we call the (i,j)th *conditional price elasticity* $(i, j \in S_g)$. Note that this elasticity holds constant the total consumption of the group DQ_{gt}.

To evaluate these elasticities we use the estimates given in Table 4–2 and the sample means of the budget shares given in (10.1). Table 4–4 contains the results. As can be seen, within meat, beef and lamb are luxuries, while pork and chicken are necessities. The own-price elasticities of demand are −0.5, −0.6, −0.7, and −2.0 for the four meats. All the cross-price elasticities are positive, indicating that the meats are all pairwise substitutes.

4.11   IS THE DIVISIA VOLUME INDEX OF MEAT A PREDETERMINED VARIABLE?

In the previous section we treated $\bar{W}_{gt} DQ_{gt}$, or DQ_{gt}, as a predetermined variable in the conditional demand equations. How is this justified?

To analyze this question, consider a finite-change version of (4.6), the composite demand equation for S_g,

$$\bar{W}_{gt} DQ_{gt} = \Theta_g DQ_t + \phi \Theta_g (DP'_{gt} - DP'_t) + E_{gt}, \tag{11.1}$$

where E_{gt} is a disturbance. It is reasonable to assume that the two variables on the right of this equation DQ_t and $(DP'_{gt} - DP'_t)$ are predetermined. This means that the only random component of $\bar{W}_{gt} DQ_{gt}$ is the disturbance E_{gt}. It then follows that $\bar{W}_{gt} DQ_{gt}$ on the right in the conditional demand equations (8.4) can be treated as a predetermined variable, provided E_{gt} is independent of the disturbances in those equations. Similar considerations apply to DQ_{gt} in the second conditional version of the Rotterdam model (9.8).

A further result of Theil's (1980) theory of rational random behavior, which was introduced in Section 3.20, is that disturbance of the composite demand equation is independent of the disturbance vector of the conditional demand system. Consequently, under rational random behavior the Divisia volume index can be treated as a predetermined variable in the conditional demand equations. It should also be noted that independence of the disturbances is entirely consistent with the idea discussed in Section 4.5 of a two-level decision hierarchy under the conditions of block independence.

4.12   EXTENSION TO BLOCKWISE DEPENDENCE

As indicated by equation (3.3), under block independence the utility function is the sum of the G group utility functions. A generalization of this specification is for the utility function to be some increasing function $f(\ )$ of these group utility functions,

$$u = f(u_1(q_1^*), \dots, u_G(q_G^*)), \tag{12.1}$$

where, as before, q_g^* is the vector of the q_i's that fall under the group S_g. Condition (12.1), known as *blockwise dependence,* has the following implications (see Theil 1975/76: Chap. 8 for proofs and further details).

In contrast to block independence, under (12.1) the marginal utility of good i depends on the consumption of good j when these goods belong to different groups. If S_g and S_h constitute two different groups, this dependence can be described in terms of how the marginal utility of a dollar spent on $i \in S_g$ changes when an extra dollar is spent on $j \in S_h$, $\partial^2 u / \partial(p_i q_i) \partial(p_j q_j)$. Under (12.1) these second derivatives take the form

$$\frac{\partial^2 u}{\partial(p_i q_i) \partial(p_j q_j)} = a_{gh} \quad i \in S_g, \ j \in S_h, \ g \neq h. \tag{12.2}$$

As the coefficient a_{gh} does not have commodity subscripts (i, j), (12.2) states that the change in the marginal utility of a dollar spent on good $i \in S_g$ caused by an additional dollar spent on $j \in S_h$ is independent of i and j. That is, this effect depends only on the two groups in question, not on the individual commodities. The utility interaction of goods is thus groupwise.

Blockwise dependence implies that the Hessian matrix of the utility function is no longer block diagonal; and the same is true for $[\theta_{ij}]$. The unconditional demand equation for $i \in S_g$ is

$$w_i d(\log q_i) = \theta_i d(\log Q) + \phi \sum_{j \in S_g} \theta_{ij} d\left(\log \frac{p_j}{P'}\right)$$

$$+ \phi \theta_i' \sum_{h \neq g} \Theta_{gh} d\left(\log \frac{P_h'}{P'}\right). \tag{12.3}$$

A comparison of this with (3.4), the corresponding equation under block independence, shows that the only difference is the addition of the last term on the right side. This term is made up of the Frisch-deflated Frisch price indexes of the groups other than S_g,

$$d\left(\log \frac{P_h'}{P'}\right) = \sum_{i \in S_h} \theta_i' d(\log p_i) - d(\log P').$$

The coefficient of this relative price of S_h in (12.3) is $\phi \theta_i' \Theta_{gh}$, where

$$\Theta_{gh} = \sum_{i \in S_g} \sum_{j \in S_h} \theta_{ij} \quad g, h = 1, \dots, G. \tag{12.4}$$

The composite demand equation for S_g under blockwise dependence is

$$W_g d(\log Q_g) = \Theta_g d(\log Q) + \phi \sum_{h=1}^{G} \Theta_{gh} d\left(\log \frac{P_h'}{P'}\right). \tag{12.5}$$

This differs from (4.6), the group demand equation under block independence, as the prices of other groups enter the substitution term of (12.5). It is to be noted that (12.5) is an "uppercase" version of the unconditional demand equation for an individual good (2.2).

In Section 4.2 we used the signs of the normalized price coefficients θ_{ij} to describe the pattern of substitutability/complementarity. Goods i and j are said to be specific substitutes (complements) if $\theta_{ij} < 0$ (> 0). The signs of the coefficients Θ_{gh} can be used in a similar manner to define the corresponding groupwise concept. As $\phi < 0$, it follows from (12.5) that an increase in the Frisch-deflated Frisch price index of S_h causes the consumption of S_g to rise if $\Theta_{gh} < 0$. Consequently, if $\Theta_{gh} < 0$ (> 0), groups S_g and S_h are said to be specific substitutes (complements). Since (12.4) states that Θ_{gh} equals the sum of the θ_{ij}'s of the two sets of constituent goods, there is thus a direct link between the specific substitutability/complementarity relationship of the two groups and the analogous relationships for the two sets of goods that are part of these groups. The $G \times G$ matrix $[\Theta_{gh}]$ is symmetric positive definite and its row sums (and column sums) are equal to the marginal shares of the groups, but these shares may be negative so that groups can be inferior under blockwise dependence. For example,

$$[\Theta_{gh}] = \begin{bmatrix} 0.1 & -0.2 \\ -0.2 & 1.3 \end{bmatrix}$$

is a symmetric positive definite matrix with row sums -0.1 and 1.1. Thus, the first group is inferior.

Combining (12.3) and (12.5) to eliminate $d(\log Q)$ yields the conditional demand equation for $i \in S_g$ under blockwise dependence,

$$w_i \, d(\log q_i) = \theta_i' W_g \, d(\log Q_g) + \phi \sum_{j \in S_g} \theta_{ij} d\left(\log \frac{p_j}{P_g'}\right). \tag{12.6}$$

This is exactly the same as (5.2), the conditional demand equation under block independence. Consequently, the results of Section 4.5 also hold under the weaker condition of blockwise dependence.

4.13   A DYNAMIC EXTENSION

Let utility now depend on consumption in three periods, the current period and the subsequent two. We write q_t^* for the n-element quantity vector of the current period t and take the multiperiod utility function to be of the form

$$u = f(u_1(q_t^*), u_2(q_{t+1}^*, q_{t+2}^*)). \tag{13.1}$$

This utility function is of the form (12.1) with $G = 2$ groups of goods, current and future consumption. Consequently, specification (13.1) exhibits blockwise dependence.

We maximize (13.1) subject to the intertemporal budget constraint,

$$p_1^{*\prime} q_1^* + p_2^{*\prime} q_2^* + p_3^{*\prime} q_3^* = M, \tag{13.2}$$

where p_t^* is the price vector in t and M is now income over the three periods. The composite demand equation for the first group of goods is (12.5) for $g = 1$ and $G = 2$:

$$W_1 \, d(\log Q_1) = \Theta_1 \, d(\log Q) + \phi^* \sum_{h=1}^{2} \Theta_{1h} d\left(\log \frac{P_h'}{P'}\right), \tag{13.3}$$

where $d(\log Q)$ is now the Divisia volume index of consumption over the three periods and $1/\phi^*$ is the elasticity of the marginal utility of three-period income with respect to three-period income; ϕ^* is the intertemporal version of ϕ. As the first group consists of currently consumed goods, the demand equation (13.3) amounts to an aggregate consumption function. By dividing (13.3) by W_1, we obtain $\phi^* \Theta_{11}/W_1$ as the own-price elasticity of demand for total current consumption.

Next, the conditional demand equation for good i consumed in the current period is of the form (12.6) for $g = 1$, which we divide by W_1:

$$\frac{w_i}{W_1} d(\log q_i) = \theta_i' d(\log Q_1) + \frac{\phi^* \Theta_{11}}{W_1} \sum_{j \in S_1} \frac{\theta_{ij}}{\Theta_{11}} d\left(\log \frac{p_j}{P_1'}\right). \quad (13.4)$$

With appropriate interpretations, equation (13.4) has the same form as the unconditional demand equation (2.2), which is obtained from one-period utility maximization. These interpretations are as follows. First, the term w_i/W_1 on the left of (13.4) is the share of good i in total current-period expenditure. This share is denoted by w_i on the left of (2.2).

Second, the coefficient θ_i' on the right in (13.4) is the marginal share of i in current-period total expenditure, which is θ_i in (2.2). Third, the Divisia volume index of S_1, $d(\log Q_1)$ in (13.4), is $d(\log Q)$ in (2.2). Fourth, since $\phi^* \Theta_{11}/W_1$ is the own-price elasticity of total current consumption and since this corresponds to ϕ in (2.2), we can identify this own-price elasticity with the income flexibility of the static model. Fifth, the normalized price coefficients θ_{ij}/Θ_{11} in (13.4) are the corresponding θ_{ij}'s in (2.2). Sixth, the Frisch-deflated prices $d[\log(p_j/P_1')]$ in (13.4) are $d[\log(p_j/P')]$ in (2.2).

Accordingly, the demand equations of the static differential approach are consistent with intertemporal utility maximization under the conditions of blockwise dependence. The unexpected result of this analysis is that the income flexibility of the static model has the interpretation as the own-price elasticity of demand for current consumption.

In Section 4.11 we stated that under rational random behavior and block independence, the Divisia volume index of the group is a predetermined variable in the conditional demand equations. It can also be shown that the blockwise specification (13.1), together with rational random behavior, imply that the change in real income is a predetermined variable in the static demand equations of the differential approach. See Theil (1980: Sec. 15.2).

Remark 1.   The multiperiod utility function (13.1) can be extended in an obvious way to any number of periods.

Remark 2.   There is no discounting of future expenditures in the intertemporal budget constraint (13.2). See Theil (1975/76: Sec. 8.7) for the introduction of such discounting.

BIBLIOGRAPHY

The publications listed below are those referred to in Chapter 4.

Barten, A.P., and S.J. Turnovsky. 1966. "Some Aspects of the Aggregation Problem for Composite Demand Equations." *International Economic Review* 7: 231–59.

Leontief, W.W. 1947a. "A Note on the Interrelation of Subsets of Independent Variables of a Continuous Function with Continuous First Derivatives." *Bulletin of the American Mathematical Society* 53: 343–50.

Leontief, W.W. 1947b. "Introduction to a Theory of the Internal Structure of Functional Relationships." *Econometrica* 15: 361–73.

Sono, M. 1961. "The Effect of Price Changes on the Demand and Supply of Separable Goods." *International Economic Review* 2: 239–71.

Theil, H. 1975/76. *Theory and Measurement of Consumer Demand*. Two volumes. Amsterdam: North-Holland Publishing Company.

Theil, H. 1980. *The System-Wide Approach to Microeconomics*. Chicago: The University of Chicago Press.

5 ALCOHOL CONSUMPTION

Kenneth W. Clements
E. Antony Selvanathan

5.1 INTRODUCTION

This chapter provides an extensive empirical application of conditional demand equations by using alcohol data pertaining to the consumption of beer, wine, and spirits in Australia, the United Kingdom, and the United States. The analysis, like that of Chapter 2, has an international comparison dimension, as it considers the question, Are tastes the same across countries? However, the analysis differs from that of Chapter 2 in that demand equations are estimated for each country with time series data.

The chapter commences by presenting the alcohol price/quantity data and their Divisia moments. We then estimate conditional demand equations in absolute prices for the three beverages and test the hypotheses of homogeneity and Slutsky symmetry. The following sections are concerned with the formulation and estimation of alcohol demand equations in relative prices and whether or not the data can be pooled across countries. Here we follow Chapter 3 and use simulation experiments to analyze the small-sample properties of the estimators. The final few sections of the chapter explore the implications of the models by tabulating the income and price elasticities as well as analyzing the role of factors other than total expenditure and prices in determining the evolution of alcohol consumption.

5.2   ALCOHOL CONSUMPTION IN THREE COUNTRIES

This section presents alcohol consumption data for Australia, the United Kingdom, and the United States. The Australian data are from Clements and Johnson (1983); the British from Selvanathan (1985), which are derived mainly from McGuinnesss (1979); and the American from Clements and Finke (1984).

Table 5-1 presents the volume of beer, wine, and spirits consumed in the three countries. These data are expressed in terms of liters per capita and are thus comparable across countries. As can be seen, the Australians are big drinkers of beer and wine, while the Americans are heavy spirits drinkers. British beer consumption always lies between that of Australia and the United States, and in most years the consumption of wine and spirits is smallest in Britain (although the differences for spirits between Australia and the U.K. are not large).

In the first three columns for each country of Table 5-2, the previous quantity data are converted to log-changes. The second set of three columns for each country contains the undeflated price log-changes. Thus, looking at the last row of the table, it can be seen that on average per capita consumption of beer, wine, and spirits in Australia increased by 1.2 percent, 4.5 percent, and 2.2 percent per annum, respectively. The corresponding average annual price increases are 5.5, 6.5, and 4.8 percent. On average, wine consumption has the fastest growth of the three beverages in each of the three countries; then follows spirits and then beer.

Table 5-3 presents the conditional budget shares for the three beverages as well as the budget share for total alcohol, all in arithmetic average form. Here, for $i = 1$ (beer), 2 (wine), and 3 (spirits),

$$\bar{w}'_{it} = \frac{\bar{w}_{it}}{\bar{W}_{gt}}, \qquad \bar{w}_{it} = \tfrac{1}{2}(w_{it} + w_{i, t-i}), \qquad (2.1)$$

where $w_{it} = p_{it} q_{it} / M_t$ is the budget share of i (p_{it} = price of i in year t, q_{it} = corresponding quantity demanded and M_t is total expenditure on all goods) and

$$\bar{W}_{gt} = \sum_{i=1}^{3} \bar{w}_{it} \qquad (2.2)$$

is the arithmetic average of the budget share for total alcohol. At sample means the Australians spend 72 percent of the alcohol budget on beer, 13

Table 5-1. Alcohol Consumption in Three Countries (Liters per capita).[a]

Year (1)	Australia Beer (2)	Australia Wine (3)	Australia Spirits (4)	United Kingdom Beer (5)	United Kingdom Wine (6)	United Kingdom Spirits (7)	United States Beer (8)	United States Wine (9)	United States Spirits (10)
1949	–	–	–	–	–	–	65.12	3.261	4.299
1950	–	–	–	–	–	–	63.76	3.364	4.735
1951	–	–	–	–	–	–	63.27	2.987	4.763
1952	–	–	–	–	–	–	63.36	3.229	4.446
1953	–	–	–	–	–	–	62.91	3.259	4.635
1954	–	–	–	–	–	–	59.78	3.238	4.430
1955	–	–	–	79.64	1.590	1.479	59.89	3.244	4.576
1956	106.0	5.337	1.998	80.44	1.665	1.570	59.18	3.304	4.847
1957	100.5	5.208	1.800	80.83	1.759	1.588	56.79	3.290	4.689
1958	100.7	5.171	1.822	78.36	1.811	1.613	56.52	3.264	4.685
1959	101.1	5.206	1.913	81.53	1.979	1.732	57.75	3.221	4.819
1960	102.9	5.253	2.081	84.83	2.287	1.839	56.99	3.326	4.936
1961	102.6	5.100	2.073	88.78	2.431	1.926	56.87	3.423	4.994
1962	102.2	5.124	2.079	88.33	2.489	1.925	57.26	3.324	5.169
1963	103.5	5.283	2.026	87.95	2.747	2.044	58.05	3.426	5.201
1964	107.0	5.532	2.186	91.40	3.120	2.195	60.11	3.547	5.464
1965	110.3	5.571	2.351	91.55	2.962	2.035	60.31	3.570	5.756
1966	110.4	6.080	2.086	92.35	3.135	2.057	62.31	3.582	5.978
1967	113.1	6.821	2.071	93.49	3.435	2.062	63.50	3.741	6.210
1968	116.9	7.570	2.326	94.46	3.828	2.150	65.35	3.880	6.573
1969	120.5	8.255	2.301	97.70	3.685	2.022	67.47	4.212	6.800
1970	123.7	8.951	2.555	99.96	3.752	2.296	69.95	4.749	6.876
1971	125.8	8.685	2.579	103.63	4.395	2.431	71.73	5.413	7.002
1972	125.7	8.852	2.729	106.05	5.037	2.783	72.95	5.912	7.123
1973	129.5	9.791	3.085	111.26	6.359	3.495	75.90	6.049	7.289
1974	138.9	10.977	3.105	114.20	6.699	3.855	79.32	6.079	7.406
1975	140.4	12.278	2.975	118.13	6.294	3.678	80.78	6.349	7.438
1976	137.5	13.057	2.872	–	–	–	81.29	6.468	7.418
1977	136.1	13.653	3.166	–	–	–	84.62	6.723	7.432
1978	–	–	–	–	–	–	87.37	7.123	7.558
1979	–	–	–	–	–	–	90.02	7.393	7.542
1980	–	–	–	–	–	–	91.84	7.872	7.488
1981	–	–	–	–	–	–	93.28	8.220	7.420
1982	–	–	–	–	–	–	92.65	8.311	7.157

a. For Australia the years end on June 30; for the other two countries the years are calendar.

percent on wine, with the remaining 16 percent devoted to spirits. All three beverages absorb 5.9 percent of total expenditure on average in Australia. In the United Kingdom and the United States, at means alcohol accounts for 6.6 and 3.9 percent of total expenditure, respectively.

Table 5-3 shows a tendency for the conditional budget shares to regress toward the mean. In each country the budget share of the beverage that starts off being the largest falls over time, and that of the beverage initially being the smallest rises. The only exception to this rule is beer in the United States, whose budget share is initially the largest; this share first falls, in accordance with the general tendency, but then rises.

The disparate behavior of the budget share of total alcohol in Table 5-3 is to be noted. In Australia $\bar{W}_g$ is more or less constant at around 6 percent. In the United Kingdom this share is also approximately constant for the first twelve years, but it then starts to rise. In the United States $\bar{W}_g$ starts off at 4.8 percent in 1949/50 and falls steadily to end up at 3.1 percent in 1981/82.

5.3   DIVISIA MOMENTS OF ALCOHOL

In Section 1.18 we introduced Divisia moments of the prices and quantities of the n goods consumed. We commence this section with a brief review of these measures and then apply conditional versions of them to the alcohol data.

The Divisia price and volume indexes are defined as

$$d(\log P) = \sum_{i=1}^{n} w_i d(\log p_i), \qquad d(\log Q) = \sum_{i=1}^{n} w_i d(\log q_i). \quad (3.1)$$

These are budget-share-weighted means of the price and quantity changes. The corresponding second-order moments are the Divisia price and quantity variances

$$\Pi = \sum_{i=1}^{n} w_i \left[d\left(\log \frac{p_i}{P} \right) \right]^2, \qquad K = \sum_{i=1}^{n} w_i \left[d\left(\log \frac{q_i}{Q} \right) \right]^2, \qquad (3.2)$$

where $d[\log(p_i/P)] = d(\log p_i) - d(\log P)$ and $d[\log(q_i/Q)] = d(\log q_i) - d(\log Q)$. These variances measure the extent to which the prices and quantities change disproportionately. Finally, the Divisia price-quantity covariance is

$$\Gamma = \sum_{i=1}^{n} w_i d\left(\log \frac{p_i}{P} \right) d\left(\log \frac{q_i}{Q} \right), \qquad (3.3)$$

which measures the co-movement of prices and quantities.

Table 5-2.   Alcohol Quantity and Price Log-Changes in Three Countries.[a]

	Australia					
	Quantities			Prices		
Year (1)	Beer (2)	Wine (3)	Spirits (4)	Beer (5)	Wine (6)	Spirits (7)
1949/50	−	−	−	−	−	−
1950/51	−	−	−	−	−	−
1951/52	−	−	−	−	−	−
1952/53	−	−	−	−	−	−
1953/54	−	−	−	−	−	−
1954/55	−	−	−	−	−	−
1955/56	−	−	−	−	−	−
1956/57	−5.36	−2.45	−10.43	14.21	5.98	0
1957/58	.21	−.73	1.22	1.23	4.88	0
1958/59	.48	.68	4.85	.37	6.11	0
1959/60	1.74	.90	8.43	.85	7.51	0
1960/61	−.29	−2.96	−.39	1.80	7.36	8.41
1961/62	−.41	.48	.29	.71	1.36	1.32
1962/63	1.24	3.04	−2.59	.59	1.58	5.66
1963/64	3.36	4.61	7.64	1.97	1.08	.89
1964/65	3.08	.71	7.27	1.37	5.81	1.98
1965/66	.05	8.74	−11.98	8.15	7.40	13.73
1966/67	2.45	11.50	−.71	4.29	4.71	−5.07
1967/68	3.30	10.43	11.59	4.11	6.95	0
1968/69	3.03	8.66	−1.07	3.03	12.28	6.77
1969/70	2.61	8.09	10.48	3.48	6.00	2.86
1970/71	1.70	−3.02	.94	6.27	9.20	3.04
1971/72	−.14	1.90	5.65	5.10	5.85	.26
1972/73	3.01	10.08	12.25	5.24	−.87	.88
1973/74	7.03	11.43	.64	7.62	2.92	20.20
1974/75	1.06	11.20	−4.27	13.33	14.99	25.66
1975/76	−2.13	6.16	−3.53	22.67	18.52	12.95
1976/77	−.97	4.46	9.77	8.94	7.75	.39
1977/78	−	−	−	−	−	−
1978/79	−	−	−	−	−	−
1979/80	−	−	−	−	−	−
1980/81	−	−	−	−	−	−
1981/82	−	−	−	−	−	−
Mean	1.19	4.47	2.19	5.49	6.54	4.76

a. All entries are to be divided by 100.

Table 5-2 continued.

	United Kingdom					
	Quantities			Prices		
Year	Beer (8)	Wine (9)	Spirits (10)	Beer (11)	Wine (12)	Spirits (13)
1949/50	—	—	—	—	—	—
1950/51	—	—	—	—	—	—
1951/52	—	—	—	—	—	—
1952/53	—	—	—	—	—	—
1953/54	—	—	—	—	—	—
1954/55	—	—	—	—	—	—
1955/56	1.00	4.63	6.01	1.59	−2.53	.82
1956/57	.49	5.50	1.10	4.07	1.83	.50
1957/58	−3.10	2.86	1.57	1.32	−2.08	1.81
1958/59	3.97	8.87	7.17	−6.91	−2.38	−.73
1959/60	3.97	14.50	5.99	−2.53	−6.96	1.02
1960/61	4.55	6.09	4.60	4.46	4.48	8.37
1961/62	−.51	2.36	−.06	9.16	−2.69	5.57
1962/63	−.43	9.86	6.01	4.06	14.32	−4.96
1963/64	3.85	12.75	7.11	5.32	3.94	5.94
1964/65	.16	−5.20	−7.58	10.05	7.95	9.85
1965/66	.86	5.68	1.11	6.14	5.36	6.11
1966/67	1.23	9.14	.23	5.31	1.44	3.03
1967/68	1.03	10.84	4.19	3.30	2.98	5.44
1968/69	3.37	−3.81	−6.18	8.05	11.66	5.98
1969/70	2.28	1.80	12.74	9.51	4.62	3.23
1970/71	3.61	15.83	5.70	7.94	3.81	3.51
1971/72	2.31	13.63	13.52	5.96	1.68	.58
1972/73	4.79	23.31	22.78	3.33	1.48	2.68
1973/74	2.61	5.21	9.82	11.00	12.17	2.31
1974/75	3.38	−6.24	−4.72	22.42	22.21	24.25
1975/76	—	—	—	—	—	—
1976/77	—	—	—	—	—	—
1977/78	—	—	—	—	—	—
1978/79	—	—	—	—	—	—
1979/80	—	—	—	—	—	—
1980/81	—	—	—	—	—	—
1981/82	—	—	—	—	—	—
Mean	1.97	6.88	4.56	5.68	4.16	4.27

Table 5-2 continued.

	United States					
	Quantities			Prices		
Year	Beer (14)	Wine (15)	Spirits (16)	Beer (17)	Wine (18)	Spirits (19)
1949/50	−2.10	3.13	9.68	.24	4.86	−4.47
1950/51	−.77	−11.91	.58	2.67	5.13	6.88
1951/52	.14	7.80	−6.89	9.85	−2.32	7.40
1952/53	−.71	.94	4.16	2.55	−7.53	−2.79
1953/54	−5.10	−.65	−4.51	2.51	7.29	3.91
1954/55	.18	.19	3.24	.60	.75	−.21
1955/56	−1.19	1.81	5.75	2.36	−7.02	.30
1956/57	−4.12	−.41	−3.30	2.52	12.62	6.33
1957/58	−.48	−.81	−.09	−.08	5.12	.66
1958/59	2.15	−1.31	2.82	.13	4.04	.76
1959/60	−1.33	3.20	2.40	1.71	−2.94	.35
1960/61	−.22	2.87	1.18	3.18	4.15	−.04
1961/62	.69	−2.93	3.43	.30	−.56	3.20
1962/63	1.38	3.04	.62	−.20	−.57	3.58
1963/64	3.48	3.46	4.95	.46	−.15	−.08
1964/65	.34	.65	5.20	.83	−.08	−.14
1965/66	3.25	.34	3.79	2.05	1.24	1.09
1966/67	1.90	4.32	3.80	−1.83	12.03	−.71
1967/68	2.88	3.65	5.68	4.16	5.11	2.89
1968/69	3.19	8.22	3.39	3.85	5.56	2.14
1969/70	3.61	12.00	1.12	5.26	9.52	4.15
1970/71	2.52	13.10	1.81	4.35	5.42	2.24
1971/72	1.68	8.82	1.71	3.28	6.20	5.06
1972/73	3.97	2.28	2.30	2.73	7.50	2.27
1973/74	4.41	.51	1.59	6.96	6.26	.47
1974/75	1.82	4.34	.43	9.03	3.37	1.43
1975/76	.63	1.86	−.27	6.57	6.35	5.76
1976/77	4.01	3.87	.20	3.94	5.26	4.54
1977/78	3.20	5.78	1.68	4.18	8.02	2.89
1978/79	2.99	3.71	−.21	11.16	9.77	5.51
1979/80	2.01	6.29	−.72	9.36	8.01	5.36
1980/81	1.55	4.32	−.91	6.74	7.00	5.12
1981/82	−.67	1.10	−3.61	3.87	3.50	3.91
Mean	1.07	2.84	1.55	3.49	4.03	2.42

Table 5-3. Arithmetic Averages of Conditional Budget Shares and Budget Share for Total Alcohol in Three Countries.[a]

Year (1)	Australia				United Kingdom				United States			
	Beer $\bar{w}'_1$ (2)	Wine $\bar{w}'_2$ (3)	Spirits $\bar{w}'_3$ (4)	Total alcohol $\bar{W}^g$ (5)	Beer $\bar{w}'_1$ (6)	Wine $\bar{w}'_2$ (7)	Spirits $\bar{w}'_3$ (8)	Total alcohol $\bar{W}^g$ (9)	Beer $\bar{w}'_1$ (10)	Wine $\bar{w}'_2$ (11)	Spirits $\bar{w}'_3$ (12)	Total alcohol $\bar{W}^g$ (13)
1949/50	—	—	—	—	—	—	—	—	50.77	5.95	43.29	4.773
1950/51	—	—	—	—	—	—	—	—	49.34	5.83	44.83	4.625
1951/52	—	—	—	—	—	—	—	—	49.97	5.51	44.52	4.625
1952/53	—	—	—	—	—	—	—	—	51.24	5.31	43.45	4.615
1953/54	—	—	—	—	—	—	—	—	51.06	5.31	43.63	4.503
1954/55	—	—	—	—	—	—	—	—	50.47	5.50	44.04	4.379
1955/56	—	—	—	—	63.50	10.12	26.39	6.338	49.75	5.26	45.00	4.303
1956/57	75.73	8.59	15.67	6.117	63.31	10.21	26.48	6.275	48.60	5.33	46.08	4.258
1957/58	76.97	8.62	14.41	6.121	62.97	10.42	26.61	6.089	47.70	5.74	46.56	4.186
1958/59	76.47	8.94	14.60	6.060	61.34	10.78	27.88	5.822	47.36	5.85	46.79	4.109
1959/60	75.50	9.35	15.15	5.935	59.52	11.31	29.17	5.697	46.95	5.81	47.24	4.031
1960/61	74.46	9.64	15.90	5.817	58.42	11.54	30.05	5.857	46.83	5.91	47.26	4.023
1961/62	73.83	9.79	16.38	5.785	58.61	11.15	30.24	6.082	46.42	5.85	47.74	4.023
1962/63	73.52	9.96	16.52	5.696	58.68	11.88	29.44	6.130	45.50	5.64	48.86	3.982
1963/64	73.14	10.06	16.80	5.622	57.56	13.37	29.07	6.292	45.05	5.60	49.35	3.941
1964/65	72.55	10.10	17.35	5.618	57.92	13.44	28.65	6.494	44.54	5.50	49.96	3.868
1965/66	72.27	10.59	17.14	5.719	58.68	13.39	27.93	6.604	44.19	5.35	50.46	3.779
1966/67	72.67	11.62	15.71	5.834	58.61	13.92	27.47	6.740	43.75	5.64	50.60	3.711
1967/68	72.30	12.74	14.96	5.907	57.88	14.71	27.41	6.811	43.02	6.06	50.92	3.676

1968/69	70.89	14.16	14.95	6.038	58.13	15.21	26.67	6.895	42.90	6.31	50.79	3.673
1969/70	69.36	15.50	15.15	6.125	59.09	14.78	26.13	7.105	43.17	7.01	49.81	3.721
1970/71	68.86	15.87	15.28	6.144	58.83	14.94	26.24	7.298	43.46	7.96	48.57	3.773
1971/72	68.96	15.97	15.07	6.065	57.89	15.84	26.27	7.319	43.18	8.81	48.01	3.750
1972/73	68.45	16.15	15.40	5.973	54.97	16.96	28.07	7.422	42.95	9.35	47.70	3.673
1973/74	67.82	16.05	16.13	5.972	52.83	18.02	29.15	7.559	44.15	9.54	46.32	3.584
1974/75	66.45	16.68	16.88	5.978	53.72	17.77	28.50	7.640	46.19	9.60	44.22	3.513
1975/76	65.76	17.87	16.37	6.065	—	—	—	—	47.33	9.73	42.94	3.437
1976/77	65.75	18.62	15.64	6.072	—	—	—	—	47.77	9.93	42.30	3.344
1977/78	—	—	—	—	—	—	—	—	48.19	10.41	41.40	3.241
1978/79	—	—	—	—	—	—	—	—	49.20	10.93	39.87	3.195
1979/80	—	—	—	—	—	—	—	—	50.65	11.39	37.97	3.203
1980/81	—	—	—	—	—	—	—	—	51.50	11.93	36.58	3.164
1981/82	—	—	—	—	—	—	—	—	52.01	12.31	35.68	3.065
Mean	71.51	12.71	15.78	5.936	58.62	13.49	27.89	6.624	47.13	7.34	45.54	3.871

a. All entries are to be divided by 100.

The within-alcohol versions of (3.1)–(3.3) in terms of finite changes are

$$DP_{gt} = \sum_{i=1}^{3} \bar{w}'_{it} Dp_{it}, \qquad DQ_{gt} = \sum_{i=1}^{3} \bar{w}'_{it} Dq_{it}, \qquad (3.4)$$

$$\Pi_{gt} = \sum_{i=1}^{3} \bar{w}'_{it} (Dp_{it} - DP_{gt})^2, \qquad K_{gt} = \sum_{i=1}^{3} \bar{w}'_{it} (Dq_{it} - DQ_{gt})^2, \qquad (3.5)$$

$$\Gamma_{gt} = \sum_{i=1}^{3} \bar{w}'_{it} (Dp_{it} - DP_{gt})(Dq_{it} - DQ_{gt}), \qquad (3.6)$$

where $\bar{w}'_{it}$ is the conditional budget share defined in (2.1), and

$$Dp_{it} = \log p_{it} - \log p_{i,t-1} \quad \text{and} \quad Dq_{it} = \log q_{it} - \log q_{i,t-1}$$

are the price and quantity log-changes. In Table 5-4 the first two columns for each country contain the Divisia volume and price indexes for alcohol, while the third column presents Divisia price-quantity correlation,

$$\rho_{gt} = \frac{\Gamma_{gt}}{\sqrt{K_{gt}\Pi_{gt}}}. \qquad (3.7)$$

For Australia 16 of the 21 correlation coefficients are negative; for the United Kingdom and the United States the corresponding figures are 16 out of 20 and 17 out of 33. This reflects the tendency of the drinker to move away from those beverages having above-average price increases. It should be noted, however, that the mean value of the correlation coefficient for the United States is a small positive number that stems mainly from the second half of the sample period.

For comparison we also give in Table 5-4 the log-change in per capita real income DQ and the log-change in the price index of all goods DP^*. This comparison is made easier in Table 5-5, which gives in log-change form relative consumption of alcohol, $DQ_g - DQ$, and its relative price, $DP_g - DP^*$. Figures 5-1, 5-2, and 5-3 are scatterplots of $DQ_g - DQ$ against $DP_g - DP^*$. These figures also give the least-squares regression lines. As can be seen, there is a distinct negative relationship between the two variables, so that total alcohol consumption grows less rapidly when its relative price rises.

The slopes of the regression lines given in Figures 5-1, 5-2, and 5-3 are (standard errors in parentheses)

Australia	−.559 (.101)	
United Kingdom	−.610 (.173).	(3.8)
United States	−.625 (.122)	

These slopes, which are all highly significant, can be interpreted as estimates of the own-price elasticity of demand for the alcoholic beverages as a group

Table 5-4.   Divisia Indexes of Alcohol Consumption, Real
Income, and General Price Index in Three Countries.[a]

| | Australia | | | | |
| | Divisia indexes of alcohol | | | Real income log-change | General price index log-change |
Year (1)	Volume DQ_g (2)	Price DP_g (3)	Price-quantity correlation ρ_g (4)	DQ (5)	DP^* (6)
1949/50	–	–	–	–	–
1950/51	–	–	–	–	–
1951/52	–	–	–	–	–
1952/53	–	–	–	–	–
1953/54	–	–	–	–	–
1954/55	–	–	–	–	–
1955/56	–	–	–	–	–
1956/57	−5.90	11.27	.67	−1.44	5.68
1957/58	.27	1.37	−.88	1.64	.98
1958/59	1.13	.83	−.17	1.42	1.57
1959/60	2.67	1.34	−.38	4.69	2.48
1960/61	−.57	3.38	−.52	−.33	4.00
1961/62	−.21	.87	.92	.49	.45
1962/63	.78	1.52	−.88	4.92	.22
1963/64	4.20	1.70	−.93	4.76	.89
1964/65	3.57	1.92	−.37	2.19	3.68
1965/66	−1.09	9.03	−.93	.48	3.55
1966/67	3.01	2.87	.52	3.09	2.63
1967/68	5.45	3.86	−.30	3.72	3.25
1968/69	3.22	4.89	.55	3.48	2.58
1969/70	4.65	3.78	.26	4.46	3.16
1970/71	.84	6.24	−.63	2.61	4.64
1971/72	1.06	4.49	−.87	1.41	6.59
1972/73	5.58	3.58	−.94	3.89	5.87
1973/74	6.71	8.90	−.98	2.87	12.17
1974/75	1.85	15.69	−.48	2.45	15.45
1975/76	−.88	20.34	−.08	4.03	12.20
1976/77	1.73	7.38	−.93	−.82	12.94
1977/78	–	–	–	–	–
1978/79	–	–	–	–	–
1979/80	–	–	–	–	–
1980/81	–	–	–	–	–
1981/82	–	–	–	–	–
Mean	1.81	5.49	−.35	2.38	5.00

a. Except for the correlation coefficients, all entries are to be divided by 100.

Table 5–4 continued.

| | United Kingdom | | | | |
| | Divisia indexes of alcohol | | | Real income log-change | General price index log-change |
Year	Volume DQ_g (7)	Price DP_g (8)	Price–quantity correlation ρ_g (9)	DQ (10)	DP^* (11)
1949/50	–	–	–	–	–
1950/51	–	–	–	–	–
1951/52	–	–	–	–	–
1952/53	–	–	–	–	–
1953/54	–	–	–	–	–
1954/55	–	–	–	–	–
1955/56	2.69	.97	−.54	.40	4.20
1956/57	1.16	2.90	−.40	1.95	3.16
1957/58	−1.24	1.10	−.40	2.05	2.81
1958/59	5.39	−4.70	.91	4.08	.55
1959/60	5.75	−1.99	−.54	3.03	1.10
1960/61	4.74	5.64	−.18	1.88	2.67
1961/62	−.05	6.75	−.98	1.03	3.90
1962/63	2.69	2.62	−.00	3.48	2.02
1963/64	5.99	5.31	−.57	2.79	3.18
1964/65	−2.78	9.71	.39	1.38	4.49
1965/66	1.58	6.03	−1.00	1.46	3.86
1966/67	2.06	4.15	−.63	1.78	2.63
1967/68	3.34	3.84	.05	2.22	4.65
1968/69	−.27	8.05	.17	.44	5.24
1969/70	4.94	7.15	−.79	2.13	6.08
1970/71	5.98	6.16	−.64	1.63	8.99
1971/72	7.05	3.87	−.99	4.87	7.00
1972/73	12.98	2.84	−.82	3.38	8.73
1973/74	5.18	8.68	−.92	−.98	14.84
1974/75	−.64	22.91	−.52	−1.54	21.69
1975/76	–	–	–	–	–
1976/77	–	–	–	–	–
1977/78	–	–	–	–	–
1978/79	–	–	–	–	–
1979/80	–	–	–	–	–
1980/81	–	–	–	–	–
1981/82	–	–	–	–	–
Mean	3.33	5.10	−.42	1.87	5.59

Table 5-4   continued.

		United States			
	Divisia indexes of alcohol				General
				Real	price
			Price-quantity	income	index
	Volume	Price	correlation	log-change	log-change
	DQ_g	DP_g	ρ_g	DQ	DP^*
Year	(12)	(13)	(14)	(15)	(16)
1949/50	3.31	−1.52	−.82	3.72	2.04
1950/51	−.81	4.70	.18	−.11	6.31
1951/52	−2.57	8.09	−.19	1.02	2.16
1952/53	1.49	−.31	−.80	1.99	1.99
1953/54	−4.61	3.37	.95	−.01	.86
1954/55	1.53	.25	−1.00	4.39	.94
1955/56	2.09	.94	−.45	1.04	1.91
1956/57	−3.55	4.81	.96	.22	3.23
1957/58	−.32	.57	−.27	−.60	2.10
1958/59	2.26	.65	−.77	3.41	1.99
1959/60	.70	.80	−.81	.99	1.83
1960/61	.62	1.72	−.48	.34	1.07
1961/62	1.79	1.63	.94	2.86	1.48
1962/63	1.10	1.62	−.81	2.32	1.55
1963/64	4.20	.16	−.86	3.97	1.32
1964/65	2.79	.30	−.92	4.18	1.74
1965/66	3.37	1.52	−.20	3.80	2.87
1966/67	3.00	−.48	.49	1.89	2.50
1967/68	4.35	3.57	−.91	3.88	4.05
1968/69	3.61	3.09	.55	2.46	4.39
1969/70	2.96	5.01	1.00	.77	4.47
1970/71	3.02	3.41	.60	2.03	4.28
1971/72	2.32	4.39	.56	4.54	3.52
1972/73	3.02	2.95	−.14	3.41	5.39
1973/74	2.73	3.88	.74	−1.66	10.31
1974/75	1.45	5.13	.44	.84	7.72
1975/76	.36	6.20	.75	5.09	4.15
1976/77	2.38	4.32	−.46	3.89	5.61
1977/78	2.84	4.05	.98	3.35	6.76
1978/79	1.79	8.75	.96	1.57	8.59
1979/80	1.46	7.69	.64	−.71	9.70
1980/81	.98	6.18	.90	1.72	8.10
1981/82	−1.50	3.84	−.69	.43	5.62
Mean	1.46	3.07	.03	2.03	3.96

Table 5-5. Relative Consumption and Price Log-Changes of Alcohol in Three Countries.[a]

Year (1)	Australia		United Kingdom		United States	
	Relative consumption $DQ_g - DQ$ (2)	Relative price $DP_g - DP^*$ (3)	Relative consumption $DQ_g - DQ$ (4)	Relative price $DP_g - DP^*$ (5)	Relative consumption $DQ_g - DQ$ (6)	Relative price $DP_g - DP^*$ (7)
1949/50	—	—	—	—	−.41	−3.56
1950/51	—	—	—	—	−.71	−1.61
1951/52	—	—	—	—	−3.59	5.93
1952/53	—	—	—	—	−.50	−2.30
1953/54	—	—	—	—	−4.60	2.51
1954/55	—	—	—	—	−2.87	−.68
1955/56	—	—	2.29	−3.24	1.05	−.97
1956/57	−4.46	5.59	−.79	−.26	−3.76	1.59
1957/58	−1.37	.39	−3.29	−1.71	.28	−1.53
1958/59	−.29	−.74	1.31	−5.25	−1.14	−1.34
1959/60	−2.02	−1.14	2.72	−3.09	−.29	−1.03
1960/61	−.23	−.62	2.86	2.97	.29	.65
1961/62	−.70	.43	−1.08	2.86	−1.08	.15
1962/63	−4.14	1.30	−.79	.60	−1.22	.08
1963/64	−.56	.81	3.20	2.13	.23	−1.16
1964/65	1.38	−1.76	−4.15	5.22	−1.39	−1.45
1965/66	−1.58	5.48	.11	2.17	−.43	−1.35
1966/67	−.09	.24	.28	1.52	1.10	−2.98
1967/68	1.73	.61	1.13	−.82	.47	−.48
1968/69	−.26	2.31	−.70	2.81	1.14	−1.30

1969/70	.19	.62	2.82	1.07	2.19	.54
1970/71	-1.77	1.60	4.35	-2.84	.99	-.87
1971/72	-.34	-2.09	2.18	-3.13	-2.22	.87
1972/73	1.68	-2.29	9.60	-5.89	-.40	-2.44
1973/74	3.84	-3.27	6.16	-6.16	4.38	-6.43
1974/75	-.60	.23	.90	1.21	.61	-2.59
1975/76	-4.91	8.14	—	—	-4.73	2.05
1976/77	2.54	-5.56	—	—	-1.51	-1.29
1977/78	—	—	—	—	-.51	-2.71
1978/79	—	—	—	—	.22	.17
1979/80	—	—	—	—	2.17	-2.02
1980/81	—	—	—	—	-.74	-1.92
1981/82	—	—	—	—	-1.93	-1.78
Mean	-.57	.49	1.46	-.49	-.57	-.89

a. All entries are to be divided by 100.

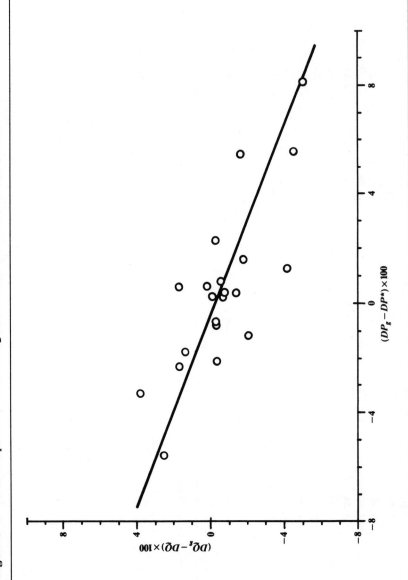

Figure 5-1.   Consumption of Alcohol against Relative Price: Australia, 1956–1977.

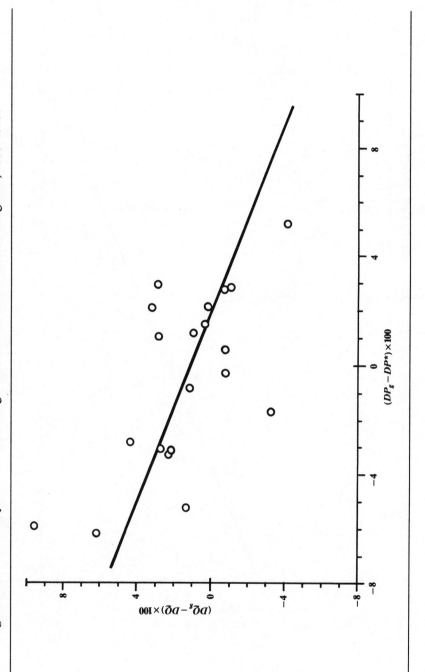

Figure 5–2. Consumption of Alcohol against Relative Price: United Kingdom, 1955–1975.

Figure 5-3. Consumption of Alcohol against Relative Price: United States, 1949–1982.

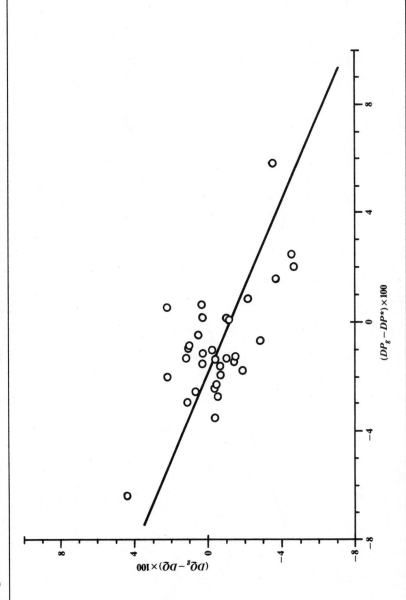

under the assumption of a unitary income elasticity. It is to be noted that these price elasticities are very similar in the three countries.

The intercepts ($\times 100$) of the regression lines are

$$
\begin{array}{lr}
\text{Australia} & -.296 \ (.308) \\
\text{United Kingdom} & 1.155 \ (.558). \\
\text{United States} & -1.126 \ (.276)
\end{array}
\tag{3.9}
$$

These intercepts are the residual exponential trend rates of growth in per capita alcohol consumption, again under the assumption of a unitary income elasticity. Consequently, Australian consumption is subject to a negative autonomous trend of 0.3 percent per annum, while consumption in the United Kingdom and United States is changing autonomously at 1.2 and -1.1 percent per annum, respectively. The U.K. and U.S. estimates are significant.

Remark 1. The log-change in per capita real income DQ given in Table 5-4 is, strictly speaking, the log-change in real total consumption expenditure per capita. It is defined as the excess of the log-change in per capital total expenditure, $\log M_t - \log M_{t-1}$, over the log-change in the price index of all goods, DP^*. For full details, see Clements and Finke (1984), Clements and Johnson (1983), and Selvanathan (1985).

Remark 2. For Australia and the United Kingdom, DP^* is the log-change in the consumer price index; for the United States, it is the log-change in the implicit price deflator for total consumption expenditure. For details, see the references given in the previous remark.

5.4   A CONDITIONAL VERSION OF WORKING'S MODEL

Working's (1943) model, introduced in Section 1.8, specifies that the budget share of each good is a linear function of the logarithm of income,

$$
w_i = \alpha_i + \beta_i \log M,
\tag{4.1}
$$

where $\sum_{i=1}^{n} \alpha_i = 1$ and $\sum_{i=1}^{n} \beta_i = 0$. The income elasticity for good i implied by (4.1) takes the form

$$
\eta_i = 1 + \frac{\beta_i}{w_i},
\tag{4.2}
$$

which shows that a good with a positive (negative) β_i is a luxury (necessity).

Equation (4.1) applies to all n goods consumed and thus can be referred to as an unconditional Engel curve. Consider now the division of the n goods into $G < n$ groups, written $S_1, \ldots, S_G$, such that each good belongs to only one group. What does (4.1) imply for the form of the conditional Engel curves that give the allocation of total expenditure on a group of goods to the commodities within the group? When the income elasticity of demand for S_g as a group is approximately unity, then for $i \in S_g$ the conditional Engel curve is

$$w_i' \approx \alpha_i' + \beta_i' \log M_g, \tag{4.3}$$

where $w_i' = w_i / W_g$ is the conditional budget share of $i \in S_g$; $W_g = \sum_{i \in S_g} w_i$ is the budget share of group g; $M_g = \sum_{i \in S_g} p_i q_i$ is total expenditure on S_g; and α_i' and β_i' are constants satisfying $\sum_{i \in S_g} \alpha_i' = 1$ and $\sum_{i \in S_g} \beta_i' = 0$.

In words, Working's model implies that the conditional Engel curves are approximately also of the Working form when the income elasticity of demand for the group as a whole is about unity. The derivation of this result, from Clements, Goldschmidt, and Theil (1985), is given in the next section. It follows from (4.3) that the conditional income elasticity for $i \in S_g$ is

$$\eta_i' = 1 + \frac{\beta_i'}{w_i'}, \tag{4.4}$$

which has the same form as the unconditional elasticity given in (4.2). Consequently, a positive (negative) β_i' means that i is a conditional luxury (necessity).

5.5   DERIVATIONS

Summing both sides of (4.1) over $i \in S_g$ yields the Engel curve for group g:

$$W_g = A_g + B_g \log M = A_g(1 + C_g \log M), \tag{5.1}$$

where $A_g = \sum_{i \in S_g} \alpha_i$, $B_g = \sum_{i \in S_g} \beta_i$, and $C_g = B_g / A_g$. We choose units such that the geometric mean of income is unity, so that $\alpha_i = w_i$ and $A_g = W_g$ at this mean. The income elasticity of demand for the group as a whole is

$$\eta_g = 1 + \frac{B_g}{W_g}$$

so that C_g is interpreted as $\eta_g - 1$ at geometric mean income.

As $W_g = \sum_{i \in S_g} w_i = M_g / M$, it follows from (5.1) that

$$\log M = \log M_g - \log A_g - \log(1 + C_g \log M).$$

When $C_g \approx 0$, which implies that $\eta_g \approx 1$ at geometric mean income, we have

$$\log M \approx \log M_g - \log A_g - C_g \log M,$$

so that

$$(1 + C_g) \log M \approx \log M_g - \log A_g,$$

or

$$\log M \approx (1 - C_g) \log \frac{M_g}{A_g}. \tag{5.2}$$

It follows from (4.1) and (5.1) that

$$\frac{w_i}{W_g} = \frac{\alpha_i + \beta_i \log M}{A_g (1 + C_g \log M)} \approx \frac{1}{A_g} (1 - C_g \log M)(\alpha_i + \beta_i \log M)$$

for $C_g \approx 0$. Ignoring the second-order term in $\log M$, which should be a satisfactory approximation if the observed income levels are not too far from their geometric mean, the above equation simplifies to

$$\frac{w_i}{W_g} \approx \frac{\alpha_i}{A_g} + \frac{\beta_i - \alpha_i C_g}{A_g} \log M$$

$$\approx \frac{\alpha_i}{A_g} + (\beta_i - \alpha_i C_g) \left(\frac{1 - C_g}{A_g} \right) \log \frac{M_g}{A_g},$$

where the second step follows from (5.2). The last equation is (4.3) with $\alpha_i' = \alpha_i / A_g - (\beta_i - \alpha_i C_g)(1 - C_g)(\log A_g)/A_g$ and $\beta_i' = (\beta_i - \alpha_i C_g)(1 - C_g)/A_g$, which are constants satisfying $\sum_{i \in S_g} \alpha_i' = 1$ and $\sum_{i \in S_g} \beta_i' = 0$.

5.6   ADDING A SUBSTITUTION TERM TO WORKING'S MODEL

Application of the conditional Working model to time series data requires the addition of a price substitution term. Our starting point is the first conditional version of the Rotterdam model in absolute prices, introduced in Section 4.8. Under block independence, the demand equation for $i \in S_g$ of that model is

$$\bar{w}_{it} Dq_{it} = \theta_i' \bar{W}_{gt} DQ_{gt} + \sum_{j \in S_g} \pi_{ij}^g Dp_{jt}, \tag{6.1}$$

where θ_i' is the conditional marginal share of i, and π_{ij}^g is the (i, j)th conditional Slutsky coefficient. The Slutsky coefficients satisfy demand homogeneity,

$$\sum_{j \in S_g} \pi_{ij}^g = 0 \quad i \in S_g, \tag{6.2}$$

and are symmetric in i and j,

$$\pi_{ij}^g = \pi_{ji}^g \quad i, j \in S_g. \tag{6.3}$$

The coefficients θ_i' and π_{ij}^g in (6.1) are specified as constants. Working's model (4.3), however, implies that the conditional marginal share θ_i' equals $\beta_i' + w_i'$, which is not constant as the budget share w_i' is variable. For a time series application we write this marginal share as $\beta_i' + \bar{w}_{it}'$. Substituting this expression for θ_i' in (6.1) and rearranging yields

$$\bar{w}_{it}(Dq_{it} - DQ_{gt}) = \beta_i' \bar{W}_{gt} DQ_{gt} + \sum_{j \in S_g} \pi_{ij}^g Dp_{jt}. \tag{6.4}$$

This is the *first conditional version of Working's model with a substitution term added.* This substitution term is formulated in terms of absolute (undeflated) prices; later in the chapter we will introduce a relative price formulation.

It will be recalled from Section 4.9 that there is also a second conditional version of the Rotterdam model that is obtained by dividing both sides of (6.1) by $\bar{W}_{gt}$:

$$\bar{w}_{it}' Dq_{it} = \theta_i' DQ_{gt} + \sum_{j \in S_g} \pi_{ij}' Dp_{jt}, \tag{6.5}$$

where π_{ij}' is a modified Slutsky coefficient with

$$\sum_{j \in S_g} \pi_{ij}' = 0 \quad i \in S_g, \tag{6.6}$$

$$\pi_{ij}' = \pi_{ji}' \quad i, j \in S_g. \tag{6.7}$$

In the second version of the model, θ_i' and π_{ij}' are taken to be constant coefficients.

Under Working's model, (6.5) becomes

$$\bar{w}_{it}'(Dq_{it} - DQ_{gt}) = \beta_i' DQ_{gt} + \sum_{j \in S_g} \pi_{ij}' Dp_{jt}. \tag{6.8}$$

This is the *second conditional version of Working's model with a substitution term.*

5.7   ALCOHOL DEMAND EQUATIONS IN ABSOLUTE PRICES

We take S_g to be the alcoholic beverages group and apply equations (6.4) and (6.8) to beer ($i = 1$), wine ($i = 2$), and spirits ($i = 3$). In effect, this amounts to assuming that these three beverages are block independent of all other commodities.

We add zero-mean error terms to the right sides of (6.4) and (6.8) and then estimate these models by maximum likelihood under the assumption that the errors are independent and multivariate normal, with a constant covariance matrix. We take total consumption of alcohol and the prices to be predetermined and use Wymer's (1977) program RESIMUL for estimation.

Tables 5-6 and 5-7 contain the estimates of (6.4) and (6.8) for each of the three countries. These are homogeneity- and symmetry-constrained estimates. Based on a preliminary analysis of the data, we have added constant terms (intercepts) to the equations where necessary; these consants take account of autonomous trends in consumption.

In the six sets of estimates, all the constant terms are significant. As the estimates of β_i' for beer are always significantly negative, beer is a conditional necessity in the three countries. Spirits is always a conditional luxury as the estimates of β_3' are always significantly positive. The estimate of β_i' for wine is insignificant in Australia and the United States, but significantly positive in the United Kingdom. Many of the Slutsky coefficients have relatively high standard errors.

We shall follow the procedure adopted in Section 4.10 and choose between the two models on the basis of a goodness-of-fit criterion, the information inaccuracy. Table 5-8 gives the averages over $t = 1, \ldots, T$ observations of

$$I_t = \sum_{i=1}^{3} w_{it}' \log \frac{w_{it}'}{\hat{w}_{it}'},$$

$$I_{it} = w_{it}' \log \frac{w_{it}'}{\hat{w}_{it}'} + (1 - w_{it}') \log \frac{1 - w_{it}'}{1 - \hat{w}_{it}'},$$

where $w_{it}' = w_{it} / \sum_{j=1}^{3} w_{jt}$ is the observed conditional budget share of beverage i and $\hat{w}_{it}'$ is the corresponding predicted value. The prediction $\hat{w}_{it}'$ from (6.8) is equal to w_{it}' minus the residual from the demand equation for i; for (6.4) the residual needs to be divided by $\bar{W}_{gt}$ before being subtracted from w_{it}'.

As can be seen from Table 5-8, there is not a great deal of difference between the two models. However, model (6.8) beats (6.4) for the three beverages combined in the United Kingdom and United States and for six out of a total of nine individual beverages. Note also that both models perform substantially better than no-change extrapolation, whereby $\hat{w}_{it}'$ is specified as $w_{i,t-1}'$. Consequently, we prefer (6.8) to (6.4).

Table 5-6. First Set of Estimates of Conditional Demand Equations for Alcoholic Beverages

$$\bar{w}_{it}(Dq_{it} - DQ_{gt}) = \alpha_i + \beta_i'\bar{W}_{gt}DQ_{gt} + \sum_{j=1}^{3}\pi_{ij}^g Dp_{jt}.\text{[a]}$$

Beverage	Constant × 1000 α_i		Conditional income coefficient β_i'	Conditional Slutsky coefficients × 100		
				π_{i1}^g	π_{i2}^g	π_{i3}^g
	Australia					
	1956/57–1964/65	1965/66–1976/77				
Beer	0	0	−.196 (.034)	−.425 (.146)	.054 (.114)	.370 (.095)
Wine	0	.456 (.080)	−.023 (.033)		−.190 (.119)	.136 (.074)
Spirits	0	−.456 (.080)	.219 (.039)			−.506 (.104)
	United Kingdom					
Beer	.366 (.133)		−.356 (.044)	−.735 (.401)	.168 (.224)	.567 (.276)
Wine	0		.126 (.025)		−.113 (.182)	−.054 (.150)
Spirits	−.366 (.133)		.230 (.039)			−.513 (.243)
	United States					
	1949/50–1967/68	1968/69–1981/82				
Beer	−.156 (.062)	.222 (.083)	−.138 (.055)	−.195 (.172)	.005 (.056)	.191 (.181)
Wine	0	.131 (.032)	−.027 (.020)		−.014 (.040)	.010 (.070)
Spirits	.156 (.062)	−.353 (.089)	.165 (.058)			−.201 (.210)

a. Asymptotic standard errors in parentheses.

Table 5-7. Second Set of Estimates of Conditional Demand Equations for Alcoholic Beverages

$$\bar{w}'_{ii}(Dq_{it} - DQ_{gt}) = \alpha'_i + \beta'_i(DQ_{gt} + \sum_{j=1}^{3} \pi'_{ij} Dp_{jt}.^{[a]}$$

Beverage	Constant × 100 α'_i		Conditional income coefficient β'_i	Modified conditional Slutsky coefficients × 10		
				π'_{i1}	π'_{i2}	π'_{i3}
	Australia					
	1956/57– 1964/65	1965/66– 1976/77				
Beer	0	0	−.194 (.034)	−.703 (.241)	.087 (.189)	.616 (.159)
Wine	0	.768 (.133)	−.023 (.033)		−.317 (.197)	.230 (.124)
Spirits	0	−.768 (.133)	.218 (.039)			−.847 (.175)
	United Kingdom					
Beer	.537 (.204)		−.347 (.046)	−1.207 (.590)	.269 (.324)	.938 (.408)
Wine	0		.126 (.025)		−.169 (.261)	−.100 (.216)
Spirits	−.537 (.204)		.222 (.040)			−.838 (.357)
	United States					
	1949/50– 1967/68	1968/69– 1981/82				
Beer	−.374 (.141)	.574 (.192)	−.115 (.051)	−.407 (.387)	.011 (.133)	.418 (.402)
Wine	0	.375 (.079)	−.025 (.020)		−.038 (.098)	.049 (.164)
Spirits	.374 (.141)	−.948 (.204)	.140 (.053)			−.466 (.468)

a. Asymptotic standard errors in parentheses.

Table 5–8.   Average Information Inaccuracies for Alcohol.[a]

Beverage (1)	Predictions based on		
	(6.4) (2)	(6.8) (3)	No-change extrapolation (4)
Australia			
All three beverages	143.8	145.9	542.5
Beer	56.7	56.4	291.9
Wine	54.2	55.4	229.4
Spirits	95.0	96.4	313.1
United Kingdom			
All three beverages	224.5	220.6	724.1
Beer	132.4	128.9	490.8
Wine	108.2	108.5	324.1
Spirits	107.6	103.6	324.9
United States			
All three beverages	120.7	114.9	381.3
Beer	70.2	66.0	195.4
Wine	44.8	44.0	148.4
Spirits	78.0	72.9	253.4

a. All entries are to be divided by 10^6.

5.8   TESTING HOMOGENEITY

Sections 3.2 and 3.5 derived various statistics for testing the hypotheses of demand homogeneity and Slutsky symmetry in the context of n unconditional demand equations. All these results carry over directly to conditional demand equations by replacing n with n_g, the number of goods in the group S_g. In this and the next section we shall apply these tests to the alcohol data by using the preferred model (6.8). We commence both sections with a brief review of the previous results with n interpreted as $n_g = 3$ alcoholic beverages.

Homogeneity takes the form

$$\sum_{j=1}^{3} \pi'_{ij} = 0 \quad i = 1, 2, 3,$$

which we write in vector form as

$$v' \gamma_i = 0 \quad i = 1, 2, 3,$$

where $v' = [0\ 1\ 1\ 1]$ and $\gamma_i = [\beta'_i\ \pi'_{i1}\ \pi'_{i2}\ \pi'_{i3}]'$. The budget constraint means that one of the three demand equations is redundant, so that we need only consider two. We write (6.8) for $i = 1, 2$ and $t = 1, \ldots, T$ (the sample size) as

$$y = (I_2 \otimes X)\gamma + \epsilon, \tag{8.1}$$

where y and ϵ are vectors consisting of 2 subvectors of T elements, namely,

$$y_i = [\bar{w}'_{it}(Dq_{it} - DQ_{gt})] \quad \text{and} \quad \epsilon_i = [\epsilon_{it}] \quad \text{for } t = 1, \ldots, T;$$

$\gamma = [\gamma'_1\ \gamma'_2]'$; I_2 is the 2×2 identity matrix; and X is a $T \times 4$ matrix whose tth row equals $(DQ_{gt}, Dp_{1t}, Dp_{2t}, Dp_{3t})$. Homogeneity can then be written for the two equations as

$$R\gamma = 0, \quad \text{where } R = I_2 \otimes v'. \tag{8.2}$$

We assume that the ϵ_{it}'s are independent and multivariate normal with zero means and a constant contemporaneous covariance matrix Σ. Let g be the LS estimator of γ, consisting of two subvectors of the form $g_i = (X'X)^{-1}X'y_i$. Also let S be the 2×2 matrix of mean squares and cross-products whose elements are $s_{ij} = e'_i e_j / (T - 4)$, where $e_i = y_i - Xg_i$ is the LS residual vector of the ith equation. Then, under the null hypothesis (8.2), the statistic

$$\frac{g'R'\Sigma^{-1}Rg/v'(X'X)^{-1}v}{\operatorname{tr} \Sigma^{-1}S} \tag{8.3}$$

is distributed as F with $n_g - 1 = 2$ and $(n_g - 1)(T - n_g - 1) = 2(T - 4)$ degrees of freedom.

The standard procedure used to apply (8.3) is to replace the unknown Σ matrix with its unbiased estimator S. This replacement means that the denominator of (8.3) becomes $\operatorname{tr} S^{-1}S = n_g - 1 = 2$, which is a constant, so that the test statistic becomes

$$g'R'S^{-1}Rg/v'(X'X)^{-1}v, \tag{8.4}$$

which is asymptotically distributed as χ^2 with $n_g - 1 = 2$ degrees of freedom.

The above results refer to the situation when constant terms are omitted from the demand equations. As the alcohol data require the addition of such terms, the homogeneity test needs to be appropriately adjusted before we apply it. Let K be the number of independent variables in each demand equation, including the constants. For Australia, we include two constant terms, one for the first part of the sample period, 1956/57–1964/65, and one for the remaining years. Consequently, there are $K = 6$ independent variables for that country, namely, the two constants, $DQ_{gt}, Dp_{1t}, Dp_{2t}$, and Dp_{3t}.

For the United Kingdom, there is one constant for the whole period, so that $K = 5$. For the United States, $K = 6$ as here also we use two constants, one for the period 1949/50–1967/68 and one for the remaining years. In all three countries, these constants are otherwise unrestricted.

The inclusion of the constants means that the following changes are required. The vectors v, γ_i, and g_i need to be redefined appropriately and X is now a $T \times K$ matrix; the elements of the S matrix become $s_{ij} = e_i'e_j/(T - K)$; and the statistic (8.3) is now distributed as F with

$$n_g - 1 = 2 \quad \text{and} \quad (n_g - 1)(T - K) = 2(T - K)$$

degrees of freedom.

The values of (8.4) are

Australia	3.55	
United Kingdom	10.66.	(8.5)
United States	9.80	

Using the asymptotic χ^2 test, these are to be compared with the critical values of $\chi^2(2)$ at the 5 and 1 percent levels of 5.99 and 9.21, respectively. On the basis of the asymptotic test, we conclude that homogeneity is acceptable for Australia at the 5 percent level; the hypothesis must be rejected for the United Kingdom and the United States.

Laitinen (1978) derived the exact (finite-sample) distribution of the statistic (8.4) under (8.2). With the constants included, this distribution is a multiple

$$\frac{(n_g - 1)(T - K)}{T - K - n_g + 2} = \frac{2(T - K)}{T - K - 1} \tag{8.6}$$

of F with $n_g - 1 = 2$ and $T - K - n_g + 2 = T - K - 1$ degrees of freedom. With T and K specified as

	T	K
Australia	21	6
United Kingdom	20	5,
United States	33	6

the values of (8.6) are

Australia	$30/14 = 2.14$
United Kingdom	$30/14 = 2.14$.
United States	$54/26 = 2.08$

Consequently, the exact 5 percent critical value for the statistic (8.4) for Australia is $(30/14) \times F(2, 14) = (30/14) \times 3.74 = 8.01$. The exact critical values, at the 5 and 1 percent levels, for all three countries are

	5 percent	1 percent	
Australia	8.01	13.95	
United Kingdom	8.01	13.95 .	(8.7)
United States	7.00	11.49	

A comparison of the values of (8.4) given in (8.5) with the critical values (8.7) shows that, according to the exact test, homogeneity can now be accepted for the United Kingdom and the United States at the 1 percent level. Of course, homogeneity remains acceptable for Australia at the 5 percent level.

5.9   TESTING SLUTSKY SYMMETRY

Our objective now is to test the hypothesis of Slutsky symmetry, given homogeneity. To do this we use $\sum_{j=1}^{3} \pi'_{ij} = 0$ to replace π'_{i3} in (6.8) for $i = 1, 2$ with $-\pi'_{i1} - \pi'_{i2}$. This yields

$$\bar{w}'_{it}(Dq_{it} - DQ_{gt}) = \beta'_i DQ_{gt} + \sum_{j=1}^{2} \pi'_{ij}(Dp_{jt} - Dp_{3t}) + \epsilon_{it} \quad i = 1, 2. \qquad (9.1)$$

We then write (9.1) in the form (8.1) with the following modifications: The matrix X is now $T \times 3$ with tth row $(DQ_{gt}, Dp_{1t} - Dp_{3t}, Dp_{2t} - Dp_{3t})$; the subvectors γ_i of γ now take the form $\gamma_i = [\beta'_i \ \pi'_{i1} \ \pi'_{i2}]'$; and $s_{ij} = e'_i e_j / (T-3)$.

Given homogeneity and with $n_g = 3$, the symmetry hypothesis takes the form $\pi'_{12} = \pi'_{21}$, which we write as

$$R\gamma = 0, \quad \text{where } R = [0 \ 0 \ 1 \ 0 \ -1 \ 0]. \qquad (9.2)$$

When Σ is known, the following statistic,

$$\frac{g'R'\{R[\Sigma \otimes (X'X)^{-1}]R'\}^{-1}Rg}{\frac{1}{2} \operatorname{tr} \Sigma^{-1} S}, \qquad (9.3)$$

is distributed as F with

$$q = \tfrac{1}{2}(n_g - 1)(n_g - 2) = 1 \quad \text{and} \quad (n_g - 1)(T - n_g) = 2(T - 3)$$

degrees of freedom under the null hypothesis (9.2).

When Σ is replaced by S, the test becomes

$$g'R'\{R[S\otimes(X'X)^{-1}]R'\}^{-1}Rg, \qquad (9.4)$$

which is asymptotically distributed as χ^2 with $q=1$ degree of freedom. In contrast to the situation regarding homogeneity, there are no exact results available for symmetry testing.

As before, we include two constant terms in each demand equation for Australia and the United States, one in each for the United Kingdom; these constants are defined in the previous section. This means that γ_i and g_i become $K\times1$ vectors, where K is the number of independent variables in each demand equation ($K=5$ for Australia and the U.S., 4 for the U.K.); X becomes a $T\times K$ matrix; R needs to be redefined appropriately; the elements of S become $e_i'e_j/(T-K)$; and (9.3) is now distributed as F with

$$q=\tfrac{1}{2}(n_g-1)(n_g-2)=1 \quad \text{and} \quad (n_g-1)(T-K)=2(T-K)$$

degrees of freedom.

The values of (9.4) are

Australia	.43	
United Kingdom	.17,	(9.5)
United States	1.61	

which are all less than the critical value of $\chi^2(1)$ at the 5 percent level of 3.84. Accordingly, symmetry is acceptable for all three countries.

5.10 HOW DO THE THREE BEVERAGES INTERACT IN THE UTILITY FUNCTION?

In this section we present some preliminary evidence about the utility interactions of beer, wine, and spirits. This evidence will be used in the next section to formulate demand equations in terms of relative prices.

In Section 4.9 we showed that the modified conditional Slutsky coefficients can be decomposed as

$$\pi_{ij}' = \nu_{ij}' - \frac{\phi\Theta_g}{W_g}\theta_i'\theta_j' \quad i,j\in S_g, \qquad (10.1)$$

where

$$\nu_{ij}' = \frac{\lambda}{MW_g}p_ip_ju^{ij} \quad i,j\in S_g \qquad (10.2)$$

is the (i,j)th modified price coefficient, λ being the marginal utility of income and u^{ij} the (i,j)th element of the inverse of the diagonal block of the

Hessian matrix of the utility function referring to S_g. That is, for $i, j \in S_g$, $[u^{ij}] = [\partial^2 u / \partial q_i \partial q_j]^{-1}$. Under block independence, the term $\phi \Theta_g / W_g$ in (10.1) is interpreted as the own-price elasticity of demand for S_g as a group; $\phi < 0$ is the income flexibility, and Θ_g is the marginal share of S_g.

The price coefficients satisfy

$$v'_{ij} = v'_{ji} \quad i, j \in S_g \tag{10.3}$$

$$\sum_{j \in S_g} v'_{ij} = \frac{\phi \Theta_g}{W_g} \theta'_i \quad i \in S_g \tag{10.4}$$

$$\sum_{i \in S_g} \sum_{j \in S_g} v'_{ij} = \frac{\phi \Theta_g}{W_g}. \tag{10.5}$$

When the beverages are ordered appropriately, if the marginal utility of i is unaffected by changes in the consumption of any other beverage, then the matrix $[\partial^2 u / \partial q_i \partial q_j]$, defined in the previous paragraph, will have zeros for all the off-diagonal elements of the ith row (and column as the matrix is symmetric). Thus, $[\partial^2 u / \partial q_i \partial q_j]$ and its inverse will both be block diagonal. It then follows from (10.2) that the matrix $[v'_{ij}]$ will also have exactly the same structure. Consequently, the pattern of $[v'_{ij}]$ reflects the interaction in the utility function of the beverages.

To construct $[v'_{ij}]$, we use (10.1) in the form

$$v'_{ij} = \pi'_{ij} + \frac{\phi \Theta_g}{W_g} \theta'_i \theta'_j. \tag{10.6}$$

We then use the estimates of $[\pi'_{ij}]$ given in Table 5–7 and set $\phi \Theta_g / W_g$ equal to -0.6 for Australia and the United Kingdom, -0.5 for the United States. These are the mean values of the own-price elasticity of alcohol from Clements and Johnson (1983: 285), Selvanathan (1985: 23), and Clements and Finke (1984: 10). These values are in broad agreement with the estimates of this elasticity presented in (3.8), which were obtained under the assumption of a unitary income elasticity. Regarding the conditional marginal shares in (10.6), under Working's model these take the form $\beta'_i + \bar{w}'_{it}$, which we shall evaluate at sample means. The resulting $[v'_{ij}]$ constructed in this manner satisfies constraints (10.3) through (10.5).

Table 5–9 presents the conditional marginal shares and price coefficients for the three countries. For Australia the two off-diagonal price coefficients involving wine, v'_{12} and v'_{23}, are both insignificant, while the coefficient v'_{13}, which refers to beer and spirits, is significant. These results suggest that the marginal utility of both beer and spirits is unaffected by wine consumption. Consequently, the beverages form two block-independent groups, (1) beer

Table 5-9.   Conditional Marginal Shares and Modified Price
Coefficients Implied by Table 5-7 Estimates at Sample Means.[a]

Beverage	Conditional marginal share θ_i'	Modified price coefficients $\times 10$		
		ν_{i1}'	ν_{i2}'	ν_{i3}'
		Australia		
Beer	.521 (.034)	−2.329 (.271)	−.237 (.186)	−.557 (.178)
Wine	.104 (.033)		−.381 (.208)	−.003 (.150)
Spirits	.376 (.039)			−1.693 (.275)
		United Kingdom		
Beer	.239 (.046)	−1.549 (.618)	−.104 (.331)	.221 (.412)
Wine	.261 (.025)		−.576 (.257)	−.882 (.226)
Spirits	.501 (.040)			−2.342 (.426)
		United States		
Beer	.356 (.051)	−1.041 (.466)	−.097 (.146)	−.643 (.394)
Wine	.048 (.020)		−.049 (.100)	−.095 (.159)
Spirits	.595 (.053)			−2.239 (.480)

a. Asymptotic standard errors in parentheses.

and spirits and (2) wine. The sign of ν_{i3}' indicates that beer and spirits are specific complements. Similarly, beer is a preference-independent beverage in the United Kingdom, while wine is again preference-independent in the United States.

5.11   DEMAND EQUATIONS IN RELATIVE PRICES

We return to the conditional demand equation for good $i \in S_g$ given by equation (9.1) of Chapter 4,

$$\frac{w_i}{W_g}d(\log q_i) = \theta_i' d(\log Q_g) + \frac{\phi \Theta_g}{W_g}\sum_{j \in S_g}\frac{\theta_{ij}}{\Theta_g}d\left(\log \frac{p_j}{P_g'}\right).$$

We take S_g to be alcohol and write the above equation as

$$w_i' d(\log q_i) = \theta_i' d(\log Q_g) + \sum_{j=1}^{3}\nu_{ij}' d\left(\log \frac{p_j}{P_g'}\right), \tag{11.1}$$

where $w_i' = w_i/W_g$ and $\nu_{ij}' = \phi\theta_{ij}/W_g$ is a modified price coefficient. These price coefficients satisfy (10.3) through (10.5). In this section we use (11.1) to formulate a relative price version of the alcohol demand equations.

In the previous section we found that the Australian data indicated that wine is a preference-independent beverage, while beer and spirits exhibited dependence. Consequently, we specify that the 3×3 symmetric matrix $[\nu'_{ij}]$ take the form

$$\begin{array}{c} \text{beer} \\ \text{wine} \\ \text{spirits} \end{array} \begin{bmatrix} \nu'_{11} & 0 & \nu'_{13} \\ & \nu'_{22} & 0 \\ & & \nu'_{33} \end{bmatrix}. \tag{11.2}$$

Under Working's model the conditional marginal share of i is $\theta'_i = \beta'_i + \bar{w}'_{it}$, so that (10.4) becomes

$$\sum_{j=1}^{3} \nu'_{ij} = \eta_{gg}(\beta'_i + \bar{w}'_{it}) \quad i = 1, 2, 3, \tag{11.3}$$

where $\eta_{gg} = \phi\Theta_g/W_g$ is the own-price elasticity of demand for alcohol as a group, which we take to be a constant.

We shall specify ν'_{13} as proportional to the geometric mean of the corresponding conditional budget shares,

$$\nu'_{13} = \kappa\sqrt{\bar{w}'_{1t}\bar{w}'_{3t}}, \tag{11.4}$$

where κ is a constant. As we previously found beer and spirits to be specific complements ($\nu'_{13} < 0$), we expect κ to be negative. It follows from (11.2) through (11.4) that

$$\nu'_{11} = \eta_{gg}(\beta'_1 + \bar{w}'_{1t}) - \kappa\sqrt{\bar{w}'_{1t}\bar{w}'_{3t}} \tag{11.5}$$

$$\nu'_{22} = \eta_{gg}(\beta'_2 + \bar{w}'_{2t}) \tag{11.6}$$

$$\nu'_{33} = \eta_{gg}(\beta'_3 + \bar{w}'_{3t}) - \kappa\sqrt{\bar{w}'_{1t}\bar{w}'_{3t}}, \tag{11.7}$$

where the last equation is also based on the symmetry of $[\nu'_{ij}]$.

We define

$$z_{it} = (\beta'_i + \bar{w}'_{it})\left[Dp_{it} - Dp_{3t} - \sum_{j=1}^{2} (\beta'_j + \bar{w}'_{jt})(Dp_{jt} - Dp_{3t})\right]$$

$$i = 1, 2, 3 \tag{11.8}$$

$$c_t = \sqrt{\bar{w}'_{1t}\bar{w}'_{3t}}(Dp_{3t} - Dp_{1t}). \tag{11.9}$$

Then (11.2) through (11.7) imply the following demand equation for beer in terms of finite changes:

$$\bar{w}'_{1t}(Dq_{1t} - DQ_{gt}) = \beta'_1 DQ_{gt} + \eta_{gg} z_{1t} + \kappa c_t. \tag{11.10}$$

The wine equation is of the same form with the last term omitted,

$$\bar{w}'_{2t}(Dq_{2t} - DQ_{gt}) = \beta'_2 DQ_{gt} + \eta_{gg} z_{2t}, \tag{11.11}$$

and the spirits equation is

$$\bar{w}'_{3t}(Dq_{3t} - DQ_{gt}) = \beta'_3 DQ_{gt} + \eta_{gg} z_{3t} - \kappa c_t. \tag{11.12}$$

The derivation of (11.10) through (11.12) is given in Section 5.14.

It follows from (11.1) that the (i, j)th Frisch price elasticity is v'_{ij}/w'_i; this is the elasticity of demand for good i with respect to the Frisch-deflated price of j. Although one might be tempted to describe this as a *conditional* elasticity, as (11.1) holds constant total consumption of the group, no such qualification is necessary. This elasticity coincides with the corresponding unconditional concept. To see this we return to equation (3.4) of Chapter 4, the unconditional demand equation for $i \in S_g$ under block independence:

$$w_i d(\log q_i) = \theta_i d(\log Q) + \phi \sum_{j \in S_g} \theta_{ij} d\left(\log \frac{p_j}{P'}\right),$$

where $d(\log Q)$ is the Divisia volume index of the change in the consumer's real income and $d[\log(p_j/P')] = d(\log p_j) - d(\log P')$, with $d(\log P') = \sum_{i=1}^n \theta_i d(\log p_i)$ the overall Frisch price index. By dividing both sides of this equation by w_i, we obtain $\phi \theta_{ij}/w_i$ as the elasticity of demand for i with respect to the Frisch-deflated price of j. This can be expressed as

$$(\phi \theta_{ij}/W_g)/(w_i/W_g) = v'_{ij}/w'_i,$$

which is the same as before. Consequently, the Frisch elasticities are invariant.

We write η'_{ij} for the (i, j)th Frisch price elasticity. Under (11.2) the two nonzero cross-price elasticities are η'_{13} (beer/spirits) and η'_{31} (spirits/beer). It follows from (11.4) and $v'_{13} = v'_{31}$ that these take the form

$$\eta'_{13} = \kappa \frac{\sqrt{\bar{w}'_{1t}\bar{w}'_{3t}}}{\bar{w}'_{1t}}, \qquad \eta'_{31} = \kappa \frac{\sqrt{\bar{w}'_{1t}\bar{w}'_{3t}}}{\bar{w}'_{3t}}.$$

Consequently, the parameter κ is interpreted as the negative of the geometric mean of the two Frisch cross-price elasticities involving beer and spirits: $\kappa = -\sqrt{\eta'_{13}\eta'_{31}}$. Had we specified the coefficients v'_{ij} as constants, the Frisch price elasticities would be inversely proportional to the conditional budget shares. The large changes in the alcohol budget shares over time would then imply unacceptable instability in these elasticities.

Equations (11.10) through (11.12) constitute the demand model for Australia, given that wine is preference-independent with respect to beer and spirits. As wine is preference-independent in the United States also, we shall apply the same model to that country. For the United Kingdom, however, beer is independent while wine and spirits interact in the utility function. For that country we shall proceed as before and specify v'_{23} (for wine/spirits) as $\kappa\sqrt{\bar{w}'_{2t}\bar{w}'_{3t}}$, where the absolute value of κ is interpreted as the geometric mean of the two Frisch cross-price elasticities η'_{23} and η'_{32}. The demand equation for beer in the United Kingdom is then (11.10) with the last term omitted; the wine equation is (11.11) with κc_t added; and the equation for spirits is (11.12). The variable c_t in the wine and spirits equations is now defined as $\sqrt{\bar{w}'_{2t}\bar{w}'_{3t}}(Dp_{3t}-Dp_{2t})$.

5.12   ESTIMATES OF THE RELATIVE PRICE VERSION OF THE MODEL

To estimate equations (11.10) through (11.12) for Australia we add constant terms, as before, and zero-mean error terms. We then apply maximum likelihood under the assumption that these errors are independent and multivariate normal with a constant covariance matrix. A similar procedure is used for the other two countries. Details of the estimation procedure are given in Section 5.14.

Columns 2 through 4 of Table 5-10 contain the estimates of the model for each country taken individually. Initial results indicated that it was not possible to obtain precise estimates of the own-price elasticity of total alcohol η_{gg}. Consequently, we fix the value of this parameter at -0.6 for Australia and the United Kingdom and at -0.5 for the United States; these are the values that were used previously in Section 5.10. The estimates of the income coefficients and constants agree reasonably well with the corresponding estimates given in Table 5-7.

We see from column 3 of Table 5-10 that the estimate of κ for the United Kingdom, which refers to the utility interaction of wine and spirits, is -0.432 and significant. The negative sign indicates that these two beverages are specific complements, as expected. From column 2 the estimate of κ for Australia, referring to beer and spirits, is -0.183. Comparing this with the estimate of the same parameter for the United States of -0.156 (column 4), we see that the two values are reasonably similar. This suggests that it may be worthwhile to specify that this parameter take the same value in the two countries. This is pursued in column 5 where the Australian and American data are pooled to estimate one value of κ for beer and spirits. The resulting estimate is -0.170, which is approximately equal to a weighted average of the two

Table 5-10.   Third Set of Estimates of Conditional Demand

Parameter (1)	Australia (2)		United Kingdom (3)
Conditional income coefficient β_i'			
Beer	−.192 (.033)		−.345 (.045)
Wine	−.045 (.025)		.119 (.024)
Spirits	.237 (.037)		.225 (.040)
Own-price elasticity of alcohol η_{gg}	−.6		−.6
κ (Beer/spirits)	−.183 (.047)		−
κ (Wine/spirits)	−		−.432 (.090)
Constant $\alpha_i' \times 100$			
	1956/57– 1964/65	*1965/66– 1976/77*	
Beer	0	0	.510 (.188)
Wine	0	.822 (.117)	0
Spirits	0	−.822 (.117)	−.510 (.188)
Beer			
Wine			
Spirits			
Beer			
Wine			
Spirits			
Log-likelihood value	208.89		186.09

a. Asymptotic standard errors in parentheses.

previous values where the weights are inversely proportional to the asymptotic standard errors. Note also that the standard error of the pooled estimate of 0.040 is below that of the two previous estimates.

The estimates given in column 5 of Table 5–10 use the data from the three countries to estimate one β_i' for each beverage. These estimates indicate that beer is a conditional necessity (as $\beta_1' < 0$), spirits a conditional luxury, while wine is approximately a borderline case as $\beta_2' \approx 0$. The estimate of κ in col-

Equations for Alcoholic Beverages.[a]

United States (4)	All three countries combined (5)
−.118 (.050)	−.183 (.024)
−.037 (.015)	−.022 (.012)
.154 (.051)	.205 (.023)
−.5	−.6 (Australia, U.K.)
	−.5 (U.S.)
−.156 (.081)	−.170 (.040)
—	−.257 (.102)

United States (4):

1949/50–1967/68	1968/69–1981/82
−.368 (.142)	.554 (.190)
0	.436 (.066)
.368 (.142)	−.991 (.195)

All three countries combined (5):

Australia

1956/57–1964/65	1965/66–1976/77
0	0
0	.756 (.105)
0	−.756 (.105)

United Kingdom

.518 (.164)
0
−.518 (.164)

United States

1949/50–1967/68	1968/69–1981/82
−.302 (.137)	.642 (.167)
0	.427 (.066)
.302 (.137)	−1.069 (.173)

336.43	719.23

umn 5 for wine and spirits uses only the British data. This estimate is −0.257 (with asymptotic standard error 0.102), while previously (in column 3) it was −0.432 (0.090). Although this discrepancy is on the high side, it is nonetheless smaller than two standard errors. The constant terms given in column 5 use the individual country data only; as is to be expected, these are quite close to the previous estimates. (Details of the estimation procedure with the pooled data are also contained in Section 5.14.)

5.13   TESTING POOLING

In this section we answer the question, Should the data be pooled across countries or should the model be estimated for each country separately?

When the model is estimated for each country separately we adjust two independent income coefficients β_i' for each country. (One β_i' is constrained by $\sum_{i=1}^{3} \beta_i' = 0$.) As there are three countries, there is a total of $3 \times 2 = 6$ independent β_i' when the data are not pooled. Under pooling each β_i' takes the same value in each country, so that we adjust only two coefficients. Consequently, pooling involves $6 - 2 = 4$ resrictions insofar as the income coefficients are concerned. Also, κ for beer and spirits is taken to be the same in Australia and the United States when we pool, which involves one additional restriction. Relative to the three individual country models, pooling therefore involves a total of five restrictions.

We shall test these restrictions by means of a likelihood ratio test. Under the null hypothesis of pooling, the statistic $-2(L_r - L_u)$ has an asymptotic $\chi^2(5)$ distribution, where L_r is the log-likelihood value with the restrictions and L_u is the unrestricted value. Under the assumption that the observations are independent across countries, the unrestricted log-likelihood value is the sum of the values for the three countries individually, given at the bottom of columns 2 through 4 of Table 5–10; thus $L_u = 208.89 + 186.09 + 336.43 = 731.41$. As the restricted log-likelihood value is 719.23, the value of the test statistic is $-2(719.23 - 731.41) = 24.36$. As this value is too high for $\chi^2(5)$ we must reject the pooled model and use the individual country models.

5.14   MORE DERIVATIONS AND THE ML PROCEDURE

To derive (11.10), the beer demand equation for Australia, we write (11.1) for $i = 1$ in the following finite-change form:

$$\bar{w}_{1t}'(Dq_{1t} - DQ_{gt}) = \beta_1' DQ_{gt} + \sum_{j=1}^{3} \nu_{1j}'(Dp_{jt} - DP_{gt}'). \tag{14.1}$$

In view of (11.2), (11.4), and (11.5) the substitution term of (14.1) becomes

$$\sum_{j=1}^{3} \nu_{1j}'(Dp_{jt} - DP_{gt}')$$

$$= [\eta_{gg}(\beta_1' + \bar{w}_{1t}') - \kappa\sqrt{\bar{w}_{1t}'\bar{w}_{3t}'}](Dp_{1t} - DP_{gt}') + \kappa\sqrt{\bar{w}_{1t}'\bar{w}_{3t}'}(Dp_{3t} - DP_{gt}')$$

$$= \eta_{gg}(\beta_1' + \bar{w}_{1t}')(Dp_{1t} - DP_{gt}') + \kappa\sqrt{\bar{w}_{1t}'\bar{w}_{3t}'}(Dp_{3t} - Dp_{1t}). \tag{14.2}$$

Using $DP'_{gt} = \sum_{i=1}^{3} (\beta'_i + \bar{w}'_{it}) Dp_{it}$ and $\sum_{i=1}^{3} (\beta'_i + \bar{w}'_{it}) = 1$, it follows that

$$Dp_{1t} - DP'_{gt} = Dp_{1t} - Dp_{3t} - \sum_{k=1}^{2} (\beta'_k + \bar{w}'_{kt})(Dp_{kt} - Dp_{3t}). \quad (14.3)$$

Using (14.3) in (14.2) we have

$$\sum_{j=1}^{3} \nu'_{1j}(Dp_{jt} - DP'_{gt})$$

$$= \eta_{gg}(\beta'_1 + \bar{w}'_{1t})\left[Dp_{1t} - Dp_{3t} - \sum_{k=1}^{2} (\beta'_k + \bar{w}'_{kt})(Dp_{kt} - Dp_{3t}) \right]$$

$$+ \kappa \sqrt{\bar{w}'_{1t}\bar{w}'_{3t}} (Dp_{3t} - Dp_{1t})$$

$$= \eta_{gg} z_{1t} + \kappa c_t, \quad (14.4)$$

where z_{1t} and c_t are defined in equations (11.8) and (11.9), respectively. Substituting (14.4) in (14.1) yields equation (11.10). Equations (11.11) and (11.12) can be obtained in a similar manner.

We now set out the maximum likelihood estimation procedure for Australia; this is very similar to that used for the cross-country demand system described in Section 2.9. We write (11.10) through (11.12), with constants and disturbances added, as

$$y_{it} = \alpha'_i Z_t + \beta'_i DQ_{gt} + \eta_{gg} z_{it} + \kappa_i c_t + \epsilon_{it} \quad i = 1, 2, 3, \quad (14.5)$$

where $y_{it} = \bar{w}'_{it}(Dq_{it} - DQ_{gt})$; α'_i is a constant satisfying $\alpha'_1 = 0$ and $\alpha'_2 = -\alpha'_3$; $Z_t = 1$ for $t = 1965/66-1976/77$, 0 otherwise; $\kappa_1 = \kappa$, $\kappa_2 = 0$ and $\kappa_3 = -\kappa$; and ϵ_{it} is a disturbance term. Summing both sides of (14.5) over $i = 1, 2, 3$ yields $\sum_{i=1}^{3} \epsilon_{it} = 0$, which indicates that one of the three equations can be deleted; we delete the third. We then write (14.5) for $i = 1, 2$ as

$$y_t = X_t \theta + \epsilon_t, \quad (14.6)$$

where $y_t = [y_{1t} \ y_{2t}]'$;

$$X_t \theta = \begin{bmatrix} 0 & DQ_{gt} & 0 & z_{1t} & c_t \\ Z_t & 0 & DQ_{gt} & z_{2t} & 0 \end{bmatrix} \begin{bmatrix} \alpha'_2 \\ \beta'_1 \\ \beta'_2 \\ \eta_{gg} \\ \kappa \end{bmatrix};$$

and $\epsilon_t = [\epsilon_{1t} \ \epsilon_{2t}]'$.

The twenty-one disturbance vectors $\epsilon_1, \ldots, \epsilon_{21}$ are assumed to be normal and independent with zero mean vector and nonsingular covariance matrix Σ. The log-likelihood function is

$$L = \text{constant} + \frac{21}{2} \log|\Sigma^{-1}| - \frac{1}{2} \sum_{t=1}^{21} (y_t - X_t\theta)'\Sigma^{-1}(y_t - X_t\theta). \tag{14.7}$$

Differentiation of (14.7) with respect to Σ^{-1} and θ' yields

$$\frac{\partial L}{\partial \Sigma^{-1}} = \frac{21}{2}\Sigma' - \frac{1}{2} \sum_{t=1}^{21} (y_t - X_t\theta)(y_t - X_t\theta)',$$

$$\frac{\partial L}{\partial \theta'} = \sum_{t=1}^{21} (y_t - X_t\theta)'\Sigma^{-1} \frac{\partial(X_t\theta)}{\partial \theta'},$$

where

$$\frac{\partial(X_t\theta)}{\partial\theta'} = \begin{bmatrix} 0 & DQ_{gt} + \eta_{gg}\dfrac{\partial z_{1t}}{\partial\beta_1'} & \eta_{gg}\dfrac{\partial z_{1t}}{\partial\beta_2'} & z_{1t} & c_t \\[2ex] Z_t & \eta_{gg}\dfrac{\partial z_{2t}}{\partial\beta_1'} & DQ_{gt} + \eta_{gg}\dfrac{\partial z_{2t}}{\partial\beta_2'} & z_{2t} & 0 \end{bmatrix}, \tag{14.8}$$

with

$$\frac{\partial z_{it}}{\partial\beta_j'} = -(\beta_i' + \bar{w}_{it}')(Dp_{jt} - Dp_{3t})$$
$$+ \delta_{ij}\left[(Dp_{it} - Dp_{3t}) - \sum_{k=1}^{2} (\beta_k' + \bar{w}_{kt}')(Dp_{kt} - Dp_{3t})\right] \quad i, j = 1, 2$$

and δ_{ij} the Kronecker delta.

The information matrix of the ML procedure is block-diagonal with respect to θ and Σ^{-1}. Consequently, the asymptotic covariance matrix of the ML estimator is equal to minus the inverse of the expectation of the derivative $\partial^2 L/\partial\theta\partial\theta'$. The expectation of this derivative is

$$K = -\sum_{t=1}^{21} \frac{\partial(X_t\theta)'}{\partial\theta}\Sigma^{-1}\frac{\partial(X_t\theta)}{\partial\theta'}, \tag{14.9}$$

so that the asymptotic covariance matrix is $-K^{-1}$.

To estimate the model with η_{gg} specified as -0.6 requires the following adjustments. We rewrite (14.6) as

$$y_t = -0.6z_t + X_t\theta + \epsilon_t,$$

where $z_t = [z_{it}]$; X_t is as before except that the second last column is omitted; and η_{gg} is now omitted from the parameter vector θ. In (14.7) and the following three equations $X_t\theta$ is replaced by $-0.6z_t + X_t\theta$. In (14.8) η_{gg} is replaced by -0.6 and the second last column is omitted. Finally, X_t and θ in (14.9) are interpreted as having their new definitions.

The ML estimates given in column 2 of Table 5–10 were then obtained by Newton's method based on successive estimates of K. The asymptotic standard errors are the square roots of the diagonal elements of $-K^{-1}$ with ML estimates substituted for the unknown parameters in K. The estimation procedure for the other two countries is similar.

When the data are pooled we specify that the income coefficients β_i' are the same across countries; $\eta_{gg} = -0.6$ for Australia and the United Kingdom, -0.5 for the United States; and that the κ parameter for beer and spirits is the same in Australia and the United States. We denote countries by a superscript (1 for Australia, 2 for the U.K., and 3 for the U.S.) and write the beer and wine equations for Australia as

$$y_{it}^1 = -.6z_{it}^1 + \alpha_i^1 Z_t^1 + \beta_i' DQ_{gt}^1 + \kappa_i^1 c_t^1 + \epsilon_{it}^1 \quad i = 1, 2, \tag{14.10}$$

where $\alpha_1^1 = 0$; $Z_t^1 = 1$ for $t = 1965/66$ through $1976/77$, 0 otherwise; and $\kappa_2^1 = 0$. These equations for the United Kingdom are

$$y_{it}^2 = -.6z_{it}^2 + \alpha_i^2 + \beta_i' DQ_{gt}^2 + \kappa_i^2 c_t^2 + \epsilon_{it}^2 \quad i = 1, 2, \tag{14.11}$$

where $\alpha_2^2 = 0$; and $\kappa_1^2 = 0$. The American equations are

$$y_{it}^3 = -.5z_{it}^3 + \alpha_{i1}^3 Z_t^3 + \alpha_{i2}^3 (1 - Z_t^3) + \beta_i' DQ_{gt}^3 + \kappa_i^3 c_t^3 + \epsilon_{it}^3 \quad i = 1, 2, \tag{14.12}$$

where $\alpha_{21}^3 = 0$; $Z_t^3 = 1$ for $t = 1949/50 - 1967/68$, 0 otherwise; and $\kappa_1^3 = \kappa_1^1$, $\kappa_2^3 = 0$. In (14.10) through (14.12) the primes have been omitted from the constant terms in order to keep the notation as simple as possible.

We define the vectors $y_i^c = [y_{it}^c]$, $z_i^c = [z_{it}^c]$, and $\epsilon_i^c = [\epsilon_{it}^c]$ for $t = 1, ..., T^c$ (the number of observations for country c) and

$$y^c = \begin{bmatrix} y_1^c \\ y_2^c \end{bmatrix}, \quad z^c = \begin{bmatrix} z_1^c \\ z_2^c \end{bmatrix}, \quad \epsilon^c = \begin{bmatrix} \epsilon_1^c \\ \epsilon_2^c \end{bmatrix}$$

for $c = 1, 2, 3$. We also define

$$y = \begin{bmatrix} y^1 \\ y^2 \\ y^3 \end{bmatrix}, \quad z = \begin{bmatrix} z^1 \\ z^2 \\ z^3 \end{bmatrix}, \quad \epsilon = \begin{bmatrix} \epsilon^1 \\ \epsilon^2 \\ \epsilon^3 \end{bmatrix},$$

$$\theta = [\alpha_2^1 \; \beta_1' \; \beta_2' \; \kappa_1^1 \; \vdots \; \alpha_1^2 \; \kappa_2^2 \; \vdots \; \alpha_{11}^3 \; \alpha_{12}^3 \; \alpha_{22}^3]',$$

and

$$X = \begin{bmatrix} 0 & DQ_g^1 & 0 & c^1 & 0 & 0 & 0 & 0 & 0 \\ Z^1 & 0 & DQ_g^1 & 0 & 0 & 0 & 0 & 0 & 0 \\ \hline 0 & DQ_g^2 & 0 & 0 & \iota_{T^2} & 0 & 0 & 0 & 0 \\ 0 & 0 & DQ_g^2 & 0 & 0 & c^2 & 0 & 0 & 0 \\ \hline 0 & DQ_g^3 & 0 & c^3 & 0 & 0 & Z^3 & \iota_{T^3} - Z^3 & 0 \\ 0 & 0 & DQ_g^3 & 0 & 0 & 0 & 0 & 0 & \iota_{T^3} - Z^3 \end{bmatrix},$$

where ι_{T^c} is a T^c-vector of unit elements; all other entries are T^c-vectors consisting of the corresponding elements. Equations (14.10) through (14.12) for $t = 1, \ldots, T^c$ can then be written as

$$y = \gamma z + X\theta + \epsilon,$$

where γ is a diagonal matrix with $-.6I_{2T^1}$, $-.6I_{2T^2}$, and $-.5I_{2T^3}$ on the diagonal.

We assume that the disturbances have zero means and are independent over time and countries. This implies that the covariance matrix

$$E(\epsilon\, \epsilon') = \Sigma$$

is block diagonal with cth block $\Sigma^c \otimes I_{T^c}$, where Σ^c is the 2×2 contemporaneous covariance matrix of country c. Under normality, the log-likelihood function is

$$L = \text{constant} + \tfrac{1}{2}\log|\Sigma^{-1}| - \tfrac{1}{2}(y - \gamma z - X\theta)'\Sigma^{-1}(y - \gamma z - X\theta),$$

which we maximize with respect to Σ and θ in the same way as before.

5.15   HOW GOOD ARE THE ML ESTIMATES?

Although maximum likelihood estimates have desirable asymptotic properties, in Section 3.11 it was demonstrated that ML estimates of nonlinear demand systems possess undesirable properties in small samples. In particular, when the Σ matrix is unknown and has to be estimated, the ML estimates have an impaired efficiency and their asymptotic standard errors overstate their precision. These problems were referred to as the two perils of not knowing Σ. These results were obtained for moderate to large-sized systems consisting of ten and fourteen equations. Do similar problems exist for the ML estimation of smaller nonlinear systems such as those used in this chapter?

To answer this question we follow the approach of Section 3.11 and use the alcohol demand models in a simulation experiment. For Australia we use the data-based ML point estimates given in column 2 of Table 5–10 as the true parameter values; and the data-based ML estimate of Σ as the true Σ of the experiment. We then draw $T^1 = 21$ independent quasi-normal error vectors with zero mean and covariance matrix Σ. Combining these errors with the observed values of the independent variables and the above-mentioned parameter values yields twenty-one new observations for each dependent variable. These values of the dependent variables and the observed values of the independent variables are then used to reestimate the model by ML. This procedure is repeated a number of times. Exactly the same approach is used for the other two countries.

Table 5-11 summarizes the results for 1000 trials. Column 2 gives the data-based ML estimates, which are the same as those contained in Table 5-10. The means over the 1000 trials are given in column 3. As these agree quite well with the true values, we conclude that the estimates are unbiased. Column 4 gives the root-mean-squared errors computed around the true values, while column 5 contains the root-mean-squared asymptotic standard errors. The RMSASEs are obtained by summing each diagonal element of the asymptotic covariance matrix over the 1000 trials, dividing by 1000, and then taking the square root. Although the RMSASEs are always below the corresponding RMSEs, the differences are not large, certainly not as large as those obtained for the ten- and fourteen-equation systems in Section 3.11. Consequently, our asymptotic standard errors provide a fairly realistic picture of the sampling variability of the estimates.

In the above experiment the data-based ML estimate of Σ was used to generate the errors. Then for each trial the new set of data was used to obtain a new estimate of this matrix. To analyze the effects of this we now redo the experiment using the original data-based ML estimate of Σ in place of the new estimate. The results are contained in columns 6 through 8 of Table 5-11. A comparison of columns 4 and 7 shows that the RMSEs are only slightly larger when Σ is estimated. Again in contrast to the results of Section 3.11, there is not much of an efficiency loss as a result of estimating Σ. (It should also be noted that the RMSASEs in column 5 of Table 5-11 are usually below those in column 8, which is in agreement with the results of Section 3.11.)

Table 5-12 shows the results of a simulation experiment for the model when the data from the three countries are pooled. The design of this experiment is the same as before with appropriate modifications. The data-based ML point estimates given in column 5 of Table 5-10 are used as the true parameter values. Following Section 5.14, Σ is now specified as a block-diagonal matrix. This matrix has three blocks on the main diagonal, one for each country of the form $\Sigma^c \otimes I_{T^c}$ where Σ^c is the 2×2 contemporaneous covariance matrix of country c and T^c is the number of observations for that country. The data-based ML estimate of Σ^c is used as the true value of this matrix in the experiment. The experiment then proceeds as before.

The results of Table 5-12 indicate that the estimates are unbiased and the efficiency loss due to Σ being unknown is minimal. These findings agree with those for the individual countries. However, when Σ is estimated there is now a tendency for the RMSASEs to understate the corresponding RMSEs by more than before (compare columns 4 and 5).

Our conclusion is that ML estimation of smaller nonlinear demand systems is on the whole satisfactory. The only qualification relates to the asymptotic standard errors of the pooled model, which we found to be too low.

Table 5-11. ML Estimation of Individual Country Models: Results for 1000 Trials.[a]

Parameter (1)	True value (2)	Σ unknown			Σ known		
		Mean (3)	RMSE (4)	RMSASE (5)	Mean (6)	RMSE (7)	RMSASE (8)
			Australia				
β'_i Beer	−.192	−.193	.033	.031	−.193	.033	.033
Wine	−.045	−.045	.026	.024	−.045	.026	.025
Spirits	.237	.238	.039	.035	.238	.038	.037
κ (Beer/spirits)	−.183	−.180	.047	.044	−.180	.045	.047
α'_i Wine	.822	.822	.124	.110	.822	.121	.117
			United Kingdom				
β'_i Beer	−.345	−.347	.048	.042	−.347	.046	.045
Wine	.119	.119	.024	.023	.119	.024	.024
Spirits	.225	.228	.040	.037	.227	.039	.040
κ (Wine/spirits)	−.432	−.432	.095	.085	−.432	.093	.090
α'_i Beer	.510	.516	.200	.172	.513	.192	.188
			United States				
β'_i Beer	−.118	−.116	.051	.046	−.116	.051	.050
Wine	−.037	−.037	.016	.015	−.037	.015	.015
Spirits	.154	.153	.052	.047	.153	.052	.051
κ (Beer/spirits)	−.156	−.149	.082	.075	−.148	.081	.081
α'_{i1} 1st beer	−.368	−.369	.152	.130	−.369	.149	.142
α'_{i2} 2nd beer	.554	.544	.191	.177	.544	.191	.190
α'_{i2} Wine	.436	.435	.069	.067	.435	.069	.066

a. All entries for the constants are to be divided by 100.

Table 5-12. ML Estimation of Pooled Model: Results for 1000 Trials.[a]

Parameter (1)	True value (2)	Σ unknown			Σ known		
		Mean (3)	RMSE (4)	RMSASE (5)	Mean (6)	RMSE (7)	RMSASE (8)
β'_i Beer	-.183	-.184	.030	.023	-.184	.029	.025
Wine	-.022	-.023	.013	.012	-.022	.012	.012
Spirits	.205	.207	.028	.023	.206	.027	.024
κ (Beer/spirits)	-.170	-.168	.043	.038	-.168	.041	.041
κ (Wine/spirits)	-.257	-.257	.109	.099	-.257	.105	.102
α'_i Australia, wine	.756	.759	.101	.101	.757	.097	.105
United Kingdom, beer	.518	.520	.158	.157	.517	.154	.165
United States, 1st beer	-.302	-.302	.133	.128	-.302	.130	.137
2nd beer	.642	.632	.161	.159	.633	.161	.166
Wine	.427	.426	.071	.068	.426	.071	.066

a. All entries for the constants are to be divided by 100.

5.16   MORE ON THE POOLING TEST

In Section 5.13 we constructed a test of pooling based on the likelihood ratio statistic $-2(L_r - L_u)$, where L_r is the log-likelihood value with the restrictions and L_u is the unrestricted value. Under the null hypothesis, this statistic has an asymptotic $\chi^2(5)$ distribution. This statistic took the value 24.36, which is much larger than the critical value of $\chi^2(5)$ at the 5 percent level of 11.07. As this is an asymptotic test, it is proper to inquire about the small-sample validity of the test.

We shall investigate this issue by means of a simulation experiment. The design of the experiment is exactly the same as that used in Section 5.15 for the pooled model. That is, we use the data-based ML point estimates and the estimate of Σ to generate new values of the dependent variables. These values of the dependent variables and the observed values of the independent variables are then used to reestimate the pooled model by ML. Now, we also use these data to reestimate the three individual country models, in addition to the pooled model. Next, we use these two sets of estimates to compute the test statistic $-2(L_r - L_u)$. This procedure is then repeated a number of times. As the null hypothesis of pooling is true by construction, the number of rejections should agree with the significance level if the test is working satisfactorily.

Table 5–13 contains the results for 1000 trials. While the rejection rates are somewhat above the significance levels, the performance of the test does not seem too bad. The last two rows of the table contain the ninety-fifth and ninety-ninth percentiles. Again, the simulated values are a little above the corresponding critical values of $\chi^2(5)$.

It is to be noted that the data-based value of the test statistic of 24.36 exceeds the simulated value of the ninety-ninth percentile of Table 5–13. In fact, the data-based value is not exceeded in any of the 1000 trials. This find-

Table 5–13.   The Pooling Test: Results for 1000 Trials.

	Simulated value	Theoretical value
Percent rejected at		
5 percent level	8.2	5.0
1 percent level	2.2	1.0
95th percentile	12.6	11.1
99th percentile	17.8	15.1

ing can be interpreted in terms of the Monte Carlo test introduced in Section 3.20. Under this procedure T_1 is defined as the data-based value of the statistic. We then simulate data sets under the null hypothesis $N-1$ times, yielding $N-1$ additional test statistics $T_2, ..., T_N$. The null hypothesis is rejected at the 5 percent significance level if T_1 is among the N' largest values of the T_i's such that $N'/N = 0.05$. In the present application, $T_1 = 24.36$, $N = 1001$, and $N' = 50$. As T_1 is the largest of the 1001 values of the test statistic, we reject the hypothesis of pooling.

To summarize, the asymptotic test of pooling has a reasonable small-sample performance. It seems fairly safe to reject pooling.

5.17   THE GOODNESS OF FIT OF THE MODEL

Table 5-14 contains the actual and predicted conditional budget shares. The predictions are from the individual country models in relative prices and are computed as the observed budget shares minus the residuals from the corresponding demand equations.

Next, following Sections 3.17 and 3.18, we measure the quality of these predictions by the information inaccuracy and its Strobel (1982) decomposition,

$$I_t = \sum_{i=1}^{3} w'_{it} \log \frac{w'_{it}}{\hat{w}'_{it}} \tag{17.1}$$

$$I_{Sit} = \hat{w}'_{it} - w'_{it} + w'_{it} \log \frac{w'_{it}}{\hat{w}'_{it}} \quad i = 1, 2, 3, \tag{17.2}$$

where w'_{it} and $\hat{w}'_{it}$ are the observed and predicted conditional budget shares of beverage i in year t. Both I_t and I_{Sit} are non-negative and increase as the predictions get worse. As $\sum_{i=1}^{3} \hat{w}'_{it} = \sum_{i=1}^{3} w'_{it} = 1$, it follows that $\sum_{i=1}^{3} I_{Sit} = I_t$.

Columns 2 through 4 of Table 5-15 give I_{Sit} for Australia, while column 5 contains I_t for that country. Column 5 indicates that the model provides excellent predictions for 1958, for example, while the worst predictions are for 1967, with most of the lack of fit coming from the spirits equation. Comparing the means of I_t given in the last row of the table, it can be seen that the predictions of the three budget shares taken together are best for the United States; but note that, relative to the other two countries, for the United States we adjust two additional parameters. Note also that these means are directly comparable with the inaccuracies for all three beverages given in Table 5-8.

The relative Strobel measure, I_{Sit}/I_t, is the proportion of the total inaccuracy of the model in year t accounted for by the misfit of the demand equation for good i. These proportions are shown in percentage form in the first three columns for each country of Table 5-16. The fourth column for each country contains the entropy of these proportions,

$$-\sum_{i=1}^{3} \frac{I_{Sit}}{I_t} \log \frac{I_{Sit}}{I_t},$$

which varies between 0 and $\log 3 \approx 1.1$. This entropy takes smaller values when the proportions I_{Sit}/I_t are more unequal, that is, when I_t is dominated by one or two equations. For Australia the entropy tends to be on the low side as the spirits equation accounts for a disproportionate share of the lack of fit of the model; on average spirits account for 55 percent, while beer and wine account for 15 and 30 percent, respectively. In the other two countries the three equations tend to contribute more equally to the inaccuracy I_t.

5.18   A CROSS-COUNTRY TIME SERIES TABULATION OF INCOME ELASTICITIES

In this and the next section we analyze the implications of the individual country models by presenting the income and price elasticities.

The conditional income elasticity of demand for beverage i is given by (4.4), which we implement in the form

$$\eta'_{it} = 1 + \frac{\beta'_i}{\bar{w}'_{it}},$$

with β'_i replaced by its estimate from Table 5-10 and where $\bar{w}'_{it}$ is the observed arithmetic average of the conditional budget share of i. These elasticities are given in the first three columns for each country of Table 5-17. At means for Australia, the conditional income elasticity for beer is 0.7, 0.6 for wine, and 2.5 for spirits. As noted previously, beer is a conditional necessity in all three countries, while spirits is a conditional luxury. The elasticities for wine are of the same order of magnitude in Australia and the United States, while they are a good deal higher in the United Kingdom. The fourth column for each country contains the Divisia variance of the conditional income elasticities,

$$V'_t = \sum_{i=1}^{3} \bar{w}'_{it}(\eta'_{it} - 1)^2 = \sum_{i=1}^{3} \frac{(\beta'_i)^2}{\bar{w}'_{it}}.$$

This V'_t is a measure of dispersion among the income elasticities. The variance is about the same in Australia and the United Kingdom, but a good deal lower in the United States. Within each country V'_t falls over time (although the fall in the U.S. is very small).

Table 5-14. Actual and Predicted Conditional Budget Shares for Alcohol in Three Countries.[a]

	Australia					
	Beer		Wine		Spirits	
Year (1)	A[b] (2)	P[c] (3)	A (4)	P (5)	A (6)	P (7)
1950	–	–	–	–	–	–
1951	–	–	–	–	–	–
1952	–	–	–	–	–	–
1953	–	–	–	–	–	–
1954	–	–	–	–	–	–
1955	–	–	–	–	–	–
1956	–	–	–	–	–	–
1957	77.04	76.65	8.51	8.54	14.45	14.82
1958	76.90	76.85	8.72	8.70	14.38	14.45
1959	76.03	76.39	9.15	8.99	14.82	14.62
1960	74.95	75.19	9.56	9.41	15.49	15.40
1961	73.97	74.42	9.73	9.90	16.31	15.68
1962	73.69	73.93	9.85	9.78	16.46	16.29
1963	73.35	73.22	10.08	9.86	16.58	16.92
1964	72.92	72.65	10.05	9.84	17.03	17.52
1965	72.17	71.96	10.16	10.15	17.67	17.89
1966	72.36	72.10	11.01	10.95	16.63	16.95
1967	72.99	72.22	12.22	11.74	14.79	16.04
1968	71.63	71.95	13.24	12.98	15.13	15.07
1969	70.17	70.19	15.06	14.57	14.77	15.25
1970	68.55	69.12	15.93	15.85	15.52	15.03
1971	69.16	68.31	15.80	16.93	15.04	14.76
1972	68.76	69.13	16.14	16.61	15.10	14.26
1973	68.14	68.37	16.15	16.25	15.71	15.38
1974	67.48	66.52	15.96	16.35	16.55	17.13
1975	65.40	66.29	17.40	16.84	17.20	16.87
1976	66.11	66.44	18.33	17.91	15.56	15.65
1977	65.37	66.32	18.91	18.95	15.72	14.73
1978	–	–	–	–	–	–
1979	–	–	–	–	–	–
1980	–	–	–	–	–	–
1981	–	–	–	–	–	–
1982	–	–	–	–	–	–
Mean	71.29	71.34	12.95	12.91	15.76	15.75

a. All entries are to be divided by 100.   b. A = actual.   c. P = predicted.

Table 5-14 continued.

Year	United Kingdom					
	Beer		Wine		Spirits	
	A (8)	P (9)	A (10)	P (11)	A (12)	P (13)
1950	–	–	–	–	–	–
1951	–	–	–	–	–	–
1952	–	–	–	–	–	–
1953	–	–	–	–	–	–
1954	–	–	–	–	–	–
1955	–	–	–	–	–	–
1956	63.15	63.58	10.04	10.30	26.81	26.11
1957	63.47	63.62	10.37	10.16	26.16	26.22
1958	62.43	64.45	10.47	10.00	27.09	25.54
1959	60.21	60.40	11.10	11.19	28.70	28.41
1960	58.83	58.54	11.52	11.32	29.65	30.14
1961	58.03	57.32	11.55	11.93	30.42	30.75
1962	59.17	59.29	10.76	10.83	30.06	29.88
1963	58.19	59.28	13.00	12.24	28.81	28.48
1964	56.96	56.63	13.72	13.56	29.32	29.80
1965	58.86	58.53	13.15	13.21	27.98	28.26
1966	58.51	58.86	13.62	13.28	27.88	27.85
1967	58.71	58.69	14.22	13.61	27.07	27.70
1968	57.06	57.89	15.20	14.49	27.74	27.62
1969	59.18	57.66	15.21	15.62	25.61	26.72
1970	59.00	58.73	14.37	15.63	26.63	25.64
1971	58.65	58.02	15.49	14.90	25.86	27.09
1972	57.12	57.41	16.19	16.16	26.69	26.43
1973	52.90	53.33	17.71	17.56	29.40	29.10
1974	52.76	52.39	18.34	18.98	28.90	28.64
1975	54.66	53.33	17.22	18.13	28.12	28.54
1976	–	–	–	–	–	–
1977	–	–	–	–	–	–
1978	–	–	–	–	–	–
1979	–	–	–	–	–	–
1980	–	–	–	–	–	–
1981	–	–	–	–	–	–
1982	–	–	–	–	–	–
Mean	58.39	58.40	13.66	13.66	27.95	27.95

Table 5–14 continued.

	United States					
	Beer		Wine		Spirits	
Year	A (14)	P (15)	A (16)	P (17)	A (18)	P (19)
1950	49.82	51.63	6.14	5.95	44.04	42.42
1951	48.84	48.72	5.52	6.20	45.64	45.08
1952	51.07	49.51	5.51	5.13	43.41	45.36
1953	51.41	51.73	5.10	5.13	43.49	43.13
1954	50.71	51.21	5.52	5.45	43.77	43.34
1955	50.21	50.31	5.47	5.48	44.32	44.21
1956	49.28	50.19	5.04	5.04	45.68	44.77
1957	47.89	48.40	5.62	5.52	46.49	46.08
1958	47.51	47.30	5.86	5.85	46.64	46.84
1959	47.21	46.67	5.84	5.93	46.95	47.40
1960	46.69	47.12	5.77	5.64	47.54	47.24
1961	46.98	46.82	6.05	5.86	46.97	47.32
1962	45.85	45.88	5.64	5.88	48.51	48.24
1963	45.14	44.65	5.63	5.51	49.22	49.84
1964	44.95	44.39	5.57	5.46	49.47	50.15
1965	44.10	44.46	5.43	5.45	50.46	50.09
1966	44.28	43.53	5.26	5.30	50.46	51.17
1967	43.21	43.05	6.04	5.73	50.75	51.22
1968	42.83	42.55	6.09	5.95	51.08	51.50
1969	42.98	43.25	6.53	6.51	50.49	50.25
1970	43.37	43.28	7.48	7.09	49.15	49.62
1971	43.56	43.92	8.44	7.91	48.00	48.17
1972	42.80	43.44	9.17	8.91	48.03	47.66
1973	43.11	42.93	9.53	9.79	47.36	47.28
1974	45.21	44.50	9.54	9.99	45.25	45.51
1975	47.18	47.09	9.65	9.78	43.16	43.13
1976	47.48	47.84	9.81	10.08	42.70	42.08
1977	48.07	47.60	10.05	10.22	41.87	42.17
1978	48.31	48.36	10.77	10.65	40.91	40.99
1979	50.08	49.62	11.09	11.18	38.82	39.19
1980	51.21	51.15	11.68	11.48	37.11	37.37
1981	51.79	51.88	12.18	12.14	36.03	35.98
1982	52.24	52.53	12.45	12.64	35.30	34.83
Mean	47.13	47.14	7.44	7.42	45.43	45.44

Table 5-15. Information Inaccuracies for Three Countries.[a]

Year (1)	Australia				United Kingdom				United States			
	Beer (2)	Wine (3)	Spirits (4)	Total (5)	Beer (6)	Wine (7)	Spirits (8)	Total (9)	Beer (10)	Wine (11)	Spirits (12)	Total (13)
1950	—	—	—	—	—	—	—	—	322.4	31.2	305.5	659.2
1951	—	—	—	—	—	—	—	—	1.4	385.0	35.0	421.3
1952	—	—	—	—	—	—	—	—	244.8	138.1	423.6	806.5
1953	—	—	—	—	—	—	—	—	10.2	.9	14.6	25.7
1954	—	—	—	—	—	—	—	—	24.7	5.0	21.1	50.8
1955	—	—	—	—	—	—	—	—	1.0	.1	1.4	2.5
1956	—	—	—	—	14.8	33.8	92.1	140.7	82.3	.0	91.6	173.9
1957	10.0	.4	45.4	55.9	1.7	21.8	.7	24.3	27.1	9.3	18.1	54.5
1958	.1	.3	1.6	2.0	319.2	108.7	459.8	887.7	4.3	.1	4.7	9.0
1959	8.4	14.1	13.5	36.0	3.2	3.8	14.8	21.8	31.5	6.6	21.9	60.0
1960	3.9	11.6	2.9	18.3	7.2	17.6	40.1	64.8	19.9	15.0	9.6	44.6
1961	14.3	14.9	125.7	154.9	44.2	62.4	17.7	124.3	2.8	30.1	13.1	46.0
1962	3.9	2.6	8.8	15.4	1.2	2.2	5.8	9.1	.1	49.6	7.8	57.5
1963	1.0	25.2	35.2	61.4	100.5	231.3	18.9	350.7	27.6	13.5	38.6	79.6
1964	5.1	22.9	68.0	96.0	9.4	8.9	39.1	57.4	35.5	11.0	45.3	91.8
1965	3.1	.0	13.6	16.7	9.4	1.2	13.5	24.0	14.1	.3	13.8	28.2
1966	4.6	1.5	29.5	35.6	11.1	42.3	.1	53.5	63.6	1.5	49.0	114.1
1967	41.1	95.8	499.8	636.7	.1	132.9	72.4	205.3	2.9	83.4	21.7	108.0
1968	7.2	26.3	1.1	34.6	60.3	170.9	2.8	233.9	9.3	15.8	17.1	42.1
1969	.0	83.1	75.4	158.5	198.4	53.6	234.6	486.6	8.2	.4	5.8	14.4
1970	23.6	2.2	78.1	103.9	6.0	519.0	189.0	714.0	.9	103.6	22.6	127.1
1971	52.2	384.7	26.8	463.7	34.3	116.8	281.5	432.6	14.7	172.1	2.9	189.8

Year												
1972	10.1	66.7	244.2	321.0	7.2	.2	12.7	20.1	46.7	38.4	14.5	99.6
1973	3.9	3.2	35.7	42.8	18.0	5.9	14.8	38.6	3.7	34.5	.7	38.9
1974	70.3	47.6	98.1	216.0	13.4	107.7	11.9	132.9	55.9	103.1	7.3	166.3
1975	60.4	92.2	32.6	185.2	164.4	234.2	30.4	429.0	1.0	8.5	.1	9.5
1976	8.3	48.8	2.5	59.6	—	—	—	—	12.9	36.1	45.4	94.4
1977	68.6	.3	323.8	392.7	—	—	—	—	23.4	14.8	10.7	48.9
1978	—	—	—	—	—	—	—	—	.2	6.8	.7	7.7
1979	—	—	—	—	—	—	—	—	21.6	3.9	17.6	43.1
1980	—	—	—	—	—	—	—	—	.3	17.5	9.0	26.8
1981	—	—	—	—	—	—	—	—	.8	.7	.3	1.8
1982	—	—	—	—	—	—	—	—	7.9	13.7	32.1	53.7
Mean	19.1	45.0	83.9	147.9	51.2	93.8	77.6	222.6	34.1	40.9	40.1	115.1

a. All entries are to be divided by 10^6.

Table 5-16. Relative Strobel Measures And Their Entropy for Three Countries.[a]

Year (1)	Australia				United Kingdom				United States			
	Beer (2)	Wine (3)	Spirits (4)	Entropy (5)	Beer (6)	Wine (7)	Spirits (8)	Entropy (9)	Beer (10)	Wine (11)	Spirits (12)	Entropy (13)
1950	—	—	—	—	—	—	—	—	48.9	4.7	46.4	.85
1951	—	—	—	—	—	—	—	—	.3	91.4	8.3	.31
1952	—	—	—	—	—	—	—	—	30.4	17.1	52.5	1.00
1953	—	—	—	—	—	—	—	—	39.6	3.6	56.7	.81
1954	—	—	—	—	—	—	—	—	48.6	9.9	41.5	.94
1955	—	—	—	—	—	—	—	—	38.8	5.4	55.7	.85
1956	—	—	—	—	10.6	24.0	65.5	.86	47.3	.0	52.7	.69
1957	17.9	.8	81.3	.51	7.2	89.8	3.1	.39	49.7	17.0	33.3	1.02
1958	6.6	14.4	79.0	.65	36.0	12.2	51.8	.97	47.5	.6	51.9	.72
1959	23.4	39.1	37.4	1.07	14.9	17.4	67.7	.85	52.5	11.1	36.5	.95
1960	21.3	63.1	15.7	.91	11.1	27.2	61.8	.89	44.7	33.7	21.6	1.06
1961	9.2	9.6	81.1	.61	35.5	50.2	14.2	.99	6.1	65.5	28.4	.80
1962	25.7	17.1	57.2	.97	12.8	23.8	63.4	.89	.2	86.3	13.5	.41
1963	1.6	41.0	57.4	.75	28.7	66.0	5.4	.79	34.6	16.9	48.5	1.02
1964	5.3	23.9	70.8	.74	16.3	15.5	68.2	.85	38.7	12.0	49.4	.97
1965	18.8	.1	81.0	.49	39.0	4.9	56.1	.84	50.1	1.0	48.8	.74
1966	13.0	4.1	82.9	.55	20.7	79.1	.2	.52	55.8	1.3	42.9	.75
1967	6.5	15.0	78.5	.65	.0	64.7	35.3	.65	2.7	77.2	20.1	.62
1968	20.7	76.1	3.3	.65	25.8	73.0	1.2	.63	22.0	37.5	40.5	1.07
1969	.0	52.4	47.6	.69	40.8	11.0	48.2	.96	56.7	3.0	40.3	.79
1970	22.7	2.1	75.2	.63	.8	72.7	26.5	.62	.7	81.5	17.8	.51
1971	11.3	83.0	5.8	.57	7.9	27.0	65.1	.83	7.8	90.7	1.5	.35

1972	3.2	20.8	76.1	.64	35.7	1.2	63.1	.71	46.9	38.5	14.6	1.00
1973	9.1	7.4	83.4	.56	46.6	15.2	38.3	1.01	9.6	88.7	1.7	.40
1974	32.5	22.0	45.4	1.06	10.1	81.0	8.9	.62	33.6	62.0	4.4	.80
1975	32.6	49.8	17.6	1.02	38.3	54.6	7.1	.89	10.2	88.5	1.3	.40
1976	13.9	81.9	4.2	.57	—	—	—	—	13.7	38.3	48.1	.99
1977	17.5	.1	82.4	.47	—	—	—	—	47.9	30.2	21.8	1.05
1978	—	—	—	—	—	—	—	—	2.7	88.2	9.0	.43
1979	—	—	—	—	—	—	—	—	50.2	9.0	40.9	.93
1980	—	—	—	—	—	—	—	—	1.2	65.3	33.5	.70
1981	—	—	—	—	—	—	—	—	42.8	39.7	17.5	1.04
1982	—	—	—	—	—	—	—	—	14.8	25.4	59.8	.94
Mean	14.9	29.7	55.4	.70	21.9	40.5	37.5	.79	30.2	37.6	32.2	.78

a. Entries in columns (2)–(4), (6)–(8), and (10)–(12) are to be divided by 100.

Table 5-17. Conditional Income Elasticities of Demand for Alcohol in Three Countries.

	Australia				United Kingdom				United States			
Year (1)	Beer (2)	Wine (3)	Spirits (4)	Divisia variance (5)	Beer (6)	Wine (7)	Spirits (8)	Divisia variance (9)	Beer (10)	Wine (11)	Spirits (12)	Divisia variance (13)
1949/50	—	—	—	—	—	—	—	—	.77	.39	1.36	.1047
1950/51	—	—	—	—	—	—	—	—	.76	.37	1.34	.1040
1951/52	—	—	—	—	—	—	—	—	.76	.34	1.35	.1054
1952/53	—	—	—	—	—	—	—	—	.77	.31	1.35	.1069
1953/54	—	—	—	—	—	—	—	—	.77	.31	1.35	.1068
1954/55	—	—	—	—	—	—	—	—	.77	.34	1.35	.1057
1955/56	.75	.48	—	—	.46	2.18	1.85	.5200	.76	.31	1.34	.1061
1956/57	.75	.48	2.51	.4303	.46	2.17	1.85	.5186	.76	.31	1.33	.1052
1957/58	.75	.50	2.64	.4608	.45	2.14	1.85	.5159	.75	.36	1.33	.1034
1958/59	.75	.52	2.62	.4552	.44	2.11	1.81	.5076	.75	.38	1.33	.1029
1959/60	.75	.53	2.56	.4408	.42	2.05	1.77	.4993	.75	.37	1.33	.1028
1960/61	.74	.54	2.49	.4234	.41	2.03	1.75	.4956	.75	.38	1.33	.1025
1961/62	.74	.55	2.45	.4132	.41	2.07	1.75	.4980	.75	.38	1.32	.1025
1962/63	.74	.55	2.43	.4101	.41	2.00	1.77	.4945	.75	.35	1.32	.1028
1963/64	.74	.55	2.41	.4045	.40	1.89	1.78	.4873	.74	.35	1.31	.1028
1964/65	.74	.57	2.37	.3943	.41	1.89	1.79	.4881	.74	.34	1.31	.1030
1965/66	.73	.61	2.38	.3975	.41	1.89	1.81	.4904	.73	.32	1.31	.1034
1966/67	.74	.65	2.51	.4253	.40	1.86	1.82	.4896	.73	.35	1.30	.1023
1967/68	.73	.68	2.58	.4419	.41	1.81	1.82	.4871	.73	.40	1.30	.1009
1968/69	.73	.71	2.58	.4416	.41	1.78	1.85	.4882	.73	.42	1.30	.1003
1969/70	.72		2.56	.4366	.42	1.81	1.86	.4915	.73	.48	1.31	.0989

1970/71	.72	.72	2.55	.4335	.41	1.80	1.86	.4906	.73	.54	1.32	.0976
1971/72	.72	.72	2.57	.4385	.40	1.75	1.86	.4882	.73	.59	1.32	.0968
1972/73	.72	.72	2.54	.4307	.37	1.70	1.80	.4808	.73	.61	1.32	.0964
1973/74	.72	.72	2.47	.4148	.35	1.66	1.77	.4779	.73	.62	1.33	.0967
1974/75	.71	.73	2.40	.4002	.36	1.67	1.79	.4793	.75	.62	1.35	.0977
1975/76	.71	.75	2.45	.4101	–	–	–	–	.75	.62	1.36	.0984
1976/77	.71	.76	2.51	.4257	–	–	–	–	.75	.63	1.36	.0987
1977/78	–	–	–	–	–	–	–	–	.76	.65	1.37	.0990
1978/79	–	–	–	–	–	–	–	–	.76	.67	1.39	.1000
1979/80	–	–	–	–	–	–	–	–	.77	.68	1.41	.1017
1980/81	–	–	–	–	–	–	–	–	.77	.69	1.42	.1031
1981/82	–	–	–	–	–	–	–	–	.77	.70	1.43	.1042
Mean	.73	.62	2.50	.4252	.41	1.91	1.81	.4944	.75	.46	1.34	.1019

Most of the elasticities are reasonably stable over time. We know from Section 1.8 that Working's model implies that all income elasticities decline with increasing affluence, prices remaining constant. Similarly, the conditional income elasticities implied by the conditional version of Working's model decline with increasing total consumption of the group if prices are held constant. However, looking at column 3 of Table 5-17, for example, we see that η_i' for wine in Australia increases from .5 to .8 over the sample period, a period of increasing total consumption of alcohol (see Table 5-4). The explanation is that these elasticities do not reflect exclusively changes in total alcohol consumption. These elasticities have been computed with the observed budget shares. As these shares incorporate the changes in tastes and relative prices that occurred over this period, in addition to increasing total alcohol consumption, it follows that the elasticities reflect the influence of all these factors.

5.19   A CROSS-COUNTRY TIME SERIES TABULATION OF PRICE ELASTICITIES

We now present price elasticities for the three beverages. Following Section 2.11, there are three such elasticities: Frisch, Slutsky, and Cournot.

We return to equation (11.1), the relative price version of the demand equation for beverage i,

$$w_i' d(\log q_i) = \theta_i' d(\log Q_g) + \sum_{j=1}^{3} v_{ij}' d\left(\log \frac{p_j}{P_g'}\right). \tag{19.1}$$

Dividing both sides of this equation by w_i' we obtain v_{ij}'/w_i' as the (i, j)th Frisch price elasticity, as stated in Section 5.11. This elasticity refers to the specific substitution effect. It will be recalled from Section 5.11 that the conditional and unconditional versions of this elasticity coincide. We implement this elasticity in the form

$$F_{ijt} = \frac{v_{ijt}'}{\overline{w}_{it}'}, \tag{19.2}$$

where the coefficients v_{ijt}' are defined in equations (11.2) and (11.4) through (11.7) after adding a time subscript to the left sides of those equations. Note that in Section 5.11 we wrote η_{ij}' for the Frisch elasticity.

The (i, j)th conditional Slutsky price elasticity refers to the total substitution effect of a change in the price of beverage j on the demand for i, total consumption of alcohol remaining constant. This can be obtained by writing $\sum_{k=1}^{3} \theta_k' d(\log p_k)$ for $d(\log P_g')$ in (19.1), so that the substitution term becomes

$$\sum_{j=1}^{3} v_{ij}' d\left(\log \frac{p_j}{P_g'}\right) = \sum_{j=1}^{3} v_{ij}'\left[d(\log p_j) - \sum_{k=1}^{3} \theta_k' d(\log p_k)\right]$$

$$= \sum_{j=1}^{3} \pi_{ij}' d(\log p_j),$$

where $\pi_{ij}' = v_{ij}' - \eta_{gg}\theta_i'\theta_j'$ is a modified conditional Slutsky coefficient. The conditional Slutsky elasticity is π_{ij}'/w_i', which we implement in the form

$$S_{ijt} = \frac{\pi_{ijt}'}{\bar{w}_{it}'}, \tag{19.3}$$

where the t subscript has been added to π_{ij}' to indicate its time dependence. The coefficients π_{ijt}' are defined as $v_{ijt}' - \eta_{gg}\theta_{it}'\theta_{jt}'$, where v_{ijt}' is defined as before; η_{gg} is the constant own-price elasticity of demand for alcohol as a group; and $\theta_{it}' = \beta_i' + \bar{w}_{it}'$.

The conditional Cournot price elasticity is the corresponding Slutsky elasticity plus the income effect of the change in the price of j. Thus, this elasticity holds constant total expenditure on alcohol in money terms and the other prices. The conditional income effect of a change in the jth price can be obtained as follows. From Section 1.9 we know that the logarithmic change in money income (M) can be decomposed into the Divisia volume index $d(\log Q)$ and the Divisia price index $d(\log P)$,

$$d(\log M) = d(\log Q) + d(\log P).$$

The conditional version of this is

$$d(\log M_g) = d(\log Q_g) + d(\log P_g),$$

where $M_g = \sum_{i=1}^{3} p_i q_i$ is total alcohol expenditure;

$$d(\log Q_g) = \sum_{i=1}^{3} w_i' d(\log q_i); \quad \text{and} \quad d(\log P_g) = \sum_{i=1}^{3} w_i' d(\log p_i).$$

Consequently, a change in p_j with M_g and the other prices constant means that the Divisia volume index equals

$$d(\log Q_g) = -d(\log P_g) = -w_j' d(\log p_j).$$

Substituting $-w_j' d(\log p_j)$ for $d(\log Q_g)$ in (19.1) yields $-\theta_i' w_j' d(\log p_j)$ for the income term of the demand equation. Dividing by $w_i' d(\log p_j)$ yields the income effect in elasticity form, $-\theta_i' w_j'/w_i'$. Adding to this the Slutsky elasticity we obtain the (i,j)th conditional Cournot price elasticity, $\pi_{ij}'/w_i' - \theta_i' w_j'/w_i'$, which we implement as

$$C_{ijt} = S_{ijt} - \frac{\theta_{it}' \bar{w}_{jt}'}{\bar{w}_{it}'}.$$ (19.4)

The relationship between the three elasticities is as follows. As

$$S_{ijt} = F_{ijt} - \eta_{gg} \frac{\theta_{it}' \theta_{jt}'}{\bar{w}_{it}'}$$ (19.5)

and $\eta_{gg} < 0$, it follows that $S_{ijt} > F_{ijt}$ since the conditional marginal and budget shares are always positive. Similarly, (19.4) implies that $C_{ijt} < S_{ijt}$. Combining (19.4) and (19.5) we obtain

$$\begin{aligned} C_{ijt} &= F_{ijt} - \eta_{it}'(\eta_{gg} \theta_{jt}' + \bar{w}_{jt}') \\ &= F_{ijt} - \eta_{it}' \bar{w}_{jt}'(\eta_{gg} \eta_{jt}' + 1), \end{aligned}$$

where η_{it}' is the conditional income elasticity of i. As these income elasticities are always positive, it follows that $C_{ijt} \gtreqless F_{ijt}$ according to whether

$$\eta_{gg} \eta_{jt}' + 1 \lesseqgtr 0 \quad \text{or} \quad \eta_{jt}' \gtreqless -\frac{1}{\eta_{gg}}$$

as $\eta_{gg} < 0$.

For Australia $\eta_{gg} = -.6$, so that $-1/\eta_{gg} \approx 1.7$, which exceeds the conditional income elasticities of beer and wine but not that of spirits (see Table 5-17). Consequently, the Cournot elasticities involving the prices of beer and wine will always be less than the corresponding Frisch elasticities, while the converse is true for spirits. In the United Kingdom where $\eta_{gg} = -0.6$ also, the η_i' for wine and spirits both exceed 1.7 in most years, so that $C_{ijt} > F_{ijt}$ for $j =$ wine and spirits; and conversely for $j =$ beer. In the United States no beverage has a conditional income elasticity above $-1/\eta_{gg} = 2$, so that $C_{ijt} < F_{ijt}$ for $j =$ beer, wine, and spirits.

Table 5-18 contains the three versions of the own-price elasticity for each beverage in the three countries. We replace all unknown parameters in equations (19.2) through (19.4) with their estimates given in Table 5-10 and interpret the $\bar{w}_{it}'$'s as the observed values of the arithmetic averages of the conditional budget shares. Spirits is usually the most price-elastic beverage in each country (no matter what version of the elasticity is used), while beer tends to be the least elastic. The elasticities for a given beverage are not too dissimilar across countries. For example, the mean elasticities are

Table 5-18. Conditional Own-Price Elasticities of Demand for Alcohol in Three Countries.

Year (1)	Australia Beer F (2)	S (3)	C (4)	Wine F (5)	S (6)	C (7)	Spirits F (8)	S (9)	C (10)
1949/50	—	—	—	—	—	—	—	—	—
1950/51	—	—	—	—	—	—	—	—	—
1951/52	—	—	—	—	—	—	—	—	—
1952/53	—	—	—	—	—	—	—	—	—
1953/54	—	—	—	—	—	—	—	—	—
1954/55	—	—	—	—	—	—	—	—	—
1955/56	—	—	—	—	—	—	—	—	—
1956/57	−.36	−.11	−.68	−.29	−.27	−.31	−1.11	−.51	−.91
1957/58	−.37	−.11	−.69	−.29	−.27	−.32	−1.16	−.56	−.94
1958/59	−.37	−.11	−.68	−.30	−.28	−.33	−1.16	−.55	−.94
1959/60	−.37	−.11	−.68	−.31	−.30	−.34	−1.13	−.53	−.92
1960/61	−.36	−.11	−.67	−.32	−.30	−.35	−1.10	−.51	−.90
1961/62	−.36	−.12	−.66	−.32	−.31	−.36	−1.08	−.49	−.89
1962/63	−.36	−.12	−.66	−.33	−.31	−.37	−1.07	−.49	−.89
1963/64	−.36	−.12	−.66	−.33	−.31	−.37	−1.06	−.48	−.88
1964/65	−.35	−.12	−.65	−.33	−.31	−.37	−1.05	−.46	−.87
1965/66	−.35	−.12	−.65	−.34	−.32	−.38	−1.05	−.47	−.88
1966/67	−.36	−.12	−.66	−.37	−.34	−.41	−1.11	−.52	−.91
1967/68	−.36	−.12	−.65	−.39	−.36	−.44	−1.15	−.55	−.94
1968/69	−.35	−.13	−.64	−.41	−.37	−.47	−1.15	−.55	−.94
1969/70	−.35	−.13	−.63	−.43	−.38	−.49	−1.15	−.55	−.94
1970/71	−.35	−.13	−.63	−.43	−.38	−.49	−1.14	−.55	−.94
1971/72	−.35	−.13	−.63	−.43	−.38	−.50	−1.15	−.55	−.94
1972/73	−.35	−.13	−.63	−.43	−.38	−.50	−1.14	−.54	−.93
1973/74	−.34	−.13	−.62	−.43	−.38	−.50	−1.11	−.52	−.91
1974/75	−.33	−.13	−.61	−.44	−.38	−.51	−1.08	−.49	−.90
1975/76	−.33	−.14	−.60	−.45	−.39	−.52	−1.10	−.51	−.91
1976/77	−.34	−.14	−.60	−.45	−.39	−.53	−1.13	−.54	−.93
1977/78	—	—	—	—	—	—	—	—	—
1978/79	—	—	—	—	—	—	—	—	—
1979/80	—	—	—	—	—	—	—	—	—
1980/81	—	—	—	—	—	—	—	—	—
1981/82	—	—	—	—	—	—	—	—	—
Mean	−.35	−.12	−.65	−.37	−.34	−.42	−1.11	−.52	−.92

Table 5–18   continued.

	United Kingdom								
	Beer			Wine			Spirits		
Year	F (11)	S (12)	C (13)	F (14)	S (15)	C (16)	F (17)	S (18)	C (19)
1949/50	–	–	–	–	–	–	–	–	–
1950/51	–	–	–	–	–	–	–	–	–
1951/52	–	–	–	–	–	–	–	–	–
1952/53	–	–	–	–	–	–	–	–	–
1953/54	–	–	–	–	–	–	–	–	–
1954/55	–	–	–	–	–	–	–	–	–
1955/56	–.27	–.19	–.49	–.61	–.32	–.54	–.85	–.30	–.79
1956/57	–.27	–.19	–.48	–.60	–.32	–.54	–.84	–.30	–.79
1957/58	–.27	–.19	–.48	–.60	–.31	–.53	–.84	–.29	–.78
1958/59	–.26	–.19	–.46	–.57	–.28	–.51	–.82	–.27	–.77
1959/60	–.25	–.19	–.44	–.54	–.25	–.48	–.79	–.24	–.76
1960/61	–.25	–.19	–.43	–.52	–.24	–.47	–.78	–.23	–.76
1961/62	–.25	–.19	–.43	–.53	–.24	–.47	–.78	–.23	–.76
1962/63	–.25	–.19	–.43	–.52	–.24	–.47	–.78	–.23	–.75
1963/64	–.24	–.19	–.42	–.50	–.21	–.46	–.77	–.22	–.74
1964/65	–.24	–.19	–.42	–.50	–.21	–.47	–.78	–.23	–.74
1965/66	–.25	–.19	–.43	–.51	–.22	–.48	–.79	–.24	–.74
1966/67	–.25	–.19	–.43	–.51	–.22	–.48	–.78	–.24	–.74
1967/68	–.24	–.19	–.42	–.50	–.21	–.47	–.78	–.23	–.73
1968/69	–.24	–.19	–.42	–.50	–.21	–.48	–.78	–.24	–.73
1969/70	–.25	–.19	–.43	–.51	–.22	–.49	–.79	–.25	–.74
1970/71	–.25	–.19	–.43	–.51	–.22	–.49	–.79	–.25	–.73
1971/72	–.24	–.19	–.42	–.50	–.20	–.48	–.78	–.24	–.72
1972/73	–.22	–.18	–.38	–.47	–.17	–.46	–.75	–.20	–.70
1973/74	–.21	–.17	–.35	–.45	–.15	–.45	–.72	–.17	–.69
1974/75	–.22	–.17	–.37	–.46	–.16	–.45	–.73	–.18	–.70
1975/76	–	–	–	–	–	–	–	–	–
1976/77	–	–	–	–	–	–	–	–	–
1977/78	–	–	–	–	–	–	–	–	–
1978/79	–	–	–	–	–	–	–	–	–
1979/80	–	–	–	–	–	–	–	–	–
1980/81	–	–	–	–	–	–	–	–	–
1981/82	–	–	–	–	–	–	–	–	–
Mean	–.25	–.19	–.43	–.52	–.23	–.48	–.79	–.24	–.74

Table 5-18 continued.

	United States								
	Beer			Wine			Spirits		
Year	F (20)	S (21)	C (22)	F (23)	S (24)	C (25)	F (26)	S (27)	C (28)
1949/50	−.24	−.09	−.48	−.19	−.19	−.21	−.51	−.11	−.70
1950/51	−.23	−.09	−.47	−.19	−.18	−.20	−.51	−.10	−.71
1951/52	−.24	−.09	−.47	−.17	−.17	−.18	−.51	−.10	−.70
1952/53	−.24	−.09	−.48	−.16	−.15	−.17	−.51	−.11	−.70
1953/54	−.24	−.09	−.48	−.16	−.15	−.17	−.51	−.11	−.70
1954/55	−.24	−.09	−.48	−.17	−.16	−.18	−.51	−.11	−.70
1955/56	−.23	−.09	−.47	−.15	−.15	−.17	−.51	−.10	−.71
1956/57	−.23	−.09	−.46	−.16	−.15	−.17	−.51	−.10	−.71
1957/58	−.22	−.09	−.45	−.18	−.18	−.20	−.51	−.10	−.72
1958/59	−.22	−.09	−.44	−.19	−.18	−.21	−.51	−.09	−.72
1959/60	−.22	−.09	−.44	−.19	−.18	−.20	−.51	−.09	−.72
1960/61	−.22	−.09	−.44	−.19	−.19	−.21	−.51	−.09	−.72
1961/62	−.22	−.09	−.43	−.19	−.18	−.21	−.51	−.09	−.72
1962/63	−.21	−.08	−.42	−.18	−.17	−.19	−.51	−.08	−.73
1963/64	−.21	−.08	−.42	−.17	−.17	−.19	−.51	−.08	−.73
1964/65	−.20	−.08	−.41	−.17	−.16	−.18	−.51	−.08	−.73
1965/66	−.20	−.08	−.41	−.16	−.16	−.17	−.51	−.08	−.74
1966/67	−.20	−.08	−.40	−.18	−.17	−.19	−.51	−.08	−.74
1967/68	−.19	−.08	−.39	−.20	−.19	−.22	−.51	−.08	−.74
1968/69	−.19	−.08	−.39	−.21	−.21	−.23	−.51	−.08	−.74
1969/70	−.20	−.08	−.40	−.24	−.23	−.27	−.51	−.08	−.74
1970/71	−.20	−.08	−.40	−.27	−.26	−.30	−.51	−.09	−.73
1971/72	−.20	−.09	−.40	−.29	−.28	−.33	−.51	−.09	−.73
1972/73	−.20	−.09	−.40	−.30	−.29	−.34	−.51	−.10	−.73
1973/74	−.21	−.09	−.41	−.31	−.29	−.35	−.51	−.10	−.72
1974/75	−.22	−.09	−.44	−.31	−.29	−.35	−.52	−.11	−.71
1975/76	−.23	−.09	−.45	−.31	−.29	−.35	−.52	−.12	−.70
1976/77	−.23	−.09	−.45	−.32	−.30	−.36	−.52	−.12	−.70
1977/78	−.23	−.10	−.46	−.32	−.30	−.37	−.52	−.13	−.70
1978/79	−.24	−.10	−.47	−.33	−.31	−.38	−.52	−.14	−.69
1979/80	−.25	−.10	−.49	−.34	−.31	−.39	−.52	−.15	−.68
1980/81	−.25	−.10	−.50	−.35	−.32	−.40	−.53	−.16	−.68
1981/82	−.26	−.10	−.50	−.35	−.32	−.41	−.53	−.16	−.67
Mean	−.22	−.09	−.44	−.23	−.22	−.26	−.51	−.10	−.71

Country	Beer			Wine			Spirits		
	F	S	C	F	S	C	F	S	C
Australia	−.4	−.1	−.7	−.4	−.3	−.4	−1.1	−.5	−.9
United Kingdom	−.3	−.2	−.4	−.5	−.2	−.5	−.8	−.2	−.7
United States	−.2	−.1	−.4	−.2	−.2	−.3	−.5	−.1	−.7
Mean	−.3	−.1	−.5	−.4	−.2	−.4	−.8	−.3	−.8

Most of the elasticities are also fairly stable over time.

Tables 5–19, 5–20, and 5–21 present the own- and cross-price elasticities. Here the own-price elasticities are the same as in the previous table and the Frisch cross-price elasticities, which are zero, are not presented.

(We also used the Table 5–10 estimates of the individual country models to calculate the characteristic roots of the matrices $[\nu'_{ijt}]$ and $[\pi'_{ijt}]$. For each country and year the three roots of $[\nu'_{ijt}]$ are negative, verifying that this matrix is negative definite; and two roots of $[\pi'_{ijt}]$ are negative while the other is zero, as required for negative semidefiniteness.)

5.20   THE ROLE OF OTHER FACTORS

Constant terms are included in all the demand equations of this chapter. These constants allow for autonomous trends in consumption; they could reflect changes in the demographic structure of the population, ethnic origin, social factors, and so on. The role of these factors in determining consumption is over and above that of prices and total expenditure on alcohol. In this section we use the demand equations to simulate consumption when these other factors are held constant. A comparison of actual and simulated consumption then shows the relative importance of the other factors.

The ith demand equation for Australia is given by (14.5), which we repeat here:

$$y_{it} = \alpha'_i Z_t + \beta'_i DQ_{gt} + \eta_{gg} z_{it} + \kappa_i c_t + \epsilon_{it}. \tag{20.1}$$

If we set the constant term α'_i equal to zero and assume that the volume index DQ_g, the prices, and the disturbances all remain unchanged, we obtain the simulated version of (20.1),

$$y^s_{it} = \beta'_i DQ_{gt} + \eta_{gg} z^s_{it} + \kappa_i c^s_t + \epsilon_{it}, \tag{20.2}$$

where the s superscript denotes a simulated value; $y^s_{it} = \bar{w}'^s_{it}(Dq^s_{it} - DQ_{gt})$;

Table 5-19. Conditional Price Elasticities of Demand for Alcohol in Australia.[a]

Year (1)	BB (2)	BS (3)	WW (4)	SB (5)	SS (6)
			Frisch		
1956/57	−.36	−.08	−.29	−.40	−1.11
1957/58	−.37	−.08	−.29	−.42	−1.16
1958/59	−.37	−.08	−.30	−.42	−1.16
1959/60	−.37	−.08	−.31	−.41	−1.13
1960/61	−.36	−.08	−.32	−.40	−1.10
1961/62	−.36	−.09	−.32	−.39	−1.08
1962/63	−.36	−.09	−.33	−.39	−1.07
1963/64	−.36	−.09	−.33	−.38	−1.06
1964/65	−.35	−.09	−.33	−.37	−1.05
1965/66	−.35	−.09	−.34	−.38	−1.05
1966/67	−.36	−.08	−.37	−.39	−1.11
1967/68	−.36	−.08	−.39	−.40	−1.15
1968/69	−.35	−.08	−.41	−.40	−1.15
1969/70	−.35	−.09	−.43	−.39	−1.15
1970/71	−.35	−.09	−.43	−.39	−1.14
1971/72	−.35	−.09	−.43	−.39	−1.15
1972/73	−.35	−.09	−.43	−.39	−1.14
1973/74	−.34	−.09	−.43	−.37	−1.11
1974/75	−.33	−.09	−.44	−.36	−1.08
1975/76	−.33	−.09	−.45	−.37	−1.10
1976/77	−.34	−.09	−.45	−.37	−1.13
Mean	−.35	−.09	−.37	−.39	−1.11

a. The notation ij at the top of columns 2–24 denotes the elasticity of demand for beverage i with respect to the price of j, where $i, j = B$ (beer), W (wine), S (spirits).

$$\bar{w}_{it}^{\prime s} = \tfrac{1}{2}(w_{it}^{\prime s} + w_{i,t-1}^{\prime s}), \tag{20.3}$$

with $w_{it}^{\prime s} = p_{it} q_{it}^s / M_{gt}^s$ and $M_{gt}^s = \sum_{i=1}^3 p_{it} q_{it}^s$;

$$z_{it}^s = (\beta_i^\prime + \bar{w}_{it}^{\prime s}) \left[Dp_{it} - Dp_{3t} - \sum_{j=1}^2 (\beta_j^\prime + \bar{w}_{jt}^{\prime s})(Dp_{jt} - Dp_{3t}) \right];$$

and

$$c_t^s = \sqrt{\bar{w}_{1t}^{\prime s} \bar{w}_{3t}^{\prime s}} (Dp_{3t} - Dp_{1t}).$$

Subtracting (20.2) from (20.1) we obtain

Table 5-19   continued.

	Slutsky								
	BB	BW	BS	WB	WW	WS	SB	SW	SS
Year	(7)	(8)	(9)	(10)	(11)	(12)	(13)	(14)	(15)
1956/57	−.11	.02	.09	.16	−.27	.11	.45	.06	−.51
1957/58	−.11	.02	.09	.17	−.27	.11	.49	.07	−.56
1958/59	−.11	.02	.09	.17	−.28	.11	.48	.07	−.55
1959/60	−.11	.02	.09	.18	−.30	.12	.46	.07	−.53
1960/61	−.11	.02	.09	.18	−.30	.13	.43	.08	−.51
1961/62	−.12	.02	.09	.18	−.31	.13	.41	.08	−.49
1962/63	−.12	.02	.09	.18	−.31	.13	.41	.08	−.49
1963/64	−.12	.02	.09	.18	−.31	.13	.40	.08	−.48
1964/65	−.12	.02	.09	.18	−.31	.14	.38	.08	−.46
1965/66	−.12	.03	.09	.18	−.32	.14	.38	.09	−.47
1966/67	−.12	.03	.09	.20	−.34	.14	.41	.11	−.52
1967/68	−.12	.04	.09	.21	−.36	.15	.42	.13	−.55
1968/69	−.13	.04	.09	.21	−.37	.16	.40	.15	−.55
1969/70	−.13	.05	.08	.21	−.38	.17	.38	.17	−.55
1970/71	−.13	.05	.08	.21	−.38	.17	.37	.17	−.55
1971/72	−.13	.05	.08	.21	−.38	.17	.38	.18	−.55
1972/73	−.13	.05	.08	.21	−.38	.17	.37	.18	−.54
1973/74	−.13	.05	.08	.21	−.38	.17	.35	.17	−.52
1974/75	−.13	.05	.08	.21	−.38	.18	.32	.18	−.49
1975/76	−.14	.06	.08	.21	−.39	.18	.32	.20	−.51
1976/77	−.14	.06	.08	.21	−.39	.18	.33	.21	−.54
Mean	−.12	.04	.09	.19	−.34	.15	.40	.12	−.52

$$y_{it} - y_{it}^s = \alpha_i' Z_t + \eta_{gg}(z_{it} - z_{it}^s) + \kappa_i(c_t - c_t^s)$$

so that

$$Dq_{it}^s = DQ_{gt}$$
$$+ \frac{\bar{w}_{it}'(Dq_{it} - DQ_{gt}) - \alpha_i' Z_t - \eta_{gg}(z_{it} - z_{it}^s) - \kappa_i(c_t - c_t^s)}{\bar{w}_{it}^{\prime s}}. \tag{20.4}$$

It follows from $w_i^{\prime s} = p_i q_i^s / M_g^s$ that

$$dw_i^{\prime s} = w_i^{\prime s} d(\log p_i) + w_i^{\prime s} d(\log q_i^s) - w_i^{\prime s} d(\log M_g^s).$$

A finite-change version of this equation is

$$w_{it}^{\prime s} - w_{i,t-1}^{\prime s} = \bar{w}_{it}^{\prime s} Dp_{it} + \bar{w}_{it}^{\prime s} Dq_{it}^s - \bar{w}_{it}^{\prime s} DM_{gt}^s. \tag{20.5}$$

Table 5-19 continued.

| | | | | Cournot | | | | |
Year	BB (16)	BW (17)	BS (18)	WB (19)	WW (20)	WS (21)	SB (22)	SW (23)	SS (24)
1956/57	−.68	−.05	−.02	−.20	−.31	.04	−1.45	−.15	−.91
1957/58	−.69	−.05	−.02	−.20	−.32	.04	−1.54	−.16	−.94
1958/59	−.68	−.05	−.02	−.21	−.33	.04	−1.52	−.16	−.94
1959/60	−.68	−.05	−.02	−.22	−.34	.04	−1.48	−.17	−.92
1960/61	−.67	−.05	−.03	−.22	−.35	.04	−1.42	−.16	−.90
1961/62	−.66	−.05	−.03	−.22	−.36	.04	−1.39	−.16	−.89
1962/63	−.66	−.05	−.03	−.22	−.37	.04	−1.38	−.16	−.89
1963/64	−.66	−.05	−.03	−.23	−.37	.04	−1.36	−.16	−.88
1964/65	−.65	−.05	−.04	−.22	−.37	.04	−1.33	−.16	−.87
1965/66	−.65	−.05	−.03	−.23	−.38	.04	−1.34	−.17	−.88
1966/67	−.66	−.05	−.03	−.25	−.41	.05	−1.41	−.18	−.91
1967/68	−.65	−.06	−.02	−.26	−.44	.05	−1.45	−.20	−.94
1968/69	−.64	−.06	−.02	−.27	−.47	.06	−1.43	−.22	−.94
1969/70	−.63	−.06	−.03	−.28	−.49	.06	−1.40	−.23	−.94
1970/71	−.63	−.07	−.03	−.28	−.49	.06	−1.38	−.23	−.94
1971/72	−.63	−.07	−.03	−.28	−.50	.06	−1.40	−.23	−.94
1972/73	−.63	−.07	−.03	−.28	−.50	.06	−1.37	−.23	−.93
1973/74	−.62	−.07	−.03	−.28	−.50	.06	−1.33	−.23	−.91
1974/75	−.61	−.07	−.04	−.28	−.51	.05	−1.28	−.23	−.90
1975/76	−.60	−.07	−.04	−.28	−.52	.06	−1.29	−.24	−.91
1976/77	−.60	−.07	−.03	−.29	−.53	.06	−1.33	−.26	−.93
Mean	−.65	−.06	−.03	−.25	−.42	.05	−1.39	−.19	−.92

Summing both sides of (20.5) over $i = 1, 2, 3$ and using $\sum_{i=1}^{3} w_{it}^{\prime s} = \sum_{i=1}^{3} \bar{w}_{it}^{\prime s} = 1$, we obtain

$$DM_{gt}^{s} = DP_{gt}^{s} + DQ_{gt}, \qquad (20.6)$$

where $DP_{gt}^{s} = \sum_{i=1}^{3} \bar{w}_{it}^{\prime s} Dp_{it}$ is the simulated Divisia price index of alcohol. In deriving (20.6) we have also used the assumption that DQ_{gt} remains unchanged, which implies that $\sum_{i=1}^{3} \bar{w}_{it}^{\prime s} Dq_{it}^{s} = DQ_{gt}$. Substituting (20.6) back into (20.5) and rearranging yields

$$w_{it}^{\prime s} = w_{i,t-1}^{\prime s} + \bar{w}_{it}^{\prime s}(Dp_{it} - DP_{gt}^{s}) + \bar{w}_{it}^{\prime s}(Dq_{it}^{s} - DQ_{gt}). \qquad (20.7)$$

We solve (20.4) and (20.7) jointly for Dq_{it}^{s} and $w_{it}^{\prime s}$ as follows. For the first observation ($t = 1$) we set $w_{i,t-1}^{\prime s}$ equal to the observed conditional budget

Table 5–20.   Conditional Price Elasticities of Demand for Alcohol in the United Kingdom.[a]

Year (1)	BB (2)	WW (3)	WS (4)	SW (5)	SS (6)
			Frisch		
1955/56	−.27	−.61	−.70	−.27	−.85
1956/57	−.27	−.60	−.70	−.27	−.84
1957/58	−.27	−.60	−.69	−.27	−.84
1958/59	−.26	−.57	−.69	−.27	−.82
1959/60	−.25	−.54	−.69	−.27	−.79
1960/61	−.25	−.52	−.70	−.27	−.78
1961/62	−.25	−.53	−.71	−.26	−.78
1962/63	−.25	−.52	−.68	−.27	−.78
1963/64	−.24	−.50	−.64	−.29	−.77
1964/65	−.24	−.50	−.63	−.30	−.78
1965/66	−.25	−.51	−.62	−.30	−.79
1966/67	−.25	−.51	−.61	−.31	−.78
1967/68	−.24	−.50	−.59	−.32	−.78
1968/69	−.24	−.50	−.57	−.33	−.78
1969/70	−.25	−.51	−.57	−.32	−.79
1970/71	−.25	−.51	−.57	−.33	−.79
1971/72	−.24	−.50	−.56	−.34	−.78
1972/73	−.22	−.47	−.56	−.34	−.75
1973/74	−.21	−.45	−.55	−.34	−.72
1974/75	−.22	−.46	−.55	−.34	−.73
Mean	−.25	−.52	−.63	−.30	−.79

a. The notation ij at the top of columns 2–24 denotes the elasticity of demand for beverage i with respect to the price of j, where $i, j = B$ (beer), W (wine), S (spirits).

share in the initial ($t = 0$) year, w_{i0}'. In the first iteration for this year we specify $\bar{w}_{it}'^{s}$ as also equal to w_{i0}' and find Dq_{i1}^{s} from (20.4). We use this Dq_{i1}^{s} in (20.7) to obtain $w_{i1}'^{s}$, which is then used in (20.3) to compute a new value of $\bar{w}_{it}'^{s}$. In the second iteration we use this new $\bar{w}_{it}'^{s}$ in (20.4) to yield a new Dq_{i1}^{s}; a new $w_{it}'^{s}$ from (20.7); and an updated value of $\bar{w}_{it}'^{s}$ from (20.3). The iterations continue until convergence is obtained, yielding final values of Dq_{i1}^{s} and $w_{i1}'^{s}$ for $i = 1, 2, 3$. To convert the changes to levels we use the initial year ($t = 0$) as the base so that $q_{i0}^{s} = q_{i0}$. Consequently, simulated consumption for $t = 1$ is

Table 5-20 continued.

				Slutsky				
Year	BB (7)	BW (8)	BS (9)	WB (10)	WW (11)	WS (12)	SB (13)	SW (14)	SS (15)
1955/56	−.19	.06	.13	.38	−.32	−.06	.32	−.02	−.30
1956/57	−.19	.06	.13	.38	−.32	−.06	.32	−.02	−.30
1957/58	−.19	.06	.13	.37	−.31	−.06	.32	−.02	−.29
1958/59	−.19	.06	.13	.34	−.28	−.06	.29	−.02	−.27
1959/60	−.19	.06	.13	.31	−.25	−.06	.27	−.02	−.24
1960/61	−.19	.06	.13	.29	−.24	−.06	.25	−.02	−.23
1961/62	−.19	.06	.13	.30	−.24	−.06	.25	−.02	−.23
1962/63	−.19	.06	.13	.29	−.24	−.06	.26	−.02	−.23
1963/64	−.19	.06	.12	.26	−.21	−.05	.25	−.02	−.22
1964/65	−.19	.06	.12	.27	−.21	−.05	.25	−.02	−.23
1965/66	−.19	.06	.12	.27	−.22	−.05	.26	−.02	−.24
1966/67	−.19	.06	.12	.27	−.22	−.05	.26	−.03	−.24
1967/68	−.19	.06	.12	.25	−.21	−.05	.26	−.03	−.23
1968/69	−.19	.07	.12	.25	−.21	−.05	.26	−.03	−.24
1969/70	−.19	.07	.12	.27	−.22	−.05	.28	−.03	−.25
1970/71	−.19	.07	.12	.26	−.22	−.05	.27	−.03	−.25
1971/72	−.19	.07	.12	.25	−.20	−.04	.26	−.03	−.24
1972/73	−.18	.06	.11	.21	−.17	−.04	.22	−.02	−.20
1973/74	−.17	.06	.11	.18	−.15	−.03	.20	−.02	−.17
1974/75	−.17	.06	.11	.19	−.16	−.04	.21	−.02	−.18
Mean	−.19	.06	.12	.28	−.23	−.05	.26	−.02	−.24

$$q_{i1}^s = q_{i0} \exp[Dq_{i1}^s] \quad i = 1, 2, 3. \tag{20.8}$$

For the second observation ($t = 2$) the iterative procedure is exactly the same except that (1) $w_{i,t-1}^{\prime s}$ in (20.3) and (20.7) now becomes the previous converged value of $w_{i1}^{\prime s}$, and (2) in the first iteration $\bar{w}_{it}^{\prime s}$ is now specified as $w_{i1}^{\prime}$. The procedure then yields final values of Dq_{i2}^s and $w_{i2}^{\prime s}$ for $i = 1, 2, 3$. To obtain q_{i2}^s we replace q_{i0} in (20.8) with q_{i1}^s and Dq_{i1}^s with Dq_{i2}^s. The procedure is then exactly the same for all subsequent observations.

Tables 5–22 and 5–23 give the actual and simulated values of consump-

Table 5-20   continued.

	Cournot								
Year	BB (16)	BW (17)	BS (18)	WB (19)	WW (20)	WS (21)	SB (22)	SW (23)	SS (24)
1955/56	−.49	.01	.01	−1.00	−.54	−.63	−.85	−.21	−.79
1956/57	−.48	.01	.01	−1.00	−.54	−.63	−.85	−.21	−.79
1957/58	−.48	.01	.01	−.98	−.53	−.63	−.85	−.22	−.78
1958/59	−.46	.01	.01	−.95	−.51	−.64	−.82	−.22	−.77
1959/60	−.44	.01	.01	−.91	−.48	−.66	−.79	−.22	−.76
1960/61	−.43	.01	.01	−.90	−.47	−.67	−.77	−.22	−.76
1961/62	−.43	.01	.01	−.91	−.47	−.68	−.77	−.22	−.76
1962/63	−.43	.01	.01	−.88	−.47	−.65	−.78	−.23	−.75
1963/64	−.42	.01	.01	−.83	−.46	−.60	−.78	−.26	−.74
1964/65	−.42	.01	.01	−.83	−.47	−.59	−.78	−.26	−.74
1965/66	−.43	.01	.01	−.83	−.48	−.58	−.80	−.27	−.74
1966/67	−.43	.01	.01	−.82	−.48	−.56	−.80	−.28	−.74
1967/68	−.42	.01	.01	−.79	−.47	−.54	−.80	−.29	−.73
1968/69	−.42	.00	.01	−.78	−.48	−.52	−.81	−.31	−.73
1969/70	−.43	.01	.01	−.80	−.49	−.52	−.83	−.30	−.74
1970/71	−.43	.00	.01	−.79	−.49	−.52	−.82	−.30	−.73
1971/72	−.42	.00	.01	−.77	−.48	−.50	−.81	−.32	−.72
1972/73	−.38	.00	.01	−.73	−.46	−.52	−.77	−.33	−.70
1973/74	−.35	.00	.01	−.69	−.45	−.52	−.74	−.34	−.69
1974/75	−.37	.00	.01	−.70	−.45	−.51	−.76	−.34	−.70
Mean	−.43	.01	.01	−.85	−.48	−.58	−.80	−.27	−.74

tion and the conditional budget shares. As before, we replace all unknown parameters in equations (20.4) and (20.7) with their estimates given in Table 5-10. The major differences between actual and simulated relate to wine consumption in Australia and the United States. In 1977, for example, actual consumption of wine in Australia is 13.7 liters per capita while simulated consumption is 6.7. Consequently, the role of other factors contribute a great deal to wine consumption. As simulated consumption of spirits is well above actual in Australia by 1977 and beer consumption is about the same, the conclusion is that most of the increase in wine due to other factors comes at the expense of spirits. A similar conclusion also holds for wine in the United States. Of course, these conclusions follow directly from the estimates of the constant terms in the demand equations of Table 5-10.

Table 5-21. Conditional Price Elasticities of Demand for Alcohol in the United States.[a]

Year (1)	BB (2)	BS (3)	WW (4)	SB (5)	SS (6)
			Frisch		
1949/50	−.24	−.14	−.19	−.17	−.51
1950/51	−.23	−.15	−.19	−.16	−.51
1951/52	−.24	−.15	−.17	−.16	−.51
1952/53	−.24	−.14	−.16	−.17	−.51
1953/54	−.24	−.14	−.16	−.17	−.51
1954/55	−.24	−.15	−.17	−.17	−.51
1955/56	−.23	−.15	−.15	−.16	−.51
1956/57	−.23	−.15	−.16	−.16	−.51
1957/58	−.22	−.15	−.18	−.16	−.51
1958/59	−.22	−.15	−.19	−.16	−.51
1959/60	−.22	−.16	−.19	−.16	−.51
1960/61	−.22	−.16	−.19	−.15	−.51
1961/62	−.22	−.16	−.19	−.15	−.51
1962/63	−.21	−.16	−.18	−.15	−.51
1963/64	−.21	−.16	−.17	−.15	−.51
1964/65	−.20	−.16	−.17	−.15	−.51
1965/66	−.20	−.17	−.16	−.15	−.51
1966/67	−.20	−.17	−.18	−.14	−.51
1967/68	−.19	−.17	−.20	−.14	−.51
1968/69	−.19	−.17	−.21	−.14	−.51
1969/70	−.20	−.17	−.24	−.14	−.51
1970/71	−.20	−.16	−.27	−.15	−.51
1971/72	−.20	−.16	−.29	−.15	−.51
1972/73	−.20	−.16	−.30	−.15	−.51
1973/74	−.21	−.16	−.31	−.15	−.51
1974/75	−.22	−.15	−.31	−.16	−.52
1975/76	−.23	−.15	−.31	−.16	−.52
1976/77	−.23	−.15	−.32	−.17	−.52
1977/78	−.23	−.14	−.32	−.17	−.52
1978/79	−.24	−.14	−.33	−.17	−.52
1979/80	−.25	−.13	−.34	−.18	−.52
1980/81	−.25	−.13	−.35	−.18	−.53
1981/82	−.26	−.13	−.35	−.19	−.53
Mean	−.22	−.15	−.23	−.16	−.51

a. The notation *ij* at the top of columns 2-24 denotes the elasticity of demand for beverage *i* with respect to the price of *j*, where *i, j = B* (beer), *W* (wine), *S* (spirits).

Table 5–21   continued.

	Slutsky							
Year	BB (7)	BW (8)	BS (9)	WB (10)	WW (11)	WS (12)	SB (13)	SW (14)	SS (15)
1949/50	−.09	.01	.08	.08	−.19	.11	.10	.02	−.11
1950/51	−.09	.01	.08	.07	−.18	.11	.09	.01	−.10
1951/52	−.09	.01	.08	.06	−.17	.10	.09	.01	−.10
1952/53	−.09	.01	.08	.06	−.15	.09	.10	.01	−.11
1953/54	−.09	.01	.08	.06	−.15	.09	.10	.01	−.11
1954/55	−.09	.01	.08	.07	−.16	.10	.09	.01	−.11
1955/56	−.09	.01	.08	.06	−.15	.09	.09	.01	−.10
1956/57	−.09	.01	.08	.06	−.15	.10	.09	.01	−.10
1957/58	−.09	.01	.08	.07	−.18	.11	.08	.01	−.10
1958/59	−.09	.01	.08	.07	−.18	.12	.08	.01	−.09
1959/60	−.09	.01	.08	.07	−.18	.12	.08	.01	−.09
1960/61	−.09	.01	.08	.07	−.19	.12	.08	.01	−.09
1961/62	−.09	.01	.08	.07	−.18	.12	.08	.01	−.09
1962/63	−.08	.01	.08	.06	−.17	.11	.07	.01	−.08
1963/64	−.08	.01	.08	.06	−.17	.11	.07	.01	−.08
1964/65	−.08	.01	.08	.06	−.16	.11	.07	.01	−.08
1965/66	−.08	.01	.08	.05	−.16	.10	.07	.01	−.08
1966/67	−.08	.01	.07	.06	−.17	.12	.06	.01	−.08
1967/68	−.08	.01	.07	.06	−.19	.13	.06	.02	−.08
1968/69	−.08	.01	.07	.07	−.21	.14	.06	.02	−.08
1969/70	−.08	.01	.07	.08	−.23	.16	.06	.02	−.08
1970/71	−.08	.02	.07	.09	−.26	.17	.06	.03	−.09
1971/72	−.09	.02	.07	.09	−.28	.19	.06	.03	−.09
1972/73	−.09	.02	.07	.10	−.29	.19	.06	.04	−.10
1973/74	−.09	.02	.07	.10	−.29	.19	.06	.04	−.10
1974/75	−.09	.02	.07	.11	−.29	.18	.07	.04	−.11
1975/76	−.09	.02	.07	.11	−.29	.18	.08	.04	−.12
1976/77	−.09	.02	.07	.11	−.30	.18	.08	.04	−.12
1977/78	−.10	.03	.07	.12	−.30	.18	.08	.05	−.13
1978/79	−.10	.03	.07	.12	−.31	.18	.09	.05	−.14
1979/80	−.10	.03	.07	.13	−.31	.18	.09	.05	−.15
1980/81	−.10	.03	.07	.14	−.32	.18	.10	.06	−.16
1981/82	−.10	.03	.07	.14	−.32	.18	.10	.06	−.16
Mean	−.09	.01	.07	.08	−.22	.14	.08	.02	−.10

Table 5-21 continued.

| | Cournot | | | | | | | | |
Year	BB (16)	BW (17)	BS (18)	WB (19)	WW (20)	WS (21)	SB (22)	SW (23)	SS (24)
1949/50	−.48	−.04	−.25	−.12	−.21	−.05	−.59	−.07	−.70
1950/51	−.47	−.04	−.26	−.11	−.20	−.05	−.57	−.06	−.71
1951/52	−.47	−.04	−.26	−.10	−.18	−.05	−.58	−.06	−.70
1952/53	−.48	−.03	−.25	−.10	−.17	−.04	−.60	−.06	−.70
1953/54	−.48	−.03	−.25	−.10	−.17	−.04	−.59	−.06	−.70
1954/55	−.48	−.04	−.25	−.10	−.18	−.05	−.59	−.06	−.70
1955/56	−.47	−.03	−.26	−.09	−.17	−.05	−.58	−.06	−.71
1956/57	−.46	−.03	−.27	−.10	−.17	−.05	−.56	−.06	−.71
1957/58	−.45	−.04	−.27	−.11	−.20	−.06	−.55	−.06	−.72
1958/59	−.44	−.04	−.27	−.11	−.21	−.06	−.55	−.06	−.72
1959/60	−.44	−.04	−.28	−.11	−.20	−.06	−.54	−.06	−.72
1960/61	−.44	−.04	−.28	−.11	−.21	−.06	−.54	−.06	−.72
1961/62	−.43	−.04	−.28	−.11	−.21	−.06	−.54	−.06	−.72
1962/63	−.42	−.03	−.29	−.10	−.19	−.06	−.53	−.06	−.73
1963/64	−.42	−.03	−.29	−.10	−.19	−.06	−.52	−.06	−.73
1964/65	−.41	−.03	−.29	−.09	−.18	−.06	−.52	−.06	−.73
1965/66	−.41	−.03	−.29	−.09	−.17	−.06	−.51	−.06	−.74
1966/67	−.40	−.03	−.30	−.10	−.19	−.06	−.51	−.06	−.74
1967/68	−.39	−.04	−.30	−.11	−.22	−.07	−.50	−.06	−.74
1968/69	−.39	−.04	−.30	−.12	−.23	−.07	−.50	−.06	−.74
1969/70	−.40	−.04	−.29	−.13	−.27	−.08	−.50	−.07	−.74
1970/71	−.40	−.04	−.29	−.15	−.30	−.09	−.51	−.08	−.73
1971/72	−.40	−.05	−.28	−.16	−.33	−.10	−.51	−.08	−.73
1972/73	−.40	−.05	−.28	−.17	−.34	−.10	−.51	−.09	−.73
1973/74	−.41	−.05	−.27	−.17	−.35	−.10	−.52	−.09	−.72
1974/75	−.44	−.05	−.26	−.18	−.35	−.09	−.55	−.09	−.71
1975/76	−.45	−.05	−.25	−.18	−.35	−.09	−.56	−.09	−.70
1976/77	−.45	−.05	−.25	−.19	−.36	−.08	−.57	−.09	−.70
1977/78	−.46	−.05	−.24	−.19	−.37	−.08	−.58	−.10	−.70
1978/79	−.47	−.06	−.23	−.20	−.38	−.08	−.60	−.10	−.69
1979/80	−.49	−.06	−.22	−.21	−.39	−.08	−.62	−.11	−.68
1980/81	−.50	−.06	−.21	−.22	−.40	−.07	−.63	−.11	−.68
1981/82	−.50	−.06	−.21	−.22	−.41	−.07	−.64	−.11	−.67
Mean	−.44	−.04	−.27	−.14	−.26	−.07	−.55	−.07	−.71

Table 5-22.   Actual and Simulated Consumption of Alcohol in Three Countries (Liters per capita).

	Australia					
	Beer		Wine		Spirits	
Year (1)	A^a (2)	S^b (3)	A (4)	S (5)	A (6)	S (7)
1949	—	—	—	—	—	—
1950	—	—	—	—	—	—
1951	—	—	—	—	—	—
1952	—	—	—	—	—	—
1953	—	—	—	—	—	—
1954	—	—	—	—	—	—
1955	—	—	—	—	—	—
1956	106.0	106.0	5.337	5.337	1.998	1.998
1957	100.5	100.5	5.208	5.208	1.800	1.800
1958	100.7	100.7	5.171	5.171	1.822	1.822
1959	101.1	101.1	5.206	5.206	1.913	1.913
1960	102.9	102.9	5.253	5.253	2.081	2.081
1961	102.6	102.6	5.100	5.100	2.073	2.073
1962	102.2	102.2	5.124	5.124	2.079	2.079
1963	103.5	103.5	5.283	5.283	2.026	2.026
1964	107.0	107.0	5.532	5.532	2.186	2.186
1965	110.3	110.3	5.571	5.571	2.351	2.351
1966	110.4	110.4	6.080	5.627	2.086	2.192
1967	113.1	113.1	6.821	5.906	2.071	2.290
1968	116.9	116.9	7.570	6.154	2.326	2.677
1969	120.5	120.3	8.255	6.391	2.301	2.786
1970	123.7	123.5	8.951	6.561	2.555	3.194
1971	125.8	125.5	8.685	5.875	2.579	3.354
1972	125.7	125.2	8.852	5.601	2.729	3.651
1973	129.5	129.2	9.791	5.789	3.085	4.226
1974	138.9	139.1	10.977	5.917	3.105	4.517
1975	140.4	140.7	12.278	6.447	2.975	4.576
1976	137.5	137.7	13.057	6.701	2.872	4.604
1977	136.1	136.3	13.653	6.672	3.166	5.079
1978	—	—	—	—	—	—
1979	—	—	—	—	—	—
1980	—	—	—	—	—	—
1981	—	—	—	—	—	—
1982	—	—	—	—	—	—

a. A = actual.   b. S = simulated.

Table 5–22 continued.

	United Kingdom					
	Beer		Wine		Spirits	
Year	A (8)	S (9)	A (10)	S (11)	A (12)	S (13)
1949	−	−	−	−	−	−
1950	−	−	−	−	−	−
1951	−	−	−	−	−	−
1952	−	−	−	−	−	−
1953	−	−	−	−	−	−
1954	−	−	−	−	−	−
1955	79.64	79.64	1.590	1.590	1.479	1.479
1956	80.44	79.79	1.665	1.665	1.570	1.600
1957	80.83	79.53	1.759	1.759	1.588	1.648
1958	78.36	76.44	1.811	1.809	1.613	1.703
1959	81.53	78.78	1.979	1.979	1.732	1.860
1960	84.83	81.18	2.287	2.285	1.839	2.008
1961	88.78	84.14	2.431	2.429	1.926	2.137
1962	88.33	83.04	2.489	2.475	1.925	2.166
1963	87.95	81.75	2.747	2.744	2.044	2.323
1964	91.40	84.02	3.120	3.115	2.195	2.529
1965	91.55	83.60	2.962	2.954	2.035	2.397
1966	92.35	83.47	3.135	3.125	2.057	2.463
1967	93.49	83.71	3.435	3.416	2.062	2.513
1968	94.46	83.48	3.828	3.807	2.150	2.658
1969	97.70	85.88	3.685	3.674	2.022	2.566
1970	99.96	86.92	3.752	3.726	2.296	2.904
1971	103.63	89.11	4.395	4.350	2.431	3.117
1972	106.05	89.85	5.037	4.968	2.783	3.560
1973	111.26	91.99	6.359	6.262	3.495	4.433
1974	114.20	93.23	6.699	6.597	3.855	4.883
1975	118.13	96.04	6.294	6.201	3.678	4.773
1976	−	−	−	−	−	−
1977	−	−	−	−	−	−
1978	−	−	−	−	−	−
1979	−	−	−	−	−	−
1980	−	−	−	−	−	−
1981	−	−	−	−	−	−
1982	−	−	−	−	−	−

Table 5–22 continued.

	United States					
	Beer		Wine		Spirits	
Year	A (14)	S (15)	A (16)	S (17)	A (18)	S (19)
1949	65.12	65.12	3.261	3.261	4.299	4.299
1950	63.76	64.24	3.364	3.365	4.735	4.697
1951	63.27	64.22	2.987	2.987	4.763	4.686
1952	63.36	64.74	3.229	3.229	4.446	4.333
1953	62.91	64.75	3.259	3.260	4.635	4.483
1954	59.78	61.98	3.238	3.239	4.430	4.247
1955	59.89	62.56	3.244	3.245	4.576	4.353
1956	59.18	62.34	3.304	3.304	4.847	4.581
1957	56.79	60.29	3.290	3.291	4.689	4.394
1958	56.52	60.45	3.264	3.264	4.685	4.353
1959	57.75	62.22	3.221	3.222	4.819	4.441
1960	56.99	61.93	3.326	3.326	4.936	4.519
1961	56.87	62.27	3.423	3.424	4.994	4.537
1962	57.26	63.23	3.324	3.324	5.169	4.662
1963	58.05	64.59	3.426	3.426	5.201	4.647
1964	60.11	67.42	3.547	3.547	5.464	4.847
1965	60.31	68.32	3.570	3.570	5.756	5.080
1966	62.31	71.09	3.582	3.583	5.978	5.237
1967	63.50	73.12	3.741	3.740	6.210	5.398
1968	65.35	75.94	3.880	3.880	6.573	5.680
1969	67.47	77.55	4.212	3.930	6.800	6.008
1970	69.95	79.42	4.749	4.187	6.876	6.198
1971	71.73	80.54	5.413	4.562	7.002	6.447
1972	72.95	81.04	5.912	4.765	7.123	6.700
1973	75.90	83.24	6.049	4.613	7.289	7.000
1974	79.32	85.79	6.079	4.351	7.406	7.269
1975	80.78	86.33	6.349	4.305	7.438	7.473
1976	81.29	85.90	6.468	4.131	7.418	7.625
1977	84.62	88.35	6.723	4.047	7.432	7.819
1978	87.37	90.14	7.123	4.136	7.558	8.128
1979	90.02	91.79	7.393	4.087	7.542	8.308
1980	91.84	92.61	7.872	4.238	7.488	8.461
1981	93.28	93.04	8.220	4.274	7.420	8.602
1982	92.65	91.44	8.311	4.126	7.157	8.523

Table 5-23. Actual and Simulated Conditional Budget Shares for Alcohol in Three Countries.[a]

	Australia					
	Beer		Wine		Spirits	
Year (1)	A[b] (2)	S[c] (3)	A (4)	S (5)	A (6)	S (7)
1949	—	—	—	—	—	—
1950	—	—	—	—	—	—
1951	—	—	—	—	—	—
1952	—	—	—	—	—	—
1953	—	—	—	—	—	—
1954	—	—	—	—	—	—
1955	—	—	—	—	—	—
1956	74.41	74.41	8.67	8.67	16.91	16.91
1957	77.04	77.04	8.51	8.51	14.45	14.45
1958	76.90	76.90	8.72	8.72	14.38	14.38
1959	76.03	76.03	9.15	9.15	14.82	14.82
1960	74.95	74.95	9.56	9.56	15.49	15.49
1961	73.97	73.97	9.73	9.73	16.31	16.31
1962	73.69	73.69	9.85	9.85	16.46	16.46
1963	73.35	73.35	10.08	10.08	16.58	16.58
1964	72.92	72.92	10.05	10.05	17.03	17.03
1965	72.17	72.17	10.16	10.16	17.67	17.67
1966	72.36	72.34	11.01	10.19	16.63	17.47
1967	72.99	73.04	12.22	10.59	14.79	16.36
1968	71.63	71.75	13.24	10.79	15.13	17.46
1969	70.17	70.34	15.06	11.70	14.77	17.96
1970	68.55	68.76	15.93	11.74	15.52	19.50
1971	69.16	69.51	15.80	10.77	15.04	19.71
1972	68.76	69.26	16.14	10.32	15.10	20.42
1973	68.14	68.64	16.15	9.64	15.71	21.72
1974	67.49	67.39	15.96	8.58	16.55	24.02
1975	65.40	64.80	17.40	9.03	17.20	26.17
1976	66.11	65.85	18.33	9.35	15.56	24.80
1977	65.37	65.50	18.91	9.25	15.72	25.25
1978	—	—	—	—	—	—
1979	—	—	—	—	—	—
1980	—	—	—	—	—	—
1981	—	—	—	—	—	—
1982	—	—	—	—	—	—
Mean	71.43	71.48	12.76	9.84	15.81	18.68

a. All entries are to be divided by 100.   b. A = actual.   c. S = simulated.

Table 5-23 continued.

| | United Kingdom | | | | | |
| | Beer | | Wine | | Spirits | |
Year	A (8)	S (9)	A (10)	S (11)	A (12)	S (13)
1949	–	–	–	–	–	–
1950	–	–	–	–	–	–
1951	–	–	–	–	–	–
1952	–	–	–	–	–	–
1953	–	–	–	–	–	–
1954	–	–	–	–	–	–
1955	63.83	63.83	10.20	10.20	25.97	25.97
1956	63.15	62.64	10.04	10.04	26.81	27.32
1957	63.47	62.46	10.37	10.37	26.16	27.16
1958	62.43	60.92	10.47	10.46	27.09	28.62
1959	60.21	58.13	11.10	11.09	28.70	30.79
1960	58.83	56.20	11.52	11.49	29.65	32.30
1961	58.03	54.84	11.55	11.50	30.42	33.66
1962	59.17	55.54	10.76	10.69	30.06	33.78
1963	58.19	54.19	13.00	13.01	28.81	32.80
1964	56.96	52.44	13.72	13.72	29.32	33.84
1965	58.86	53.83	13.15	13.15	27.98	33.02
1966	58.51	52.97	13.62	13.60	27.88	33.43
1967	58.71	52.72	14.22	14.20	27.07	33.09
1968	57.06	50.50	15.20	15.15	27.74	34.35
1969	59.18	52.17	15.21	15.22	25.61	32.61
1970	59.00	51.69	14.37	14.39	26.63	33.92
1971	58.65	50.98	15.49	15.51	25.86	33.51
1972	57.12	49.12	16.19	16.21	26.69	34.66
1973	52.90	44.41	17.71	17.72	29.40	37.88
1974	52.76	44.06	18.34	18.49	28.90	37.45
1975	54.66	45.39	17.22	17.34	28.12	37.27
1976	–	–	–	–	–	–
1977	–	–	–	–	–	–
1978	–	–	–	–	–	–
1979	–	–	–	–	–	–
1980	–	–	–	–	–	–
1981	–	–	–	–	–	–
1982	–	–	–	–	–	–
Mean	58.65	53.76	13.50	13.50	27.85	32.73

Table 5–23 continued.

	Beer		Wine		Spirits	
Year	A (14)	S (15)	A (16)	S (17)	A (18)	S (19)
1949	51.67	51.67	5.77	5.77	42.56	42.56
1950	49.82	50.19	6.14	6.14	44.04	43.68
1951	48.84	49.58	5.51	5.52	45.64	44.91
1952	51.07	52.18	5.51	5.51	43.41	42.31
1953	51.41	52.87	5.10	5.10	43.49	42.03
1954	50.71	52.55	5.52	5.52	43.77	41.94
1955	50.21	52.41	5.47	5.47	44.32	42.12
1956	49.28	51.85	5.04	5.03	45.68	43.12
1957	47.89	50.83	5.62	5.62	46.49	43.55
1958	47.51	50.81	5.86	5.86	46.64	43.33
1959	47.21	50.87	5.84	5.85	46.95	43.28
1960	46.69	50.72	5.77	5.77	47.54	43.51
1961	46.98	51.36	6.05	6.04	46.97	42.60
1962	45.85	50.62	5.64	5.64	48.51	43.74
1963	45.14	50.31	5.63	5.64	49.22	44.05
1964	44.95	50.48	5.57	5.58	49.47	43.94
1965	44.10	50.00	5.43	5.44	50.46	44.57
1966	44.28	50.54	5.26	5.26	50.46	44.21
1967	43.21	49.80	6.04	6.04	50.75	44.16
1968	42.83	49.77	6.09	6.09	51.08	44.14
1969	42.98	49.35	6.53	6.09	50.49	44.56
1970	43.37	49.17	7.48	6.59	49.15	44.24
1971	43.56	48.80	8.44	7.10	48.00	44.10
1972	42.80	47.49	9.17	7.39	48.03	45.12
1973	43.11	47.26	9.53	7.27	47.36	45.47
1974	45.21	48.83	9.54	6.82	45.25	44.35
1975	47.18	50.25	9.65	6.53	43.16	43.23
1976	47.48	50.00	9.81	6.25	42.70	43.76
1977	48.07	50.04	10.05	6.04	41.87	43.92
1978	48.31	49.79	10.77	6.25	40.91	43.96
1979	50.08	51.08	11.09	6.14	38.82	42.79
1980	51.21	51.70	11.68	6.30	37.11	42.00
1981	51.79	51.78	12.18	6.35	36.03	41.88
1982	52.24	51.66	12.45	6.20	35.30	42.14
Mean	47.27	50.49	7.39	6.00	45.34	43.51

United States

BIBLIOGRAPHY

The publications listed below are those referred to in Chapter 5, supplemented by some other publications that are directly related to the topics discussed.

Clements, K.W., and R. Finke. 1984. "The Demand for Beer, Wine and Spirits in the United States." McKethan-Matherly Discussion Paper MM4, The University of Florida at Gainesville.

Clements, K.W., and L.W. Johnson. 1983. "The Demand for Beer, Wine, and Spirits: A System-Wide Analysis." *Journal of Business* 56: 273–304. Reprinted in T.J. Coyne ed. 1985. *Readings in Managerial Economics,* 4th ed., 127–55. Plano, Tex.: Business Publications, Inc.

Clements, K.W.; P.S. Goldschmidt; and H. Theil. 1985. "A Conditional Version of Working's Model." *Economics Letters* 18: 97–99.

Goldschmidt, P.S. 1983. "Running the TRANSF and RESIMUL Programs at The University of Western Australia." Department of Economics, The University of Western Australia. Mimeo.

Laitinen, K. 1978. "Why Is Demand Homogeneity So Often Rejected?" *Economics Letters* 1: 187–91.

McGuinness, T. 1979. "An Econometric Analysis of Total Demand for Alcoholic Beverages in the U.K., 1956/75." Scottish Health Education Unit Report. Published without the data listing in *Journal of Industrial Economics* 29: 85–109.

Pearce, D. 1986. "The Demand for Alcohol in New Zealand." Discussion Paper No. 86-02, Department of Economics, The University of Western Australia.

Selvanathan, E.A. 1985. "The Demand for Alcohol in the U.K.: An Econometric Study." Discussion Paper No. 85-06, Department of Economics, The University of Western Australia.

Strobel, D. 1982. "Determining Outliers in Multivariate Surveys by Decomposition of a Measure of Information." *Business and Economic Statistics Section, Proceedings of the American Statistical Association,* pp. 31–35.

Working, H. 1943. "Statistical Laws of Family Expenditure." *Journal of the American Statistical Association* 38: 43–56.

Wymer, C.R. 1977. "Computer Programs: RESIMUL Manual." Washington, D.C.: International Monetary Fund. Mimeo.

EPILOGUE

Henri Theil
James Seale, Jr.
Denzil G. Fiebig

This Epilogue will illustrate that further explorations of the subject matter of this book can be quite rewarding.

THE DEMAND FOR ENERGY

In Chapter 2 we considered ten broad groups of goods. These groups correspond with standard classifications, but it frequently occurs that the analyst is interested in a different grouping. One of the advantages of the procedure and tables of Kravis and his colleagues is that such regroupings can be performed easily. This is a matter of adding the appropriate items both in national currency and in international dollars; by dividing the former sum by the latter we obtain the price of the new group in question.

Fiebig, Seale, and Theil (1986a) applied this procedure to the demand for energy by taking fuel out of "gross rent and fuel" and gasoline (plus oil and grease) out of "transport and communication," and then combining fuel and gasoline into "energy." This raises the number of groups from $n = 10$ to $n = 11$, but the model of Section 2.6 is otherwise unchanged. The ML estimates of the α_i's and β_i's of the eight goods that are not directly affected remain virtually unchanged, and so does the income flexibility ϕ. The β_i of energy has an ML estimate of 0.016 with an asymptotic standard error of 0.003.

The income elasticity of the demand for energy increases from about 1.25 at the U.S. and Western European per capita income levels to about 1.6 at those of India and Pakistan. The own-price elasticity of the demand for energy (both Frisch and Slutsky and Cournot) is about one-half of these values, apart from sign. For further details see Fiebig, Seale, and Theil (1986a), including a comparison with income and price elasticities of energy obtained by other analysts.

THE FOUR PHASES OF THE INTERNATIONAL COMPARISON PROJECT

In Section 2.1 (first paragraph) we mentioned that Kravis and his colleagues considered successively 10, 16, and 34 countries, which are commonly referred to as Phases I, II, and III of the International Comparison Project. They were followed by Phase IV, conducted by the United Nations Statistical Office, which covered 60 countries.

The dependence of the food budget share on real income is by far the most spectacular feature of the cross-country comparisons. Therefore, Seale and Theil (1986) decided to test Working's model for food graphically for each of the four phases. The results in the form of four graphs (one for each phase) are shown in Figure E-1. In each graph the budget share of food is measured vertically and per capita real income (on a logarithmic scale) horizontally. Note that the outliers indicated are all African countries; otherwise the fit of Working's model is remarkably good. The African exceptions should cause no surprise, since the data for many of these countries are so unreliable. This holds even for population data. For example, the 1984 population estimates by the Ethiopian government based on past censuses differed from the actual census account in mid-1984 by no less than 9 million persons out of a population of 42 million (*The Economist,* July 20, 1985: 30).

COMBINING SUCCESSIVE PHASES

An interesting question is to what extent the model of Section 2.6 remains applicable when we use it for the data of other phases or to all these data jointly. Fiebig, Seale, and Theil (1986b) approached this problem by considering the 30 countries whose Phase III data were used in Chapter 2. The α_i and β_i estimates in column 3 of Table E-1 are identical to those of Table 2-5.

Figure E–1.   Working's Model for Food in Four Phases of the International Comparison Project.

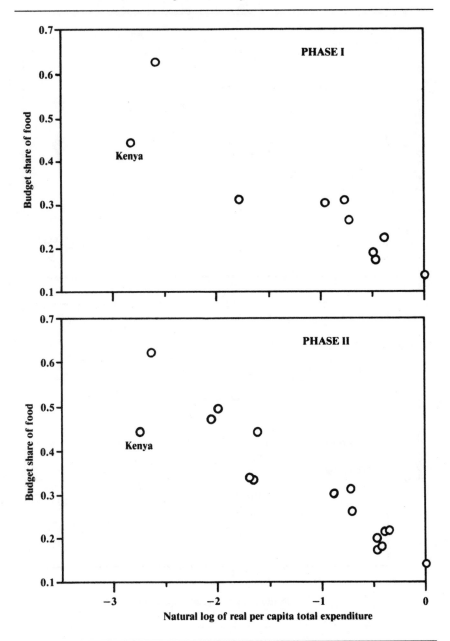

Figure E-1   continued.

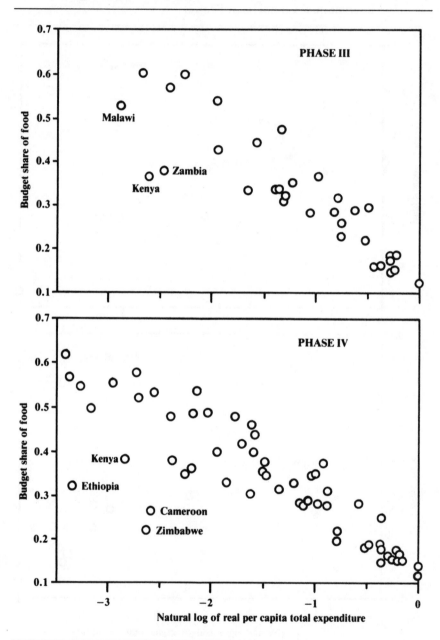

Table E-1. ML Parameter Estimates for Three Phases.

Good or parameter (1)	Phase II (2)	Phase III (3)	Phase IV (4)	Pooled (5)
		Coefficient ϕ		
Income flexibility	−.737 (.039)	−.526 (.037)	−.592 (.043)	−.663 (.027)
		Coefficients β_i		
Food	−.155 (.010)	−.154 (.010)	−.140 (.010)	−.140 (.008)
Beverages, tobacco	.002 (.005)	.001 (.005)	−.003 (.005)	−.001 (.004)
Clothing, footwear	.004 (.005)	−.005 (.005)	−.003 (.004)	−.006 (.003)
Gross rent, fuel	.025 (.008)	.032 (.006)	.029 (.007)	.025 (.005)
House furnishings, operations	.023 (.006)	.025 (.004)	.017 (.004)	.018 (.003)
Medical care	.024 (.004)	.024 (.003)	.026 (.005)	.019 (.003)
Transport, communications	.029 (.009)	.030 (.005)	.028 (.009)	.033 (.005)
Recreation	.024 (.003)	.019 (.003)	.012 (.004)	.018 (.003)
Education	.003 (.006)	−.004 (.005)	.002 (.007)	.004 (.005)
Other	.021 (.007)	.033 (.006)	.032 (.007)	.030 (.005)
		Coefficients α_i		
Food	.138 (.015)	.162 (.012)	.175 (.011)	.175 (.010)
Beverages, tobacco	.059 (.007)	.056 (.006)	.053 (.006)	.054 (.005)
Clothing, footwear	.090 (.007)	.084 (.006)	.078 (.004)	.081 (.004)
Gross rent, fuel	.152 (.012)	.145 (.008)	.144 (.008)	.141 (.006)
House furnishings, operations	.097 (.008)	.098 (.005)	.085 (.004)	.090 (.004)
Medical care	.089 (.005)	.089 (.004)	.088 (.004)	.083 (.004)
Transport, communications	.117 (.013)	.118 (.007)	.128 (.009)	.124 (.007)
Recreation	.075 (.004)	.069 (.004)	.064 (.004)	.067 (.003)
Education	.064 (.007)	.054 (.006)	.059 (.006)	.062 (.005)
Other	.119 (.009)	.126 (.007)	.126 (.007)	.124 (.006)

Out of these 30 countries, 15 were represented in Phase II and 24 in Phase IV. Accordingly, columns 2 and 4 of Table E-1 give the parameter estimates for the 15 or 24 countries of these two phases. Note that Phases II, III, and IV refer to 1970, 1975, and 1980, respectively. Since we normalize the per capita incomes of 1975 so that the U.S. value equals 1, it thus follows from the Divisia volume indexes in Table 2-13 that we must normalize those of 1970 and 1980 so that the U.S. values in these two years are 0.905 and 1.127, respectively.

Are the estimates in columns 2, 3, and 4 compatible with each other? On the whole the agreement seems to be reasonably close, although the discrepancy of the ϕ estimates in columns 2 and 3 looks large relative to their asymptotic standard errors. However, recall from Section 3.11 that such a standard error tends to underestimate the true variability of the ϕ estimate. Here we follow Fiebig, Seale, and Theil (1986b) by postulating that the parameter values underlying the estimates of columns 2 to 4 are the same. We add a subscript t to the variables in equations (6.6) and (6.7) of Section 2.6 to distinguish between the three phases,

$$y_{ict} = \alpha_i + \beta_i \log Q_{ct} + \phi(w_{ict} + \beta_i)$$

$$\times \left[\log(p_{ict}/\bar{p}_i) - \sum_{j=1}^{10} (w_{jct} + \beta_j) \log(p_{jct}/\bar{p}_j) \right] + \epsilon_{ict},$$

where

$$y_{ict} = w_{ict} - w_{ict} \left[\log(p_{ict}/\bar{p}_i) - \sum_{j=1}^{10} w_{jct} \log(p_{jct}/\bar{p}_j) \right],$$

and we note that $\bar{p}_i$ (as in Section 2.6) stands for the geometric mean of the prices of good i in the thirty countries in 1975 (i.e., in Phase III).

If the error terms ϵ_{ict} were independent both over countries and over phases, the ML procedure applied to the above model would be a straightforward extension of that of Section 2.9. But it seems plausible that the 1970 and 1975 errors of each country will be correlated, and similarly the 1975 and 1980 errors, and even (though to a lesser degree) the errors of 1970 and 1980. A first-order autoregressive model with one parameter ρ is the simplest solution. Accordingly, we extend the contemporaneous covariance matrix Σ of Section 2.9 to a partitioned matrix,

$$\begin{bmatrix} \Sigma & \rho\Sigma & \rho^2\Sigma \\ \rho\Sigma & \Sigma & \rho\Sigma \\ \rho^2\Sigma & \rho\Sigma & \Sigma \end{bmatrix},$$

where the first set of rows and columns refers to 1970, the second to 1975, and the third to 1980. Then, under the assumption of multivariate normality, we maximize the likelihood function with respect to the α_i's, β_i's, ϕ, ρ, and Σ. The ML estimate of ρ is 0.72 and a 95 percent confidence interval, based on the asymptotic chi-square distribution of minus twice the log-likelihood ratio for variations in ρ, is (0.65, 0.77). Thus, the autoregressive parameter is significant (although the qualifications regarding the use of asymptotic theory are obvious). The implied pooled estimates of the α_i's, β_i's, and ϕ are shown in the last column of Table E-1. See Fiebig, Seale, and Theil (1986b) for further details.

BIBLIOGRAPHY

Fiebig, D.G.; J. Seale; and H. Theil. 1986a. "The Demand for Energy: Evidence from a Cross-Country Demand System." McKethan-Matherly Discussion Paper MM21, University of Florida.

Fiebig, D.G.; J. Seale; and H. Theil. 1986b. "Cross-Country Demand Analysis Based on Three Phases of the International Comparison Project." McKethan-Matherly Discussion Paper MM22, University of Florida.

Seale, J., and H. Theil 1986. "Working's Model for Food in the Four Phases of the International Comparison Project." *Economics Letters* 22: 103–104.

INDEX

ABOUT THE AUTHORS

Henri Theil pioneered the mathematical testing of economic theories. Presently at the University of Florida in Gainesville, Professor Theil holds the first Eminent Scholar Chair to be instituted at that university. Originally from the Netherlands, he was appointed at the University of Chicago in 1966, where he held the post of university professor and director of the Center for Mathematical Studies in Business and Economics. He is a past president of the Econometric Society, a fellow of the American Academy of Arts and Sciences and of the American Statistical Association, a corresponding member of the Royal Netherlands Academy of Sciences, and an elected member of the International Statistical Institute. He holds four honorary doctorates: University of Chicago (1964), Free University of Brussels (1974), Erasmus University in Rotterdam (1983), and Hope College in Michigan (1985). A prolific scholar, Professor Theil has written more than 10 books and 200 articles in several languages.

Kenneth W. Clements has been professor of economics at the University of Western Australia since 1981. He was educated at Monash University in Melbourne and the University of Chicago where he completed a Ph.D. in economics. He was on the faculty of the Graduate School of Business at the University of Chicago from 1977 until 1979; during this period he began his collaboration with Henri Theil. From 1979 until 1981 he was at the Research Department of the Reserve Bank of Australia in Sydney. His research interests are in international economics, business economics, and econometrics.

ABOUT THE CONTRIBUTORS

Denzil G. Fiebig is senior lecturer of econometrics at the University of Sydney in Australia. He obtained his Ph.D. at the University of Southern California, Los Angeles, in 1982. He is co-author, with Henri Theil, of *Exploiting Continuity,* which is Volume 1 of this series.

James L. Seale, Jr., is assistant professor of food and resource economics at the University of Florida. He obtained his Ph.D. at Michigan State University in 1985. He spent six years in Egypt, Sudan, and Zaire, working for the Peace Corps and three American and Egyptian Universities.

E. Antony Selvanathan is a senior tutor at the University of Western Australia. He is a native of Sri Lanka.